PENGUIN CLASSICS

A HISTORY OF MY TIMES

ADVISORY EDITOR: BETTY RADICE

XENOPHON was an Athenian country gentleman born about 430 B.C. He is sometimes thought to have helped to publish Thucydides' *History*, and certainly wrote his own *Hellenica* as a continuation of it. By his own (possibly reliable) account he was a fine officer and outstanding leader, but having chosen to serve under Cyrus in his revolt against the King of Persia, he was exiled. The Spartans gave him an estate at Scillus, and he settled down to enjoy the life of a landed aristocrat; it was during this period that he began to write histories, biographies, memoirs and specialist treatises, of which *The Persian Expedition*, *A History of My Times* and *Conversations of Socrates* are published in Penguin Classics. The defeat of Sparta in 371 forced him to move to Corinth where he probably lived for the rest of his life.

REX WARNER was a Professor of the University of Connecticut from 1964 until retirement. He was born in 1905 and went to Wadham College, Oxford, where he gained a 'first' in Classical Moderations, and took a degree in English Literature. He taught in Egypt and England, and was Director of the British Institute, Athens, from 1945 to 1947. He wrote poems, novels and critical essays, worked on films and broadcasting, and translated many works, of which Xenophon's *History of My Times* and *The Persian Expedition*, Thucydides' *History of the Peloponnesian War*, and Plutarch's *Moral Essays* and *Fall of the Roman Empire* have been published in Penguin Classics. Rex Warner died in 1986.

GEORGE CAWKWELL is a Fellow Emeritus of University College, Oxford. He has specialized in the history of the fourth century B.C.

XENOPHON

A HISTORY OF MY TIMES
(HELLENICA)

**TRANSLATED BY
REX WARNER**

*With an Introduction
and Notes by*
GEORGE CAWKWELL

PENGUIN BOOKS

PENGUIN BOOKS

Published by the Penguin Group
Penguin Books Ltd, 27 Wrights Lane, London W8 5TZ, England
Penguin Books USA Inc., 375 Hudson Street, New York, New York 10014, USA
Penguin Books Australia Ltd, Ringwood, Victoria, Australia
Penguin Books Canada Ltd, 10 Alcorn Avenue, Toronto, Ontario, Canada M4V 3B2
Penguin Books (NZ) Ltd, 182–190 Wairau Road, Auckland 10, New Zealand

Penguin Books Ltd, Registered Offices: Harmondsworth, Middlesex, England

This translation first published 1966
Reprinted with new Introduction and Notes 1979
11 13 15 17 19 20 18 16 14 12

Translation © Rex Warner, 1966
Introduction and Notes © George Cawkwell, 1979
All rights reserved

Set in Bembo Monotype
Printed in England by Clays Ltd, St Ives plc

CONTENTS

INTRODUCTION

THE Fourth Century B.C. is a fascinating period of Greek history. It began with Sparta triumphant over Athens and seemingly secure; it ended with all Greece subject to Macedon – dramatic changes which are of special appeal to an age which has seen and fears yet to see similar reversals of power and fortune. No one who cares for liberty can contemplate with detachment the decline of the city-states of Greece before the national state of Macedon, and the rise of Philip II in the 350s and the 340s will always have prior claim on men's interest, but if one is properly to understand it one must understand also how in the first four decades of the century the city-states reached a balance of impotence. Sparta undone by Thebes ceased to be a world power and became a mere Peloponnesian wrangler. Thebes proved unequal to her great pretensions and prompted a resistance in Central Greece which she could not easily suppress. Athens, dreaming of and constantly scheming to recover her Fifth-Century empire, wasted her resources and her credit, and by the accession of Philip in 359 was approaching bankruptcy and general contempt. Thus the first four decades of the century ended in 'uncertainty and confusion in Greece', which must be understood if we are to understand the sequel. Nor is the period without interest for itself. If Philip had died young and Macedon had remained disunited and weak, the age of Lysander, Agesilaus and Epaminondas would still have had wide appeal.

Of these troubled decades Xenophon's *Hellenica* (commonly translated *The History of Greece*, here less closely but more aptly *A History of My Times*) is the only surviving formal account. There are fragments of other histories and

7

late epitomes; there are speeches and inscriptions; and the study of these has led to a sharp decline in Xenophon's credit. All this will become evident and the reader must be warned at the outset that he will be seriously misled if he believes all he reads in the *Hellenica* and if he neglects to read between the lines. But it should also be stated that, although we would not be without knowledge of the period if the works of Xenophon had perished, it would hardly seem worth the knowing. For all its faults as history, *A History of My Times* closely studied is a most engaging work, which stimulates great interest in the period it covers.

THE LIFE OF XENOPHON*

Xenophon was born in Athens in the early years of the Peloponnesian War into the class of the Knights, men rich enough to maintain a horse and so render military service in the cavalry, which was at that stage 1,200 strong compared to the near 30,000 of military age in the *hoplite* class and to the unnumbered mass of those liable for service in the fleet or in the light-armed forces (Thucydides II.13). Such men of property found much to discontent them in the war. Their estates were liable to Spartan ravaging; those of military age were liable to the costly duty of commanding a ship in the Athenian navy: so they had a special interest

*All references unless otherwise stated are to the *Hellenica*. The following abbreviations of Xenophon's works are used in the Introduction.

> *Memorabilia* – *Mem.*
> *Anabasis* – *Anab.*
> *Agesilaus* – *Ages.*

In addition, Diod. is used for Diodorus, whose works are to be found in the Loeb Classical Library series, and Tod, *G.H.I.* is used for M. N. Tod, *Greek Historical Inscriptions*, II (Oxford, 1948).

in the ending of the war when opportunity offered. It did so in 425 but was rejected, and, although peace was made in 421, within a few years the disastrous Sicilian Expedition had brought Athens itself near to ruin. The oligarchic revolution of 411 was the consequence, and, although it failed to maintain itself, the closing years of the war did nothing to make a young man of Xenophon's sort an admirer of the Athenian system. We may presume that he had grown up amidst grumbling discontent at the very least; we may be sure that as a young man he conceived a lively contempt for democracy as it displayed itself in the last years of the Peloponnesian War. To judge by the precise detail of his account of a cavalry action in Ionia (I.2.1 ff.), which suggests autopsy, he was already old enough for military service by 409 and for the right to attend the debates in the assembly. It is therefore possible that he was present in person at one of the most discreditable performances of the Athenian democracy, the trial of the generals after the naval-battle of Arginusae in 406 (I.7.1 ff.); they were, in defiance of the law and Socrates' attempt to uphold it (§15), condemned *en bloc*. Whether Xenophon was present or not, clearly enough he was appalled, his sympathies being attested, as is his manner, by the length of the speech he put into the mouth of Euryptolemus (§§16–33) pleading for respect for the due procedure of the law. Indeed there can be no doubt that he despised democracy. Although he had nothing but contempt for the leader of the oligarchic revolution of 404, as emerges perhaps from his account of the arrest and execution of Theramenes (II.3.15–56), certainly from the account he gave in the *Memorabilia* of the relations of Critias and Socrates (*Mem.* I.2.12–48), yet he did not, it would seem, leave Athens with the supporters of democracy in 404; the prominence of the Knights in his account of 404 and 403 and its detail (cf. II.4.8 f. and 24 ff.) suggest that he was one of them, and there is no evidence to suggest that he did not remain in the city.

So he must have in some degree shared the hostility to democracy characteristic of the Knights, which made them suspect to the democracy restored in 403 (III.1.4).

Broadly speaking, his sympathies may have been with the moderate oligarchs. Although his account of Theramenes' part in the making of peace with Sparta in 404 is bitterly hostile (II.2.16 ff.), this was perhaps due to his friendship with Euryptolemus and the feeling that Theramenes was really to blame for unjust treatment of the generals of Arginusae (I.7.8). It is notable that, in describing the return to Athens in 407 of Euryptolemus' cousin, Alcibiades (I.4.11 ff.), Xenophon reported the two views of Alcibiades' conduct but gave the favourable view at length, the critical quite curtly, whilst in the *Memorabilia*, when he defended Socrates against the charge of being responsible for the doings of Critias and Alcibiades, he had much to say of the former's violence in 404 but very little about the latter and absolutely nothing about his lack of patriotism when he lent his services to Sparta and to Persia (*Mem.* I.2.12 ff.). So perhaps he was a moderate critic of the democracy, for whom, as for Alcibiades (Thuc. VI.89.6), democracy was 'generally acknowledged folly'. This after all was only to be expected with a disciple of Socrates. The extent to which the *Memorabilia* recorded what he himself had heard from Socrates is doubtful; only one conversation (*Mem.* I.3.8 ff.) explicitly involved him, and much is clearly hearsay; on the other hand at one point he spoke as if he had regularly been a bystander (*Mem.* I.2.31) and there are a number of trivial remarks (cf., e.g., *Mem.* III.13 and 14) that are likely to have been included because they record what Xenophon himself had heard. But it is certain that he was a follower and admirer. He declared that he consulted Socrates about whether he should accept the invitation to join the army of the young Cyrus in Asia Minor (*Anab.* III.1.5), and all his Socratic writings argue a mind deeply imbued with Socratic ideas.

Inevitably he followed his master in being critical of Athenian democracy.

It was therefore, we may guess, no great sadness to him when in late 402 or early 401 he left the Athens of restored democracy to seek fortune and adventure under Cyrus, brother of the Great King, who shortly revealed that he planned no less than to march to the heart of the Persian Empire and seize the throne. The long march up-country (the 'Anabasis' to use the Greek word), the death of Cyrus on the battlefield of Cunaxa not far from Babylon in September 401, the perilous situation in which the Ten Thousand Greeks found themselves, the arrest and murder of their captains, the appointment of new captains the youngest of whom was Xenophon, the long march through mountainous and barbarous lands in mid-winter to the Black Sea and then along the coast to the Bosporus in the following summer, mercenary service in Thrace for the remnants now under the sole command of Xenophon from the winter of 400 until the summer of 399 when he and they joined the Spartan army operating in Asia Minor against the Persian governors ('satraps') – all this is the subject of Xenophon's masterpiece, the *Anabasis*, which, written after about thirty years' interval, delights all by its freshness and vigour and deceives only those who cannot read between the lines.* In 399, however, thoughts of literature were far from Xenophon's mind. He was rather in a quandary. The expedition had been adventurous enough and he had acquired a taste for captaincy, but no great fortune had come to him. He had wanted the Ten Thousand to found a city on the Black Sea (*Anab*. IV.6.15), a proposal indignantly rejected by the majority who had had their fill of barbarians and barbary, and he was ready for almost anything

*Xenophon's *Anabasis* is translated by Rex Warner in Penguin Classics under the title *The Persian Expedition* (reprinted in 1972 with a new introduction by G. L. Cawkwell).

rather than to return home to Athens. But his captaincy of the rabble remnant at the Bosporus and in Thrace had earned him a bad reputation. The Spartans, who at that period had all the cities of the Greek world in thrall, blamed Xenophon for his troops' indiscipline, and at one moment he was in danger of being put to death if he was caught (*Anab.* VII.6.4 and 43). He even thought of going home (*Anab.* VII.7.58). Service with the Spartans in Asia Minor saved him from that, but the Spartans continued to regard him with suspicion (III.2.6) and it was not until the Spartan king, Agesilaus, came out in summer 396 at the head of a large army to manage the war (III.4.1 ff.) that Xenophon's fortune changed.

It changed decisively. Between Xenophon and Agesilaus there sprang up a warm friendship which was to decide the whole of Xenophon's future. They shared both a sentimental longing to see Greece unite in a crusade against Persia and a belief in the supremacy of landed aristocracy, and events would never divide them. More than that, Agesilaus was to Xenophon, as he would declare nearly forty years later in his encomium on the king, a 'completely good' man (*Ages.* I.1), and the king in return accorded favour, fortune and intimacy. Xenophon fought in Agesilaus' army in Asia, as many references in Books III and IV show, and, when in 394 Agesilaus was recalled to deal with the general uprising against the Spartan empire, Xenophon went with him and took part in the battle of Coronea against, amongst others, the Athenians (*Ages.* II.11). This may have caused him some distress, but, as Socrates had shrewdly surmised (*Anab.* III.1.5), service under Cyrus, Sparta's close friend and patron in the last years of the Peloponnesian War, was held against him by the Athenians, and had earned him exile (cf. Diogenes Laertius II.58, and *Anab.* VII.7.57). So he had to stay with the man on whom his future depended.

Agesilaus duly rewarded him with an estate at Scillus, a

mere two and a half miles south of Olympia (*Anab.* V.3.7 ff.), and for over two decades he lived there in great contentment.* At first, he probably served in various campaigns, to judge by the fullness and precision of some of the chapters of the *Hellenica* (cf. IV.5 and 6), but once Sparta had regained her supremacy and secured it by the King's Peace of early 386, he was able to settle down to the idyllic life he described in the third chapter of Book V of the *Anabasis*. Hunting and fishing, dogs and horses, festivals and entertainment were wholly congenial to him. His two sons shared in the sport, until they were old enough to be sent to Sparta to receive as favoured 'strangers' the severe education of the full Spartan youth, so widely admired by the aristocrats of Greece (Diogenes Laertius II.54). No doubt he visited Sparta frequently enough, as 'the best men' of the Peloponnese would do at festivals, especially the Festival of the Naked Youths (cf. *Mem.* I.2.61); he may even have witnessed the remarkable display of the Spartan version of stiff upper lip at the celebration of 371, when the horrifying news arrived of the defeat of Sparta by the Thebans at Leuctra (VI.4.16). There at Sparta intimacy with Agesilaus made familiar to him not just the inside of the king's house (*Ages.* VIII.7) but also the whole circle of Agesilaus, Spartans and non-Spartans alike. Altogether Xenophon was very comfortably situated, a prosperous country gentleman who was well in with the people who really mattered in his world.

Then came Leuctra, and very shortly afterwards, as part of the general turmoil that the defeat occasioned in the Peloponnese, Xenophon was ejected from his estate. He then did something of very great importance if he and his book are to be fully understood. He did not go home to Athens. The date at which the decree of exile from Athens was revoked is not known (the claim that it was in 369 has

*The site has recently been conjecturally fixed.

little to support it), but it certainly was revoked (Diogenes Laertius II.59). Yet Xenophon, expelled from Scillus, chose to remain in the Peloponnese and live and die in Corinth. In his last years the condition of Athens engaged his attention, and his treatise of 355, *The Revenues*, was the result. But he 'died at Corinth'. He had become a Peloponnesian, one of 'those who really cared for the Peloponnese' (VII.4.35 and 5.1), a man like the famous Fifth-Century advocate of concord between Athens and Sparta, Cimon, whose 'very cast of mind was Peloponnesian' (Plutarch *Cimon* 4.5). Friendship with Agesilaus and all it implied was not lightly to be put aside.

In Corinth he had much to engage his attention and much to make him grieve. The Thebans under Epaminondas, having inflicted the crushing defeat on the Spartans on the plain of Boeotia, came into the Peloponnese and did, in Xenophon's opinion, immense damage. They did not succeed in destroying Sparta, though they invaded the land, inviolate for centuries; but they did cripple her by setting free the inhabitants of Messenia, on the products of whose servile labour Spartans had for over three hundred years lived and been free to devote themselves to war. Then too, under Theban patronage, there was the flowering of Arcadian nationalism, the foundation of a great bastion of Arcadian independence from Sparta, Megalopolis, and the refoundation of Mantinea. In the good old days Sparta had checked urbanization – with its attendant dangers of large populations out of reach of immediate reprisals and free to follow political trouble-makers. Now Thebes fostered such things and on all sides there was 'uncertainty and confusion'. Xenophon looked for a resolution on the field of battle and in 362 the powers of good and evil faced each other on the battlefield of Mantinea. He sent his own sons to join the Athenian cavalry and fight the good fight. One of them, Gryllus, died gloriously in a skirmish outside Mantinea (see below, p. 400, and cf. n. on VII.5.16 f.), but it was all in vain. The battle resolved nothing, and in his old age Xenophon had to live with 'uncertainty and confusion'. He died, it is to be presumed, in the later 350s.

At what stage in life he began to write is uncertain. Surely enough it was not before he was settled at Scillus, but there he had the time and leisure to begin the writing of what is, by ancient standards, a fairly large body of work. Perhaps among his earliest tasks was the vindication of the memory of Socrates. By the late 380s and the 370s much had been written about him. His execution must have stirred Xenophon deeply, and it is likely enough that he felt moved to contribute what he could to the discussion. It is frequently asserted that the so-called *Memorabilia* were written in the 360s, but the passage adduced to prove it (*Mem.* III.5.1 ff.) does no such thing and nothing forbids our putting the work in the Scillus period. Perhaps too *The Education of Cyrus* belongs there – save for the bitterly disillusioned last chapter, which dates itself to the late 360s. Both works are stylistically somewhat similar, and are both unlike what can be shown to belong to Xenophon's latest period. The *Anabasis* is more dubitable: it could belong to the late 370s or to the early 360s. The *Agesilaus* was written shortly after the king's death in 360 or 359. *The Revenues* is later still. Where in this literary development does the *Hellenica* belong? When and how was it composed?

THE COMPOSITION OF THE *Hellenica*

No work of ancient literature has in this century suffered so sharp a decline in reputation as Xenophon's *Hellenica*. In the nineteenth century it was generally agreed that his obvious defects as a historian were more than balanced by his obvious merits; although he made little effort to correct or even restrain his hatred of Thebes and his admiration of Sparta, and although his historical judgements were superficial, his interests narrow, and his omissions astounding even within the range of his interests, he was nonetheless residing in the Peloponnese and an intimate of Agesilaus, peculiarly well placed to know what was afoot and why; where he admired he could also censure, for a naïve belief in divine retribution kept him from the crudest apologia and downright dishonesty; his experience of war fitted him to record an age of wars; all in all, a plain man without intellectual subtlety, he was safe; with discreet use of the remains of the Fourth-Century historian, Ephorus, which were to be found in the history of the First-Century-B.C. historian, Diodorus the Sicilian, the gaps in Xenophon could be filled, and for the rest he was not likely seriously to mislead. Few scholars would have dissented from the view that he was 'a really well-informed and truthful reporter'. The publication in 1909 of the papyrus fragments of a hitherto unknown historian, which were found in the sands of Egypt at Oxyrhynchus, has utterly changed all that. It was immediately apparent that, whoever the Oxyrhynchus Historian was, he was of the first rank, far superior to Xenophon, and, directly or indirectly, in part or in whole, the source of the parts of Diodorus Book XIV that did not concern Sicily. The age-old, complacent preference for Xenophon where he differed from Diodorus was no longer possible. With the publication of further fragments in 1949 the same devaluation of Xenophon happened in relation to Diodorus Book XIII. So far we can only guess who this new historian is. Further fragments have recently been identified, and we may hope to know more about him.[*] Already, however, we know enough to say that Xenophon is not reliable. Like the grin of the Cheshire Cat, his literary charm remains, but his high esteem as a reliable historian is a thing of the past.

[*] Cf. L. Koenen, *Studia Papyrologica*, 15, 1976, pp. 55 ff.

The precise points of conflict between the *Hellenica* of Xenophon and that of the Oxyrhynchus Historian are noted in the text.* The major one concerns Xenophon's account of the campaign of Agesilaus in summer 395 B.C. (III.4.20–25). It is almost certain that Xenophon was in the army of Agesilaus. Yet he seems to have omitted to mention the great battle in which the army of the Persian satrap was defeated and the road 'up-country' opened to the Greeks. To postulate so startling an omission has often seemed incredible to scholars and lame attempts have been made to reconcile the account of Xenophon with that of the Oxyrhynchus Historian. But it has all been in vain. Whatever one makes of the battle, it is beyond dispute ,that Xenophon has entirely omitted Agesilaus' march 'up-country' after the battle, which most curiously came to nothing, and this suffices to call in question in the most radical way the value of Xenophon's account. The same may be said of Xenophon's account of Agesilaus' campaign of autumn and winter 395 (III.4.26 ff., and IV.1.1–41). Again there are the most startling omissions. The Oxyrhynchus Historian gives details which are not only lacking in Xenophon but also transform our conception of what Agesilaus was about, while Xenophon plays prettily with picturesque scenes. Xenophon has been shown up for what he is or rather for what he is not. No one in future will describe him as 'a really well-informed and truthful reporter'. But is that the explanation of it all? What was the *Hellenica*? How and why was it composed?

*

The first point to make clear is that the main part of *Hellenica*, i.e. from II.3.10 to the end, was composed very late in Xenophon's life, in the 350s.

If there is one thing on which Xenophontic scholarship is agreed, it is that there was a break in the composition with

*Cf. nn. at I.5.14, III.4.24, 29 and 5.2, 3, IV.1.1, 15.

Lysander's return to Sparta in late summer 404 B.C. The theory is based on the study of Xenophon's linguistic usages.* The details need not concern us here, for the case is overwhelming. So the *Hellenica* has to be treated almost as two separate works, the first of which poses some especially awkward problems to which we must come in due course. For the present it is the second part that is under discussion, and here there has been far less agreement. Some have professed to discern a number of 'breaks', as if Xenophon a number of times laid down his pen, thinking he had concluded his history, and had on each occasion to take it up again, moved by events to say more; if that view were correct, Xenophon would have to be regarded as a man who began early to write history far from well and continued without improvement to the end. Others have argued that the part from II.3.10 to the end was composed as a unit and, because at VI.4.37 Xenophon alluded to events of the mid 350s, was written late in Xenophon's life; in which case his method of describing events many long years afterwards needs careful consideration. Of these two positions, with all the firmness which I can employ, it is here argued that the second is correct. The part from II.3.10 to the end was indeed composed, and wholly composed, in the 350s.†

The argument is two-fold. First there is the evidence provided by various passages in the *Hellenica*. They are noted in the text.‡ Only VI.4.37 clearly alludes to the 350s, but the tendency of the other passages is to bring the date of

*Cf. M. Maclaren, *American Journal of Philology*, 55, 1934, pp. 121–39, 249–62.

†It need cause no surprise that Part I should end in the middle of Book II. There was a different division into books in antiquity. Harpocration cited the name Theognis, which occurs only at II.3.2, as coming from 'Book II', but the word *penestai* in the sentence in which it occurs at II.3.36, as coming from 'Book III'.

‡Cf. nn. at II.4.43, III.1.2 and 5.25, IV.2.12 and 3.16, V.1.35, 2.7, 4.1, 33 and 64, VI.4.37.

composition down. The reference to the valour of Cleonymus at the battle of Leuctra in 371 (V.4.33) shows that the account of early 378 was written after 371. The seemingly gratuitous comment on the upright conduct of Timotheus on Corcyra in 375 (V.4.64) has point if it was written after the scandalous conduct of another Athenian general, Chares, in the same place in 361 (Diod. XV.95.3). So Book V seems to be 'late'. The note about the death of the Spartan King, Pausanias, in Tegea (III.5.25) must have been written after the death of his son, Agesipolis, in whose honour he erected a memorial at Delphi (Tod, *G.H.I.* no. 120), and if the reference to the *Anabasis* of one Themistogenes (III.1.2) is, as is generally supposed, a reference to Xenophon's own *Anabasis*, he must have begun Book III later than the late 370s at the earliest. There has always been a temptation to regard the King's Peace of 387–6 as so obvious a break in Greek history that Xenophon might well have thought to round off his history at that point, if he was composing it, in the manner of Thucydides, as events unfolded: just as the great Fourth-Century historian, Callisthenes, began in 387–6, so Xenophon at one period of his life might have intended to finish there. But this consideration could only apply if he had reached the end of Chapter 1 of Book V before the Spartan domination began to crumble as it did with the Liberation of Thebes in winter 379–8; from then onwards the King's Peace must have seemed the end of a chapter and not the end of a book. Now, in Xenophon's account of the King's Peace there is one very tell-tale remark. At V.1.35 he said 'Thus after the war which followed the destruction of the walls at Athens' (i.e. in 404) 'there occurred this first peace'. The remark seems to suggest that when Xenophon wrote his account of the King's Peace, he knew of the second peace at the least, i.e. the peace of 375 described at VI.2.1, and so he must have written his account of 387–6 after the King's Peace had ceased to seem so decisive a turning point in Greek affairs. Nor is there any good argument for an 'early' date for the composition of the history of the period down to the King's Peace; the two passages which have been used are not decisive (cf. nn. at II.4.43 and IV.3.16). Of course much of what has been said in this paragraph might be consistent with Xenophon beginning to compose his history in the late 370s, rather than in the 350s. But there is one fairly strong indication that that was not so, *viz.* that Xenophon appears to have written his account of the Liberation of Thebes with knowledge of the events of the 360s. Xenophon knew that there were seven conspirators (V.4.1); he named three of them, making Melon the chief (V.4.2 f.), but he wholly omitted mention of the most celebrated, Pelopidas, to whom 'all agreed in assigning the leading part in the attempt' (Diod. XV.81.1). This is of a piece with Xenophon's studied omission elsewhere of the name of the man who played so notable a part in the battle of Leuctra and in the invasion of the Peloponnese in winter 370–69. Only in connection with the negotiations with the Great King at Susa in 367 did the name of Pelopidas receive mention. Xenophon cannot have failed to know about him or have thought him unimportant. Pelopidas' fame as the victor of the battle of Tegyra in 375 (cf. n. at VI.1.1) precludes that possibility. His refusal to mention his name in connection with the Liberation of Thebes stems in all probability from the accursed part played by Pelopidas in the dismantling of Spartan power in the early 360s. So the composition of Chapter 4 of Book V is 'late', or at the least fairly 'late'. All in all, there is nothing to suggest that any section of the work after II.3.10 was written at a different period from the latest pages which, as already remarked, were explicitly written in the 350s (VI.4.37).

The second part of the argument derives from consideration of the relation of the *Hellenica* and the *Agesilaus*, which was written in praise of Agesilaus after his death in 360–59.

Some parts of Books III and IV of the *Hellenica* are almost word for word identical with parts of the first two chapters of the *Agesilaus*, but there are curious variations. Which version was written first? The matter is too detailed and technical to be treated here. In my view the *Agesilaus* passages are the original, but it might be contested. What is beyond contest is the evidence of Xenophon's use of words. Some words and phrases are known to be characteristic of Xenophon's style in the period when he wrote the *Anabasis*, whereas in the last books of the *Hellenica* alternative expressions are largely preferred, and if one compares the overlapping passages of the two works one finds that the *Agesilaus* is akin to the style of the *Anabasis*, and the passages from Books III and IV of the *Hellenica* tend to the style of the later books. The conclusion must be that the whole of the *Hellenica* from II.3.10 onwards was written after the *Agesilaus*, i.e. after 359.

The *Hellenica* must, therefore, be declared a work of his last years, and save for the *Revenues* almost the last thing he wrote, the vision of an old man. Consistently with this view, one can discern no development of historical method within Books III to VII. Chronologically vague before the King's Peace, Xenophon is no less sc after. Nor is there any sign that he took more pains to collect material as time went on. His method, or lack of method, in recounting battles is very striking. The three great land battles of the Corinthian War were variously and unsystematically reported; when he came to what must have been for him the most important battle of his lifetime, the battle of Leuctra, there is no improvement; he appears to have made no effort whatsoever to discover what happened on the Theban side. Of course it may be countered that on any hypothesis he wrote the first part of the *Hellenica* (i.e. I–II.3.10) before, and probably well before, the 350s, and if that did not teach him the need for accuracy, he was incorrigible, and his later errors do not disprove that the errors of Books III and IV were not committed to paper well before the 350s. But at least those who would argue that those books were written 'early' can find no development of method to support their claim. The case that the *Hellenica* from II.3.10 onwards was composed wholly in the 350s stands. All that might be advanced against it would be the general presumption that Xenophon is hardly likely to have sat down in the 350s to record events of forty to fifty years past. But that presumption is wrongheaded, as discussion of how he wrote Part II will now show.

It cannot be proved but it is very probable that Xenophon did not use literary sources for the history of the years 404 to 362 B.C. There was one source, at least, he could have used, the *Hellenica* of the Oxyrhynchus Historian, but he did not; otherwise he would not have fallen into the various errors which the few fragments we have of that work have exposed. Doubtless there were other histories; although, when he professed knowledge of the works of 'all the historians' (VII.2.1), he may have been thinking principally of the historians of the Fifth Century, we have names of Fourth-Century historians, mere shadows to us, whom he might have used. But he did not. He was not in our sense a scholarly historian. In his *Anabasis*, although he shows that he had some acquaintance with the account of the Cunaxa campaign given by Ctesias (cf. *Anab.* I.8.26), he clearly did not use it in writing his own account; otherwise he would have avoided the muddle which he makes of the battle; he preferred to draw on his own memories. In the *Hellenica* at no point does he even hint at the use of others' histories. His account is essentially lopsided and personal. He did not feel the need to use others. He himself knew.

The *Hellenica* in a broad sense is entirely Xenophon's own experience. The very title is a sham. He made no pretence of writing the history of Greece in his time. The whole

Theban expansion into Thessaly, for example, potentially so dangerous, is alluded to only once (VII.1.28), and that in report of a debate at Corinth that Xenophon himself might well have heard. The Athenian preoccupation in the 360s with the attempt to recover Amphipolis is never even hinted at; the name of the city is mentioned only once, at a moment clear in his memories of the return from Asia in 394 (IV.3.1). Of the capture of Samos and the Athenian settlement there (a so-called *cleruchy*), which aroused great apprehension in some Athenian minds and stirred the Thebans under Epaminondas to thoughts of intervention in the Aegean, not a word. Xenophon cared for none of those things. His theme in Part II was Sparta and the Peloponnese, where he lived and chose to remain to die. The work had been more justly styled *Peloponnesiaca*, a History of the Peloponnese.

But not just in this broad sense is the *Hellenica* personal. A great deal of the book records events in which he himself participated. The plainest case is his account of the Spartan operations in Asia Minor from 399 to 394 in Books III and IV. There are ample signs of autopsy in the length and footling detail of Dercyllidas' few days' campaign in the Troad in 399 (III.1.10 ff.), the picture of Ephesus in 395 become 'the workshop of war', the betrothal of Spithridates' daughter (IV.1.4 f.), the meeting with Pharnabazus (IV.1.29 f.). Caution is necessary, for Xenophon had a vivid pen, but few will question that a great deal of these two books reflects his own experiences. For instance, both the Acarnanian campaign of 389 (IV.6.1 ff.) and the invasion of the Argolid in 388 (IV.7.2 ff.) have the fullness and touch suggestive of autopsy. The full account of the campaign of Agesilaus in 390 (IV.5.1 ff.) contrasts strangely with the scanty notice of the family triumph of 391 (IV.4.19), when Agesilaus and his step-brother Teleutias converged by land and sea on the port of Corinth, Lechaeum; perhaps Xenophon took part in the one but not the other. But there is no need to labour the point. His own experiences inform much of his narrative.

That is not an end to the matter. By the King's Peace in 387–6, Xenophon must have been about forty-four years old, and military service much later is unlikely. There is therefore no justification for finding in the full account of, for instance, the Spartan operations of the 370s a sign of his presence. There is in Books V to VII a very great deal that Xenophon could not have witnessed in person. But for the understanding of the *Hellenica* it is essential to realize that Xenophon, as it were, experienced by hearsay. His intimacy with Agesilaus enabled him to meet Agesilaus' friends, Spartan and non-Spartan, his step-brother Teleutias, for instance, who takes up a number of pages, or Phoebidas who took his chance at Thebes in 382 (V.2.25 ff.), or Procles of Phlius (V.3.13) whose speeches are not excluded (VI.5.38–48, VII.1.2–11). Amongst such men Xenophon would have heard told and retold the stories of Spartan valour. It was, as the Xenophontic *Constitution of the Spartans* (V.6) declares, 'the custom of the city for whatever noble deeds anyone in the city did to be told in the messes'. For anyone who did not share Xenophon's dislike of intellectual discussion (cf. *Art of Hunting* 13), this would have been singularly boring, but for Xenophon it was all part of the good life of the landed aristocracy and very informative. He was sufficiently accepted even to get the full story of the conspiracy of Cinadon (III.3.4 ff.), and it is not difficult to imagine him absorbing such stories as how Pausanias betrayed Sparta's interests at Athens in 403 (II.4.28 ff.), how Lysander fought and lost the battle of Haliartus (III.5.17 ff.), how Teleutias, so admirable a commander in many ways (V.1.3 ff. and 13 ff.), lost his temper and so his life at Olynthus (V.3.3 ff.), and a great deal else. Nor was this 'experience by hearsay' confined to visits to Sparta. Settled at Scillus, Xenophon doubtless regularly attended the festival at Olympia, where every four years 'the best men' (to translate literally a common term in the *Hellenica* – cf. IV.4.1, V.2.6, etc.) would assemble for the games, for improving Panhellenist orations of the sort familiar to us from Isocrates' *Panegyric,* and for society. We may safely presume that Xenophon did his share of entertaining (cf. *Anab.* V.3.6 f.) and so heard the talk – of how, for instance, Phlius had fared in the Corinthian War (IV.4.15), what Mantinea had done to deserve its punishment in 385 (V.2.2), perhaps an account of the liberation of Thebes (V.4.2 ff.), and so on. Nor did his opportunities for 'experience by hearsay' end when he was ejected from his estate at Scillus. At Corinth he was at the headquarters of the Spartan alliance (cf. n. at VII.1.28) and the centre of operations. Armies passed and repassed. He again became an eye-witness and at moments a participant. Certainly he must have followed keenly the course of affairs, exulting over the success of the allied light-armed troops against the Theban Sacred Band (VII.1.19) which he could probably see from the walls, fuming at the incompetence of the commander of the Spartan division (the Polemarch) who let the Thebans through the Isthmus in summer 369 and whose name Xenophon therefore suppressed (VII.1.17), thrilling at reports of the gallantry of Phlius and giving what aid he could for the loading of supplies for that city when the call came one night (VII.2.23). Book VII is, in fact, as 'personal' to Xenophon as any other part of the work. Even diplomacy was seen from a Corinthian viewpoint; the Common Peace of 366–5 was represented as an essentially Corinthian affair (VII.4.6 ff.). All this is obvious enough. So too are the advantages of residence at Corinth for one who had friends and interest in Phlius and Sicyon (VII.2 and 3). A very great deal of Book VII is beyond dispute Xenophon's Corinthian Memoirs. But it is not just in Book VII that his Corinthian experience is reflected. At Corinth, which had been the chief battleground of the Corinthian War described in Books III and IV, he could meet men like Pasimelus who had brought the Spartans within the Long Walls of Corinth in 392 and was still alive in the 360s (IV.4.4 ff., and VII.3.2). With such acquaintances it happened naturally enough that to the memories of the 390s and the 380s was joined 'experience by hearsay' of things long past.

Thus, certainly for much of the *Hellenica*, Xenophon was spared the trouble of comparing what others had said or doing research for himself – the alternatives of *collatio* ('compilation') and *inquisitio* ('research') in Pliny's celebrated letter on the writing of history (*Ep.* V.8.12). He knew it well himself. A test case is provided by what he tells us about Thessaly. As already noted, he entirely neglects the expansion of Theban power in Thessaly save for a single passing allusion (VII.1.28), but he is quite full on the relations between Pharsalus and Jason of Pherae, and the later history of the Pheraean dynasty is recounted in some detail. How did he get this information? Alexander of Pherae was murdered in 357–6 (Diod. XVI.14.1). Varied talk, current when Xenophon was writing, went into the *Hellenica* (VII.4.37), and it is impossible to say how he came to hear it. But for earlier affairs it is notable that much of the information is retailed through the mouth of Polydamas of Pharsalus, the 'representative' (*proxenus* – VI.1.4) of Sparta, whom Xenophon introduces in a highly laudatory fashion (VI.1.2 f.). It is a reasonable presumption that what he had to say about Thessaly came not from careful historical research but from the conversation in Sparta and Olympia of Spartan sympathizers in Pharsalus; for Xenophon's excursion into Thessalian affairs of the 370s is essentially concerned with Pharsalus. If he had been systematically collecting material, Pheraean relations with the other leading Thessalian city, Larisa, would have been more prominent. But Xenophon did not systematically collect. He had heard tell of enough for his purposes.

Much then was 'personal', but will this formula suffice for the whole of the work after II.3.10? There is a residue of passages which concern matters seemingly so far outside Xenophon's 'personal' experience that one has somewhat to strain to find an explanation of how these matters could have come to him in the casual course of friendship. It would be tedious and inappropriate here to examine in detail. I believe that these passages are explicable, and there the matter must for the moment rest save for one category which is of special interest – *viz*. those passages that concern Athens itself. Was this Athenian material 'personal', as readily and casually acquired as information about Corinth and the Peloponnese? Names of his Athenian contacts can be suggested – friends of his youth, men like Callias, so prominent in Athenian diplomatic history (VI.3.4, V.4.22 and cf. *Symp*. VIII.39), whom he could have met in Corinth or at Olympia – quite apart from Athenian commanders of the 360s whose business took them to Corinth (cf. VI.5.49). Sources there were of course. But did Xenophon casually take in what they had to say of things past and present, or did he carefully collect material to use in his history? An answer is to be found in a study of the Athenian names given in the *Hellenica*. They are fitfully distributed: seven for the period of his residence in Corinth, eleven for the period 387–6 to 370, twenty-one for the period between his departure from Athens in 401 and 387–6. Perhaps this last figure reflects Xenophon's interest in the men he knew of before he left Athens, but, whatever the correct explanation, it is striking how few names he had for the later period. If one is collecting material for a history, names are indispensable. Is it likely that a historian collecting material for a history of Greece between 387–6 and 362 would name only sixteen different Athenians, seven of whom represent the curiously incomplete list of ambassadors to Sparta in 376 (cf. n. to VI.3.2), and most of the rest men assuredly familiar to anyone living in Corinth or visiting Sparta? This looks, to me at any rate, more like an old man remembering than a historian at work.

When Xenophon sat down in the 350s to complete his *Hellenica*, he knew a great deal and all he felt he needed to know. Confident in his memory, the man who had written up his *Anabasis* had no hesitation in writing the history of his times. When Agesilaus died, he had been moved to give an account of his hero which began in more detail than he felt it appropriate to continue, and when he moved on to the *Hellenica* he used what he had written and added to it in the same vein. Old men forget. No wonder difficulties arise for modern historians of Greece. He is principally what we have to rely on, and again and again puzzles present themselves. For the *Hellenica* is not history. It is essentially Memoirs.

THE PROBLEM OF I–II.3.10

It is not possible to say exactly when the first part of the *Hellenica* was written. With the aid of the computer, stylistic comparisons may be made with other works of Xenophon, and one can assert that it was probably amongst the earliest of his writings. However, since it is quite uncertain exactly when they were written, that does not get us very far. What one can assert with confidence, despite modern hypotheses to the contrary, is that he did not begin the *Hellenica* while he was still in Athens. It is in ample measure composed of material which reflects purely Spartan sources. The most notable instance is his account of the battle of Notium (I.5.11). A fragment of the *Hellenica* of Oxyrhynchus shows that the account given by Diodorus reflects, albeit inaccurately, that historian, but apart from a disagreement about the number of ships lost by the Athenians, Xenophon's version, rightly understood, is entirely consonant with that of Oxyrhynchus but recounts the story from the viewpoint of the Spartans (cf. n. *ad loc.*). He gives no explanation of the Athenians' actions, which presumably he would have done if he had heard of the battle while he was in Athens. There is much else purely Spartan. The account of the period of Callicratidas as Spartan admiral (*nauarch*), including a speech and various remarks (I.6.1 ff.), is almost entirely seen from the Spartan side. Likewise the story of the Spartan commander on Chios, Eteonicus, quelling a mutiny (II.1.1 ff.), the defeat of the Athenians at Aegospotami (II.1.17 ff.), and much else. This mass of material argues plainly that Xenophon wrote the first part of the *Hellenica* after he had begun to have access to Spartans and talk of Spartan deeds. Whether he wrote at Scillus or in Corinth is hardly important here, but, since in the second part he manifests a sympathetic attitude to Theramenes in sharp contrast to the bitterness of his earlier account (cf. n. at II.2.16), enough time must be allowed for this change of heart. One may note too that there is no trace in the first part of the hatred Xenophon conceived for Thebes after the battle of Leuctra (cf. III.5.3 and IV.2.18, and *v.i.*). It is likely enough therefore that Xenophon wrote the first part at Scillus.

'It is said that by publishing the books of Thucydides which were unknown Xenophon made him famous, although he could have filched them for himself.' Thus Diogenes Laertius II.57, and from an early date the temptation to treat Xenophon as some sort of literary executor or heir of Thucydides has beguiled critics. Some of the manuscripts of Xenophon bear in their title 'the missing portions of Thucydides',* and the fact that Xenophon was one of the continuators of Thucydides was too obvious to miss (cf. Marcellinus, *Life of Thucydides* §45). Thucydides stopped in mid-campaign in 411, and the last six years of the Pelopon-

*Cf. J. Hatzfeld, *Revue de Philologie*, 4, 1930, p. 117.

nesian War cried out for treatment. What more natural for
Xenophon than to fill the gap? His political awareness and
his military experience roughly began where Thucydides'
ceased, and he had known, or come to know of, the leading
figures of the period. But to take the remark of Diogenes
Laertius literally is folly. Xenophon was not the only man to
'continue' Thucydides. The mysterious Cratippus, the most
likely suggestion for the authorship of the *Hellenica* of
Oxyrhynchus, was also declared to be a contemporary of
Thucydides and to have 'put together the portions missed
out by him' (Dionysus of Halicarnassus *On Thuc.* 16). Only
wanton translation of the phrase here rendered 'the missing
portions' can make of Xenophon a literary executor.

In some ways the first part of the *Hellenica* is Thucydidean.
For instance, Xenophon made some attempt to follow the
practice of dividing up the narrative by summers and win-
ters, though he proved much less able consistently to maintain it than the Oxyrhynchus Historian (cf. I.3.1 and 4.2).
His language too was perhaps influenced by his model. In
essentials, however, his performance is almost as un-
Thucydidean as one could imagine. If one makes a detailed
synopsis of the first part of the work, the lopsidedness and
fitfulness of it all is immediately apparent, and a parallel
synopsis of Book XIII of Diodorus makes Xenophon's in-
adequacy starkly clear. Yet some have supposed that these
scraps were material left by Thucydides, the master of
method supremely accurate; which is a hypothesis discredit-
ing only its authors. If proof is demanded that Xenophon
was not using Thucydidean material, formal conflict between
Thucydides Book VIII and the first book of the *Hellenica*
can be adduced. Xenophon would have us believe that
Clearchus (later captain of the Ten Thousand) was sent out
to Byzantium in 410 (I.1.35); Thucydides was explicit about
his arrival in 411 (Thuc. VIII.80), which is confirmed by
Diodorus (XIII.51) who has Clearchus taking part in the

battle of Cyzicus, described by Xenophon before the note of the despatch of Clearchus (I.1.16). Again, the appearance of the Spartan King, Agis, before the walls of Athens in 410 (I.1.33 f.) looks suspiciously like the event described by Thucydides (VIII.71) under 411; Xenophon has the Athenian general, Thrasyllus, meet the emergency, while in Thucydides' account he was far away in Samos when Agis made his demonstration; while it is possible that Agis pointlessly repeated in 410 his somewhat unfortunate move of 411, it is also possible and, one judges, more probable that Xenophon was confused.* But no matter. If one wants to find the true heir of Thucydides, one has only to read the *Hellenica* of the Oxyrhynchus Historian, a lack-lustre copy of the master but a copy. A Thucydides and a Xenophon are 'clean different things'.

Thucydides wrote history; Xenophon, in the sense already discussed, wrote memoirs. In the first part, too, personal experience suffices to explain much; such matters, for instance, as the campaign of Thrasyllus in Ionia (I.2.1 ff.), Alcibiades' return to Athens (I.4.10 ff.), the trial of the generals after the battle of Arginusae (I.7.1 ff.). 'Experience by hearsay', too, accounts for much of the Spartan material, for which a key figure was perhaps the Megarian, Hermon, who had been steersman of the Spartan flagship under Callicratidas (I.6.32) and then under Lysander (Pausanias X.9.7). (Steersmen were professionals who virtually commanded Greek warships, and the steersman on the admiral's ship had special status (cf. I.5.11) and doubtless had much to tell about naval campaigns.) Xenophon spoke in the *Oeconomicus* (IV.20 f.) of Lysander on a visit to Megara telling a story about Cyrus to a 'friend' (in Greek, a *xenos*). Perhaps the 'friend' was Hermon, who told Xenophon not just about Lysander's conversation but about a multitude of things that he had seen and done as admiral's steersman.

*Cf. n. at I.1.33, and also n. at I.1.27.

31

In any case there were many Spartans whom Xenophon could have heard talking about the war, especially the wrangle between supporters of Callicratidas and supporters of Lysander; it is no surprise that Callicratidas' disgust at depending on Persia for money (I.6.7) is echoed by Teleutias just before the King's Peace (V.1.17); that was the way they talked no doubt in the circle of Agesilaus. For much of the Athenian material the cousin of Alcibiades, Euryptolemus, to whose speech at the trial of the generals Xenophon gave ample space (I.7.16 ff.), may have been a man whom Xenophon entertained at Scillus; in his conversation the exploits of Alcibiades, which figure largely in the early pages of the *Hellenica*, would have been fully discussed. But Xenophon's circle of friends at Athens had been well acquainted with affairs, and many of them no doubt took the opportunity of the Olympic Games to renew acquaintance. One has no difficulty in imagining sources of information.

Thus without laborious inquiry Xenophon was able to accumulate in his mind the large bulk of the material in the first part. The residue of passages which require explanation is small. There are a number of what might be termed chronographic notices (I.2.1 and 19, 3.1, 5.21, 6.1, II.3.4, 5, 9 and 10) which are so out of character with the rest of the work that they have been generally, and probably rightly, regarded as interpolations. For the rest, three brief notes might suggest the hand of a recorder of information rather than of the writer of memoirs, but all three are concerned with Sparta, the sort of thing Xenophon might have heard discussed (cf. nn. at I.1.32 and I.2.18). If he had been assembling material for a history as we conceive the task, there would surely have been a great deal more.

The first part of the *Hellenica* is not radically different from the second. But it is nonetheless different. Within the narrative, which I have suggested caused Xenophon no pains to assemble, there is a lot of detail, notably the numbers of ships engaged, and it is not to be excluded that, when he sat down to complete the history of Thucydides, he began to question more precisely. But overall his method was to write up what he already knew about, not to find out what he did not know. In that sense the first part too is memoirs rather than history.

*

For us, however, the *Hellenica* is a major historical source of which we must perforce make the best. Two precautions must be stated.

First, Xenophon was a man of uncommon reserve. It would be a grave error to suppose that what he did not mention he did not know about. His silences speak loud, if not always clear. When he recounted the Athenian cavalry action that took place outside the walls of Mantinea in 362 (VII.5.15–17), a preliminary to the great battle, he abstained from naming the man most celebrated for his gallantry that day, his own son Gryllus, who was commemorated in paint, marble and encomiastic prose. 'Good men among them were killed.' Perhaps here silence was more creditable. Elsewhere it is more surprising. Although he lived for twenty years at Scillus before the place was seized and he himself expelled by the Eleans after Leuctra, he makes no mention of the expulsion and only a single allusion to the Elean claim (cf. VI.5.2). He will not whine for himself. In less personal matters his reserve is puzzling. He recounts the debate at Sparta over the succession to King Agis, in which the lame-footed Agesilaus triumphed. Lysander stopped the move to exclude Agesilaus by arguing that an oracle warning against 'the lame Kingship' referred to the dangers of someone acceding who was not of the royal line (III.3.3). Xenophon must have known that Lysander later wished, or was claimed to have wished, that the Kingship be opened to a form of election, but what he thought about the whole affair he kept

33

to himself (cf. n. *ad loc.* and n. at V.2.3). Another challenging silence concerns his sojourn in Corinth. At VII.4.6 he recounts the Corinthians' decision to assemble a force of mercenaries and their use in defence of the city, but no more. Yet these same mercenaries were the instrument of a famous fratricide (cf. n. at VII.4.6) and one would like to have been told what Xenophon thought of the man who had his brother murdered to free the city. Again and again Xenophon's reserve leaves us in ignorance and uncertainty. We should not think that he was similarly placed.

Secondly, Xenophon's manner is allusive. He wrote for men who knew, and felt no need to explain to those who did not know. For instance, the Corinthian War that engaged his attention in Books III and IV was fought against Sparta by a Grand Alliance, the formal establishment of which is described for us in Diodorus (XIV.82). Xenophon eschews such directness, though his account of the debate at Corinth before the battle of Nemea in 394 shows that he fully understood (cf. n. at IV.2.13, and also n. at VI.5.6 for a parallel case). The famous protest of Socrates against the trial of the generals *en bloc* in 406–5 is another instance (cf. n. at I.7.15). Xenophon may be a plain man, but he is rarely obvious. His comments come obliquely. Agesilaus had been accused of putting Phoebidas up to seizing the Cadmea, the citadel of Thebes. Xenophon by implication denied this; Phoebidas, he declared, lacked intelligence and good sense (V.2.28). When he was writing in the 350s, Greece was in a state of outrage over events at Delphi, where the Phocians had seized control of the temple: some excused; others accused. Xenophon made perhaps a complex comment. Controlling the temple might in his view be excusable; laying hands on its treasures was not. So, when he reported (VI.4.30) the alleged plan of Jason of Pherae to intervene at Delphi, he added that the oracle declared that, should anyone take of Apollo's sacred wealth, Apollo 'would look after that matter himself'. Jason was slaughtered in the next sentence (of which readers in Phocis might well have taken note). To those who can read between the lines there is much to attend to. The *Hellenica* is for connoisseurs.

After these precautions, one may address oneself respectfully to the most astonishing thing about the *Hellenica*, its omissions. The text of the serious student of Xenophon is peppered with *caret* and exclamation marks, and much of his business is to fill in the gaps and explain why Xenophon so wrote. A full list of the omissions would involve too much detail for this discussion (though many of them are indicated in the notes to the text). Some general points, however, can be made. The restricted range of Xenophon's interests has already been remarked. The great obsession of Athenian foreign policy, *viz.* the recovery of as much of the Fifth-Century empire as circumstances allowed the Athenians to hope for, has no part in his work. If it were not for a chance phrase (cf. n. at VI.3.19), at no point in the *Hellenica* would one even suspect that from 378 Athens was the head of an organization of allies, the Second Athenian Confederacy: the reason for this omission may not be merely restriction of interest, but that is surely part of it. Athenian foreign affairs, save in so far as they concerned the Peloponnese, were beyond his ken.

The rise of Thebes under Epaminondas and Pelopidas was, by contrast, all too well-known to him, and his omissions here are striking indeed. As already remarked, Pelopidas is named only in connection with the negotiations with the Great King in 367 (VII.1.33–38), although, as Plutarch's *Life of Pelopidas* shows, there was a great deal to say about him. Xenophon cannot have failed to know about his share in the Theban intervention in the Peloponnese in winter 370–69, even if he lacked precise knowledge about earlier actions, but he kept silence. Similarly with Epaminondas, the dominating figure of his age in the judgement both of contemporaries and of posterity: Xenophon gave him scant notice indeed. He did, as he had to, accord him due praise in his account of the campaign of Mantinea in the fifth chapter of Book VII; the greatest soldier in Greek history could no longer be ignored by the student of the art of war. He is mentioned too in connection with his commendable moderation in the campaign in the north of the Peloponnese in 367 (VII.1.41), but from earlier matters his name is, astonishingly, entirely absent. One might excuse the omission in the account of the battle of Leuctra; evidently Xenophon took no trouble to find out what had happened and contented himself with blaming the Spartan commander (VI.4.13). He must however have known about Epaminondas' share in the peace negotiations at Sparta shortly before Leuctra and his famous and ominous altercation with Agesilaus (cf. n. at VI.3.18), and he knew all too well about the Theban army's doings in the Peloponnese in winter 370–69, which set Xenophon's world in turmoil. But the name is withheld and no one could be prepared by the pages of Xenophon to understand the famous couplets on the statue of Epaminondas in Thebes:

'By my counsels is Sparta shorn of its glory
And holy Messene at last takes back her children.
Yea, by the arms of Thebes the Great City* has been crowned
And all Greece is independent and free.' (Paus. IX.15.6)

Xenophon knew, loathed and kept silence. So too with lesser Theban heroes of the age. In the whole *Hellenica* only thirteen Thebans are named, and the great achievements whereby Sparta was transformed from a world power to a Peloponnesian wrangler scantily treated. He wholly omitted the refoundation of Messene which took from Sparta the products of serf labour that sustained the military caste, and the foundation of Megalopolis, which became a bastion of

*i.e., Megalopolis (cf. n. at VII.1.32).

independence from Spartan domination. These were matters too painful to recount. Elsewhere his hatred of the Thebans breaks through. They, not Sparta, had broken the peace in 395 (III.5.3) and ruined Agesilaus' attack on Persia (III.5.1, V.2.35). Their dealings with Persia were, unlike those of Sparta, moved by base self-interest and ambition (VII.1.33). As to their great military renown, he shows them timid when they and not others had to do the fighting (III.5.21, IV.2.18 and 13), and in the invasion of Sparta in 362 a hundred Spartans cooled the ardour of these glorious fire-eaters (VII.5.12). The real battle had been Coronea (IV.3.16), not Leuctra. In both what he said and what he did not say, his hatred and contempt were manifest.

By contrast, Sparta could be fully treated and his intimate knowledge and sympathy make the *Hellenica* uniquely precious for the understanding of Sparta and the Spartan world. He is never at a loss for a Spartan term and feels no need to explain himself. Pylos, so familiar to Athenians, is called quite simply Coryphasium (I.2.18), which, Thucydides saw fit to explain, was the Spartan name. 'The so-called Spartan-trained' (*trophimoi*), 'the bastards', 'the lower-grade Spartans' (*hypomeiones*) each make one solitary appearance in his pages, the last occurring only here in the whole of classical literature; all three have played a vital part in illuminating the social structure of Sparta (cf. nn. at III.3.6 and V.3.9). The significance of 'the Little Assembly' (III.3.8) is unknown. Xenophon knew all about it. Indeed no more telling proof of intimacy in and with Sparta could be adduced than Xenophon's account of the conspiracy of Cinadon (III.3.4–11); Thucydides succeeded in breaking 'the secretiveness of the state' sufficiently to know of a mass murder of Helots, but remained unable exactly to date it (Thuc. IV.80); Xenophon's friendship with Agesilaus made him privy to the *arcana imperii*. Nor was he ever short of a name. The number of Spartiates (i.e. members of the ruling

37

military caste) in Xenophon's day was not many more than one thousand; he probably met many of the most influential in the company of Agesilaus, and heard tell of the rest. Eighty-two are named in the second part of the work and, when he withheld a name, it was, one supposes, not due to ignorance. For instance, the polemarch, whose division was cut to pieces at the Lechaeum disaster of 390 (IV.5.11 ff.), was not named, nor the polemarch who made a mess of blocking the Theban passage of the Isthmus of Corinth in summer 369 (VII.1.15 ff.). But for the most part the deeds of the Spartans are amply reported. When he is reticent, he is covering up – mostly for his friend and hero, Agesilaus. For instance, the scandal of the Spartan occupation of the Theban Cadmea in 382 was not that Phoebidas seized it, arguably a justifiable act, but that Sparta continued to hold it; in his own way Xenophon absolved Agesilaus from the charge of instigating the seizure (v.s.) but omitted to mention that it was Agesilaus who persuaded the Spartans to maintain the occupation (Plutarch, *Life of Agesilaus* 23.11). Nor did he say that it was Agesilaus who opposed the plan to evacuate Central Greece in 371 and so brought on the battle of Leuctra (VI.4.2); Plutarch (*ibid.* 28.6) enlightens us. Perhaps the omission of the great battle of the Hermus and Agesilaus' abortive march 'up-country' in 395, so fully treated by the Oxyrhynchus Historian (v.s.) was all part of this defence of Agesilaus; the victory removed all obstacles to the march and to turn back when the omens were not favourable was perhaps not entirely creditable; he could have waited until they were; there is a suspicion that despite all the trumpetings Agesilaus' performance was less than marvellous, though of course other explanations of Xenophon's omissions could be advanced.

In general, however, Xenophon felt no need to omit Spartan history. The Spartans were for him essentially good men, and their ordered life the best climate for virtue.

Critias could be made to declare (II.3.34) 'It is agreed that the best constitution is that of Sparta', and this was the common opinion of aristocratic Greece, which abhorred large cities and the power of demagogues; Sparta, the city without walls, and the landed aristocracy of the Peers was the ideal arrangement. Nothing is more revealing of the nature and values of the Spartan order or of Xenophon's attitude to it all than the comment he made on the reaction of the Mantinean men of property to the settlement of 385, whereby Mantinea's walls were pulled down and the city population made to live again in villages (V.2.7). The words, seemingly trivial, disclose much of the secret of Spartan power, and Xenophon concludes with a sneer at people who could not realize what was good for them. Xenophon could, and he sent his sons to get the benefits of a Spartan education, which was staggeringly severe; the flogging was appalling; both Plutarch and Cicero saw boys flogged to death in a competition as to who could endure the most; they were kept on short rations and so encouraged to steal although if they were caught they were flogged (*Anab.* IV.6.14 f. and [Xen.] *Constitution of the Spartans* II.6 f.). Of formal education they had no more than the practical business of Spartan life required (Plutarch, *Mor.* 237A), none of the training in the use of words to persuade, so characteristic of the sophistic education (*Art of Hunting* 12 and 13). This was what he chose for his son who in due course died a hero's death. The choice says much about Xenophon. For him, as for many others of the landed gentry of the Peloponnese (cf. n. at V.3.17), the Spartan way of life was best. Sparta and Agesilaus could not have had a more faithful satellite.

With Agesilaus, he had yet another bond. Both of them shared in the fashionable and sentimental folly of Panhellenism, the belief that the Greeks could and should find peace and concord for themselves by uniting in a great crusade against Persia – which brings us to one of the most challenging aspects of the *Hellenica*. Despite what starry-eyed Panhellenists said to each other, the hard fact was that Sparta did come to terms with Persia for the sake of domination in Greece, and not until the Great King had transferred his patronage to Thebes, as he did in 367 (VII.1.36), and given his blessing to Messenian independence, did Spartan interest and Panhellenist talk coincide. In the *Hellenica* Xenophon is astonishingly curt about the King's Peace of 387–6 and its various renewals. One would never guess from his account of the events of 387–6 that a representative of the Great King had shared in the exchange of oaths, nor from his account of the peaces of 375 and 371 that peace was made in response to threats of Persian intervention (cf. nn. at V.1.32, VI.2.1 and 3.18). If the Peace of Thebes in 366 (VII.4.10) is rightly seen as a form of King's Peace, it too is greatly underdone; there certainly was more to it than Xenophon lets on (cf. n. *ad loc.*). The most striking case of all however is the abortive peace negotiations of 392–1. In Xenophon's account they came to a stop when the Great King's terms were announced in Sardis (IV.8.12–15); there is ample and incontrovertible evidence that there was another Congress in Sparta when the Great King's wishes in slightly different form were made clear and the peace came very near to being accepted (cf. n. at IV.8.15). There can be only one explanation of all this. The whole business of dealing with Persia had become too distasteful to recount. Spartan 'medizing' had been a grave mistake and silence was best. Not so when Thebes 'barbarized' (V.2.35). No scruples, no distaste deterred him from a full statement about a Persian at Thebes reading a Royal Rescript and the Thebans ordering 'those who wanted to be friends of the King and of themselves' to swear submission (VII.1.39). In so far as such shameful scenes had occurred at holy Sparta, the least said the better.

Xenophon had, with regard to Persia too, kept in step

with Agesilaus. Agesilaus had gone to Asia Minor in 396 with the grandest pretensions (cf. n. at III.4.2), and shortly proceeded to make truces and deal with the hated Persian (III.4.5, 25). Only when negotiation had failed, did he plan really to attack (IV.1.41). His Panhellenism was plainly of the common milk-and-water variety, and, though he did not initiate or bear the responsibility for the making of the King's Peace and may even have continued to disclaim it (cf. Isocrates, *Epistle* IX.11), he was probably content enough with the position the Peace secured for Sparta. Once Persia changed her policy and supported Thebes, fashionable sentiment turned in a trice to passionate hatred. Although he was well into his seventies, he set out to fight for any enemy of the Great King that needed him, and died in Egypt aged nearly eight-five, a somewhat ridiculous figure but undeniably a 'Persian-hater' (*misopersês*) to the last (*Ages.* II.25 ff., VII.7). As Agesilaus in deed, so Xenophon in word.* One of his earlier works was the *Education of Cyrus*, which notoriously betrays no strong feelings against Persians or the Persian Empire, until the very last chapter, which contains a reference to events of 362 B.C. and in which Persia is declared corrupt, faithless and in decline. The chapter must be a late addition. Xenophon too has been converted by events in the 360s and in that spirit wrote the second part of the *Hellenica*. Hence those thundering silences.

Less readily explained is his attitude to Athens and Athenians. The preponderance of Athenian over Spartan names in his account of events before he left to join the Ten Thousand is reversed for the period afterwards, and this reflects, as has already been remarked, the balance of his experience. But many of the Athenians influential in the first three decades of the Fourth Century must have been known to Xenophon in youth and one might expect

*For Xenophon's Panhellenism, cf. Cawkwell's Introduction to the Penguin *Anabasis* (*The Persian Expedition*, 1972) pp. 23–6.

Xenophon to have listened with some interest to accounts of how they had turned out. For instance, Agyrrhius born about 440 B.C. was prominent enough by 405 to be alluded to by Aristophanes in the *Frogs* (l.367 and Schol.), and from 392 to 386 he was a figure of major importance. He is named once only in the *Hellenica* (IV.8.31). Another major figure of the 390s is not even mentioned, Epicrates (cf. n. at III.5.2). Thrasybulus the Stirian is amply treated and is commended at his death (cf. n. at IV.8.31). This imbalance argues political approval and disapproval; Thrasybulus had had no truck with Persian gold or Persian arms. Thus perhaps Xenophon distributed praise and blame among the men he had known, or known of as a young man. By the 370s they would have been at the zenith of their importance. Xenophon must have known something of them and their policies. He recounted the embassy sent by the Spartans in 378, which from other evidence may be inferred to have been aimed at stopping the Second Athenian Confederacy (V.4.22); surely enough he knew their business. But, as already remarked, only a single phrase hints at the existence of the Confederacy (VI.3.19), and to preserve this silence must have taken some care in writing (cf. nn. at V.4.63 and 64). One may guess an explanation. The Confederacy was, at least in part, the work of 'the pro-Boeotian party' (V.4.34). These men are alluded to by this general term, but never named. One of them, Cephalus, had a long and illustrious political career, denied to the readers of the *Hellenica*. In particular, he proposed the decree which sent the Athenians out to save Thebes from Spartan reprisals in winter 379–8 (cf. n. at V.4.19); all of which is passed over in silence by Xenophon. Only when Athens turned in 369 to saving Sparta, did her foreign policy begin to engage his pen (VI.5.33–52, VII.1.1–14). Indeed the events of the 360s made it possible to forgive and less bitterly to remember.

The theme of Xenophon's omissions is a large one and

for the present what has been said must suffice. It can with some confidence be asserted that to say nothing was his principal means of censure. Conversely, speaking generally, one may look for his approval in those who get names and space. A notable exception is Critias (II.3.24–34) whom Xenophon condemned; the Thebans are given space to persuade the Athenians to war in 395 (III.5.8–15), although he deplored the war and found Thebes guilty of treachery to Greece; two speeches critical of Sparta are included (VI.3.7–9, VII.1.12–14). These are however exceptions which may be variously explained. For the most part, it is Xenophon's friends and heroes who are accorded space – Callicratidas, Euryptolemus, Thrasybulus, Teleutias, Procles to name the most obvious. His method was to commemorate the commendable, and by silence to censure.

The *Hellenica* thus requires delicate handling by the historian. What it says, and the way it says it, is always to be weighed against what it does not say, and the reason why it does not. One is tempted to wonder what Xenophon thought he was at. He evidently meant to carry on where Thucydides left off; the opening of Book I presumes that the reader is aware of Thucydides' last chapters (cf. n. on I.1.1). But Xenophon must have known that he was not in any important sense doing the sort of thing Thucydides had done. Thucydides had been, historiographically speaking, a monster. No one before him had taken such pains to discover the truth and, although he had his descendants, notably the Oxyrhynchus Historian in the Fourth Century, Hieronymus of Cardia in the Third and Polybius in the Second, most historians of the Fourth Century were far from a single-minded obsession with truth and Xenophon is with them rather than with his great predecessor. His primary purpose is the moral one of depicting virtue. When in Book VII he embarks on his excursus about the small northern Peloponnesian city of Phlius, he excuses himself for involving himself in such trifling matters thus: 'If one of the great powers does some fine and noble action, all the historians write about it; but it seems to me that if a state which is only a small one has done numbers of great and glorious things, then there is all the more reason for letting people know about them' (VII.2.1). He then proceeds to recount various instances of Phliasian steadfastness and valour, including in considerable detail the business of a single day (VII.2.5–9). The relevance of all this to the development of Peloponnesian history is not explained. The comment is rather this: 'There is no question that men who did deeds like this must be called noble men and great warriors' (VII.2.16). After further Phliasian heroics, he concludes: 'This completes my account of the Phliasians, of their fidelity to their friends, of their valour in war, and of how, though short of everything themselves, they remained steadfast in the alliance' (VII.3.1). This is all very revealing. Xenophon saw his task as in large measure the depiction of virtue. His final comment on the death of Theramenes (II.3.56) is moral commendation. Indeed he is prepared, we may infer, to disregard acknowledged canons of historical writing. When Teleutias left the fleet there were extravagant scenes (V.1.3 f.); Xenophon, having described them, added 'I know that I am not telling of anything which cost money or involved danger or showed any particular skill', i.e. the conventional matters, 'but, by Zeus, I think it is very well worth a man's while to consider this question – how had Teleutias conducted himself so as to make the men under his command feel like this about him?' (After his own fashion, he delays the answer – cf. V.1.14 f.) That is, his real concern is with virtue and vice. The latter is, occasionally, frankly declared. The same Teleutias damaged his army and lost his life out of sheer bad temper, which should not be indulged even by masters dealing with slaves (V.3.6 f.). Normally, however, as has been seen, censure is by silence. When, introducing the account of the naval operations after 394 B.C., Xenophon declared 'I shall pass over those actions that are not worth mentioning, dealing only with what deserves to be remembered', he was not making a flat and otiose remark; it was the formal profession of a judge of virtue and vice. Whatsoever things are of good report, think on these things; the rest is silence.

His main purpose is thus moralistic. The assessment of commanders is part of it. With experienced eye he appraises the conduct of, for example, Iphicrates and Epaminondas (VI.2.27-39, 5.51, VII.5.8), and all sorts of military matters arouse his interest. In this, superficially he resembles Thucydides, but at bottom he is not a military historian. He has no consistent method of describing battles and what must have challenged every fibre of a true military historian, *viz.* the battle of Leuctra, Xenophon had clearly taken no trouble over at all. That defeat was due to the hand of God (VI.4.3 and 8).

The hand of God is an explanation that dulls the quest for truth, but it is the explanation to which Xenophon, so unlike Thucydides, readily had recourse. The hand of God checked the success of Epaminondas (VII.5.13), provided foes for the slaughter (IV.4.12), directed the Arcadian nationalist trouble-maker to land where his political enemies were encamped (VII.4.3), and so on. Failures were due to neglect of religious duties (cf. IV.8.36, VII.1.27) and above all to impious acts, the supreme example being the Spartan defeat at Leuctra (V.4.1). Though Xenophon hoped for the resolution of the conflict of good and evil at the battle of Mantinea, God willed otherwise (VII.5.26 f.). Xenophon was a deeply religious man. Hence his concern with the depiction of virtue. But all this kept him from becoming a historian. With bland confidence in his memory and in the unimportance of exact truth, he wrote his memoirs. The

Hellenica in all its oddness and with its melancholic conclusion is the result. But at the end of his life he was perhaps not discontented. The last words of the *Revenues* were perhaps the last words he wrote. 'For, if things are done under the guidance of God, it is to be expected that our doings will ever prosper.' He was fortunate to die before Philip of Macedon could shake his confidence.

University College, Oxford   G. L. CAWKWELL
September 1977

SELECT BIBLIOGRAPHY

(excluding works in German and Italian)

(a) On Xenophon

ANDERSON, J. K., *Xenophon*, London, 1974.
CAWKWELL, G. L., *Xenophon: The Persian Expedition* (tr. R. Warner), Penguin Classic; new introduction 1972.
DELEBECQUE, F., *Essai sur la vie de Xénophon*, Paris, 1957.
HENRY, W. P., *Greek Historical Writing*, Chicago, 1966.

(b) On the history of the period covered by the *Hellenica*

 (i) Books

ANDERSON, J. K., *Military theory and practice in the age of Xenophon*, University of California Press, Berkeley, Los Angeles, 1970.
HAMMOND, N. G. L., *History of Greece to 322 B.C.*, Oxford, 1959.
LARSEN, J. A. O., *Greek Federal States*, Oxford, 1968.
RYDER, T. T. B., *Koine Eirene*, Oxford, 1965.
SEALEY, B. R. I., *A history of the Greek city-states, 700–338 B.C.*, University of California Press, Berkeley, Los Angeles; London, 1976.
WESTLAKE, H. D., *Thessaly in the Fourth Century*, London, 1935.

 (ii) Articles

ANDREWES, A., 'Two notes on Lysander', *Phoenix*, 25, 1971, pp. 206–26.
ANDREWES, A., 'The Arginousai trial', *Phoenix*, 28, 1974, pp. 112–22.
CAWKWELL, G. L., 'The Common Peace of 366–5', *Classical Quarterly*, 12, 1962, pp. 80–86.
CAWKWELL, G. L., 'Notes on the Peace of 375–4', *Historia*, 12, 1963, pp. 84–95.
CAWKWELL, G. L., 'Epaminondas and Thebes', *Classical Quarterly*, 22, 1972, pp. 254–78.

CAWKWELL, G. L., 'The foundation of the Second Athenian Confederacy', *Classical Quarterly*, 23, 1973, pp. 47–60.

CAWKWELL, G. L., 'Agesilaus and Sparta', *Classical Quarterly*, 26, 1976, pp. 62–84.

CAWKWELL, G. L., 'The imperialism of Thrasybulus', *Classical Quarterly*, 26, 1976, pp. 270–77.

GRIFFITH, G. T., 'The union of Corinth and Argos', *Historia*, 1, 1950, pp. 236–56.

PARKE, H. W., 'The development of the Second Spartan Empire', *Journal of Hellenic Studies*, 50, 1930, pp. 37–79.

PERLMAN, S., 'The causes and the outbreak of the Corinthian War', *Classical Quarterly*, 14, 1964, pp. 64–81.

ROY, J., 'Arcadia and Boeotia in Peloponnesian affairs, 370–362 B.C.', *Historia*, 20, 1971, pp. 569–99.

SEAGER, R., 'Thrasybulus, Conon and Athenian imperialism, 396–386 B.C.', *Journal of Hellenic Studies*, 87, 1967, pp. 95–115.

SEAGER, R., 'The King's Peace and the balance of power in Greece, 386–362 B.C.', *Athenaeum*, 52, 1974, pp. 36–63.

SEALEY, B. R. I., 'Callistratus of Aphidna and his contemporaries', *Historia*, 5, 1956, pp. 178–203.

SMITH, R. E., 'The opposition to Agesilaus' foreign policy', *Historia*, II, 1953/4, pp. 274–88.

A NOTE ON THE NOTES

A historical commentary on the *Hellenica* would require a larger volume than the text itself, and those who wish to study the history of the period 411–362 B.C. can here only be referred to Diodorus Books XIII–XV as a basic text and to a general history such as N. G. L. Hammond's *History of Greece*. The scope of the notes provided here is almost entirely historiographical, to elucidate Xenophon's mind and methods. The not infrequent reference to my own articles on the period is not so much a mark of self-satisfaction as a kind of shorthand.

G. L. C.

BOOK ONE

CHAPTER 1

Operations in the Hellespont. Victories of Alcibiades
(end of 411 and 410 B.C.)

SOME days later* Thymochares arrived from Athens with a 1
few ships, and the Spartans and Athenians immediately
fought another naval action in which the Spartans, under
the command of Agesandridas,† were victorious.

Soon after this and at the beginning of winter Dorieus, the 2
son of Diagoras, sailed into the Hellespont. He had come
from Rhodes with fourteen ships. He arrived at dawn and
was sighted by the Athenian observer on duty for the day,
who signalled his arrival to the Athenian commanders.
They put to sea against him with twenty ships and Dorieus
fled from them in the direction of the land. As soon as he
had got his triremes clear of the enemy he ran them ashore
near Rhoeteum and, when the Athenians sailed in close, his 3
men fought back both from the shore and from their ships.
In the end the Athenians, without having achieved anything, sailed away to Madytus to rejoin the rest of their
fleet.

But Mindarus, who was sacrificing to Athena at Ilium, 4
had observed the fighting. He hurried down to the sea,
launched his triremes and set sail in order to pick up Dorieus
and his ships. The Athenians sailed out to meet him and 5
engaged him off shore near Abydus. The battle went on
from morning till late in the afternoon, with successes and

*The gap between the end of Thucydides VIII and the first events
of the *Hellenica* is much greater than an innocent reader might suppose.
†Thuc. VIII.95.2.

losses on both sides. Then Alcibiades* with eighteen ships
6 sailed into the Hellespont in support of the Athenians, and
the Spartans turned and ran for shelter towards Abydus.
Pharnabazus rode up along the shore in their support and
joined the fighting, urging his horse into the sea as far as it
could go and shouting out orders to the rest of his cavalry
7 and infantry. The Spartans made a barrier of their ships,
formed up in line and fought from the land. Finally, the
Athenians sailed away to Sestus. They had captured thirty
enemy ships without their crews, and had recovered all their
8 own ships which had been previously lost.† Then the
Athenian ships, except for forty which were left behind,
sailed out of the Hellespont from Sestus and went off on
different missions to collect money, and Thrasyllus, who
was one of the generals, sailed to Athens to report what had
happened and to ask for more troops and ships.

9   After this Tissaphernes‡ arrived at the Hellespont, and
Alcibiades with one trireme went to visit him. He took with
him gifts and tokens of friendship, but Tissaphernes had him
arrested and shut up in Sardis, saying that the King's orders
10 were that he should make war on the Athenians. Thirty days
later, however, Alcibiades with Mantitheus, who had been
taken prisoner in Caria, made his escape. They had managed
to find horses and got away by night to Clazomenae.

11   The Athenians at Sestus could see that Mindarus was planning to sail against them with sixty ships, so they slipped
away by night and made for Cardia. Here they were joined
by Alcibiades, who had come from Clazomenae with five
triremes and a rowing-boat. Hearing that the Spartan fleet
had left Abydus and was sailing to Cyzicus, he himself went
overland to Sestus, and ordered the ships to sail round and
12 meet him there. After they had arrived he was just on the

*Thuc. VIII.108.1.
†For a different account of the battle of Abydus, see Diod. XIII.45 ff.
‡Cf. Thuc. VIII.109.

point of putting out to sea in order to bring the enemy to
action when Theramenes sailed in from Macedonia with
twenty ships and Thrasybulus from Thasos with twenty
more. Both officers had been out collecting money. Alcibia- 13
des told them to clear for action and to follow after him,
and set out himself for Parium. Here the whole fleet,
eighty-six ships in all, assembled and set sail on the following
night. Next day about breakfast-time they arrived at
Proconnesus, when they discovered that Mindarus was at 14
Cyzicus as was Pharnabazus with his land forces. They stayed
at Proconnesus for that day, and on the following day
Alcibiades called an assembly at which he told the men that
they would have to fight by sea, on land and against the
fortifications. 'The fact is,' he said, 'that we have no money
at all, while the enemy have plenty which they have got
from the king.' He had already on the previous day, when 15
they came to anchor, taken over and put under guard all
ships in the harbour, big or small, so that no one could report
the size of the fleet to the enemy, and he had issued a proclamation that anyone caught trying to sail across the strait
to the other side would be put to death.

After the assembly he made ready for battle and, in a 16
heavy rainstorm, set out for Cyzicus. By the time they were
near, the sky had cleared and the sun came out. He could see
Mindarus' fleet, sixty ships altogether, engaged in training
exercises some way out from the harbour and already cut off
from it by his own fleet. The Peloponnesians, seeing that 17
they were faced with many more Athenian triremes than
before and that they were already close to the harbour, fled
towards the shore, moored their ships close together and
fought back against the Athenians as they sailed down on
them. But Alcibiades with twenty ships sailed right round 18
and landed on the shore. Seeing this, Mindarus also landed.
He was killed while fighting on shore, and the men with
him took to flight. The Athenians captured the entire

Peloponnesian fleet except for the Syracusan ships which were burned by their crews. They then sailed off to Proconnesus, taking the ships with them.*

19 Next day they sailed out against Cyzicus. The town had been evacuated by the Peloponnesians and Pharnabazus, and the townspeople received the Athenians inside the walls.

20 Alcibiades stayed there for twenty days and raised large sums of money from the citizens. Then, without doing any other harm to the place, he sailed back to Proconnesus and went on

21 from there to Perinthus and Selymbria. The people of Perinthus allowed his forces inside their walls, and the people of Selymbria, while not letting them inside, contributed money.

22 Next they went on to Chrysopolis, in Calchedonia, and built fortifications there. They established a customs house in the city and began to levy a ten-per-cent tax on all cargoes sailing out through the Bosporus.† They left behind there as a garrison thirty ships with two of the generals, Theramenes and Eumachus. Their duties were to look after the fort, to levy the tax on outgoing ships and to do any other harm they could to the enemy. The other generals then went back to the Hellespont.

23 Meanwhile Hippocrates, Mindarus' vice-admiral, had sent a letter to Sparta. This letter was captured and taken to Athens. It was as follows: 'Ships lost. Mindarus dead. Men starving. Don't know what to do.'‡

*For a different account of the battle of Cyzicus, see Diod. XIII.49 ff. Cf. R. J. Littmann, 'The strategy of the battle of Cyzicus', *Trans. Amer. Philol. Ass.*, 99, 1968, pp. 265–72.

†Cf. Diod. XIII.64.2. Despite Polybius IV.44.4, the institution of a customs-house at the Bosporus probably went back to the Periclean period (cf. *Greek Historical Inscriptions*, ed. Meiggs and Lewis, 58 A, l.7). It was reinstituted by Thrasybulus in the late 390s (IV.8.27). A small squadron of the Athenian navy probably enforced payment (cf. Meiggs and Lewis, *op. cit.*, 65, l.39).

‡Diod. XIII.52 f. records a Spartan offer of peace with Athens after the battle of Cyzicus, which was rebuffed at the instigation of Cleophon. If it happened, it is one of Xenophon's more astonishing omissions. He eschews the part played by Cleophon in the last years

Pharnabazus, however, did his best to keep up the spirits of 24
the whole army of the Peloponnesians and their allies. He
told them that so long as their lives were theirs they should
not be discouraged because of the loss of ships' timbers, since
there were plenty more of these in the King's dominions.
He gave each man a cloak and two months' rations; and he
armed the men who had served in the fleet and put them on
guard duty along his own coastline. He then called to- 25
gether the ship-captains and the generals from the various
cities and instructed the men from each city to build at
Antandrus the same number of triremes as those which
they had lost. He himself supplied the money, and told them
to take the timber from Mount Ida. While this work was 26
being done the Syracusans helped the men of Antandrus to
finish part of their fortifications, and in the duties of defence
made themselves more popular than anyone else. As a result
they now enjoy the privilege of benefactors and the rights
of citizens at Antandrus. After making these arrangements
Pharnabazus set out at once to relieve Calchedon.

The Syracusan generals now received the news from home 27
that they had been exiled by the democratic party.* So they
called an assembly of their soldiers at which Hermocrates
spoke for them all. He expressed their deep sorrow at what
had happened to them and claimed that the sentence of exile
passed against them all as a body was both unwarranted and
unconstitutional. He urged the soldiers to show in the future
the same spirit that they had shown in the past and to act like
good men in carrying out every order that was given, and
he told them to elect new commanders to hold office until
those chosen to replace them should arrive from Syracuse.

---

of the war, mentioning him only once (I.7.35 and n.). He also omits
to notice the end of the Constitution of Theramenes and the re-
establishment of the full democracy at Athens (cf. Andocides I.96),
again astonishingly.

*Either noticed proleptically by Thuc. VIII.85.3, or, more prob-
ably, Xenophon has misplaced the event.

28 The men, however, especially the captains, marines and
steersmen, protested loudly and asked the existing generals
to hold on to their commands. But they refused. 'We ought
not,' they said, 'to form an opposition party to our own
government. But if anyone has any charges to bring against
us, then you should allow us to speak in our defence.
Remember all the naval battles you have won and all the
ships you have captured when fighting entirely by yourselves,
and how often afterwards in an allied command you have
shown yourselves invincible under our leadership, and how
you have held the place of honour in the line of battle because of our skill and your own daring and willing spirit
which has made itself evident both on land and sea.'

29 No one brought any charges against them, and at the request of the men they stayed on until the generals arrived to
replace them. These were Demarchus, the son of Epicydes,
Myscon, the son of Menecrates, and Potamis, the son of
Gnosis. On their arrival the men said good-bye to the outgoing generals and sent them away with freedom to travel
where they liked. Most of the captains took an oath that,
when they got back to Syracuse, they would see to it that
these generals were recalled from exile. They had all been
30 popular, but Hermocrates was particularly badly missed by
those who had been in close contact with him and who now
felt the loss of his guiding authority, his readiness to help
and his ability to mix with his men. Every morning and
every evening he had been in the habit of inviting to his own
tent a select body of those whose acquaintance he had made,
both captains and steersmen and marines, and he would discuss with them whatever he was planning to say or to do.
He would explain his reasons and then ask them sometimes
to express their opinions at once, sometimes to go away and
31 think it over first. Hermocrates, as a result of this, had a very
high reputation in the general assembly. He was regarded
there as the best speaker and the most reliable planner.

In the past he had spoken against Tissaphernes in Sparta and, with Astyochus backing him up, had convinced the Spartans that what he said was true. So that now when he went to visit Pharnabazus he was given money even before he asked for it. With this he began to provide himself with mercenaries and triremes in order to secure his recall to Syracuse. Meanwhile the new Syracusan generals arrived at Miletus and took over command of the ships and the army.

About this time there was a revolution in Thasos,* and the 32 Spartan governor Eteonicus together with the pro-Spartan party was driven out. The Spartan Pasippidas was accused at Sparta of having plotted the organization of this revolt with Tissaphernes, and was forced to go into exile. Cratesippidas was sent out from Sparta to take over the fleet which Pasippidas had raised from the allies, and took over his command at Chios.

Also about this time, when Thrasyllus was still in Athens, 33 Agis, from his base at Decelea, led his troops out on a raid right up to the city wall. Thrasyllus led out the Athenian and all other forces available, and drew them up in line by the Lyceum with the intention of engaging the enemy if he should come any nearer.† When he saw this, Agis quickly 34 withdrew, and a few men from his rear-guard were killed by the Athenian light troops. As a result of this action the Athenians were all the more willing to give Thrasyllus what he had come to ask, and they passed a vote authorizing him to call up for service 1,000 hoplites,‡ 100 cavalry, and 50 triremes.

Meanwhile, from Decelea Agis could see the ships carrying 35

---

*The part played by Tissaphernes suggests that 'Thasos' is a corruption of 'Iasos', a small town on the Asiatic coast some twenty miles to the north of Halicarnassus (cf. Thuc. VIII.28.2 f., 29.1).

†Is this a confusion of the events of Thuc. VIII.71 or of those of Diod. XIII.72 f.?

‡Heavy-armed troops.

grain that were constantly sailing in to Piraeus, and he remarked that there was no use in his men going on spending so much time in cutting the Athenians off from their land unless it were possible also to control the sources from which food was being brought in to them by sea. He therefore proposed to send Clearchus,* the son of Rhamphias, to Calchedon and Byzantium. Clearchus was the man who looked after

36 the diplomatic interests of Byzantium in Sparta. This proposal was approved. Fifteen ships, designed rather as troop-carriers than as warships, were manned by the Megarians and the other allies, and with these Clearchus set out. Three of his ships were sunk in the Hellespont by the nine Athenian ships always on patrol there to guard their merchantmen, but the rest got away to Sestus and from there got safely to Byzantium.

37 So the year ended.

This was the year in which the Carthaginians, under Hannibal, invaded Sicily with an army of 100,000 men, and in a campaign lasting three months captured two Greek cities, Selinus and Himera.†

---

*According to Thuc. VIII.80, Clearchus had been sent out in 411, and, according to Diod. XIII.51, he took part in the battle of Cyzicus (*v.s.* I.1.11 ff.).

†This paragraph is generally thought not to have been written by Xenophon. Cf. n. at I.2.1.

CHAPTER 2

409 B.C. Thrasyllus in Ionia. Alcibiades and Thrasyllus join forces

THE following year was that of the ninety-third Olympiad 1
in which Euagoras of Elis won the two-horse race (a newly
added event) and Eubotas of Cyrene won the 200-yard foot
race. Euarchippus was ephor at Sparta and Euctemon archon
at Athens.* In this year the Athenians fortified Thoricus. At
the beginning of the summer Thrasyllus sailed from Athens
to Samos with the ships that had been voted to him. He had
equipped 5,000 of his sailors as peltasts.† After staying three 2
days in Samos he sailed to Pygela, where he laid the country waste and made an assault on the fortifications. However,
some troops from Miletus arrived to reinforce the people of
Pygela, and put to flight some Athenian light troops whom
they came upon when they were out of formation. But 3
the peltasts and two companies of hoplites came up in relief
and destroyed the Milesian force almost to the last man.
They captured about two hundred shields and set up a
trophy.

Next day they sailed to Notium and from there, after 4
making the necessary preparations, marched to Colophon
and won the town over peaceably.

* Such chronological notices (cf. I.3.1, 6.1; II.1.10, 3.1 and 9 f.)
were almost certainly inserted in the text of Xenophon by a later
hand, as probably were the notes concerning Sicilian and Oriental
history etc. (I.1.37, 2.19, 5.21; II.1.8 f., 3.4 f.). For a discussion of the
chronology of these years, cf. *Cambridge Ancient History*, V, p. 483 ff.

† 'Peltasts' were light-armed infantry, equipped with spear and
the crescent moon-shaped Thracian shield, used ever more frequently
in the Peloponnesian War. Thrasyllus' action was an important
development (cf. J. G. P. Best, *Thracian Peltasts*, 1969, esp. p. 36 f.);
in certain circumstances the peltast was to prove superior to the hoplite (cf. IV.5.13 f.).

It was now the time when the corn was growing ripe, and in the following night they made a raid inland into Lydia. They burned a number of villages and captured large quanti-
5 ties of money, slaves and other kinds of property. However, the Persian, Stages, was in the area, and when the Athenians left camp and set off to get plunder, each man for himself, he captured one of them and killed seven others, though the
6 cavalry came up in support. After this Thrasyllus led the army back to the coast. He intended next to sail on to Ephesus, but Tissaphernes got to know of the plan and got together a large force to deal with it. He sent horsemen all round the country with instructions that everyone should move on Ephesus for the protection of Artemis.
7 It was on the seventeenth day after his raid that Thrasyllus sailed in to Ephesus.* He landed the hoplites at the foot of Mount Coressus and the cavalry, peltasts, marines and all the rest near the marsh on the other side of the city. At dawn he
8 gave orders for both divisions to advance. But those in the city came out to meet him. There were the Ephesians them-selves, the allied force brought up by Tissaphernes, the Syra-cusans (both the crews of the original twenty ships and also of five others under the command of Eucles, the son of Hip-pon, and Heraclides, the son of Aristogenes, which happened to have just arrived) and the crews of the two ships from
9 Selinus.† The whole of this force moved first against the hop-lites at Coressus and put them to flight, killing about a hun-dred and pursuing the rest to the shore. They then turned against the Athenians by the marsh, and these, too, were
10 routed and about three hundred of them killed. The Ephe-sians put up a trophy at this spot and another one at Coressus.

---

*For a newly-discovered papyrus fragment concerning Thrasyllus at Ephesus, very probably from the *Hellenica Oxyrhynchus*, cf. L. Koenen, *Studia Papyrologica*, XV, 1976, pp. 55 ff.
†Thuc. VIII.26.1.

They awarded the prizes for valour to the Syracusans and to the men of Selinus, since both had fought with particular distinction. The prizes given were to individuals as well as to the troops as a whole. They also gave them the right, if any of them wished to avail themselves of it, to live in Ephesus tax free. And after Selinus had been destroyed they gave the Selinuntines the right of Ephesian citizenship as well.

The Athenians took up the bodies of their dead under a 11 truce and sailed back to Notium where they buried them. They then set sail for Lesbos and the Hellespont. While they 12 were at anchor at Methymna in Lesbos they caught sight of the twenty-five Syracusan ships from Ephesus, which were sailing past. They put out to sea against them, captured four ships together with the crews, and chased the rest back to Ephesus. Thrasyllus sent all the prisoners back to Athens 13 except for one of them, an Athenian called Alcibiades who was stoned to death. He was a cousin of Alcibiades the general and had been in exile with him. From there Thrasyllus sailed to Sestus to join the rest of the army, and from Sestus the whole force crossed over to Lampsacus.

It was now nearly winter, and in the course of this winter 14 the Syracusan prisoners, who had been shut up in the stone quarries at Piraeus, dug through the rock and escaped by night. Most of them got away to Decelea, though some went to Megara.

At Lampsacus, meanwhile, Alcibiades wanted the whole 15 army to serve together as one unit, but the old soldiers refused to serve in the same ranks with those who had come with Thrasyllus. They themselves, they said, had never been defeated, while these others had just arrived from a defeat. However, both detachments joined in fortifying Lampsacus, where they spent the winter. They also made an expedition 16 against Abydus, and Pharnabazus, who had brought up a large force of cavalry to its defence, was defeated in battle and put to flight. Alcibiades with the Athenian cavalry and 120 hop-

lites under Menander pursued him till darkness made it pos-
17 sible for him to get away. As a result of this battle the troops
got together of their own accord and the old soldiers began
to fraternize with Thrasyllus' men. During the winter several
other raids were made into the interior, and some damage
was done to the king's territories.

18 At this time the Spartans reached an agreement with the
helots* who had revolted and fled from Malea to Co",ypha-
sium.† They were allowed to leave Coryphasium under a
safe conduct. Also at this time the colonists of Heraclea in
Trachis were betrayed by the Achaeans in a battle in which
both they and the Achaeans had gone into action against the
Oetaeans. As a result of Achaean treachery about seven hundred of the men of Heraclea, including Labotas, the Spartan
governor, were killed.

19 So the year ended. It was the year in which the Medes who
had revolted from Darius, king of the Persians, were again
brought into subjection.

*Spartan serfs, for the most part descendants of the ancient Messen-
ians (cf. Thuc. I.101.2).

†Unlike Xenophon, Thucydides (IV.3.2) saw fit to explain that
Coryphasium was the Spartan name for Pylos.

CHAPTER 3

Sieges of Calchedon and Byzantium

DURING the following year the temple of Athena at Phocaea 1
was struck by lightning and set on fire. In this year Pantacles
was ephor and Antigenes archon,* and the war had lasted
for twenty-two years.

After the winter was over and at the very beginning of
spring the whole Athenian force sailed to Proconnesus, and 2
from there set out against Calchedon and Byzantium. They
made their camp near Calchedon. Meanwhile the citizens of
Calchedon, who had heard that the Athenians were coming,
had entrusted all their portable property to their neighbours,
the Bithynian Thracians. Alcibiades, however, ordered the 3
ships to sail after him along the coast and, taking the cavalry
and a few hoplites with him, went to the Bithynians and
demanded that they should give up the property, and said
that he would make war on them if they refused. They accordingly handed it over, and Alcibiades, after making a 4
treaty with them, came back to camp with the booty. He
then employed the whole army in blockading Calchedon.†
A wooden stockade was built from sea to sea and brought as
close as possible to the line of the river which intersected
it.

At this point Hippocrates, the Spartan governor, led his 5
men out from the city to fight. The Athenians drew up in
order of battle to meet him, and Pharnabazus, from his
position outside the blockading lines, came up with a large
force of infantry and cavalry to help him. Fighting went on 6

---

*Antigenes was archon at Athens in 407–6. The interpolator has
blundered. Cf. n. at I.2.1.

†For another account of the blockade, see Diod. XIII.66.

for a long time between the hoplite armies of Hippocrates and Thrasyllus, but then Alcibiades with the cavalry and a few hoplites came to the help of Thrasyllus. Hippocrates was

7 killed and his men fled back into the city. At the same time Pharnabazus also withdrew. He had been unable to join up with Hippocrates because of the lack of room for manoeuvre, since the stockade came down close to the river, and he now retired to his camp at the Heracleium in Calchedonian territory.

8   Alcibiades went away after this to the Hellespont and the Chersonese to raise money, and the other generals came to an agreement with Pharnabazus that they would spare Calchedon if he paid them twenty talents and also conducted

9 Athenian ambassadors to the King. It was also agreed (and oaths were exchanged on both sides) that Calchedon should pay the Athenians the same amount of tribute as they used to pay in the past and should make up all arrears of payment, and that the Athenians would take no hostile action against Calchedon until the ambassadors had returned from the King.

10   At the time when these oaths were exchanged Alcibiades was away at Selymbria. He captured this city and then moved on to Byzantium. He had with him the whole army of the people of the Chersonese, some Thracian troops and more

11 than 300 cavalry. Pharnabazus considered that Alcibiades ought to give his oath, too, to the agreement, and so he waited at Calchedon for him to return from Byzantium. However, when he did get back he said he was not going to swear an oath to Pharnabazus unless Pharnabazus also swore

12 an oath to him. Later he gave his oath at Chrysopolis in the presence of two representatives of Pharnabazus, Mitrobates and Arnapes; and Pharnabazus gave his oath at Calchedon in the presence of Alcibiades' representatives, Euryptolemus and Diotimus. The oaths not only covered the original general agreement but also included specific pledges given by each man to the other.

Directly afterwards Pharnabazus left Calchedon and in- 13
structed the Athenian ambassadors to meet him at Cyzicus.
This Athenian embassy consisted of Dorotheus, Philocydes,
Theogenes, Euryptolemus and Mantitheus, together with
the two Argives, Cleostratus and Pyrrolochus; on the
Spartan side Pasippidas and others went along too, and with
them was Hermocrates, now an exile from Syracuse, and
his brother Proxenus.

Pharnabazus then set out with his party, and the Athenians 14
went on with the siege of Byzantium. They had built siege
works all round the place and launched attacks on the fortifications both at long range and at close quarters. Inside the 15
city was the Spartan governor Clearchus, who had with him
some Laconian Perioeci,* and a few helots who had won
their freedom,† one contingent of Megarians, and one of
Boeotians. The Megarians were commanded by their fellow-
countryman Helixus, and the Boeotians by Coeratadas.

The Athenians, after finding that their efforts to take the 16
city by force were getting them nowhere, persuaded some of
the Byzantines to betray the place to them. This was a thing 17
which Clearchus, the governor, imagined that no one would
do; and so, after having made what seemed to him the best
possible arrangements for the defence, he left Helixus and
Coeratadas in charge and went across the straits to visit
Pharnabazus in order to get money from him to pay the
army and also to raise more ships. His plan was to get together the ships which had been left behind by Pasippidas and
which were on patrol in the Hellespont, and also the ships
at Antandrus and those which were operating on the coast
of Thrace under the command of Agesandridas, one of

*i.e. Lacedaemonians who were not full Spartan citizens although
they fought beside Spartans in the hoplite phalanx, but who belonged
to the many small communities within Laconia, the territory of
Sparta.
†The so-called *neodamodeis*.

Mindarus' junior officers.* He would also have other ships
built, and then with the whole fleet combined would make
attacks on the Athenian allies with a view to forcing the Athen-
18 ians to withdraw their forces from Byzantium. However,
the men who were organizing the betrayal of the city got to
work as soon as Clearchus had sailed away. These men were
19 Cydon, Ariston, Anaxicrates, Lycurgus and Anaxilaus. Because of the betrayal Anaxilaus was afterwards put on trial
for his life at Sparta, but was acquitted. His defence was that
he was a Byzantine, not a Spartan; he had seen women and
children dying of hunger, since Clearchus gave all the food
there was in the city to the Spartan and allied soldiers; and
this was why he had admitted the enemy – not because he
had been bribed, nor out of hatred for the Spartans.
20   What happened was this. When the conspirators had made
their plans, they opened the gates at night (the ones leading
to what is known as 'the Thracian square') and then let in the
21 Athenian army with Alcibiades. Helixus and Coeratadas,
quite ignorant of what was happening, led all their men into
the market place to resist the enemy. But when they found
that the enemy were in control everywhere and that their
22 position was hopeless, they surrendered.† They were all sent
to Athens. Coeratadas,‡ when they were disembarking at
Piraeus, managed to slip away in the crowd and got away
safely to Decelea.

*Xenophon uses the Spartan term, *epibatês*, without explanation
(cf. *Hell. Oxy.* 22.4).

†For another account of the capture of Byzantium, see Diod.
XIII.66 f.

‡He later appeared at Byzantium in 400 as a mercenary general
(*Anab.* VII.1.33 ff.), and was in 395 a leading Theban politician (*Hell.
Oxy.* 17.1).

CHAPTER 4

Arrival of Cyrus. Alcibiades' return to Athens (407 B.C.)

THE news of what had happened at Byzantium reached Phar- 1
nabazus and the ambassadors while they were spending the
winter at Gordium in Phrygia. At the beginning of the spring 2
they were on their way again to the King, but met with
another party on its way back. These were the Spartan ambassadors, Boeotius and those with him, and the other messengers. Their report was that the Spartans had got everything
that they wanted from the King; also that Cyrus had been 3
appointed to take command of the whole coastline and to
help the Spartans in the war. Cyrus had a letter with him,
bearing the King's seal and addressed to all the inhabitants of
the coastal areas. Among other things it contained the following words: 'I am sending Cyrus down to the coast as *caranus*
[a word which means "lord"] of all those whose mobilization centre is Castolus.'

After the Athenian ambassadors had heard this news and 4
had seen Cyrus himself, they wanted in the first place, and if
it were possible, to go on and see the King; and if this were
not possible, to return home. Cyrus, however, did not want 5
the Athenians at home to know what was going on and he
told Pharnabazus either to leave the ambassadors in his
charge, or at any rate not to let them go home yet. So 6
Pharnabazus, in order to avoid trouble with Cyrus, kept the
ambassadors with him for the time being. Sometimes he
pretended that he was just on the point of taking them to see
the King and at other times that he was just getting ready to
escort them home, adding 'so you won't have to blame me'.
So three years went by.* In the end Pharnabazus asked Cyrus 7

* Cyrus' presence must have been well known long before three

69

to release them, saying that he had sworn an oath that he would take them back to the coast if he could not take them to the King. So the ambassadors were sent to Ariobarzanes, who was instructed to escort them. Ariobarzanes conducted them to Cius, in Mysia, and they sailed from there to rejoin the Athenian army.

8 Alcibiades, meanwhile, wanted to sail home accompanied by his own troops. First he went to Samos and, taking twenty 9 ships, sailed to the Gulf of Ceramus, in Caria. There he raised 100 talents before returning to Samos.

Thrasybulus, with thirty ships, went to the Thracian coast where he reduced all the places which had revolted and gone over to the Spartans. Among these was Thasos which, what with war, revolution and famine, was in a very miserable condition.

10 Thrasyllus, with the rest of the fleet, sailed home to Athens. Before he arrived the Athenians had elected as generals Alcibiades, though he was still in exile, Thrasybulus, who was absent, and, from those actually present in Athens, Conon.

11 Alcibiades now set sail from Samos with his twenty ships and the money. He went first to Paros and from there straight on to Gytheum to find out what he could about the triremes which, as was reported, were being fitted out there by the Spartans. At the same time he was waiting to find out what the feeling in Athens was likely to be about his coming 12 back. He soon realized that the city was friendly towards him, the people had elected him as general and his friends

---

years had elapsed and Pharnabazus could hardly so long have claimed that he was not guilty of breach of faith. So 'three years' is probably a corruption of the text and the Euryptolemus involved (I.3.13) may well have been back in Athens to welcome Alcibiades (I.4.19). He was perhaps one of Xenophon's principal informants (cf. the space accorded to his speech at the trial of the generals – I.7.16–33 – and the sympathetic view of his cousin at I.4.13 ff., etc.).

were constantly sending him messages on their own, urging him to return. So he set sail and put in to Piraeus on the day when the festival of the Plynteria was being celebrated. On this day the statue of Athena is covered up from sight, and many people took the coincidence of Alcibiades' arrival with this day as a bad omen both for him and for the city; for no Athenian would venture to start doing anything important on that day.

Dense crowds of people, not only from Piraeus but from Athens itself, gathered around the ships as he sailed in. Everyone wanted to see and to wonder at the sight of the great Alcibiades. He, it was said, was the best citizen they had got and he alone had been banished not because he deserved it but because of the intrigues of people who were inferior to him in power, who lacked his abilities to speak and whose only political principle was their own self-interest. Alcibiades, on the other hand, was always doing good to the state as a whole, and he used both his own private resources and the resources of the public to that end. He had been perfectly willing at the time to stand his trial immediately and when the charge against him of having profaned the Mysteries was quite fresh, and quite clearly he was entitled to do so. His enemies, however, had managed to put the trial off, and then, when he was absent, had robbed him of his rights as a citizen. In the time of his exile he had been the helpless slave of necessity and, being every day in danger of losing his life, had no other course but to make himself agreeable to those whom he hated most. Meanwhile, he saw the mistakes that were being made by those whom he loved best – his fellow-citizens, his kinsmen, the whole city; but he was an exile, shut off from them, and could do nothing to help them. Nor was it in the character of people like Alcibiades to work for revolution or any violent change; his position under the democracy had been that of a man who had been more distinguished than any of his contemporaries and no less distinguished than any of his elders; his enemies, on the other hand, were not thought any more highly of after his banishment than they had been before; true that, once they had gained power, they had destroyed all the best men and, since only they were left, they were accepted by the citizens for the simple reason that better men were not available.

17 That was one view. Others said that Alcibiades, and Alcibiades alone, was responsible for the troubles of the past, and that the chances were that he, too, would turn out to be the chief cause for all the perils of the future.

18 Alcibiades meanwhile brought his ship to anchor close to the shore, but did not land at once as he was still apprehensive about his enemies. Standing on deck he looked round to see
19 whether his friends were present. When he caught sight of his cousin Euryptolemus, the son of Peisianax, and his other relatives and his friends with them, he landed from the ship and went up to Athens, surrounded by a party ready to pro-
20 tect him from any attempt at arrest. He then made speeches both in the Council and the Assembly in his own defence, stating that he had not been guilty of sacrilege and claiming that he had been unjustly treated. More of the same sort was said, and no one said a word in contradiction; the Assembly would not have tolerated it if anyone had. Alcibiades was then proclaimed supreme commander with authority over all the other generals. He, it was thought, was the man who had the ability to re-establish the former power of Athens.

His first act was to organize the procession to Eleusis for the Mysteries. Previously, because of the war, the procession had gone by sea; but Alcibiades led out the whole army and escorted it by land.

21 After this he raised a force of 1,500 hoplites, 150 cavalry and 100 ships. Then, four months after his return to Athens, he set sail for Andros, which had revolted from the Athenian alliance. Aristocrates and Adimantus, the son of Leucolo-

phides, were sent out with him as the generals chosen to operate by land.

Alcibiades landed his army at Gaureum in Andros. The 22 men of Andros and the Laconians who were with them came out to oppose the Athenians, but were routed and penned up inside the city. The Athenians killed a few of them and 23 Alcibiades set up a trophy. Then, after staying on at Andros for a few days, he sailed to Samos, which he was making his base for the prosecution of the war.

CHAPTER 5

Lysander. Athenian Defeat at Notium. Alcibiades deposed (406 B.C.)

1 NOT long before this the Spartans had sent out Lysander as admiral to replace Cratesippidas, whose term of office had expired. Lysander went to Rhodes, where he took over the ships stationed there, and then sailed to Cos, Miletus and Ephesus, where he remained with seventy ships until Cyrus

2 arrived at Sardis. He then went inland to visit Cyrus, and took with him the ambassadors from Sparta. They lost no time in telling Cyrus how badly, in their opinion, Tissaphernes had behaved, and they begged him to take a really serious

3 and energetic part in the war. 'That,' said Cyrus, 'is exactly what my father has asked me to do and that is what I mean to do myself. I shall do all that I can.' He told them that he had brought 500 talents with him. If that was not enough, he said, he would use his own money, which had been given him by his father, and if that also ran out, he would break up the throne of silver and gold on which he sat.

4 The ambassadors thanked him for these words. They then suggested that he should fix the pay at one Attic drachma a day for each sailor, pointing out that, if this was the wage offered, the Athenian crews would desert their ships and so he would save money in the long run.

5 Cyrus replied that, though this was a good idea, it was not possible for him to act contrary to the instructions he had received from the King. The present agreement, he said, was that, however many ships the Spartans wished to keep in service, the King would provide thirty minae a month for each ship.

6 Lysander said no more about this matter at the moment,

but after dinner, when Cyrus drank his health and asked him what he could do for him which would please him most,* he replied: 'You would please me most if you were to add one obol to each sailor's pay.'

From that time on the pay was increased from three to 7 four obols a day. Cyrus also settled all arrears and in addition gave them a month's pay in advance. The result was a great improvement in the men's morale.

All this was depressing news for the Athenians, and they 8 sent ambassadors to Cyrus, using Tissaphernes as a go-between. Cyrus, however, refused to receive them, in spite 9 of the entreaties of Tissaphernes, who urged him to follow his own policy (which he had adopted on the advice of Alcibiades) – namely, to guard against the emergence of any single strong Greek state by seeing that they were all kept weak by constantly fighting among themselves.

After Lysander had reorganized the fleet, he dragged 10 ashore the ninety ships which were at Ephesus and remained inactive while they were being dried out and refitted. Alci- 11 biades, meanwhile, had heard that Thrasybulus had sailed out from the Hellespont and was organizing a blockade of Pho-caea from the land. He sailed across to see him and left his own pilot Antiochus in command of the fleet with orders not to bring about an engagement with Lysander's ships. But Antiochus with his own ship and one other put out from 12 Notium into the harbour of Ephesus, and then went sailing along right past the prows of Lysander's fleet. At first 13 Lysander launched a few ships and sent them in pursuit of Antiochus and then the Athenians came up with more ships to support him. Finally, Lysander launched all the ships he had, put them in line of battle and went into action. The Athenians then launched all the rest of their triremes at Notium and put out to sea one after another, just as they

*For the friendship of Lysander and Cyrus, cf. *Oeconomicus* IV.20 ff.

14 were launched. Thus in the battle that followed one side was fighting in good order while the Athenians were in no sort of order at all. In the end they turned and fled with the loss of fifteen triremes. Most of the crews got away, though some were taken prisoner. Lysander took over the captured ships and sailed across to Ephesus, after having put up a trophy at Notium. The Athenians then sailed to Samos.*

15 After this Alcibiades arrived at Samos. He put to sea with the whole fleet and made for the harbour of Ephesus, where he formed his ships up in order of battle at the harbour's mouth as a challenge to the enemy to fight. But Lysander, whose fleet was greatly inferior in numbers, did not take up the challenge. Alcibiades then sailed back to Samos. Soon after this the Spartans captured Delphinium and Eion.

16 When the news of the naval battle reached Athens, the Athenians were furious with Alcibiades. In their view it was because of his carelessness and the general irregularity of his character that the ships had been lost.† They then elected ten new generals, Conon, Diomedon, Leon, Pericles, Erasinides, Aristocrates, Archestratus, Protomachus, Thrasyllus and

17 Aristogenes. So Alcibiades, who was now unpopular in the

*The account of Diodorus XIII.71 plainly derives from *Hell. Oxy.* 4, for the understanding of which the key word is the partially preserved word for a sea-ambush (*nau]lochein*). Antiochus did not disobey orders, but took a small squadron of ten ships, put eight of them behind a headland, and tried to lure out 'the three ships' which Lysander had used previously as a patrol; the plan miscarried; the eight Athenian ships, Xenophon's 'more ships', were chased home and the Athenian fleet forced suddenly to get out and try to rescue them, with disastrous results. Xenophon gives the story from a purely Spartan viewpoint, an important indication of the date at which he wrote Book I. See Introduction p. 28 f.

†Diod. XIII.73 says that the naval reverse was only part of the case against Alcibiades, and describes an abortive raid on Cyme, a member of the Athenian Empire, as well as the threat of a number of private legal actions.

army as well, sailed off with one trireme to his castles in the Chersonese.

After he had gone, Conon sailed from Andros with his 18 own twenty ships and came to Samos to take over the command of the fleet in accordance with the decrees passed by the Athenians. They had sent Phanosthenes to Andros with four ships to replace Conon, and on his way there he fell in 19 with two Thurian triremes and captured them, together with their crews. These men were all put in prison by the Athenians except for their commander, Dorieus. At this time Dorieus was a citizen of Thurii, but he had been born a Rhodian and then, some time previously, been exiled from both Rhodes and Athens. In fact, the Athenians had passed a vote condemning him and all his family to death. Now, however, they had pity on him and let him go free without even demanding a ransom.

When Conon arrived at Samos he found that the fleet was 20 in a poor state of morale. He fully manned seventy triremes instead of the number (more than 100) which had been in service before and then, taking the other generals with him, set sail with these. He made a number of landings at various points in enemy territory and carried off plunder.

So the year ended. This was the year in which the Cartha- 21 ginians invaded Sicily with 120 triremes and an army of 120,000 men. Though defeated in a pitched battle, they forced Acragas to surrender through hunger, after having besieged it for seven months.*

*Cf. n. at I.2.1.

CHAPTER 6

Battle of Arginusae (406 B.C.)

1 THE following year was the one in which there was an eclipse of the moon one evening and the old temple of Athena at Athens was burned. Pityas was ephor at Sparta and Callias archon at Athens.*

In the summer of this year the Spartans sent out Callicratidas to take over the command of the fleet from Lysander, whose term of office had expired. The war had now gone on
2 for twenty-four years. When Lysander gave up his command he told Callicratidas that he was doing so as master of the sea and as conqueror in battle. Callicratidas then told him to sail along the coast from Ephesus, with Samos, the Athenian naval base, on his left, and bring the ships to him at Miletus. 'If you do this,' he said, 'I shall be quite prepared
3 to recognize that you are master of the sea.' But Lysander replied that, since someone else was in command, all this was none of his business.

So Callicratidas, acting on his own, manned with crews from Chios and Rhodes and other allied states fifty ships in addition to those he had taken over from Lysander, and with the whole force together, 140 ships in all, prepared to engage
4 the enemy. He found, however, that his authority was being undermined by Lysander's friends, who were not only slow in carrying out orders but were also spreading abroad in all the cities their own views, which were to the effect that the Spartans were making a very serious mistake in changing their admirals; in place of men who were really showing ability, they said, men who were just becoming proficient in naval warfare and who knew well how to treat those under

*Cf. n. at I.2.1.

their command, the Spartan government was too apt to send
out people who knew nothing of the sea and were themselves
unknown to the men on the spot; and this policy was likely
to end in disaster.

In this situation Callicratidas called a meeting of all the
Spartans present and spoke to them as follows: 'Personally I 5
am perfectly content to stay at home. And if Lysander or anyone else wants to claim a superiority in the knowledge of sea
warfare, I, for my own part, have no objection. However,
it is I who have been commissioned by the state to command
the fleet, and I have no alternative except to carry out my
orders to the best of my ability. What I want you to do now
is to weigh up in your minds the questions of my ambition
and of the criticisms made against Sparta (you know these
just as well as I do), and then give me the best advice you can:
am I to stay here, or am I to sail back home and report on the
conditions which I find here?'

No one ventured to suggest any other course of action 6
except that he should obey the authorities at home and carry
on the work for which he had been appointed. He then went
to Cyrus and asked him for the pay for the sailors, but Cyrus
told him to wait two days. Callicratidas was furious at being 7
put off and at having to keep behaving like a courtier. It was
a sad day for the Greeks, he said, when they had to make up
to foreigners for the sake of money, and he declared that if
he got home safely he would do his best to make peace between Athens and Sparta.* He then sailed away to Miletus,

* The rivalry of Lysander and Callicratidas reflected a wide difference
in Spartan views about the conduct of the war. Lysander, the intimate
of Cyrus (I.5.6 and n.), did not scruple to depend on Persian aid;
Callicratidas, whose reported dictum here is echoed by the Panhellenist Teleutias (V.1.17), would prefer to come to terms with Athens.
(Cf. Cawkwell, *Yale Classical Studies*, XXIV, 1975, p. 63 f.) He was
a character who appealed to Xenophon; hence the full account including a number of colourful dicta (I.6.3, 14, 15, 32) as well as the
two speeches.

8 and from there sent triremes to Sparta to ask for money.
Next he called an assembly of the people of Miletus and
addressed them as follows: 'What I have to do, men of
9 Miletus, is to obey my home government. As for you, I
think that you ought to show the greatest possible willingness
to help in this war, since you live surrounded by foreigners
and you have suffered a great deal from them in the past.
It is up to you to give a lead to the other allies and show
them how we can do most damage to the enemy in the
shortest time, until my messengers return from Sparta. I sent
10 them there to get money, since Lysander, before going away,
gave back to Cyrus all the money he had as though we had
enough already. I went to Cyrus, but he kept on avoiding an
interview with me and I could not bring myself to hang
11 around his court. But I promise you that I shall show a fitting
gratitude in return for all successes that we win during the
time that we are waiting for the money from Sparta. Let us,
then, with the help of heaven, show the foreigners that, even
without paying excessive attention to them, we can still
make our enemies suffer for what they have done.'

12 After his speech a number of Milesians rose to speak, and
especially those who were accused of opposing Callicratidas.
In some alarm they proposed a grant of money and went out
of their way to make personal contributions. Callicratidas
took this money and also secured from Chios a sum of five
drachmas for each of the sailors. He then sailed to the city of
13 Methymna, in Lesbos, which was in enemy hands. Here the
citizens refused to surrender. There was an Athenian garrison
inside the town and the government was pro-Athenian.
14 Callicratidas attacked and took the place by storm. All the
property in the town was taken as plunder by his soldiers,
and all the prisoners were herded together into the market
place. Callicratidas was urged by his allies to sell as slaves the
Methymnaeans as well as the Athenians, but he refused.
While he was in command, he said, no Greek should be sold
as a slave, if he could help it.

Next day, therefore, he let all Methymnaean citizens go 15
free, but sold the men who had formed the Athenian garrison
and those among the prisoners who had been slaves before.
He then sent the following message to Conon: 'I am going
to put a stop to your fornication with the sea. She belongs
to me.'

At dawn he caught sight of Conon putting out to sea and
went after him with the aim of cutting him off so that he
could not retire to Samos. Conon fled away from him at a 16
good speed, since his few ships were manned by the best
rowers chosen out of the crews of many, and he got away to
Mytilene, in Lesbos, with two more of the ten generals, Leon
and Erasinides, in his company. But Callicratidas was right
after him with 170 ships and entered the harbour at the same
time as Conon, who, finding that his way was barred, was 17
forced to engage the enemy at the mouth of the harbour. He
lost thirty ships in the fighting, but their crews got away
safely to the land, and he dragged up his remaining forty
ships under the shelter of the fortifications of the city. Calli- 18
cratidas anchored inside the harbour and blockaded him on
that side by cutting off his way out to the sea. As for the land
side, he ordered the Methymnaeans to come up in full force
and also brought over his army from Chios. And now the
money arrived from Cyrus.

Conon now found himself under blockade from land and 19
sea; he could see no prospect of feeding his men; the population of the city was large; and the Athenians, knowing
nothing of what had happened, would not be doing anything
to help. He therefore launched two of his fastest ships and
had them manned during the night, picking out for them the
best rowers in the whole fleet. The marines were sent below
and side-screens were put up. They stayed aboard during the 20
day and were put ashore in the evening, when it became
dark, so that the enemy should not know what was going on.
On the fifth day they put aboard a moderate supply of food
and at noon, when the blockading force had relaxed their

vigilance and were, in many cases, enjoying a sleep, they
sailed out of the harbour, one ship making for the Hellespont
21 and one for the open sea. The blockaders, who had been
having their meal ashore, got their ships clear one after another, cutting away their anchors, shaking off their sleep and,
in a disorganized sort of way, tried to do the right thing.
When they were aboard, they set off after the ship that had
headed for the open sea and overhauled her at sunset. They
captured her after a fight and then took her in tow and
22 brought her back with all her crew to their station. But the
ship that had made for the Hellespont got away and reached
Athens to give news of the blockade.

Meanwhile Diomedon, in the hope of helping Conon's
blockaded force, had anchored in the straits of Mytilene with
23 twelve ships. But Callicratidas made a sudden attack and captured ten of them. Diomedon himself escaped with his own
ship and one other.

24 When the Athenians heard of what had happened and of
how Conon was under blockade they voted in favour of
sending 110 ships to his relief, and put aboard these ships all
men of military age, slave or free. Within thirty days the
ships were manned and had set out. There were even many
men who were entitled to serve in the cavalry who took part
25 in this expedition. After leaving Athens they sailed to Samos
and there picked up ten Samian ships; more than thirty
others were collected from the rest of the allies, the crews
being made to embark whether they liked it or not; and in
the same way they took over any Athenian ships that happened to be abroad on various missions, so that altogether
they had more than 150 ships.

26 As soon as Callicratidas heard that the relief force was at
Samos, he left behind at Mytilene fifty ships under the command of Eteonicus and set out himself with the remaining
120. They stopped for their midday meal at Cape Malea in
27 Lesbos and it so happened that the Athenians on the same

day were taking their meal on the islands of Arginusae, which lie opposite Mytilene. Callicratidas saw their fires 28 during the night and when he was informed by various people that these were, in fact, the Athenians, he planned to put to sea about midnight so as to fall upon them unexpectedly. However, a thunderstorm with heavy rain prevented him from putting out. When the weather cleared at dawn he set sail for the Arginusae islands.

The Athenians sailed out to meet him. Their left wing was 29 out to sea and they were in the following order: Aristocrates commanded the left wing and led the way with fifteen ships; next to him was Diomedon with fifteen; Pericles was stationed behind Aristocrates and Erasinides behind Diomedon; next to Diomedon were the ten Samian ships in a single line; and next to them, also in single line, were the ten ships commanded by the taxiarchs; behind them were the three ships commanded by the navarchs and also some allied ships. Protomachus, with fifteen ships, was in command of the 30 right wing; next to him was Thrasyllus, also with fifteen ships; Lysias, with the same number, was stationed behind Protomachus, and Aristogenes behind Thrasyllus. The reason 31 for adopting this formation was to prevent the enemy from breaking through the line, since the Athenians were inferior in seamanship. The Spartan ships, on the other hand, with their more skilful crews, were all drawn up in a single line so as to be able to execute the manoeuvres of breaking through and wheeling back on the enemy. Their right wing was under the command of Callicratidas. His steersman, a 32 Megarian called Hermon, told him that it would be wise to retire, since the Athenian triremes were much more numerous than his; but Callicratidas replied, 'If I die, Sparta will go on just the same; what is disgraceful is to run away.'

So battle was joined and the fighting went on for a long 33 time. At first the ships were in close order, but later they became separated. Finally, Callicratidas, as his ship was ramming an enemy ship, fell overboard and disappeared in the water; Protomachus and those with him on the right wing defeated the Spartan left, and, at this point, there was a general flight of the Peloponnesians back to Chios, though many of them went in the direction of Phocaea. The Athenians on their side sailed back to the Arginusae islands.

34 They had lost twenty-five ships with all their crews, except for a few men who were carried ashore. The Peloponnesians lost nine out of the ten Spartan ships and more than sixty allied ships.*

35   After the battle the Athenian generals decided that Theramenes and Thrasybulus, who were ship-captains, and some of the taxiarchs should sail with forty-seven ships to the aid of the disabled ships and the men on board them, and that the rest of the fleet should sail against the blockading force under Eteonicus at Mytilene. However, the wind rose and a heavy storm came on so that they were unable to do as they had planned. They therefore set up a trophy and spent the night where they were.

36   Meanwhile a fast dispatch-boat had reached Eteonicus and given him the full story of what had happened in the battle. Eteonicus ordered the boat to sail away and told those aboard to sail out quietly and not to say a word to anyone while they were leaving the harbour; they were then to sail straight back again to his fleet, wearing garlands and shouting out that Callicratidas had won a great victory and that the whole

37 Athenian fleet had been destroyed. They carried out these instructions and, as they came sailing in, Eteonicus began to offer sacrifices of thanksgiving for the good news. He told the soldiers to take their meal, and ordered the traders to put their goods quietly aboard their ships and then set sail (as the

*Diod. XIII.76–9 and 97–100 gives a much fuller and more systematically developed account of the nauarchy of Callicratidas; his version of the battle of Arginusae is notably different from that of Xenophon.

wind was in the right quarter) for Chios; the triremes were
to follow them at full speed. He himself set fire to the camp 38
and led the army back to Methymna.

Conon, finding that the enemy had gone, launched his
ships and, as the wind had slackened, went to meet the Athenians, who by now had set out from the Arginusae islands.
He told them what Eteonicus had done. The Athenians first
put in to Mytilene and then sailed out again against Chios,
where they failed to accomplish anything. They then sailed
back towards Samos.

CHAPTER 7

Debate on the Generals (406 B.C.)

1 IN Athens the people deposed all these generals except Conon.
They appointed two new generals as his colleagues, Adiman-
2 tus and Philocles. Two of the generals who had taken part
in the battle – Protomachus and Aristogenes – did not return
to Athens. The other six – Pericles, Diomedon, Lysias, Aristocrates, Thrasyllus and Erasinides – did. On their return
Archedemus, who at that time was the leading popular politician and controlled the two-obol relief fund, brought
Erasinides before the court and charged him first with having
in his possession public money from the Hellespont and,
secondly, with misconduct as general. The court sentenced
3 Erasinides to prison. After this the generals made statements
in front of the Council both about the battle and about the
great storm that had arisen after it. Timocrates then proposed
that these generals, too, should be imprisoned and handed
over to the Assembly for trial. The Council adopted this
4 proposal and a meeting of the Assembly was held soon afterwards. Many speakers attacked the generals, and no one
more vigorously than Theramenes, on the ground that they
should be held responsible for not picking up the shipwrecked. As evidence that they could not shift the blame on
to anyone else he produced a letter which they had sent to
the Council and to the Assembly, in which they had given
no other reason for what had happened except the storm.
5 Each of the generals then spoke in his own defence. These
speeches were short, since they were not allowed to speak
for the length of time permitted by law. In their account of
what had taken place they pointed out that they themselves
were to sail against the enemy and they had given the job

of recovering the shipwrecked to various responsible men
among the ship-captains, men who had served as generals in
the past – Theramenes, Thrasybulus and others. If, therefore, 6
anyone was to be blamed at all, it was impossible to blame
anyone else except these men to whom the job had been
given. 'But,' they said, 'we are not going to tell a lie and
say that they are to blame, simply because they are accusing
us. The fact is that what prevented the recovery was the
violence of the storm.' For this they produced as witnesses
many of the steersmen and others who had sailed with them,
and their arguments were proving effective. A number of 7
citizens rose up and offered to give bail for them. However,
it was decided to put off the decision until another meeting
of the Assembly, since by this time it was late in the day and
it would have been impossible to count the hands when it
came to voting. The Council was instructed to review the
matter and then to bring in a proposal as to what sort of
trial the men should have.

After this came the festival of the Apaturia, at which 8
fathers and their families meet together. At this festival Theramenes and his party made arrangements by which a number
of people, dressed in black and with hair close-shaven, should
attend the Assembly, pretending to be kinsmen of those who
had been lost after the battle. They also bribed Callixenus
to attack the generals at the meeting of the Council. They 9
then called a meeting of the Assembly at which the Council
brought in the following proposal. It was introduced by
Callixenus: 'That, since in the previous Assembly the
speeches in accusation of the generals and the speeches of the
generals in their own defence have been heard, the Athenians
shall now all proceed to voting by tribes; that for each tribe
there shall be two voting urns; that in each tribe a herald
shall proclaim that whoever judges the generals guilty for
not picking up the men who won the victory in the sea
battle shall cast his vote in the first urn, and whoever judges

10 them not guilty shall cast his vote in the second urn; and, if they are adjudged guilty, they shall be punished with death and handed over to the Eleven, and their property shall be confiscated to the state and the tenth part of it shall belong to the goddess.'

11 Then a man got up and said that he had been saved by clinging on to a barrel that and others, who were drowning, had told him, if he got away safely, to report to the people that the generals were doing nothing to rescue men who had fought most gallantly for their country.

12 Euryptolemus, the son of Peisianax, and a few others now intervened with a summons against Callixenus for putting forward an unconstitutional proposal, and some sections of the Assembly clearly backed them in this. However, the great mass shouted out that it was an intolerable thing if the

13 people was not allowed to do what it wanted to do. Lyciscus took up this theme and proposed that unless the sponsors of the summons withdrew it, they, too, should be judged by the same vote as the generals. They were thus forced to withdraw the summons.

14 Next some members of the presiding committee declared that they would not put the motion, since it was an illegal one, to the vote. Callixenus then mounted the platform again and put forward the same charge against them, and the crowd shouted out that, if they refused, they should be pro-

15 secuted. At this all the members of the committee except Socrates, the son of Sophroniscus, were terrified and agreed to put the motion to the vote. Socrates said that he would do nothing at all that was contrary to the law.*

---

*The 'presiding committee' (the fifty *prytaneis*) were in a sense in charge of the Assembly as well as of the Council (cf. Aristophanes *Acharnians* 167 ff.), but the 'president' (the *epistates*) was normally in charge. The question of whether the motion here was to be put to the vote or not could only have been discussed and decided by the *prytaneis*, because the *epistates* had refused to put it to the vote. All

Then Euryptolemus rose up to speak and spoke as follows 16
in defence of the generals: 'Men of Athens, in this speech I
shall have something to say against Pericles, although he is a
relation of mine, and against Diomedon, although he is my
friend. I shall also have something to say in their defence;
and, finally, I shall give you what, in my view, is the best
advice for the city as a whole. What I have to say against 17
them is this: they persuaded their colleagues in the command
to change their minds about the letter to be sent to the Council and to you; for the original intention had been to state
that Theramenes and Thrasybulus with forty-seven triremes
had been given the duty of picking up the shipwrecked and
had not done so. And now are these generals to share the 18
blame for what Theramenes and Thrasybulus, on their own
responsibility, failed to do? Are they, in return for the kind-
ness which they showed to these men, to be put in danger of

---

the *prytaneis* save Socrates were in favour of yielding to the popular
demand. He said he would 'do' nothing that was contrary to the law.
That is, he refused to put it to the vote. He was *epistates*. Plato
Gorgias 473ᵉ confirms this view: Socrates failed 'to put it to the vote'.
Plato *Apology* 32ᵇ shows that there was a great uproar against him
for taking his contrary stand, and this can only be because he was
not a mere one in fifty, but the one who really mattered, the *epistates*.

In *Mem.* I.1.18 and IV.4.2 Socrates is said to have been *epistates* on
this occasion. Why does Xenophon not say so here? The answer is
that, although he implied it ('would *do* nothing'), he saw no need to
explain what everyone knew. Xenophon wrote for those who knew.
His method was allusive. Cf. Introduction p. 34.

But, if Socrates was *epistates* and refused to put such a motion to
the vote, how was it that the debate was proceeded with? The answer
is suggested by the spurious Platonic *Axiochus* 368ᵈ: the debate was
adjourned to the next day when there was a new *epistates*. The words
that begin the following paragraph (*meta tauta*), here translated
'then', often in Xenophon should be understood to mean 'the next
thing I choose to tell you is that . . .'

It is only fair to add that although the view developed in this note
has often been held, it is not at present fashionable.

losing their lives because of the intrigues of these men them-
19 selves and certain others? Certainly not, if you will follow
my advice and do what is just and right and what will best
enable you to learn the truth and best preserve you from
finding out later to your sorrow that it is you yourselves who
have been guilty – guilty to the gods and guilty to yourselves.
Now my advice is this: give these men at least one day, if not
more, to speak in their own defence, and put your trust not
in others but in yourselves. In this way you cannot be deceived either by me or anybody else and you will be able,
with full knowledge, to inflict on the guilty any punishment
you like, either on all of them together or on each one
separately.

20 'You all know, men of Athens, the extremely severe terms
of the decree of Cannonus. It provides that if anyone does
harm to the people of Athens, he shall make his defence in
chains before the Assembly, and if he is found guilty, he shall
be put to death by being thrown into the pit, his property
shall be confiscated, and a tenth part of it shall belong to the
21 goddess. It is according to this decree that I propose that you
should judge the generals, and, by Zeus, if you will have it so,
let my kinsman Pericles be the first to stand his trial. For I
should be ashamed to put his interests before those of the city
as a whole.

22 'But if you are against this proposal, then try them under
the law applying to temple-robbers and traitors, which provides that those who are traitors to the state or who have
stolen property sacred to the gods shall be tried before the
courts and, if found guilty, shall not be buried in Attica and
shall have their property confiscated.

23 'Choose whichever one of these laws you like, men of
Athens, but let each prisoner have a separate trial, and let the
day be divided into three parts – one for the prosecution, one
for the defence, and one for deliberating and voting on
whether the accused are innocent or guilty.

'In this way the guilty will be punished with the utmost 24
severity and the innocent will be set free by you, men of
Athens; and will not be unjustly put to death. Moreover, the 25
trial will be in accordance with the law and you will be acting
with proper reverence to the gods and to the oaths which you
have sworn. Nor will you be fighting on the same side as the
Spartans, as you would be doing if you put to death, illegally
and without a trial, men who have defeated the Spartans in
battle and destroyed seventy of their ships.

'And what reason have you for this excessive haste? What 26
are you frightened of? Is it that, if you act legally, you will
not be able to condemn or absolve anyone you like, whereas
you can do so if you act illegally by the method which Callixenus managed, by just one vote, to induce the Council to
recommend to the Assembly? Yes, but suppose you put to 27
death an innocent man? Just remember how painful it is and
how useless indeed to regret what one has done. And how
much more so when one's mistake has cost a man his life! In 28
the recent past you gave Aristarchus* a whole day in which
to defend himself as he pleased and allowed him all his other
legal rights. Yet he had destroyed the democracy and had
then betrayed Oenoe to your enemies, the Thebans. It would
be a monstrous thing if you did not grant these same rights to
the generals who in all their actions have carried out your
purposes and who have inflicted a defeat on the enemy. You 29
are Athenians, and Athenians do not act like this. The laws
are your own creation and it is the laws, above all, which
have made you great. Abide by them and never attempt to do
anything without their sanction.

'And now I want you to come back to the actual facts of
the situation in which the generals are supposed to have done
wrong. After winning their victory they sailed in to the
shore. Then Diomedon proposed that they should all put to
sea in line and pick up the wreckage and the shipwrecked

*Thuc. VIII.90–98.

men. Erasinides, on the other hand, was in favour of the whole fleet sailing as fast as possible against the enemy at Mytilene. At this point Thrasyllus suggested that both plans could be carried out if some ships were left behind while the

30 rest sailed against the enemy; if this suggestion were accepted, he proposed that each of the eight generals should leave behind three ships from his own command and that they should also leave the ten ships of the taxiarchs, the ten from Samos and the three of the navarchs. These come to forty-seven ships altogether – four for each of the twelve ships lost.

31 And among the captains left behind were Thrasybulus and also Theramenes, the man who made a speech accusing the generals at the last meeting of the Assembly. It was the generals' intention to sail against the enemy with the rest of the ships.

'Now what fault can possibly be found with any of these arrangements? Is it not fair, then, that if anything went wrong with the action against the enemy those people who were given this assignment should be held responsible, and, on the other hand, that those people who had the job of recovering the shipwrecked should be the ones tried for not doing so, if

32 they failed to carry out the orders of the generals? I can, however, say this for both parties; in fact, the storm made it impossible for either of them to carry out what the generals had planned. And as evidence for this I can refer you to those who were saved by pure chance. Among these is one of our generals who managed to get safely to land on a sinking ship. And now they are asking you to try him, who was in need of being rescued himself, by the same vote by which you are trying those who did not do what they were ordered to do.

33 'Men of Athens, you have won a great and fortunate victory. Do not act as though you were smarting under the ignominy of defeat. Do not be so unreasonable as not to recognize that some things are in the hand of heaven. These men are helpless; do not condemn them for treachery. They

were simply unable because of the storm to do what they had been ordered to do. Indeed, it would be a very much fairer thing to crown these victors with garlands than to punish them, at the instigation of rogues, with death.'

After making this speech Euryptolemus put forward a 34 motion that each of the men should be given a separate trial in accordance with the decree of Cannonus. The Council's motion, of course, was that they should all be tried together by one vote. When a vote was taken on these two motions they at first decided in favour of the proposal of Euryptolemus. Menecles then lodged an objection under oath; another vote was taken, and this time the Council's proposal was approved. Then they voted on the eight generals who had taken part in the naval action and found them guilty. The six who were in Athens were put to death.*

Quite soon afterwards the Athenians regretted what they 35 had done and voted that complaints should be lodged against those who had deceived the people; that those against whom complaints were lodged should have to provide sureties for themselves until their cases came up for trial, and that Callixenus should be included among them. Complaints were lodged against four others apart from him and all were put in confinement by their guarantors. Late, however, in the course of the disturbances in which Cleophon† was put to death,

*The whole affair is somewhat differently reported by Diodorus (XIII.101 f.) and there are good reasons for distrusting Xenophon. Cf. Andrewes, 'The Arginousai Trial', *Phoenix*, 28, 1974, pp. 112 ff.

† The only mention in the *Hellenica* of the leading Athenian statesman of the closing years of the Peloponnesian War is also somewhat baffling; the phrase 'in the course of the disturbances' hardly suits the account of Cleophon's trial and execution given by Lysias XIII.12. Xenophon's failure to say more of him must be deliberate. Cf. Diod. XIII.53 and n. at I.1.23. Aristotle *Constitution of Athens* 34.1 places a Spartan appeal for peace directly after the battle of Arginusae, which if correct casts a queer light on the trial of the generals and an even queerer light on Xenophon's account of it all. In view of the

they escaped before being brought to trial. Callixenus did come back again at the time when the Piraeus party returned to the city; but everyone loathed him and he died of starvation.

---

readiness to treat with Athens implied by Callicratidas' remark at I.6.7, a Spartan offer to negotiate is not inconceivable despite the silence of Diodorus, who did not choose to epitomize everything in his sources. Only innocence and ignorance could argue that in view of Xenophon's silence it did not happen. But perhaps Aristotle is confused and was really thinking of what happened after the battle of Cyzicus (Diod. XIII.53 and cf. n. at I.1.23).

BOOK TWO

CHAPTER 1

Recall of Lysander. Athenian Disaster at Aegospotami
(406–405 B.C.)

THE troops in Chios under Eteonicus could support them- 1
selves during the summer months from the seasonal produce
and could get money by hiring out their labour in the island.
But when winter came on they found themselves short of
food, clothing and footwear. So they got together and planned to make an attack on Chios. It was agreed that all in
favour of the plan should carry a reed so that they could see
what their numbers were. Eteonicus heard of the plot, but 2
there were so many of the men carrying reeds that he did not
know what to do about it. To proceed against them openly
seemed to him a risky business. They might run to arms and
occupy the city; then, as declared enemies, they would, if
they got the upper hand, ruin everything. If, on the other
hand, he put to death so many men who were allies, that also
seemed dangerous. Sparta would get a bad name among the
other Greeks and the troops would become disaffected. What 3
he did was to make his way through the city accompanied
by fifteen men armed with daggers. On his way he met a
man suffering from ophthalmia who was coming away from
the doctor's. This man was carrying a reed and Eteonicus had
him killed. In the ensuing disturbance people asked why he 4
had been killed, and Eteonicus had it proclaimed that it was
because he was carrying the reed. As a result all those with
reeds in their hands threw them away, everyone, as he heard
the announcement, being afraid that he might be seen with
one. Next Eteonicus called together the people of Chios and 5
told them to raise money so that the sailors could be paid
and so would not do anything violent. The people of Chios

raised the money, and then Eteonicus gave the signal for the men to go aboard the ships. He went round the whole fleet, ship by ship, giving his instructions and making long encouraging speeches, as though he knew nothing at all about what had happened, and he gave everyone a month's pay.

6   Afterwards the people of Chios and the other allies held a meeting at Ephesus at which they discussed their situation and decided to send ambassadors to Sparta to report what was happening and to ask that Lysander should be sent out to take over the command. He was very popular with the allies because of his conduct during his previous term of office, when

7 he also won the battle of Notium. So the ambassadors were sent and were accompanied by messengers from Cyrus who supported their request. The Spartans sent Lysander out with the office of vice-admiral, with Aracus as admiral. This was because they have a law forbidding the same man to be admiral twice. However, the ships were in fact under the command of Lysander.

8   The war had now lasted twenty-five years. It was in this year, too, that Cyrus put to death Autoboesaces and Mitraeus, the sons of Darius' sister (daughter of Xerxes, the father of Darius).* He did this because when they met him they failed to push their hands through the *corê* – a gesture that is made only in the presence of the king. (The *corê* is a kind of sleeve, longer than the *cheiris*, and anyone with his hands inside it

9 would be incapable of doing anything.) Hieramenes and his wife then told Darius that it would be a disgrace if he were to overlook such an act of violence and of arrogance, and Darius sent messengers to summon Cyrus, pretending that he was ill.

*Cf. n. at I.2.1. (It is to be noted that the Greek form of Darius used in the text is that found in Ctesias, a prime source of Oriental information for this period, but differs from that used at I.2.19.) The information about Darius' illness is given below in §13 and points the more plainly to this notice being an interpolation by a later hand.

Next year was the year in which Archytas was ephor and 10
Alexias was archon at Athens. Lysander arrived at Ephesus
and instructed Eteonicus to meet him there with the fleet
from Chios. He himself got together all the ships that he
could lay his hands on anywhere, and started refitting them
and building others at Antandrus. He also went to see Cyrus 11
and asked him for money. Cyrus pointed out that all the
money supplied by the King had been already spent, and
indeed a great deal more besides, and he gave him an account
of the sums which each of the admirals had received. However, he did give him money and Lysander, when he had got 12
it, appointed captains for each trireme and paid the sailors
all the pay that was due to them. Meanwhile the Athenian
generals at Samos were also getting their fleet ready for
action.

Cyrus now sent for Lysander. The messenger had arrived 13
from his father saying that he was ill and wanted to see him.
At this time Cyrus was in Thamneria, in Media, near the
territory of the Cadusians, who had revolted and against
whom he had been marching. When Lysander arrived, Cyrus 14
advised him not to fight any action with the Athenians unless he found himself with a great numerical superiority. He
pointed out that both the King and he himself had plenty of
money, so that, so far as that was concerned, it would be
possible to man a great many ships. He then allotted to
Lysander all the tribute from the cities to which he personally
was entitled and also gave him all the surplus which he had
by him.* After reminding him of the friendly feelings he
entertained both for Sparta and for Lysander himself, he set
out on the journey inland to his father.

After Cyrus had given Lysander all the money in his pos- 15
session and had set out, as requested, to visit his sick father,

*According to Andocides (III.29), the Persians gave the Spartans
5,000 talents for the war (an immense sum). But, until the coming of
Cyrus, they were niggardly (cf. Thuc. VIII.29; Hell. Oxy. 19). The
intimacy of Lysander and Cyrus changed all that (cf. I.5.6 f.).

Lysander paid his men and set sail to the Gulf of Ceramus in Caria. Here he attacked a city called Cedreae which was an ally of Athens. On the second day's assault he took the place by storm and sold the inhabitants as slaves. The population 16 was a mixed one of Greeks and natives. From there he sailed to Rhodes.

The Athenians meanwhile, still based on Samos, were raiding the King's territory and sailed out against Chios and Ephesus. They were also getting ready to fight a naval action and had chosen three more generals in addition to those they had already; the new generals were Menander, Tydeus and Cephisodotus.

17 Lysander now sailed from Rhodes along the Ionian coast to the Hellespont. His object was to intercept the merchant ships coming out of the Pontus* and to deal with the cities in the area which had revolted from Sparta. The Athenians also set out there, keeping out in the open sea from Chios, 18 since Asia was in enemy hands.

Lysander sailed along the coast from Abydus to Lampsacus which was an ally of Athens. He had land support from the forces from Abydus and other cities and these troops were 19 under the command of a Spartan, Thorax by name. They made an assault on the city and took it by storm. It was a rich city, full of wine and grain and other supplies, and it was given over to the soldiers to plunder, though Lysander released all the prisoners who were free men.

20 The Athenians had been sailing close behind and, with their fleet of 180 ships, came to anchor at Elaeus in the Cher-

---

*The merchant ships 'came out' of the Pontus and down through the Bosporus, as we learn from Demosthenes L.4–6, etc., in the second half of the summer and the autumn (the date of the corn-harvest in South Russia having varied somewhat in the course of two thousand years). So this passage provides a pointer to the date for the final campaign of the war, as well as to Lysander's sound strategic judgement, for Athens depended on imports of Pontic corn.

sonese. It was here, while they were having their morning meal, that they received the news about Lampsacus. They 21 set out at once for Sestus where they took provisions aboard and then went straight on to Aegospotami, which is opposite Lampsacus. The Hellespont here is about two miles wide. It was here that the Athenians had their evening meal.

The night passed and at dawn Lysander ordered his men to 22 have breakfast and embark. He had the side-screens put up on the ships and made all preparations for battle, but gave orders that no one should leave his position or put out into the open sea.

As soon as the sun rose the Athenians came up with their 23 fleet in line of battle to the mouth of the harbour. However, Lysander did not put to sea against them, so, when it was late in the day, they sailed back again to Aegospotami. Lysander 24 then instructed some of his fastest ships to follow the Athenians and, when they had disembarked, to observe what they were doing and then to report back to him. He did not allow his own men to go ashore until these ships had returned.

Both he and the Athenians did the same thing for four days. All this time Alcibiades was in his castle and he could see 25 from there that the Athenians were moored on an open shore with no city behind them and that they were getting their supplies from Sestus, which was about two* miles away from the ships, while the enemy, inside a harbour and with a city at their backs, had everything they wanted. He therefore told the Athenians that they were in a very poor position and advised them to shift their anchorage to Sestus, where they would have the advantages of a harbour and a city. 'Once you are there,' he said, 'you can fight whenever you please.'

*The correct distance from Aegospotami is more like 15 miles. The figure in the text, 15 *stades* (here translated 'two miles', more exactly 1.72 miles), may be due to corruption of 115, or to Xenophon himself.

26 The generals, however – particularly Tydeus and Menander – told him to go away. 'We are in command now,' they said, 'not you.' So Alcibiades went away.

27 On the fifth day as the Athenians sailed up, Lysander gave special instructions to the ships that were to follow them. As soon as they saw that the Athenians had disembarked and had scattered in various directions over the Chersonese – as they were now doing more freely every day, since they had to go a long way to get their food and were now actually contemptuous of Lysander for not coming out to fight – they were to sail back and to signal with a shield when they were half-way across the straits. These orders were carried out

28 and, as soon as he got the signal, Lysander ordered the fleet to sail at full speed. Thorax and his men went with the fleet.

When Conon saw that the enemy were attacking, he signalled to the Athenians to hurry back as fast as they could come to their ships. But they were scattered in all directions; some of the ships had only two banks of oars manned, some only one, and some were not manned at all. Conon himself in his own ship with seven others and also the state trireme *Paralus* did get to sea fully manned and in close order. All the rest were captured by Lysander on land. He also rounded up nearly all the crews, though a few managed to escape into various fortified places in the neighbourhood.*

29 Conon, escaping with his nine ships, could see that for the Athenians all was over. He put in at Abarnis, the headland off Lampsacus, and there seized the cruising masts of Lysander's fleet. Then, with eight ships, he sailed away to King Evago-

---

*The whole of Lysander's second period of command is treated much more comprehensively in Diodorus XIII.104 ff. and the account of the battle is quite different. (Cf. C. Ehrhardt, *Phoenix*, 24, 1970, pp. 225–8.) According to Diodorus, Alcibiades demanded a share of the command. Another account (Plutarch *Lysander* 9) made the mutilation proposed by Philocles of 'right thumbs', not of 'right hands', which seems, surgically speaking, more likely.

ras in Cyprus. The *Paralus* sailed to Athens to report what had happened.

Lysander brought the ships, the prisoners and all his other 30 prizes into Lampsacus. Among the prisoners were Philocles, Adimantus and others of the generals. And on the very day of the victory he sent Theopompus, the Milesian pirate, to Sparta to report what had happened. Theopompus arrived with the news in three days.

Next Lysander called a meeting of his allies and asked them 31 for their views as to what should be done with the prisoners. Very many bitter speeches were now made about the Athenians, both with regard to all the crimes they had committed in the past and about the decree which they had passed to the effect that, if they won the naval action, they would cut off the right hand of every man taken alive; there was also the fact that, after capturing two triremes, one from Corinth and one from Andros, they had thrown every man in the crews overboard. It was Philocles, the Athenian general, who had had these men killed. Many other such stories were told, and 32 in the end it was decided that all the prisoners who were Athenian should be put to death with the one exception of Adimantus. He had been the only man in the Assembly who opposed the decree for cutting off the hands of prisoners. He was also, it should be said, accused by some people of having betrayed the fleet. As for Philocles, who had thrown the Andrians and Corinthians overboard, Lysander first asked him this question: 'What do you deserve for having been the first to act like a criminal towards your fellow-Greeks?' He then had his throat cut.

CHAPTER 2

Surrender of Athens (405 B.C.)

1 AFTER making the necessary arrangements at Lampsacus, Lysander sailed against Byzantium and Calchedon. Both places submitted to him and the Athenian garrisons were allowed to go away under safe conduct. At the time the people who had betrayed Byzantium to Alcibiades fled to Pontus, though later they came to Athens and were granted

2 Athenian citizenship. Lysander sent all Athenian garrisons and any other Athenians whom he found back to Athens, allowing them safe conduct to go there, but nowhere else. He knew that the more people there were in the city and in Piraeus, the sooner the food supplies would run out. Then, leaving behind a Spartan, Sthenelaus, as governor of Byzantium and Calchedon, he sailed back to Lampsacus and refitted his ships.

3 It was at night that the *Paralus* arrived at Athens. As the news of the disaster was told, one man passed it on to another, and a sound of wailing arose and extended first from Piraeus, then along the Long Walls until it reached the city. That night no one slept. They mourned for the lost, but more still for their own fate. They thought that they themselves would now be dealt with as they had dealt with others – with the Melians, colonists of Sparta, after they had besieged and conquered Melos, with the people of Histiaea, of Scione, of

4 Torone, of Aegina and many other states.* Next day they held an Assembly at which it was decided to block up all the harbours except one, to repair and man the walls, and to take all other measures to put the city into a state of readiness for a siege.

*Thuc. V. 116; I.114; V.3; V.32; II.27.

While the Athenians were occupied in this way, Lysander 5
sailed out of the Hellespont with 200 ships. Coming to Lesbos,
he settled matters in Mytilene and the other cities and sent
Eteonicus with ten triremes to Thrace. Eteonicus brought all
the places in that area over to Sparta. Indeed, directly after 6
the battle every state in Greece except Samos had abandoned
the Athenian cause. In Samos the people slaughtered the
aristocratic party and held control of the city.

Lysander then sent word to Agis at Decelea and also to 7
Sparta that he was sailing to Athens with 200 ships. At the
same time Pausanias, the other king of Sparta, the whole
army of the Spartans and all the rest of the Peloponnesians,
except the Argives,* took the field. When the whole force 8
was concentrated, Pausanias led them to Athens and camped
in the Academy. Meanwhile Lysander arrived at Aegina and, 9
gathering together as many of the people of Aegina as he
could, gave the island back to them. He did the same thing
for the people of Melos and for all the others who had been
deprived of their own states. Then, after devastating Salamis,
he anchored at Piraeus with 150 ships and closed the harbour
to all merchant ships.

The Athenians were now besieged by land and by sea. 10
They had no ships, no allies and no food; and they did not
know what to do. They could see no future for themselves
except to suffer what they had made others suffer, people of
small states whom they had injured not in retaliation for anything they had done but out of the arrogance of power and
for no reason except that they were in the Spartan alliance.
They therefore continued to hold out. They gave back their 11
rights to all who had been disfranchised and, though numbers
of people in the city were dying of starvation, there was no
talk of peace.

However, when their food supplies were entirely exhausted they sent ambassadors to Agis, saying that they were

* Allies of Athens in 420 and 416. Thuc. V.47 and 82.

willing to join the Spartan alliance if they could keep their walls and Piraeus, and that they were prepared to make a trea-
12 ty on these terms. Agis told them to go to Sparta, saying that he himself had no authority to negotiate. This reply was reported back to the Athenians by the ambassadors and they
13 were sent on to Sparta. However, when they were at Sellasia, near the Laconian border, and the ephors heard what their proposals would be – i.e. the same that they had made to Agis – they told them to go back again and, if they really wanted peace, to think again and return with better proposals than
14 these. When the ambassadors got back to Athens and made their report, there was general despondency. The people saw nothing but slavery in front of them and knew that, while another embassy was on its way, many would die of famine.
15 But still no one wanted to make any proposal offering to destroy the walls. In fact, when Archestratus said in the Council that the best thing to do would be to make peace on the terms offered by Sparta (these being that ten stades * of each of the Long Walls should be pulled down), he was thrown into prison. And a decree was passed forbidding anyone to make such proposals. †

16   It was in this situation that Theramenes made a speech in the Assembly saying that, if they were willing to send him to Lysander, he would go and return with information as to whether the Spartan insistence on the demolition of the walls was because they wanted to enslave the population of Athens or merely wanted a pledge of Athenian good faith. He was sent to Lysander and stayed with him more than three months,‡ waiting for the moment when the Athenians, with

* About 2,000 yards.

† Xenophon withholds the name of Cleophon as the inspirer of Athenian intransigence (cf. Aeschines II.76, Lysias XIII.8). Cf. n. at I.7.35.

‡ It is hard to accept that, if Theramenes was with Lysander for over three months, the Athenians did not send someone to inquire what was afoot but just waited and starved. In Lysias XIII, where a simi-

no food left, would agree to any terms whatsoever. In the 17
fourth month he returned and reported to the Assembly that
Lysander had kept him there all this time and had then told
him to go to Sparta. He had explained that only the ephors,
not he, had authority to give Theramenes the information
which he required. Theramenes, with nine others, was then
chosen to go as ambassador with full powers to Sparta.
Lysander meanwhile sent an Athenian exile called Aristoteles 18
with some Spartans to the ephors to tell them that he had
advised Theramenes that it was they who were the only
people empowered to make peace or war.

At Sellasia Theramenes and the other ambassadors were 19
asked to define the purpose of their mission. They replied
that they had come with full powers to treat for peace and
the ephors then gave orders that they should be summoned
to Sparta. On their arrival the ephors called an assembly at
which many Greek states, and in particular the Corinthians
and Thebans, opposed making any peace with Athens. The
Athenians, they said, should be destroyed. The Spartans, 20
however, said they would not enslave a Greek city which had
done such great things for Greece at the time of her supreme
danger. They offered to make peace on the following terms:
the Long Walls and the fortifications of Piraeus must be
destroyed; all ships except twelve surrendered; the exiles to
be recalled; Athens to have the same enemies and the same
friends as Sparta had and to follow Spartan leadership in any
expedition Sparta might make either by land or sea.*

larly hostile view of Theramenes is presented, the long delay is said
to have been at Sparta, which is wholly credible; Sparta may well
have summoned all her allies, which were by now spread all over the
Greek world, to a peace conference, and not just the members of the
Peloponnesian league (cf. II.2.19); so Theramenes and Athens had to
wait, and malignity could blame him for what was inevitable.
Xenophon maligned and misremembered – hence the muddle about
the failure of the corn supply (cf. §11).

*The course of the negotiations is obscure; Plutarch *Lysander* 14
claims to quote a decree of the ephors which left the exact size of the

21 Theramenes and his fellow ambassadors brought these terms back to Athens. Great masses of people crowded round them as they entered the city, for it was feared that they might have come back unsuccessful and it was impossible to delay any longer because of the numbers who were dying of hun-
22 ger. Next day the ambassadors reported to the Assembly the terms on which Sparta was prepared to make peace. Theramenes made the report and spoke in favour of accepting the Spartan terms and tearing down the walls. Some people spoke in opposition, but many more were in favour* and so
23 it was decided to accept the peace. After this Lysander sailed into Piraeus, the exiles returned, and the walls were pulled down among scenes of great enthusiasm and to the music of flute girls. It was thought that this day was the beginning of freedom for Greece.
24 So the year ended. In the middle of this same year Diony-sius of Syracuse, the son of Hermocrates, became tyrant. This was after the Syracusans had defeated the Carthaginians in battle. The Carthaginians, however, had captured Acragas after the city had been reduced by starvation and abandoned by the Sicelians.†

Athenian fleet to be determined. Perhaps the peace was not made until Athens had voted to accept in broad outline the proposed peace terms. The peace itself must have been much fuller than Xenophon lets on. Aristotle *Ath. Pol.* 34.3 says that it contained a clause about the 'ancestral constitution', which in view of Sparta's method elsewhere is wholly likely; democracy was neither to be trusted nor to be tolerated. Xenophon is very unhelpful on the whole business.

*Lysias XIII.13 ff. represented the peace negotiated by Theramenes to be as bad as could be, but since he had secured that the walls of Athens itself were left intact, it is not surprising that he was widely commended.

†This paragraph is an interpolation. Cf. n. at I.2.1.

CHAPTER 3

Tyranny of the Thirty. Death of Theramenes (404 B.C.)

THE Olympic Games were held in the following year. At this Olympiad Crocinas the Thessalian was winner in the stadium. Eudius was ephor in Sparta and Pythodorus archon in Athens. However, since Pythodorus was chosen during the oligarchy, the Athenians do not use his name for this year. They call it 'the year without an archon'. *

The oligarchy came into power in the following way. It 2 was decided in the Assembly that thirty men should be elected to codify the ancient laws as a basis for a new constitution. The men chosen were Polychares, Critias, Melobius, Hippolochus, Eucleides, Hieron, Mnesilochus, Chremon, Theramenes, Aresias, Diocles, Phaedrias, Chaereleos, Anaetius, Pison, Sophocles, Eratosthenes, Charicles, Onomacles, Theognis, Aeschines, Theogenes, Cleomedes, Erasistratus, Pheidon, Dracontides, Eumathes, Aristoteles, Hippomachus, Mnesitheides. After their election Lysander sailed off to 3 Samos and Agis withdrew his troops from Decelea and allowed his men to disperse to their cities.

It was about this time, when there was also a solar eclipse, 4 that Lycophron of Pherae, who was ambitious to gain control over the whole of Thessaly, defeated in battle those Thessalians (the people of Larissa and others) who opposed him and killed large numbers of them.

Also at this time Dionysius, the tyrant of Syracuse, was 5 defeated in a battle against the Carthaginians and lost Gela and Camarina. Soon afterwards the people of Leontini too, who had been living in Syracuse, revolted from Dionysius

---

* This chronographic note is an interpolation. Cf. n. at I.2.1.

and went back to their own city. Dionysius immediately
sent the Syracusan cavalry to Catana.*

6   The people of Samos were now completely blockaded by
Lysander. At first they refused to come to terms, but when
Lysander was on the point of launching a general assault,
they came to an agreement that every free man should be
allowed to leave, keeping just one cloak; everything else was
to be surrendered. On these conditions they left the city.

7 Lysander gave it back with everything it contained to the
exiled party and appointed a governing body of ten men to
see to its security.† He then dismissed the naval contingents

8 of his allies to their various cities and himself sailed to Sparta
with the Laconian ships. He took with him the prows of all
captured ships, the triremes from Piraeus, except twelve, the
crowns which various cities had given to him as personal
gifts, the balance of the tribute which Cyrus had made over
to him as a war fund (this came to 470 talents in money) and

9 everything else which he had acquired in the war. All this he
handed over to the Spartan government at the end of the
summer.

    So ended the twenty-eight years and six months of the war.
The eponymous ephors for these years were as follows: first
Aenesias, in whose ephorate the war began, in the fifteenth
year of the thirty years' truce signed after the conquest of

10 Euboea; and after him Brasidas, Isanor, Sostratidas, Exarchus,
Agesistratus, Angenidas, Onomacles, Zeuxippus, Pityas,
Plistolas, Clinomachus, Ilarchus, Leon, Chaerilas, Patesia-
das, Cleosthenes, Lycarius, Eperatus, Onomantius, Alexippi-

---

*These two paragraphs are probably interpolations. Whether the
list of the Thirty was given by Xenophon is debatable; the names
seem to be in the official order of the Athenian tribes. Such precision
is perhaps due to an interpolator, as is perhaps the list of Spartan
ephors in §§ 9 and 10.

†For Lysander's infamous 'Councils of Ten' (*decarchies*), see n. at
III.4.2.

das, Misgolaidas, Isias, Aracus, Euarchippus, Pantacles, Pityas, Archytas and Eudius. It was in Eudius' term of office that Lysander sailed home after the accomplishments described above.

At Athens the Thirty were elected directly after the demo- 11 lition of the Long Walls and the walls of Piraeus.* Though they were elected to frame laws for a new constitution they kept on putting things off. No laws were framed or published, and meanwhile they appointed members of the Council and other magistrates just as they saw fit. Their first 12 measure was to arrest and put on trial for their lives all who were generally known to have made a living during the time of the democracy by acting as informers and had made a practice of attacking the aristocrats. The Council was glad enough to condemn these people to death and no objections were raised by the public in general – or at least not by those who had no guilty consciences in the matter themselves. Next, however, the Thirty began to consider how they 13 could get the power to do exactly what they liked with the state. They sent Aeschines and Aristoteles to Sparta to persuade Lysander to support their request that a Spartan garrison should be sent just until, so they said, they had got rid of 'the criminals' and had established a new consitution; and they undertook to pay for the garrison themselves. Lysander 14 agreed, and helped them to secure the sending of a garrison with Callibius to act as governor. Then, when they had got

* This sentence is the opening of Part II of the *Hellenica*. See Introduction p. 17 f. It is to be noted that the appointment of the Thirty had already been reported in § 2 – which confirms the view that the break in the composition of the work is to be found here.

The whole question of how exactly the Thirty were set up and what part Theramenes played has aroused great debate. Cf. C. Hignett, *History of the Athenian Constitution*, Ch. XI and Appendix xiii, unfortunately tainted by Nineteenth-Century idolatry of Xenophon. The evidence of Diodorus XIV.3 f. and Lysias XII (esp. §§71 ff.) suggests that Xenophon has left us greatly under-informed.

their garrison, they made themselves as agreeable as they possibly could to Callibius so as to get him to approve of everything they did. He gave them troops to go with them and they began to arrest all whom they wished to arrest. And now it was no longer a question of the so-called 'criminals' or of people whom no one had heard of. Those arrested now were the people who, in the view of the Thirty, were the least likely to submit to being pushed out of politics and who could count on the greatest support if they chose to take action.

15 At first Critias and Theramenes shared the same views and were personal friends. But when Critias, acting as one who had himself been exiled by the democracy,* began to show this lust for putting people to death, Theramenes opposed him. 'There is no sense,' he said, 'in putting a man to death simply because he has been honoured by the democracy and when he has done the aristocracy no harm at all. After all, both you and I have often said and done things in order to make ourselves popular with the citizens.'

16 At this stage Critias was still on friendly terms with Theramenes. 'It is,' he said, 'quite impossible for those who want to gain power to avoid getting rid of those people who are most likely to form an opposition. And it is pure simplicity on your part if you think that, just because we are thirty and not one, we have to keep a less close watch on the government than is done by an absolute dictator.'

17 So more and more people were put to death, and put to death unjustly, and it became clear that many citizens were getting together in opposition and were wondering what the state was coming to. Theramenes then spoke again and expressed the view that the oligarchy could not possibly survive, unless they brought in a reasonable number of others to share in the government.

18 By this time Critias and the rest of the Thirty were alarmed,

*See n. at II.3.36.

and they were particularly afraid of Theramenes, in case the
citizens might turn to him as a leader. So they enrolled a body
of 3,000 citizens who, according to them, were to be asso-
ciated in the government. Theramenes, however, objected 19
to this move too. 'In the first place,' he said, 'it seems ridiculous to me, when we want to bring the best men into the
government, to fix the number at 3,000, as though this
number must necessarily comprise all the good people*
there are, and as though there cannot possibly be a number
of excellent people who are not included and a number of
rogues who are. And secondly, it appears to me that we are
trying to do two absolutely inconsistent things at once – to
organize a government based on force, and at the same time
to make it weaker than its subjects.'

So Theramenes expressed himself. The Thirty, however, 20
proceeded to hold a review under arms. The Three Thousand paraded in the market place and the other citizens in
various other parts of the city. The order was given to pile
arms, and when the men were off duty, the Thirty sent their
Spartan troops and other people who were on their side,
seized the arms of all who were not included among the
Three Thousand, carried them up to the Acropolis and
stored them in the temple. Once this was done they 21

---

*Behind this phrase, 'the good people' (*kaloi kai agathoi*), lies the
real conflict between Critias and Theramenes. The latter claimed, and
many historians believe that the claim was just, to have consistently
sought a restriction of the vote to those rich enough to qualify for
hoplite service (cf. II.3.48). Critias was the idealizer of Sparta. He
wrote two accounts of the Spartan way of life (cf. Diels, *Vorsokratiker*,
no. 88), which lauded all things Spartan; he imitated the narrow
Spartan education system (*Mem.* I.2.31), and went so far in his
'Spartanizing' as to wish to see Athens, like Sparta, unwalled. His
3,000 'good people' were to correspond to the Spartan 'peers'
(*homoioi*) who, educated in virtue, did the fighting. Like Sparta,
Athens too was to expel foreigners (*xenêlasia*); hence Critias' violence.
Cf. §21 for the persecution of 'resident-aliens' (*metics*).

considered that they were now free to act exactly as they liked, and they began to put people to death in great numbers,
some because they were personal enemies, some for the sake
of their money. It was necessary, too, to find money to pay
the Spartan garrison, and so they decided that each one of
them should arrest one of the resident aliens, put him to
22 death and confiscate his property. They told Theramenes
also to select someone and arrest him. Theramenes made the
following reply: 'In my view it is dishonourable for those
who call themselves "the best people" to act worse than
the informers did. The informers took money from their
victims, but did at least allow them to stay alive. Are we, in
order to get money, going to kill people who have done
nothing wrong? Is not this worse in every way?'

23   The Thirty now came to regard Theramenes as an obstacle
in the way of their complete liberty to do as they liked, and
so they began to intrigue against him. In private conversations with various members of the Council they kept on
undermining his position, telling one man after another that
he was a menace to the government. Then they called a
meeting of the Council, after having instructed some young
men, chosen for their toughness and lack of scruple, to stand
24 by with daggers hidden under their arms. When Theramenes
appeared at the Council, Critias rose to his feet and made
the following speech:

   'Gentlemen of the Council, if there is anyone here who
has the impression that more people are being put to death
than is warranted by the situation, I ask him to reflect that
in periods of revolution this is a thing that always happens.
And it is inevitable that we, who are setting up an oligarchy
in Athens, should meet with the most numerous opposition,
both because this state is the most highly populated in Greece
and because the people have been brought up here in free-
25 dom for a longer time than any other people. Now we have
come to the conclusion that for men like ourselves and like

you, <u>democracy is an oppressive form of government</u>. We
realize that while the democracy could never become friends
with our preservers, the Spartans, the aristocrats would continue always loyal to them. And therefore, with the full
approval of Sparta, we are setting up the present system of
government. If we find anyone opposed to the oligarchy, we
do our best to get rid of him. And in particular, if we find 26
that one of our own number is interfering with the order we
have set up, we consider it right and proper that he should
be punished.

'And now we find Theramenes here doing everything he 27
can to destroy us and to destroy you. Consider the matter,
and you will see that this is true. You will find that, whenever
we want to get rid of some demagogue, it is always Theramenes who objects and opposes us. Now if these had been
his views from the beginning, he was certainly an enemy,
but it would have been wrong to call him a scoundrel. As it 28
happens, however, it was Theramenes himself who took the
initiative in establishing friendly and loyal relations with
Sparta and in overthrowing the democracy; it was Theramenes who took the lead in urging you to punish the first
batch of people who were put on trial. And now, when both
you and we have obviously incurred the hatred of the democrats, Theramenes has begun to disapprove of what is going
on, his idea being, of course, to get on the safe side again himself and leave us to face the punishment for what has been
done. <u>I say therefore that he should be punished not only as 29
an enemy but as a traitor – a traitor to you and to us.</u> We
have much more horror of a traitor than of an enemy, since
it is harder to guard against hidden dangers than open ones.
And we hate traitors more than enemies, since with our
enemies we can make peace and become friends again, but
when we find that we have been betrayed by someone, we
can never under any circumstances make peace with him
and can never trust him again.

30   'In order that you may realize that this behaviour of Theramenes is nothing new, but that he is a born traitor, let me
remind you of what he has done in the past. This man started
his career in high favour with the democracy, like his father
Hagnon; he then became an enthusiast for replacing the
democracy by the oligarchy of the Four Hundred and became the leading man in it. However, he observed that there
was some opposition gathering against the oligarchy, and so
he took the lead again, this time for the democrats and
against the oligarchs. This, of course, is why he has been
31 nicknamed "the stage boot"; for boots worn on the stage
look identical for both feet and seem to face both ways. But,
Theramenes, a man who deserves to stay alive ought not to
be so clever at leading his comrades into difficult situations
only to change round again at once, if something goes wrong;
what he ought to do is to stick to the job in hand, as one does
on board ship, until the wind fills the sails again. For sailors
would never make the port for which they were bound if,
at the first sign of difficulty, they turned round and sailed in
32 the opposite direction. It is true, certainly, that in every
change of government people are going to get killed; but
you, Theramenes, because of your remarkable facility in
changing sides have to share in the blame both ways – for all
the oligarchs killed by the democrats and for all the democrats killed by the aristocracy. And this Theramenes, you
will recall, was also the man to whom the generals gave the
job of picking up the Athenians who were drowning after
the battle of Lesbos. He did not do so, and yet it was he who
prosecuted the generals and had them condemned to death,
just so that he could save his own skin.

33   'How, I ask you, can it possibly be right to show mercy to
a man who so obviously is always looking out for his own
advantage without the least consideration for honour or for
his own friends? We know how he is always changing sides.
Ought we not to take precautions to prevent him doing the

same thing to us? We therefore accuse him, on the charge
that he is plotting against and betraying both you and us.
Consider this further point which will indicate that what we
are doing is right and proper. I suppose that it is agreed that 34
the best constitution is that of Sparta. Suppose that there one
of the ephors should venture to go against the majority and
to object to the government and oppose what it was doing.
Would not the whole state, and not only the ephors themselves, consider that he deserved the severest possible punishment? So you, if you are wise, will show no mercy to
Theramenes. Show it rather for yourselves. To allow him to
remain alive would be to encourage the ambitions of numbers of your opponents; but to destroy him would mean
cutting short the hopes of all of them, whether here in
Athens or outside.'

After making this speech, Critias sat down. Theramenes 35
then rose and spoke as follows: 'I shall begin, gentlemen,
with the last point that Critias made against me. He says that
I brought about the deaths of the generals by my accusation.
But, as you are well aware, it was not I who started proceedings against them.* In fact, it was they who accused me.
They said that they had given me the job of rescuing those
unfortunate men after the battle off Lesbos, and I had failed
to do so. I, in my defence, pointed out that because of the
storm it was impossible to put to sea at all, let alone rescue
the men, and the state came to the conclusion that, while
what I said was perfectly reasonable, it looked as though the

*A lot has been made of the failure of Xenophon to recount a
letter (or letters) sent by the generals denouncing Theramenes which
is recounted by Diod. XIII.101 and here alluded to. Cf. Andrewes,
Phoenix, 29, 1974, pp. 112 ff. However, if Xenophon was one of the
Knights sent out to the relief of Mytilene (cf. I.6.24), he probably
came home with the generals and so missed the preliminary charges
and counter-charges. His account of the trial in I.7.1 ff. may be no
more and no less than personal memories, with perhaps some confusion about a letter alluded to in one debate (I.7.4).

generals were accusing themselves. For, after claiming that it was possible to save the men, they had sailed away and left
36 them to their fate. However, I am not surprised that Critias has got things wrong. He did not happen to be here at the time. Instead, he was in Thessaly where he and Prometheus were setting up a democracy and arming the serfs against
37 their masters. I hope that none of the things he did there will ever take place here.

'On this point, however, I do agree with him. It is quite right that the severest punishment should be given to any man who wants to put an end to your government and who is strengthening those who are intriguing against you. But which of us two is actually doing this? You will best be able, I think, to decide this point if you look into the past record and the present conduct of both Critias and myself.
38 'The fact is that we were all in agreement on policy up to the time when you became members of the Council and the magistrates were appointed and the known informers were brought to justice. It was only when these Thirty began to arrest people who were good men and men of standing that
39 I, too, began to take a different view of things. Take the case of Leon of Salamis,* a man with a great and deserved reputation, who had done nothing wrong at all. When he was put to death I realized that people like him would be terrified and in their turn would turn against the government. Then there was Niceratus, the son of Nicias, a man of property who, like his father, had never been in any sense of the word a demagogue. When he was arrested it was clear to me that
40 others like him were going to hate us. Antiphon, too, was

*Theramenes had no occasion to mention here that Socrates had been ordered to arrest Leon and had defied the Thirty (Plato, *Apology* 32ᶜ). The incident was decisive for Plato in dissuading him from actively supporting the Thirty (Plato *Epistle* VII p. 324 f.). It is amazing that Xenophon did not describe it when he spoke of the violent acts of the period (cf. II.3.21 f.).

put to death by us. During the war he had supplied us with
two fast triremes out of his own resources. I could see that
all those who in the past had been willing to help the state
would now begin to look on us with suspicion. I also object- 41
ed when they said that each of us must arrest one resident
alien. It was clear enough that if these were put to death
every other resident alive in Athens would become hostile
to the government. I also objected when they disarmed the
people, because I do not think that we ought to weaken our
state. I could see that when the Spartans saved our lives they
did not do it for this reason – that we should become few in
number and consequently incapable of being of any use to
them. If this had been what they wanted, it was in their
power. They had only to keep on the pressure of famine for
a little longer and no one would have been left at all. Nor 42
was I in favour of hiring Spartan guards. We could have
raised an equal number of men from our own citizens and
kept them until we, the rulers, had quite comfortably gained
control of the rest. And then, when I saw that many people
in Athens hated this government and many were going into
exile, it did not seem to me a good thing to banish Thrasybulus or Anytus or Alcibiades.* I saw that this meant
strengthening the opposition; the mass of exiles would get
capable leaders, and those who wanted to lead would find
plenty of supporters.

'Now how ought one to think of a man who quite openly 43
gives this advice? As a well-wisher or as a traitor? Let me tell
you, Critias, that the people who strengthen the opposition
are not those who prevent one from making a lot of enemies
and who show one how to gain most friends. Far from it. It
is the people who confiscate property illegally and who put

*For Alcibiades' second banishment, see Isocrates XVI.37, and
Justin V.8.12. Xenophon nowhere notices the murder of Alcibiades in
Phrygia on Spartan prompting (Diod. XIV.11, and Plut. *Alcibiades*
38 f.).

the innocent to death who are the ones that are increasing the
opposition and acting as traitors both to their friends and to
44 themselves, and all for the sake of dishonest gain. And if you
cannot see already that what I say is true, look at it this way.
Do you think that Thrasybulus and Anytus and the other
exiles would rather see us in Athens following the lines which
I am suggesting or the course which these people are actually
taking? Personally, I fancy that they must think that for them
the whole city is full of potential allies, whereas, if the best
people in the state were on our side, they could scarcely
imagine that they could so much as set foot in the country.

45 'And now with regard to Critias' assertion that I am the
sort of man who is always changing sides, I should like you
to consider the following points. As you all know it was the
democracy itself which voted in the government of the Four
Hundred, and this was because they had been told that the
Spartans* would never have any confidence in any demo-
46 cratic form of government. However, the Spartans went on
with the war just the same, and meanwhile it was seen that
Aristoteles, Melanthius, Aristarchus and their fellow-generals
were building fortifications at the entrance to Piraeus. What
they wanted to do was to let the enemy in and so gain control of the state for themselves and their friends. I saw what
was going on and I put a stop to it. Do you call this being a
traitor to one's friends?

47 'He calls me "the stage boot" because, according to him, I
try to fit both parties. What in the name of heaven should we
call a man who pleases neither? In the days of the democracy
you, Critias, were regarded as the most rabid hater of the
people; now, under the aristocracy, you have become the
48 most rabid hater of the upper classes. But I, Critias, have always been consistently opposed to those who think there can
be no good democracy until the slaves and the sort of people

*The question in 411 was how to gain the confidence of the King
of Persia (Thuc. VIII.53).

who would sell their country if they needed a drachma take part in the government; and I have also equally been opposed to those who think there can be no good oligarchy until the state is brought into the condition where a few men rule with absolute power. To me the best thing is to organize the government in company with those who, whether in the class of cavalry or in the class of hoplites, are able to be of use. This was what I thought in the past and I have not changed today. Name one instance, Critias, if you can, when I have 49 joined forces with either the extreme left or the extreme right wing and helped them to deprive decent people of their citizenship. If I am proved guilty of behaving like this now or of ever having behaved like this in the past, then I admit that I deserve the supreme punishment of death.'

When Theramenes had concluded his speech, the Council 50 made it clear by their applause that they were on his side and Critias realized that, if he allowed them to vote on the case, Theramenes would be acquitted. Not being able to bear the thought of this, he went and held a brief consultation with the Thirty. He then went out and told the men with daggers to stand at the railing separating the Council from the public. He then rejoined the Council and said: 'Members of the 51 Council, in my view if a man who is a true leader sees that his friends are being deceived, he will not allow this to happen. And this is what I am going to do. Besides, these men who are standing by the railings say that they will simply not allow us to let go a man who is so obviously doing harm to the oligarchy. Now in the new laws it is provided that without your vote no one on the list of the Three Thousand may be put to death, but that the Thirty has power of life and death over all not on the list. And therefore, with the full approval of the Thirty, I am striking off this man Theramenes from the list. And we, the Thirty, now condemn him to death.'

When he heard this Theramenes sprang to the altar. 'And 52

121

I,' he said, 'ask for nothing but justice – that it should not be in the power of Critias to strike my name from the list or the name of anyone of you whom he may wish to remove. These men themselves made the law about those on the list. Let the decision be made in accordance with that law, both
53 in my case and in yours. By heaven,' he added, 'I am indeed aware that this altar is not going to help me, but I want to make this point clear too – that these people respect the gods no more than they do men. Nevertheless, you gentlemen of Athens, I must own to surprise at your conduct in not being willing to defend yourselves, though you must know that it is just as easy to strike any of your names from the list as it is to strike out mine.'

54   At this point the herald of the Thirty ordered the Eleven to seize Theramenes, and they came in with their henchmen led by Satyrus, the greatest ruffian and the most shameless character of the lot. Critias then said, 'We are putting into your custody this man Theramenes, who has been condemned in accordance with the law, and we ask you, the Eleven, to arrest him and take him to the proper place and then do what follows next.'

55   After Critias had spoken Satyrus and the rest dragged Theramenes forcibly away from the altar. Theramenes, as was natural, kept calling on gods and men to be the witnesses of what was happening. But the Council members made no move. They could see that the men standing by the railings were of the same sort as Satyrus was and they were aware that they had come armed with daggers. They could see, too, that all the space in front of the Council chamber was packed with troops.

56   So the Eleven led Theramenes away through the market place, and he shouted out at the top of his voice, telling everyone how he was being treated. It is reported that one of the things he said was this. When Satyrus told him that if he did not keep quiet he would suffer for it, he replied: 'Shall I

not still suffer, if I do?' And when he was forced to die and drank the hemlock, they said that he threw the dregs out of the cup, as one does when playing *Kottabos*,★ and said: 'And here's to that delightful fellow, Critias.'

Of course, I realize that these remarks are not really worth mentioning; but I do think it admirable in the man that, with death hanging over him, his spirit never lost either the ability to think or the taste for making a joke.

★ A game. One threw the last drops of wine in the cup into a basin while wishing the health of a loved one.

CHAPTER 4

Thrasybulus in Piraeus. Rout of the Thirty. End of the
Civil War in Athens

1 AFTER Theramenes had been put to death in this way, the
Thirty began to act on the assumption that they now had
nothing to fear and could behave as tyrants. They issued a
proclamation forbidding all who were not on the list to enter
the city and, in order to secure their land for themselves and
their friends, they evicted them from their estates. Many of
those who sought refuge in Piraeus were driven out from
there too. Both Megara and Thebes were full of refugees.

2   It was at this stage that Thrasybulus, with about seventy
men, left Thebes and seized the strong fortress of Phyle. The
Thirty marched out against him from Athens with the Three
Thousand and the cavalry. It was particularly fine weather
when they marched and, when they reached Phyle, some of
the young men were so confident in themselves that they
went straight in to attack the fortifications. But they achieved
nothing and, after a number of them had been wounded, fell

3 back again. The intention of the Thirty was to blockade the
place and reduce it by siege after cutting off all sources of supply, but during the night there was a heavy fall of snow and
it went on snowing throughout the next day. So they returned to Athens in the snow after losing a good many of
their camp-followers who were raided by the men in Phyle.

4 It was clear to the Thirty that the enemy would also get plunder from the country estates unless there were forces available
to protect them, so they sent out nearly the whole of the
Spartan garrison and two divisions of cavalry and stationed
them in the outlying districts about two miles from Phyle.
This force made its camp in a place where there was some

shelter from trees and bushes and kept a watch on the neighbourhood.

By this time about seven hundred men had joined Thrasy- 5
bulus in Phyle. With the whole of this force he came down
by night and grounded arms about half a mile from the
Spartan guards. They waited in silence until it was nearly 6
dawn and the enemy troops were beginning to get up and
leave their positions on their various occasions, and the
grooms were making a lot of noise as they were currying the
horses. At this moment Thrasybulus' men snatched up their
arms and ran in to the attack. They cut down some of the
enemy and routed the rest, pursuing them for nearly a mile.
They killed more than 120 of the hoplites and among the
cavalry they killed Nicostratus, who was called 'the beautiful', and two others, having surprised them before they had
time to get out of bed. After coming back from the pursuit 7
they put up a trophy, collected all the arms and equipment
which they had captured, and returned to Phyle. Thus, when
cavalry reinforcements came up from Athens, there was no
enemy in sight. The cavalry stayed there and did not go back
to the city until the bodies of the dead had been taken up by
their relatives.

After this the Thirty no longer regarded their position as 8
secure. They now wanted to take over Eleusis for themselves
so as to have a place to retire to if that became necessary. So
Critias and the rest of the Thirty ordered out the cavalry and
went with them to Eleusis, and held a review of the people
there with the cavalry all round them. They pretended that
they wanted to check the numbers of the population so as to
find out what size of a garrison would be needed, and ordered everyone to register his name. As each man registered,
he was to go out from the gate in the wall in the direction of
the sea. They then posted cavalry detachments on the shore
at each side of the gate and, as each man came out, he was
seized and bound by the servants in attendance on the cavalry.

When they had all been seized the Thirty ordered Lysimachus, the commander of the cavalry, to take them to Athens and hand them over to the Eleven.

9 Next day they called a meeting in the Odeum of all the hoplites and cavalry whose names were on the list, and Critias rose and spoke as follows: 'My friends, we are organizing this government in your interests as well as in our own. It is right that, just as you share in the privileges, so you should share in the dangers. And so, in order that you may have the same hopes and same fears as we have, you must now pass the death sentence on these men of Eleusis who have been captured.'

He then showed them where to vote and gave instructions
10 that the votes were to be cast openly and in full view. One half of the Odeum had been filled with Spartan troops, all carrying their arms. It was a way of doing things which caused pleasure to those citizens whose one thought was of their own advantage.*

By now about a thousand men had gathered together at Phyle with Thrasybulus, and soon after the events described above, he led them down and marched by night to Piraeus. As soon as they heard of this the Thirty went out against them with the Spartan garrison, the cavalry and the hoplites. They moved on Piraeus by the carriage road which leads up
11 to the town, and for some time the men from Phyle tried to prevent their coming up it. However, they realized that the great circuit of the town wall needed a large force for its defence and that their numbers were still not sufficient for the task. They therefore gathered together in a body on the hill of Munychia.

The men from Athens advanced to the market place of Hippodamus and formed into line of battle so as to fill the

* If Xenophon was with 'the cavalry' (the Knights), as is to be presumed, he saw and took part in enough to make him hate the acts of the Thirty.

road leading to the temple of Artemis and the shrine of Bendis in Munychia. Their line was not less than fifty shields deep and, when they had taken up their positions, they advanced up the hill.

The men from Phyle also filled up the road, but their line 12 of hoplites was not more than ten deep. Behind them, however, were the peltasts and light javelin throwers, and behind them the slingers, of whom there were a great many, since this was the district where they lived.

As the enemy were coming forward, Thrasybulus told his men to ground their shields. Then, putting down his own shield, but otherwise fully armed, he spoke to them as follows, standing in the centre of the line: 'Fellow citizens, I 13 want to remind some of you and to inform others that those on the right wing of the enemy's advance are the men whom four days ago you defeated and put to flight. Now for the extreme left. Yes, that is where the Thirty are, the men who robbed us of our city though we have done nothing wrong, the men who drove us out of our homes and who, by their proscriptions, have victimized our dearest friends. And now they find themselves just where they never expected to be and just where we used to pray that they would be. For we 14 are face to face with them and we have arms in our hands. In the past we were seized and arrested when we were asleep, or eating our meals or going about our business in the market; we were exiled when we have not only done nothing wrong but were not even in the city. And because of this the gods are quite evidently on our side now. In the middle of fair weather they send us a snowstorm to help us, and when we attack, few against many, it is we who are granted the right to set up the trophies. So now they have brought 15 us to a position where these enemies of ours, because they are advancing uphill, cannot throw their spears and javelins over the heads of the front ranks, while we, with spears, javelins and stones all thrown downhill, cannot miss our

16 mark and are certain to inflict casualties. One might have thought that at least with their front rank we should have to fight on even terms. But in fact we have only got to do the right thing and let our weapons fly with full force, and not one of us will miss his man, since the whole road is packed with them. They will be cowering under their shields trying to keep out of the way, so that you will be able to thrust at them wherever you like, as though they were blind men, and then leap in on them and cut them down.

17 'And now, my friends, I want each one of you to act so that afterwards he will know that he was the man who won the victory. For this, please God, will be a victory that will give us back our country, our homes, our freedom, our honour and, for those who have them, our wives and children. Happy indeed will those of us be who, after the victory, will see the light of the gladdest day of our lives. Fortunate, too, will be the man who dies; for no one, however rich, could acquire for himself so splendid a memorial.

'Now at the right moment I shall strike up the paean, and when we call on the War God, then let us all be of one mind, and let us make these men suffer for the insolent wrong that they have done us.'

18 After saying this he turned about to face the enemy. As yet he made no move, because the prophet had told them not to attack until one of their own number was either killed or wounded. 'When that has happened, however,' he had said, 'we shall lead you on. You will follow and victory will be yours. But for me, so far as I can see, it will be death.'

19 His prophecy came true. When they had taken up their shields, he, inspired, it seems, by some kind of fate, sprang forward in front of them, fell upon the enemy and was killed. He lies buried at the ford of the Cephisus.

The others, however, were victorious and drove the enemy down the hill to the level ground. Two of the Thirty, Critias and Hippomachus, were killed in the fighting, and

one out of the ten rulers in Piraeus, Charmides, the son of
Glaucon, and of the rest about seventy lost their lives. Thrasybulus' men took the arms of the fallen, but did not strip the
tunic from any citizen. While this was going on and they
were giving back the bodies of the dead under a truce, many
people on both sides approached each other and got into
conversation. And Cleocritus, the herald of those initiated 20
into the mysteries, a man with a remarkably fine voice,
called for silence and then spoke as follows: 'Fellow-citizens,
why are you driving us out of the city? Why do you want
to kill us? We have never done you any harm. We have
shared with you in the most holy religious services, in sacrifices and in splendid festivals; we have joined in dances with
you, gone to school with you and fought in the army with
you, braving together with you the dangers of land and sea
in defence of our common safety and freedom. In the name 21
of the gods of our fathers and mothers, of the bonds of kin-
ship and marriage and friendship, which are shared by so
many of us on both sides, I beg you to feel some shame in
front of gods and men and to give up this sin against your
fatherland. Do not give your obedience to those wicked
men, the Thirty, who, just for their own private profit, have
in eight months come close to killing more Athenians than
all the Peloponnesians did in ten years of war. These men, 22
when there is nothing to prevent our living peaceably together in our city, have brought on us war among ourselves,
and there can be nothing more shameful than this, nothing
more unbearable, more unholy and more hateful to gods
and men alike. Yet all the same you can be sure that we as
well as you have wept much for some of those whom we
have just killed.'

Cleocritus made this appeal, but the surviving officers of
the Thirty led their men back to the city, largely because they
were listening with attention to what he said. Next day the 23
Thirty met in the Council chamber. They were now feeling

their isolation and were in a singularly subdued state of mind. As for the Three Thousand, they were quartered in various parts of the city and each detachment began to quarrel among themselves. Those who had committed notable acts of violence and were therefore frightened insisted that there should be no giving in to the party in Piraeus, while those who knew that they had done nothing wrong came to the conclusion that all these evils were quite unnecessary and tried to convince the others of this, saying that they ought not to obey the Thirty any longer nor allow them to bring the state to ruin. In the end they voted that the Thirty should be deposed and another government elected; and they chose a committee of ten, one man from each tribe.

24   The Thirty now retired to Eleusis, and the Ten, with backing from the cavalry commanders, took over the command of the men in the city, who were in a very disorderly state and distrustful and suspicious among themselves. Indeed, even the cavalry stood on guard by night in the Odeum, keeping both their horses and their shields with them. The failure of confidence was such that they patrolled the walls from dusk to dawn armed as hoplites and at dawn on horseback. There was constant apprehension that some attack might be launched by the men in Piraeus, who by now amounted to a large number of people of all sorts and conditions. In fact, they were busy making shields of wood or wickerwork and in painting them. Within ten days, however, they took the field, after exchanging oaths that every man serving with them, whether he was a foreigner or not, should be taxed on an equal basis. They had a large force both of hoplites and of light troops, and had acquired about seventy cavalry. They spread over the country collecting wood and provisions and went back to Piraeus to sleep. No one in the city came out in arms against them, except the cavalry, who captured a few of the foragers from Piraeus and inflicted some casualties on the main body. They also

came across some people from Aexone who were going to
their own farms to get provisions. In spite of their pleas for
mercy and in spite of the strong opposition of many of his
own men, Lysimachus, the cavalry commander, had these
people put to death. In retaliation the men in Piraeus put to 27
death a cavalryman, Callistratus of the tribe of Leontis, whom
they had captured in the country.

Indeed, by this time they were so full of confidence that
they ventured to make attacks on the city walls. It is perhaps
worth mentioning here what the city engineer did when he
heard that the enemy were planning to bring up their siege
engines by the race track leading out of the Lyceum: he
ordered each of his wagon teams to bring up one stone big
enough to fill the wagon, and to unload these stones anywhere they liked on the track. The result was that each single
stone caused the enemy a good deal of trouble.

Now both the Thirty in Eleusis and the men on the list of 28
the Three Thousand in Athens sent ambassadors to Sparta to
ask for help on the grounds that the democrats were revolting
from the Spartan alliance. Lysander calculated that it would
be possible to force the men in Piraeus to come to terms
quickly by blockading them by land and sea and cutting off
all their supplies. He therefore supported the ambassadors
and arranged that a loan of 100 talents should be made to the
oligarchs, that he himself should be sent out by land as governor and that his brother Libys should have command of
the fleet. He then came to Eleusis and began to get together 29
a large force of hoplites from the Peloponnese, while his
brother kept watch on the sea so that no provisions could be
brought in that way. So the party in Piraeus were soon in
difficulties again, while the party in Athens, relying on Lysander, regained all their old confidence.

Affairs had reached this stage when the Spartan king Pausanias himself led a field force out of Sparta. He was jealous
of Lysander and feared that his success in this undertaking

would not only win him fame but would also result in his taking Athens as his personal property. Pausanias had won
30 over three of the five ephors to his point of view,* and all the allies marched out with him except for the Boeotians and Corinthians, who claimed that for them to march against the Athenians, who were not breaking the peace treaty in any way, would, in their view, be an act contrary to the oaths they had sworn. In fact, they acted as they did because they had concluded that the intention of the Spartans was to take over for themselves the territory of Athens and to keep it.

Pausanias made his camp in the plain near Piraeus which is called Halipedum. He commanded the right wing himself, and Lysander, with his mercenaries, commanded the left.
31 Next Pausanias sent ambassadors to the men in Piraeus and told them to disperse to their homes. They refused and Pausanias attacked – at least he went forward to the point where the battle cry is raised – and he did this so that it should not be evident that in fact he was well-disposed to them.† He then retired, after this 'attack' of his had accomplished nothing.

Next day, with two Spartan regiments and the Athenian cavalry from three tribes, he went along the shore to the Still Harbour to see where was the best place to build a wall to
32 blockade Piraeus. On his return some of the enemy attacked him and gave him some trouble. Pausanias became angry and ordered the cavalry to charge them at a gallop and the infantry in the age groups 20 to 30 to follow the cavalry. He himself came up in support of them with the rest of the infantry.

His men killed nearly thirty of the enemy's light troops and
33 drove the rest back to the theatre in Piraeus, which was just where, as it happened, all the peltasts and hoplites of the

*For the role of the ephors in the despatch of armies, cf. V.1.33, and 4.14, and Thuc. VIII.12.3.

†Here and in §35 Xenophon reflects probably the views and the prejudices of Agesilaus and his circle. Cf. III.5.25, V.2.3 and 6, V.3.10–16 and 23 ff., and Cawkwell, Classical Quarterly, XXVI, 1976, p. 74 f.

Piraeus party were getting armed. The light troops went into action at once, throwing javelins, hurling stones, shooting arrows and slinging. The Spartans, hard pressed and with many of them wounded, fell back in good order, and the army of the Piraeus attacked all the more fiercely. In this fighting two colonels, Chaeron and Thibrachus, were killed; also Lacrates, a winner at Olympia, and other Spartans who now lie buried in the Cerameicus outside the gates of Athens. And now Thrasybulus came up with the hoplites. He had 34 seen what was happening and they quickly formed up in line of battle, eight deep, in front of the others. Pausanius was hard pressed and fell back about a mile to a hill. He then sent orders to the Spartans and allies to come up in support, and, when they had arrived, drew up his phalanx in great depth and advanced on the Athenians. At first the Athenians stood up to him in close fighting, but in the end some of them were forced on to the muddy ground in the marsh of Halae and others gave way. About a hundred and fifty of them were killed.

Pausanias put up a trophy and retired to his camp. Even 35 now he felt no animosity towards the Piraeus party. Indeed, he sent to them secretly and urged them to send ambassadors to him and to the ephors who were with him, at the same time advising them what they should say. The men in Piraeus acted on his advice, and meanwhile he was causing a split in the party at Athens. He told them to come with as many people as possible to him and the ephors, and to say that they had no wish to make war on the men in Piraeus, and that they wanted to come to terms with them and then follow a common policy of friendship with Sparta. Nau- 36 cleidas too, who was one of the ephors, was very pleased to hear these proposals. For it is the Spartan custom that two of the ephors accompany the king on a campaign, and on this occasion Naucleidas and one other were with Pausanias. Both of them favoured Pausanias' policy rather than that of

Lysander. So they were very glad to send to Sparta the ambassadors from Piraeus with their proposals for peace, and also two representatives from the party in the city, Cephisophon and Meletus, who went as private individuals.

37 However, when they had set out for Sparta, the authorities in the city sent another delegation on their own. They were to say that they were surrendering the fortifications which they held and themselves unconditionally to the Spartans, and that they regarded it as right that the people in Piraeus too, if they claimed to be friendly to Sparta, should also surrender Piraeus and Munychia.

38 The ephors and the Spartan Assembly heard all these delegates and then sent fifteen men to Athens with instructions to act in conjunction with Pausanias in making what seemed to them the best settlement. An agreement was effected on these terms: that the two parties should be at peace with each other and that everyone should return to his home except for the Thirty, the Eleven and also the Ten who had been in command in Piraeus. It was also decided that if any of the people in the city felt apprehensive about themselves they should be free to settle in Eleusis.

39 When these arrangements had been made Pausanias disbanded his army and the men from Piraeus, carrying arms, went up to the Acropolis and sacrificed to Athena. When they had come down, the generals called an Assembly and

40 then Thrasybulus made the following speech: 'This is the piece of advice I want to give to the men of the city: know yourselves. And you will best be able to do so if you try to consider what right you have to be so arrogant as to attempt to make us your subjects. Are you morally better? Then why is it that the common people, though poorer than you are, never did you any harm for the sake of money, whereas you, who are richer than all of them, have committed many disgraceful crimes for the sake of your own profit? Well then, since you can lay no claim to morality, is it, do you think,

courage which entitles you to feel so proud? I think that the 41
best test we can find of this is in the fighting which took place
between us. Or will you say, perhaps, that it is in intelligence
that you are so superior, you who, with the advantages of
fortifications, arms, money and Spartan allies, have been defeated by men who had none of these? Perhaps it is the Spartans themselves you count on to make good your right to be
arrogant? I cannot quite see how. The Spartans have gone
away and left you to the mercy of this people whom you
have wronged, just as one ties a clog to the neck of a dog that
is apt to bite and then hands him over to a keeper. All the
same, my friends, I am not the man to ask you to go back on
any of your sworn assurances. All I ask is that you should give 42
us an exhibition of just one more virtue in addition to all your
other ones. Show us that in all good faith you can keep your
promises.'

So Thrasybulus spoke and added more to the same effect,
pointing out that there was no need for anyone to feel un-
easy and that all they had to do was to live in accordance with
the established laws. He then dismissed the Assembly. Magis- 43
trates were appointed, and for the time being life went on
normally. Later, however, when they heard that the people
in Eleusis were raising an army of mercenaries, the Athenians
marched out against them in full force and put their generals
to death when they had come to a conference. They then
sent the friends and relatives of the rest into Eleusis and persuaded them to come to a peaceful settlement. Oaths were
sworn that there should be an amnesty for all that had happened in the past, and to this day both parties live together as
fellow-citizens and the people abide by the oaths which they
have sworn.*

* Some have thought that these words would not have been written
in the 350s, and argued that this part of Book II must have been
written earlier. Demosthenes XX.48 (of 355-4 B.C.) shows otherwise.

BOOK THREE

CHAPTER 1

Death of Cyrus (401 B.C.) .Thibron in Asia (399 B.C.).
Successes of Dercylidas in Asia (399 B.C.)

NOT long after the civil war in Athens had ended, as de- 1
scribed above, Cyrus sent messengers to Sparta and appealed
to the Spartans to show themselves as good friends to him as
he had been to them in their war with Athens. The ephors
regarded this as a perfectly fair request and sent orders to
Samius, who was then in command of their fleet, telling him
to help Cyrus in any way that was required. Samius on his
side was very willing to do what Cyrus asked. He and his
fleet sailed with Cyrus' fleet round the coast to Cilicia and
prevented Syennesis, the governor of Cilicia, from employing
his land forces against Cyrus while he was marching against
the king of Persia. Themistogenes of Syracuse has recorded 2
the story of that campaign – of how Cyrus collected an army
and marched inland against his brother, of the battle* in
which Cyrus was killed, and how afterwards the Greeks
came safely to the sea.†

In this war of Cyrus against his brother, Tissaphernes was 3
considered to have shown himself extremely valuable to the
king and was sent down to the coast as satrap not only of the
provinces which he had governed before but also of those
which had been under Cyrus. His first act was to demand the
submission of all the Greek cities in Ionia. These cities not

*Cunaxa, in 401 B.C.
†It is generally agreed that Themistogenes is a pseudonym for
Xenophon himself. If so, this passage shows that he wrote the begin-
ning of Book III of the *Hellenica* after the *Anabasis* was written in the
later 370s at the earliest. Cf. Introduction to Xenophon's *The Persian
Expedition*, Penguin Classics, 1972, p. 16.

only wanted to be free but were frightened of Tissaphernes, because, instead of following him, they had chosen to support Cyrus while he was alive. So they refused to allow him into their cities and sent ambassadors to Sparta asking the Spartans, as the leading power in Greece, to take them also, the Greeks of Asia, under their protection, to save their land
4 from being laid waste and to maintain their freedom. The Spartans sent out Thibron to them as a governor and gave him an army of 1,000 emancipated helots and 4,000 other troops from the Peloponnese.* Thibron also asked the Athenians to send him 300 cavalry and promised to pay for them himself. The Athenians sent some of the men who had served in the cavalry under the Thirty, thinking that for them to live and die in foreign parts would be all to the good of the democracy.
5 When they had arrived in Asia Thibron also raised troops from the Greek cities on the mainland; for at that time the cities would obey any order that a Spartan might give. With this army Thibron, considering the enemy's strength in cavalry, did not venture to come down on to the plain but was content merely with preventing them from laying waste whatever part of the country he happened to
6 be in. Later, however, he was joined by the Greeks who had marched into the interior with Cyrus and had come safely back again, and now he did form up in line of battle against Tissaphernes even on level ground. He also gained possession of various cities. Pergamus came over to him voluntarily, as did Teuthrania and Halisarna, which were ruled over by Eurysthenes and Procles, who were descendants of Demaratus the Spartan. The land had been given to Demaratus by the king of Persia as a reward for accompanying him on his expedition against Greece. Thibron was also joined by the brothers Gorgion, rulers of Gambrium and Palaegambrium, and Gongylus, ruler of Myrina and Gryneum. These cities,

*Cf. *Anab.* VII.6.1, 7.57, 8.24 for the remnants of the Ten Thousand under Xenophon joining up with Thibron.

too, had been given by the king to the earlier Gongylus, who had been the only one of the Eretrians to join the Persians and had therefore been exiled. There were also some weak cities 7 which Thibron took by storm. The place known as Egyptian Larissa, however, would not give in to him and he surrounded it with his army and besieged it. After other methods had failed, he sunk a shaft and from it dug a tunnel so as to cut off the water supply. However, the enemy kept sallying out from their fortifications and throwing wood and stones into the shaft. Thibron then constructed a wooden shed and had it placed to cover over the shaft, but this also was destroyed by the townspeople, who came out at night and set it on fire. Then, since he did not appear to be doing anything valuable, the ephors ordered him to leave Larissa and march against Caria.*

He was already at Ephesus and preparing for this campaign 8 when Dercylidas arrived to take over the command of the army. Dercylidas had the reputation of being a singularly clever and subtle man; in fact, he was nicknamed 'Sisyphus'. After his arrival Thibron returned to Sparta where he was condemned and exiled. He had been accused by the allies of allowing his troops to plunder their friends.

Dercylidas was aware that Tissaphernes and Pharnabazus 9 each viewed the other with suspicion and, as soon as he had taken over the army, he came to an arrangement with Tissaphernes, and then led his troops away into the territory of Pharnabazus, electing to make war against one of them rather than against both together. He had also been an enemy of Pharnabazus for some time. He had been governor of Abydus when Lysander was admiral and had then been slandered by Pharnabazus and, as a result, been forced to stand on guard carrying his shield. This is normally the punishment for insubordination and is regarded by distinguished Spartans as a

*Diod. XIV.36 recounts operations of Thibron in Caria, seemingly before Xenophon joined him.

141

great disgrace. He was therefore particularly pleased to be
10 marching against Pharnabazus now. And from the very
beginning his conduct in the command showed a marked
contrast to that of Thibron. He led his army through friendly
country all the way to the Aeolis, in Pharnabazus' territory,
and his troops did no harm to the allies on the march.

This Aeolis was indeed part of Pharnabazus' province, but
Zenis of Dardanus had, while he was alive, governed it for
him as satrap. After he fell ill and died, Pharnabazus had
planned to give the satrapy to someone else, but Mania, the
wife of Zenis, who was also from Dardanus, set out to visit
him with a great company of attendants and with gifts for
Pharnabazus himself and for use in winning the favour of his
concubines and of the most influential people at his court.
11 She was granted an interview with him and spoke as follows:
'Pharnabazus, my husband was always a good friend to you
and used to pay you all the tributes due. For this you praised
and honoured him. Now if I serve you just as loyally as he
did, what need is there to appoint anyone else as satrap? And
if I fail to please you, surely it is in your power to take the
satrapy away from me and give it to someone else.'
12 After hearing this, Pharnabazus decided that the woman
should be satrap. She, when she had taken over her province,
paid the tribute just as regularly as her husband had done and,
in addition, never visited Pharnabazus without bringing gifts
for him. And whenever he came down to her country, she
gave him a far more splendid and enjoyable reception than
13 did any of his other governors. She not only kept loyal to
him all the cities which she had taken over but gained control over other cities on the coast which had not been subject
to him before – Larissa, Hamaxitus and Colonae. She used a
Greek mercenary force for these operations and, while they
were attacking the walls, used to look on from a carriage.
Anyone who won her approval would be rewarded with the
most splendid gifts, so that this force of hers was magnifi-

cently equipped. She also used to join forces with Pharnabazus even when, in retaliation for raids on the King's territory, he invaded the land of the Mysians and the Pisidians. In return for all this, Pharnabazus gave her special honours and privileges and sometimes called her in as a counsellor.

When she was more than forty years old, her daughter's 14 husband, Meidias, found it intolerable to hear people saying that it was a disgrace for the country to be ruled by a woman and for him to be merely an ordinary individual. Against other people Mania always took the precautions that are normal for an absolute ruler, but she trusted Meidias and was fond of him, as a woman naturally would be of her son-in-law. He was therefore able, so it is said, to make his way into her presence and to strangle her. He also killed her son, who was a remarkably good-looking boy of about seventeen. Next 15 he seized the fortresses of Scepsis and Gergis, where Mania had kept most of her treasure; but the other cities refused him entry and were held for Pharnabazus by their garrisons. Meidias then sent gifts to Pharnabazus and claimed that he should be appointed ruler of the province just as Mania had been. But Pharnabazus told him to keep his gifts and look after them well. 'I shall come soon,' he said, 'to take them and you too. For, if I fail to avenge Mania, I would rather not live.'

This was the state of affairs when Dercylidas arrived upon 16 the scene. He took action immediately, and in one day secured the voluntary submission of the coastal cities of Larissa, Hamaxitus and Colonae. He sent to the cities of Aeolis also and urged them to free themselves, to admit him inside their walls and to become allies. The cities of Neandria, Ilium and Cocylium did as he asked. They were all garrisoned by Greek troops and these had not been treated at all well since the death of Mania. However, the officer in command of the 17 garrison of the extremely strong fortress of Cebren refused to admit Dercylidas. In his view, he was likely to be

143

rewarded with high honours by Pharnabazus if he could keep the city in allegiance to him.

Dercylidas, angry at this refusal, made preparations for an assault on Cebren. On the first day the sacrifices that he made did not turn out favourably, so he sacrificed again on the second day. Again they were unfavourable, and he tried once more on the third day and then for the fourth day too. He was exceedingly impatient at this delay since he was in a hurry to gain control of the whole of Aeolis before Pharnabazus came to its rescue.

18 One of his captains, Athenadas of Sicyon, considering that this delay on the part of Dercylidas was stupid and that he was capable by himself of cutting off the water supply of Cebren, ran forward with his own company and tried to block up the spring from which they drew their water. But the people in the town sallied out, killed two of his men, wounded him himself and drove back the rest of his company in close fighting and with missiles. Dercylidas was vexed at this set-back, thinking that now, when it came to an assault, the troops would be less enthusiastic; but just at this moment heralds came from the walls from the Greeks in the city. Their message was that the Greeks were opposed to the actions of their commander; they themselves would rather be on the side of their fellow-Greeks than on that of the

19 foreigners. While this conference was still going on, another messenger came out, this time from their commander himself, who declared that he also was in agreement with what the others were saying. It happened that on that day Dercylidas' sacrifices had turned out favourably, so he ordered his men to take up their arms at once and then led them towards the gates. Those inside opened the gates and let him in. Then, leaving a garrison here too, he marched immediately against Scepsis and Gergis.

20 By this time Meidias was not only expecting Pharnabazus to arrive but was also frightened of his own citizens. He sent

to Dercylidas and said that he was prepared to come and
negotiate with him if Dercylidas would give him hostages.
Dercylidas sent him one man from each of the allied cities
and told him to choose out of them as many as he liked.
Meidias took ten men and then came out from the city and,
in a conference with Dercylidas, asked him what terms he
would offer if he became an ally of Sparta. Dercylidas replied that the terms were that Meidias should allow his citizens to be free and independent; and, while he was still
speaking, he continued to move forward towards Scepsis.
Since it was clear to Meidias that, against the will of his citi- 21
zens, he could do nothing to prevent it, he allowed Dercylidas inside the city. Dercylidas first sacrificed to Athena on the
acropolis of Scepsis, and then led Meidias' garrison troops
outside the walls. He gave over the city to its citizens and
made a speech to them in which he encouraged them to organize their political life as Greeks and free men should do.
He then left Scepsis and advanced against Gergis, accompanied on his way by numbers of the people of Scepsis, who
were delighted with what he had done and wished to show
him honour. Meidias, too, went along with him, and on the 22
way claimed that Dercylidas should hand Gergis over to him.
Dercylidas, however, merely replied: 'You can be sure that
you will lose nothing of what really belongs to you.' He
said this as he was already approaching the gates of Gergis,
with Meidias by his side and the army following in double
file, as though there was no hostility to be expected.

The men on the towers, which were extremely high,
could see Meidias with Dercylidas and so they did not dis-
charge their missiles. Dercylidas then said: 'Order them to
open the gates, Meidias, so that you may lead the way and I
can go with you to the temple and sacrifice here, too, to
Athena.'

Meidias did not at all like the idea of opening the gates. On
the other hand, he was frightened of being arrested on the

23   spot, and so he gave the order for them to be opened. When
he had entered the city, Dercylidas, still keeping Meidias at
his side, went up to the acropolis and, with his immediate
following, sacrificed to Athena. He told the rest of his troops
to take up position along the walls. When the sacrifice was
over, he announced that the spearmen in Meidias' bodyguard were to fall in at the van of his own army and were in
future to enter his service as mercenaries. 'Meidias,' he told
them, 'has nothing to fear.'

24   Meidias, however, was at his wits' end. 'Well,' he said, 'I
think I'll go away now, and organize some entertainment for
you.'

'Oh no,' said Dercylidas, 'by Zeus, it would be disgraceful
for me just after I have sacrificed to accept your hospitality
rather than offer you some of my own. You must really stay
with me. And while dinner is being prepared, you and I will
discuss what is the fairest way for us to act towards each other,
and then we will do as we have decided.'

25   When they had sat down, Dercylidas asked, 'Tell me,
Meidias, did your father leave all his property to you?'

'He certainly did,' said Meidias.

'And how many houses were there? How many farms?
How much pasture land?'

Meidias then began to make a list, but the citizens of Scepsis
who were present said: 'Dercylidas, he's not telling you the
truth.'

26   Dercylidas turned to them and said: 'All the same, you
must not be too particular about details,' and then, when a
list of all Meidias' inheritance had been drawn up, he said:
'Tell me, to whom did Mania belong?'

They all replied that she belonged to Pharnabazus.

'Then,' he said, 'does not her property belong to Pharnabazus too?'

'It certainly does,' they answered.

'In that case,' said Dercylidas, 'it must now belong to us,

since we are the conquerors and Pharnabazus is our enemy. And now,' he went on, 'will someone show me the way to where this property of Mania, or rather of Pharnabazus, is stored?'

Then they led him to Mania's house, which Meidias had 27 taken over, and Meidias, too, went with them. After entering the house Dercylidas summoned the stewards and ordered his servants to seize them. He then told them that if they were caught concealing any of Mania's property, they would have their throats cut on the spot, and they showed him everything there was. When he had seen it all he shut the house, put a seal on it and posted guards. And on his way out, 28 meeting some of the colonels and captains at the gates, he said: 'My friends, we have earned nearly a year's pay for the army – for 8,000 men; and if we earn any more, we'll add that to the total too.' He made this statement because he knew that when the soldiers heard of it there would be a great improvement in discipline and in morale.

Meidias now asked: 'But what about me, Dercylidas? Where am I to live?'

Dercylidas replied: 'Just where you have a perfectly good right to live, Meidias. In your native city of Scepsis and in the house you inherited from your father.'

CHAPTER 2

Further campaigns of Dercylidas (398 and 397 B.C.).
The Elean War

1 AFTER these accomplishments – he had taken nine cities in eight days – Dercylidas considered how he could avoid being a burden to his allies, as Thibron had been, by quartering his troops among them for the winter, and at the same time not expose the Greek cities to damage from Pharnabazus' cavalry, which he would use if he felt strong enough. So he sent to Pharnabazus and asked which he preferred, peace or war. Pharnabazus chose to make a truce, since it seemed to him that Aeolis was now a formidable base directed against
✓ Phrygia, where he lived himself.*

2 After this Dercylidas went to Bithynian Thrace and spent the winter there. Pharnabazus was far from displeased with this, as the Bithynians were constantly making war against him. For most of the time Dercylidas was able to plunder Bithynia with complete impunity and had all the supplies he wanted. His only set-back was after a force of Odrysians came to him as allies from Seuthes from the other side of the strait – about two hundred cavalry and three hundred peltasts. These troops of Seuthes built a camp and fortified it with a stockade about two and a half miles from the Greek camp. They then asked Dercylidas for some of his hoplites to guard their camp, and set out themselves on raiding expeditions, bringing in a number of slaves and a great quantity of
3 property, so that their camp was full of all the prisoners they had taken. The Bithynians now discovered how many went out on raids and how many Greeks were left behind as a garrison; they then got together all the cavalry and peltasts

*Diod. XIV.38 says the truce was for eight months.

that they could, and at dawn made an attack on the Greek
hoplites, who were about two hundred strong. When they
got within range they hurled spears and javelins at the Greeks,
who, shut up inside the stockade which was only about the
height of a man, found themselves unable to do anything
and were killed or wounded on all sides. Finally, they broke
down their own fortifications and charged the Bithynians.
They, however, being peltasts, could easily escape from hop- 4
lites; wherever the Greeks charged, they gave ground and
meanwhile kept on hurling their javelins from both flanks,
striking down numbers of them on every occasion they
charged out. In the end the Greeks were shot down like
cattle in a pen. About fifteen of them, however, escaped to
the Greek camp, and they only managed to do so because
they had seen at once what the position was and had slipped
away in the middle of the fighting without being noticed by
the Bithynians.

After this quick victory, the Bithynians killed the Odry- 5
sian Thracians who were guarding the tents, recovered all
the booty and went away. So by the time that the Greeks had
heard the news and come to the rescue, there was nothing to
be seen in the camp except naked corpses. However, when
the Odrysians got back, they buried their dead, drank a great
deal of wine in their honour and held horse races. For the
future they joined camp with the Greeks and then went on
ravaging Bithynia with fire and sword.

At the beginning of spring* Dercylidas moved out of 6
Bithynia and came to Lampsacus. While he was there commissioners arrived from the government in Sparta – Aracus,
Naubates and Antisthenes. They had come to get a general
view of the situation in Asia and to tell Dercylidas to remain
in command for the coming year; they were also to tell him
that they had been instructed by the ephors to call together
the soldiers and give them the following message: 'The

* That is, spring 397 B.C.

ephors look with disapproval on your past behaviour, but for your good conduct at present they commend you. As for the future they will not tolerate any ill-treatment of the allies, but if you behave well to them, they will commend you.'

7 When they had called together the soldiers and delivered this message, the man* who had been the leader of the troops that had served with Cyrus stood forward and made the following reply: 'I think, Spartans, that it should be pointed out that we are the same men now as then. The difference is that we have another commander now. You can therefore judge for yourselves why it is that there is no fault to be found at present, though there was in the past.'

8 While the commissioners were staying in camp with Dercylidas, one of Aracus' party happened to mention that they had left at Sparta some ambassadors from the people of the Chersonese. They had said that at the present time they were unable to cultivate their land, as it was constantly being raided by the Thracians; if, however, a wall were to be built across their peninsula from sea to sea, they would not only have plenty of good land for themselves to cultivate but there would also be plenty for any Spartans who wanted some.† And so, the commissioners said, it seemed quite likely that some Spartans would be sent out by the state with an army to carry out this operation.

9 Dercylidas said nothing to the commissioners about what he had in mind when he heard this. He sent them on their way through the Greek cities to Ephesus and was very pleased at the thought that they would see all these cities in a state of peace and contentment. And so they went on their way.

*That is, Xenophon himself, who was putting the blame for the indiscipline of 399 on Thibron. Cf. IV.8.22 for a sour note about Thibron after his death. Xenophon had been suspect at Sparta as captain of the Ten Thousand who were regarded as a gang of roughs. Cf. *Anab.* VII.1.7 ff., 6.4, etc.

†Some settlers were sent to the Chersonese under Spartan auspices (IV.8.5). Characteristically, Xenophon did not formally record their despatch.

Now that he knew he was to stay in Asia, Dercylidas sent again to Pharnabazus and asked whether he wanted war or would prefer the winter's truce to remain in force. Once again Pharnabazus chose the truce and so Dercylidas, leaving behind him the cities at peace in this area also, crossed the Hellespont into Europe with his army.

After marching through the friendly part of Thrace, where he was entertained by Seuthes, he came to the Chersonese. Here he discovered that there were eleven or twelve towns 10 and that the land was excellent and capable of producing everything, although, as had been reported, it had been laid waste by the Thracians. He found that the isthmus was nearly five miles across, and without any further delay offered a sacrifice and began to build a wall across it. Each contingent of troops had its own section to build, and prizes were offered to those who were the first to complete their section and to others whose work deserved it. Thus, though the wall was not begun until spring, it was finished before the time of harvest. By this wall he had given protection to eleven towns, many harbours and a great deal of good land for sowing, and great stretches of magnificent pasture where animals of all sorts could be raised. When the work was over, he 11 crossed back again into Asia.*

In the course of his inspection of the cities of Asia he found that they were all doing well, with the exception of Atarneus

*Perhaps Xenophon was left in Lampsacus, while Dercylidas was in the Chersonese. Otherwise one would expect rather more about a second dinner with Seuthes (cf. *Anab.* VII.3.15–33) with whom Xenophon had had a great deal to do (*Anab.* VII.1.5 *et passim*). Also there is no hint that the building of the wall was restoration work (cf. Herodotus VI.39 for the Sixth-Century wall, and Plut. *Pericles* 19 for the earlier Fifth-Century wall; it needed restoration because it was of earth, according to Procopius *Buildings* 4.10.5 ff.). Xenophon had friends in Lampsacus (*Anab.* VII.8.1) and may have been in charge to await the army's return. So he heard what happened, remaining perhaps uncertain, or indifferent, about the exact number of cities to be counted as in the Chersonese. According to Diod. XIV.38.7, Dercylidas had to drive Thracians out before he began to build.

which was a strong place and had been occupied by exiles from Chios who were using it as a base from which to make raids on the rest of Ionia, and who were living on the proceeds of these raids. He discovered, too, that they had got together great quantities of grain. After surrounding the place with his troops he laid siege to it, and in eight months forced them to come to terms. He put Dracon of Pellene in charge of the city, and filled the place with great stocks of supplies of all kinds so that he could use it as a centre for rest and re-equipment whenever he came that way. He then went on to Ephesus, which is three days' march from Sardis.

12 Up to this time there had been peace between Tissaphernes and Dercylidas and also between the Greeks and the foreigners in this area. Now, however, ambassadors from the cities of Ionia came to Sparta and pointed out that Tissaphernes had the power, if he chose, to allow the Greek cities to enjoy their independence. They said that in their view, if Caria, where he had his own establishment, were to suffer, that would be the quickest way of getting him to act. After hearing this, the ephors sent out to Dercylidas with orders that he and his army should cross into Caria, and that the admiral, Pharax, should sail along the coast with his fleet in support.

13 As it happened Pharnabazus was visiting Tissaphernes at this time. This was partly because Tissaphernes had been appointed to the supreme command, and partly because he wanted to assure him that he was ready to join forces with him and fight at his side in order to drive the Greeks out of the king's territories. He had various reasons for being jealous of Tissaphernes' position as supreme commander, and particularly resented the fact that he had been driven out of Aeolis. When Tissaphernes had heard what he had to say, he replied: 'First of all, then, cross over into Caria with me, and

14 then we will discuss the whole position.' However, when they got to Caria, they decided to garrison all the strong points and then cross back again into Ionia.

Dercylidas, when he heard that they had come back again over the Maeander, told Pharax that he was afraid that Tissaphernes and Pharnabazus might overrun the land in its undefended state and seize what they wanted; so he also crossed into Ionia. While on the march and with the army in no sort of battle formation (since it was assumed that the enemy were some distance ahead in the territory of Ephesus), they suddenly saw scouts on the burial mounds in front of them. They 15 sent men up to the mounds and the towers near their own line of march, and now they could see an army drawn up in line of battle right across their road. There were Carians with their white shields, all the Persian troops that were available, all the Greek troops serving with either Pharnabazus or Tissaphernes and a great mass of cavalry, those of Tissaphernes on the right wing and those of Pharnabazus on the left.

When Dercylidas saw what the position was, he ordered 16 the divisional commanders and the captains to form up their men in a line eight deep, and to station the peltasts on each wing together with the cavalry he had, which was not impressive either in numbers or in quality. Meanwhile he himself offered sacrifice. All those soldiers in the army who came 17 from the Peloponnese made ready for battle in a quiet and orderly way. Very different was the conduct of the men from Priene and Achilleum, from the islands and the Ionian cities. Some of them just ran away, leaving their arms on the ground in the deep corn that grows in the plain of the Maeander; and those who did stay in their positions were quite clearly not going to stay there long.

On the other side, Pharnabazus, so it was said, was in 18 favour of launching an attack. Tissaphernes, however, could remember how the Greek troops with Cyrus had fought against the Persians. He imagined that all Greeks were like them, and so was unwilling to join battle. Instead, he sent to Dercylidas saying that he would like to have a conference

with him. Dercylidas went forward to meet the messengers,
taking with him some of the best-looking troops, both cavalry and infantry, in his service. 'As you see,' he said, 'I myself
was ready enough to fight. However, if he wants a conference, I am not going to raise any objection. But if this is
to take place, there must be an exchange of pledges and
hostages.'

19   His proposals were adopted and carried out and then both
armies went away, Tissaphernes' and Pharnabazus' men to
Tralles in Caria, and the Greeks to Leucophrys. In this place
there was a very holy temple of Artemis and a lake about two
hundred yards long, with a sandy bottom and a constant
supply of warm water, good to drink.

After this interim arrangement, the commanders came on
the following day to the agreed meeting place and decided
to find out from each other on what terms they were each
20 prepared to make peace. Dercylidas stated that his conditions
were that the King should allow the Greek cities their independence; Tissaphernes and Pharnabazus then stated their
conditions – that the Greek army should leave the country
and the Spartan governors should be withdrawn from the
cities. After stating these terms they made a truce which was
to last until the proposals had been reported to Sparta by
Dercylidas, and to the King by Tissaphernes.

21   At the same time* as these campaigns of Dercylidas in
Asia, Sparta was having trouble with Elis. The Spartans had
been angry for a long time with the Eleans for the following
reasons. First Elis had made an alliance with Athens, Argos

*Xenophon's synchronism is wildly inexact. By his own account
the war fell before the death of King Agis (III.3.1), who was succeeded by his brother Agesilaus in 400 B.C. or earlier. For another
case of lax chronology, cf. n. at V.2.2. More alarming still is the fact
that the account in Diod. XIV.17 and 34 is irreconcilably different.
Since the discovery that at least part of Diodorus Book XIV is de-
rived indirectly from the *Hellenica Oxyrhynchia*, it would be foolhardy
to assert that Xenophon's account must be preferred.

and Mantinea,* then they had debarred the Spartans from competing in the horse races and athletic contests at the Olympic Games, the pretext being that a judgement had been awarded against Sparta.† And they had gone further than this. Lichas, a Spartan, had made over his chariot to the Thebans and the Thebans had been announced as the winners; but when Lichas came in to put the garland on the head of the charioteer, the Eleans had beaten him, though he was an old man, and driven him out. After this, when Agis had 22 been sent, in obedience to an oracle, to sacrifice to Zeus, the Eleans refused to allow him to pray for victory in war, saying that it was an ancient and established principle that Greeks should not consult the oracle with regard to a war waged against Greeks. So Agis had to go away without having sacrificed.

With all these reasons for anger, the ephors and the Assem- 23 bly decided to make the Eleans see reason. They therefore sent ambassadors to Elis to say in the view of the Spartan government it was only right that the Eleans should grant independence to all outlying cities now in their control. The Eleans replied that they would do no such thing, since these cities were theirs by right of conquest. The ephors then ordered mobilization on a war basis, and Agis, at the head of the army, advanced into Elean territory by way of Achaea, along the Larisus. The army had only just arrived in enemy 24 country and was beginning to lay the land waste when there was an earthquake. Agis regarded this as a sign sent from heaven, and so he fell back again and disbanded the army. The effect of this was to make the Eleans still bolder, and they began to send embassies round to all states which they knew to be unfriendly to Sparta. However, in this same year the 25 ephors again ordered a general mobilization against Elis and, with the exception of the Boeotians and the Corinthians, all the allies, including the Athenians, joined Agis in this

*Thuc. V.47. †Thuc. V.49.

expedition. He invaded Elis by way of Aulon and immediately the Lepreans revolted from Elis and came over to him. So did the Macistians and then the Epitalians. Then, while he was crossing the river, the Letrinians, Amphidolians and Marganians also came over.

26   He then went to Olympia and sacrificed to Olympian Zeus – this time no one made any effort to stop him. After the sacrifice he marched on the city of Elis, cutting down the trees and burning the crops on the way. Very great numbers of cattle and of slaves were captured in the country, with the result that, as this news spread, many more of the Arcadians and Achaeans came as volunteers to join his army and get a share of the plunder. Indeed, this expedition turned out to be a kind of process for restocking the whole Peloponnese.

27   When he reached the city Agis did a certain amount of damage to the suburbs and to the very beautiful gymnasia. The city itself was unfortified,* and it is thought that Agis was unwilling, rather than unable, to capture it. In the city was Xenias, the man of whom they say that he measured out the money he got from his father by the bushel, and he and his party were anxious to get the credit for bringing the city over to the Spartans. So, while the country was being ravaged and Agis' army was in the neighbourhood of Cyllene, Xenias and his friends, with swords in their hands, rushed out of a house and began a massacre of their oppo-

*The translation follows the conventional interpretation. For another interpretation, see Cawkwell, *Classical Quarterly*, XXVI, 1976, p. 75 n. 3, where the distinction in the text between the *astu* and the *polis* is equated with the distinction in VII.4.14 ff. between the *polis* and the *acropolis*; Diod. XIV.17.10 f. implies that the town was walled and Pausanias III.8.5 says that one of the terms of the peace was that the wall of the *astu* had to be pulled down; the *acropolis* was by ancient custom inviolable, and was unwalled until 313 B.C. (Diod. XIX.87). The translation of §30 follows the text as conventionally emended; the text of the manuscripts is consistent with the alternative interpretation.

nents. After killing a man who looked like Thrasydaeus, the
leader of the democratic party, they imagined that it was
really Thrasydaeus whom they had killed, and so the democratic party lost heart and put up no resistance, while the 28
murderers assumed that there was nothing more to be done,
and those who shared their views came out and paraded
under arms in the market place. In fact, however, Thrasydaeus had been drinking and was still sleeping it off, and as
soon as the people realized that he was not dead they crowded round his house on all sides, as a swarm of bees crowds
round its leader. Thrasydaeus put himself at their head; there 29
was a battle in which the democrats were victorious, and
those who had tried to seize power by violence fled to the
Spartans. Later Agis crossed the Alpheus again and withdrew,
but he left a garrison behind at Epitalium near the Alpheus,
with Lysippus as governor and with him the exiles from Elis.
Agis then disbanded the army and returned to Sparta. For the 30
rest of the summer and the following winter the land of Elis
was ravaged by Lysippus and his men. But during the next
summer, Thrasydaeus sent to Sparta and offered to destroy
the fortifications of Phea and Cyllene, to grant independence
to the Triphylian cities of Phrixa and Epitalium; also to the
Letrinians, Amphidolians and Marganians; also to the Acrorians and to the city of Lasion, which was claimed by the
Arcadians. The Eleans, however, considered that they had a
right to retain possession of Epeum, the city between Heraea
and Macistus; they said that they had bought the whole territory for thirty talents from the people who owned the city at
the time, and that the money had been paid over. The Spar- 31
tans, however, decided that it was just as unfair to take property from the weaker party by a forced purchase as by a
forcible seizure, and so they compelled them to give this city
its independence too. But they did not deprive them of their
position as guardians of the temple of Olympian Zeus, even
though this was not a right which had always belonged to

them. This was because they considered that the rival claimants were a peasant community and not qualified to hold the position. These terms were agreed upon, and peace and alliance were concluded between Elis and Sparta. And so this war between the two states came to an end.

CHAPTER 3

Death of Agis. Accession of Agesilaus. Conspiracy of
Cinadon (397 B.C.)

AFTER this Agis went to Delphi, and made an offering of 1
the tenth part of the booty to the god. He was now an old
man and on the way back, at Heraea, he became ill. He was
carried back to Sparta still alive, but died soon after his arrival. His burial was of a grandeur that seemed to go beyond
what a mere man could claim or expect.

After the due period of mourning it became necessary to
appoint a new king and this position was claimed by both
Leotychides,* who professed to be a son of Agis, and by
Agesilaus, a brother of Agis.

Leotychides said: 'But, Agesilaus, the law is that the king- 2
ship goes to the son, not to the brother of the king. The
brother can only become king if there is no son.'

'Then,' said Agesilaus, 'it is I who should be king.'

'How can that be,' said Leotychides, 'so long as I am alive?'

'Because,' Agesilaus replied, 'the man you call your father
said that you were not his son.'

'But my mother knows far better than he does,' said
Leotychides, 'and to this day she says that I am his son.'

'But,' said Agesilaus, 'Poseidon made it clear that you are
entirely mistaken. He drove your father out of your mother's
bedroom into the open air by an earthquake. And his evidence is supported by what is known as the truest of all witnesses, namely, time. For you were born in the tenth month
from the time when he fled from the bedroom.'

With these arguments on both sides, Leotychides received 3

*Xenophon refrains from mentioning that it was generally believed
that Leotychides was the son of Alcibiades (Plut. *Alcibiades* 23, etc.).

some support from Diopithes, a man with great knowledge of oracles. Diopithes said that there was also an oracle of Apollo warning them 'to beware of the lame kingship'.*

Lysander, however, speaking on behalf of Agesilaus, objected to this. He said that in his opinion the oracle did not mean that they should beware if some king of theirs pulled a muscle and became lame; what was meant was that they should beware lest someone not of the royal blood should become king. For the kingship really would be lame if people other than the descendants of Heracles were to be leaders of the state.†

4   After hearing these and similar arguments from both sides, the state chose Agesilaus king.

In the first year of his reign, while he was making one of the official sacrifices on behalf of the state, the prophet said that the gods were revealing that there was some very terrible conspiracy afoot. He sacrificed again, and the prophet said that the signs were worse still. Then, when he had sacrificed for the third time, he said: 'Agesilaus, the signs that I read here are just as they would be if we were surrounded by enemies.' After this they made sacrifices to the powers who turn evil aside and to the powers who preserve us from evil, and it was some time before they obtained favourable omens and stopped sacrificing. Within five days of these sacrifices someone brought information to the ephors not only of the existence of a conspiracy but also of the name of the leader of

5   the whole affair. This leader was a young man called Cinadon, strong, healthy and with plenty of courage, but not one

---

* Agesilaus was lame.

† One would never guess from Xenophon's account of the succession that Lysander was later credited with seeking to throw the kingship open to some sort of election (Plut. *Lysander* 24–6). Xenophon must have known. He passed over another occasion for similar comment when he recounted the arrogant behaviour of Lysander in Asia in 396 B.C. (III.4.7 ff.); cf. Plut. *Agesilaus* 8.

of the regular-officer class. In reply to the ephors' question of how Cinadon proposed to carry his plan into effect, the informer told them that Cinadon had taken him to the edge of the market place and then told him to count how many Spartans of the officer class were there. 'And I,' said the informer, 'counted up the king and the ephors and the members of the Council and about forty others, and then asked him "What was the point, Cinadon, in asking me to make this count?" Then he said, "I want you to consider these men as your enemies and all the others in the market place, who are more than 4,000, as your allies."' Then too, the informer said, Cinadon would comment on the people they met in the streets, pointing out sometimes one, sometimes two as 'enemies', all the rest being 'allies'. And in looking over the people who happened to be on the country estates belonging to the officer class, he would point out one more, namely, the owner, as an 'enemy', but would find on each estate a great many 'allies'.

The ephors then asked how many people, according to 6 Cinadon, were in the plot with him and the informer told them that on that point Cinadon had said that those actually in the plot with himself and the leaders were not very many, though they were trustworthy; it was rather the case, the leaders claimed, that they were in the plot with everyone else – helots, freedmen, lower-grade Spartans* and Perioeci – since all these people showed clearly enough, if there was ever any mention of the Spartan officer class, that they would be glad to eat them up raw.

*'Lower-grade Spartans' is the translation of a Spartan term that occurs nowhere else (*hypomeiones*), presumably designating a class of *déclassé* Spartans of the top class (the so-called *Spartiates*). Xenophon is never at a loss for a Spartan term. In §8 he refers to the so-called 'Little Assembly', about which we can only guess. His whole account of this conspiracy argues his great familiarity with Spartan life. Without this chapter the obscurity surrounding ancient Sparta would be ten times more opaque.

7   The next question of the ephors was 'Where did they say they would get arms?' and the informer replied that Cinadon had said: 'Those of us who are in the army, of course, have arms of our own. As for the mob, I will show you.' He had then taken him into the iron market and pointed out to him the great supply of knives, swords, spits, axes, hatchets and sickles. 'All tools,' he said, 'which are used for work in agriculture, forestry or stonework are also weapons, and most of the other industries, too, use implements which are perfectly good weapons, especially against unarmed men.' Cinadon had also said, when asked what date had been set for action, 'My orders are to remain in the city.'

8   After hearing all this, the ephors came to the conclusion that this plot of which they had been told had been thoroughly thought out, and they were extremely alarmed. They did not even call together the members of what is known as the Little Assembly; instead, they made their plans with a small group selected by them individually from the Council of Elders. It was decided to send Cinadon with a detachment of the younger men to Aulon, with instructions to bring back from there various citizens of Aulon and helots whose names were written in the despatches he was to carry. He was also told to bring back the woman who was said to be the most beautiful of all the women in Aulon, but one who was believed to be corrupting all the Spartans, young and old alike,

9 who came there. Cinadon had already done work of this kind for the ephors in the past; so on this occasion, too, they handed over to him the official despatch in which were written the names of those to be arrested. When Cinadon asked which of the young men he was to take with him, they said: 'Go to the senior guard commander and ask him to let you have six or seven of the men he happens to have available.' They, meanwhile, had seen to it that the guard commander knew whom to send, and that the men to be sent knew that the one to be arrested was Cinadon himself. They also told

Cinadon that they would send with him three wagons so that it would not be necessary to bring back his prisoners on foot. In fact, they did everything they could to conceal the fact that there was only going to be one prisoner, and that was he. They did not have him seized inside the city because they did not know how far the conspiracy had spread, and also they wanted to hear from Cinadon the names of his fellow-conspirators before they could learn that they had been informed upon, so that they would not be able to escape. The arrangement was that Cinadon should be arrested and held. When his captors had found out from him the names of his fellow-conspirators, they were to write them down and send them to the ephors as quickly as possible. The affair was regarded so seriously that the ephors also sent out a regiment of cavalry to support the party who had gone to Aulon.

So Cinadon was seized and a cavalryman rode back to Sparta with the list of names which he had given them. The ephors immediately put under arrest the prophet Tisamenus and the most important of the other conspirators. Cinadon was then brought back for interrogation. He admitted everything and told them the names of those who were in the plot. Finally, they asked him: 'But what was it you hoped to achieve by this?' He replied: 'To be equal to the best in Sparta.' After this, however, his hands were immediately bound and his neck fixed fast in a collar. Beneath lashes and spear-thrusts he and those with him were dragged through the city, and so they got their punishment.*

*Xenophon omits to mention what most surely is to be presumed, *viz.* that the punishment was completed by execution. Plut. *Agesilaus* 32 shows how Xenophon's hero would deal with disaffection.

CHAPTER 4

Agesilaus in Asia (396–395 B.C.)

1 IT was after this that news arrived from a Syracusan called Herodas. He had been in Phoenicia with a shipowner there and had observed Phoenician triremes sailing in from different directions, while others were being manned or being got ready for sea on the spot. After hearing, too, that there were to be 300 of them, he sailed on the first boat leaving for Greece and reported to the Spartans that the King and Tissaphernes were preparing to use this force in action; what its objective was, he did not know.

2 This was disturbing news to the Spartans, and they began to mobilize their allies and make plans for what should be done. In the view of Lysander the Greeks would be greatly superior on the sea, and he also took into account the land force which had marched into the interior with Cyrus and got safely back again. He therefore persuaded Agesilaus to campaign against Asia,* if the Spartans would give him thirty Spartans of the officer class, 2,000 of the helots who had been granted their freedom and a force of 6,000 allied troops. This was his estimate, but he had his own reasons, too, for wanting to accompany Agesilaus on the expedition.

*By 'Asia' Xenophon meant 'the Persian Empire' (cf. III.5.13, IV.8.5) as did the Greeks generally (cf. Herodotus I.4.4) and as the Great King himself showed in Rescripts and treaties (cf. V.1.13 and Thuc. VIII.58.2). Agesilaus' grandiose intention is spelled out in the *Agesilaus* (1.8) and made plain by his plan to sacrifice at Aulis like Agamemnon before him. What he actually did shows a more circumspect approach, but such 'Panhellenism' became a strong bond between him and Xenophon (cf. Cawkwell, *Classical Quarterly*, 26, 1976, pp. 66–71). For the development of Xenophon's attitude to Persia, see Introduction pp. 39 ff.

The Councils of Ten, which had been set up in the cities when he was in command, had been dissolved by the ephors, who had proclaimed that all cities should return to their traditional constitutions.* Lysander now wanted, with the help of Agesilaus, to bring back these Councils into power.

Agesilaus stated that he was ready to go on this campaign, 3 and the Spartans gave him all the forces for which he had asked and provisions for six months. He then set out, after having made all the proper sacrifices, including the ones required before crossing the frontier. Messengers were sent round to the various cities with instructions as to the number of men required from each area and when they were to report. Agesilaus himself wanted to go and sacrifice at Aulis, where Agamemnon had sacrificed before sailing to Troy. However, when he got there the commanders of the Boeo- 4 tian League, who had heard that he was sacrificing, sent out cavalry and told him to stop; they took the victims which had already been offered and threw them down from the altar. Agesilaus, in great anger, called on the gods to witness their behaviour. He then embarked on his trireme and sailed away. At Gerastus he got together as much of his army as he could and went on his way to Ephesus.

As soon as he arrived there, Tissaphernes sent to him and 5 asked him why he had come. Agesilaus answered: 'So that the cities in Asia may be independent as are the cities in our part of Greece.' In reply to this Tissaphernes said: 'Then if you will make a truce until I can send to the King, I think you will be able to achieve your purpose and then, if you would like to do so, sail home again.'

*One should not suppose that Xenophon's words refer to a recent action by the board of ephors. The most likely date for the dissolution of these so-called *decarchies* is 403–2, when King Pausanias succeeded in persuading a majority of the five ephors to let him have his way at Athens (cf. II.4.29). For the whole subject, see A. Andrewes, *Phoenix*, 25, 1971, pp. 206–16. Xenophon's words illustrate well the casualness of his methods (cf. n. at III.2.21).

'I should certainly like to do so,' said Agesilaus, 'if I could be quite sure I was not being deceived by you.'

'I am prepared,' said Tissaphernes, 'to give you a solemn pledge that I will do what I have undertaken to do in all good faith.'

'And I,' said Agesilaus, 'am prepared to give you a solemn pledge in all good faith that, if you do as you say, we will do no harm to any part of your territory during the period of the truce.'

6 On the strength of this agreement Tissaphernes on his side gave his solemn oath to the commissioners sent to him (Herippidas, Dercylidas and Megillus) that he would negotiate the peace in all good faith, and they, acting on behalf of Agesilaus, gave their solemn oaths to Tissaphernes that, if he did so, Agesilaus would strictly observe the terms of the truce.

(Tissaphernes broke all his promises immediately.) Instead of keeping the peace he sent to the King for a large army in addition to the one he had already. Agesilaus, though he knew what was going on, nevertheless continued to keep the truce.

7 During this time, when Agesilaus was in Ephesus with no urgent business on his hands, there was much confusion in the cities with regard to their constitutions. There were no longer democracies, as there had been when Athens was in control, nor were there the Councils of Ten, as under Lysander. Since Lysander was so generally known, he was being constantly approached by people asking him to help them to get what they wanted from Agesilaus, and as a result there was always a great crowd of courtiers around Lysander wherever he went, so that it looked as though Agesilaus was an ordi-

8 nary individual and Lysander was the king of Sparta. It was not until later that Agesilaus showed how infuriated this made him; but the thirty Spartans of the officer class who were with him were too jealous to keep quiet. They went to

Agesilaus and told him that Lysander was offending against
the laws of Sparta; he was behaving with a pomp and splen-
dour that would be excessive even in royalty.*

Lysander now began to introduce his clients to Agesilaus
personally, but Agesilaus invariably sent away empty-handed
all those for whose interests he knew that Lysander was
working. Lysander grasped what the situation was when he
found that things always went exactly contrary to his wishes;
he no longer allowed a crowd to follow him about and he
plainly told those who wanted to make use of his influence
that they would do better without it. But he found his dis- 9
grace hard to bear and said to the king, 'Agesilaus, you certainly know how to make your friends look small.'

'Yes, indeed I do,' said Agesilaus, 'when the friends
concerned are people who want to make themselves look
greater than I am. But when a friend adds to my greatness,
I should be ashamed if I did not know how to honour him in
return.'

'It may well be,' said Lysander, 'that you are behaving
with more good sense than I did. But may I ask you for just
one thing? Send me off somewhere else, so that I need not be
in your way and need not feel ashamed of my lack of influence with you. Wherever I may be, I shall try to be of
service to you.'

When he had said this, Agesilaus also thought that this 10
would be the right course to take, and he sent Lysander to
the Hellespont. Here Lysander found out that the Persian
Spithridates had been insulted in some way by Pharnabazus,
so he went to Spithridates and persuaded him to revolt and
to take with him his children, all the money he had available
and about two hundred cavalry. Leaving everything else behind at Cyzicus, he took Spithridates himself and his son
aboard a ship and came with them to Agesilaus. When he
saw them Agesilaus was very pleased with what Lysander

*See n. at III.3.3.

had done and began at once to make inquiries about Pharnabazus' territory and his system of government.

11   Tissaphernes was now full of confidence because of the army from the King which had marched down to him to the coast, and he informed Agesilaus that war would be declared unless he withdrew from Asia. Both the allies and the Spartans with Agesilaus were obviously ill at ease, as they thought that the army of Agesilaus was no match for the King's army; Agesilaus, however, looked positively radiant. He told the ambassadors to convey the following message to Tissaphernes: 'I am deeply grateful to you. By breaking your oath you have made the gods your enemies and our allies.' He thus immediately issued orders for the soldiers to pack up for a campaign, and sent instructions to all cities on the route to Caria that they should make a market available for his army. He also ordered the people of Ionia, Aeolis and the Hellespont to send troops to him at Ephesus to join in the campaign.

12   Tissaphernes knew that Agesilaus had no cavalry (and it was difficult for cavalry to operate in Caria); he also believed that Agesilaus was angry with him for deceiving him. He therefore assumed that he was in fact going to move into Caria against his own establishment there; so he brought his whole infantry back across the river into Caria, and led his cavalry round into the plain of the Maeander, imagining that he was strong enough to grind the Greeks into the ground with this arm alone before they ever reached the areas where cavalry could not operate.

Agesilaus, however, so far from marching on Caria, turned immediately in the opposite direction and advanced on Phrygia. He picked up further contingents of troops to follow him on his march, gained control of the cities and, since his invasion was entirely unexpected, secured great quantities

13   of booty. For most of the march he went through the country in perfect safety. There was one occasion however, when he was near Dascylium, when his cavalry in the vanguard

had ridden on ahead to a hill to see what was in front; and it so happened that Pharnabazus' cavalry also, under the command of Rhathines and Bagaeus, his bastard brother, had been sent forward by Pharnabazus and rode to the top of the very same hill. They were a force about equal to the Greeks in number. When they saw each other, only about four hundred feet apart, at first, both sides halted. The Greek cavalry was drawn up four deep in a phalanx formation, and the natives were in a column with a front of not more than twelve but many more deep. Then the natives charged, and 14 when they got to close quarters every Greek who hit his man broke his spear, but the natives with their javelins of cornel wood soon killed twelve men and two horses. At this the Greek cavalry broke and fled, but Agesilaus came up in support with the hoplites, and then the natives retired, with the loss of one man.

The day after the cavalry battle Agesilaus sacrificed with a 15 view to advancing farther, but it was discovered that the livers of the victims were without a lobe. It was a clear sign, and Agesilaus altered direction and marched to the sea. He realized that without an adequate force of cavalry he would be unable to campaign in the plains, and so he decided that he must acquire such a force rather than have to fight a campaign in which he must always be, as it were, on the run. He therefore had a list made of all the richest people in the area and told them to provide horses. It was proclaimed that whoever produced a horse, arms and a good man would be exempted from military service himself, and, as people were very willing indeed to find others to die instead of them, the result of this proclamation was that the plan was carried out with remarkable efficiency.

After this, at the first signs of spring, he brought the whole 16 army together at Ephesus. As part of his training programme he offered prizes for the division of hoplites which was in the best physical condition and for the cavalry division which showed the best horsemanship. Prizes were also offered to the peltasts and archers for excellence in their particular departments. One could now see all the gymnasia full of men at their exercises, the hippodromes full of riders, and continual practice going on among the javelin throwers and archers.

17 In fact, he made the whole city where he was a sight worth seeing. The market was full of all kinds of horses and weapons for sale; copper-workers, carpenters, smiths, leather-workers, painters were all engaged on making weapons, so that one might have thought that the city was in fact one great arma-

18 ment factory. And here was another sight to warm the heart – the soldiers, with Agesilaus at the head of them, coming back from the gymnasia with their garlands and then dedicating them to Artemis. For where you find men honouring the gods, disciplining themselves for war and practising obedience, you may be sure that there everything will be full of good hope.

19 Agesilaus also believed that contempt for one's enemy will help to inspire courage in battle and he instructed the heralds that all natives captured by Greek raiding parties should be put up to sale naked. And when the Greeks saw their skin all white because they never took off their clothes and that they were soft and flabby because they always rode in carriages, they came to the conclusion that fighting against them would be much the same thing as having to fight with women.

20 Since the year was now ended since Agesilaus had sailed to Asia, Lysander and the thirty Spartans of the officer class sailed back home. They were replaced by thirty others under Herippidas, and out of these men Agesilaus appointed Xenocles and one other* to command the cavalry, Scythes to

* Some have supposed that the 'one other' was Xenophon himself, modestly not named, as at III.2.7. But this other person was one of the new thirty *Spartiates*. Xenophon withheld his name perhaps because he disapproved of him (cf. IV.5.11, VII.1.17). What then happened to Xenophon? Herippidas took command of the remnant

command the helot hoplites, Herippidas to the army that had fought with Cyrus, and Mygdon to the troops from the allied cities. By proclaiming that he proposed to march immediately and by the shortest route into the heart of the country he encouraged them to become from that very moment physically and morally prepared for battle.

Tissaphernes, however, imagined that he was saying this 21 just to deceive him again, and thought that this time he really would invade Caria; so, just as he had done before, he brought his infantry across into Caria and stationed his cavalry in the plain of the Maeander. But Agesilaus was not practising any deception. He moved straight on to the area of Sardis, just as he said he would. For three days he marched without seeing an enemy and had plenty of supplies for the army, but on the fourth day the enemy cavalry put in an appearance. Their commander instructed the leader of his 22 baggage train to cross the river Pactolus and make a camp there. Meanwhile, the cavalry themselves killed a number of Greek camp-followers whom they could see scattered about the plain in search of plunder. When Agesilaus saw what was happening, he ordered his own cavalry up in support, and at the sight of the approaching reinforcements the Persians drew together and formed up against the Greeks in line of battle, with squadron after squadron of cavalry.

Agesilaus was aware that the enemy were still without 23 their infantry, while he had every branch of his newly trained army at his disposal. Now, therefore, he thought, was the moment to bring the enemy to battle, if he could. So, after he had made the sacrifices, he led his phalanx directly against the line of cavalry that was facing him. He ordered the hoplites in the age group 20 to 30 to run and close with them and

of the Ten Thousand. So either Xenophon held a subordinate command or went on to Agesilaus' staff. It would be better for his reputation (cf. n. at III.4.24) if he could be shown to have been left behind in Ephesus, but there is no reason to think he was.

told the peltasts to take the lead at the double. He also
ordered the cavalry to charge, telling them that he and the
24 whole army were following them in support. This charge of
the cavalry was held by the Persians, but when they found
themselves confronted by the whole force and fury of the
attack, they broke. Some of them were killed on the spot
while crossing the river and others fled. The Greeks followed
them up and captured their camp as well. Here the peltasts,
naturally enough, began to give their attention to the plunder, but Agesilaus made the circuit of his own camp big
enough to cover everything, enemy property as well as
Greek. Altogether, it was a large haul and it fetched more
than seventy talents. It was here, too, that the camels were
captured which Agesilaus took back with him later to
Greece.*

25   Tissaphernes was in Sardis when this battle was fought,
and the Persians accused him of having betrayed them. Also
the Persian king himself came to the conclusion that Tissaphernes was responsible for the reverses which his cause was
suffering. He therefore sent Tithraustes down to the coast
with instructions that Tissaphernes should be beheaded.
When this had been done, Tithraustes sent ambassadors to
the Spartans with the following message: 'Agesilaus, the man
who was responsible for the trouble which both you and we
have had has paid the penalty. The king now proposes that
you should sail home and that the Greek cities in Asia should
be self-governing, and should pay to him the tribute that
they used to pay in the past.'

26   Agesilaus replied that he could not do this without authority from his home government.

'Then at least,' said Tithraustes, 'you can leave this district
and go into the territory of Pharnabazus, until you hear from
Sparta. Remember that it is I who have taken vengeance on
your enemy.'

*See Appendix, p. 405.

'In that case,' said Agesilaus, 'I ask you to give me supplies for my army on the march there.'

Tithraustes gave him thirty talents, which he took and then set out for the parts of Phrygia which were under the control of Pharnabazus.

When he was in the plain above Cyme, he received orders 27 from the home government to take over command of the fleet in addition to the army, and to use it as he thought fit; he was to appoint an admiral of his own choice. The Spartans had taken this measure on the theory that both army and fleet would be much more effective under a unified command – the army, because of the added strength of the fleet, and the fleet because the army could appear in support wherever needed. On receiving these instructions, Agesilaus' 28 first action was to send to the cities on the islands and the coast ordering each of them to build as many triremes as they wished. As a result 120 new triremes were constructed, some by the local governments, some by private individuals who wanted to please Agesilaus. He appointed as admiral Peisan- 29 der,* his brother-in-law, an ambitious man with plenty of resolution, but not very experienced in the kind of organiza- tion that was required. Peisander then went away to take up his naval responsibilities, and Agesilaus resumed his march to Phrygia.

*Some have wished to argue on the strength of *Hell. Oxy.* 22.4 that Xenophon has misdated the appointment of Peisander, but cf. Cawkwell, *Classical Quarterly*, 26, 1976, p. 67 n. 24.

CHAPTER 5

Coalition against Sparta in Greece. Death of Lysander (395 B.C.)

1 TITHRAUSTES had now convinced himself that Agesilaus
was not impressed by the King's power and, so far from
having any intention of leaving Asia, had great hopes of
overpowering the King himself. Not knowing how to deal
with the situation, he sent Timocrates of Rhodes to Greece
with gold to the value of fifty talents of silver and told him
to distribute this money, on the basis of receiving very firm
guarantees, to the leading men in various states on the understanding that they would make war on Sparta. Timocrates
came to Greece and gave his money, at Thebes, to Androclidas, Ismenias and Galaxidorus; at Corinth to Timolaus and
2 Polyanthes; and at Argos to Cylon and his party. No money
went to the Athenians, but they were ready enough for the
war in any case, as they thought that empire was their own
prerogative. Those who had received the money now began
to foment anti-Spartan feeling in their own cities and planned, once they had induced a general feeling of hatred
against the Spartans, to organize an alliance of the most
powerful states.*
3   In Thebes the leading men were well aware that the Spar-

*The *Hellenica Oxyrhynchia* 7.5 appears to make Pharnabazus the
satrap who sent Timocrates to Greece. Tithraustes would have been
appointed too late in the summer of 395 to excite a war in Greece
which involved the ravaging of corn just before it was due to be
harvested (Pausanias III.9.9). Xenophon has failed yet again?

Xenophon also differs from the *Hell. Oxy.* 7.2 in the claim that
none of Timocrates' gold was accepted in Athens. Perhaps this is a
mark of his sympathy for Thrasybulus who took Athens into the
Grand Alliance of the Corinthian War (cf. III.5.16 and IV.8.31), for
which see n. at IV.2.1.

tans would never break their treaties with their allies, unless someone committed an act of war first. They therefore induced the Opuntian Locrians* to levy money from some territory of which both they and the Phocians claimed to be the owners. The Theban view was that, if this happened, the Phocians would invade Locris, and in this they were quite right. The Phocians invaded Locris immediately, and seized property worth much more than what the Locrians had taken. Androclidas and his party now persuaded the Thebans to 4 come to the help of the Locrians on the ground that the Phocians had invaded, not a piece of disputed territory, but Locris itself, which was admitted to be a friendly and allied state. The Thebans thus made a counter-invasion of Phocis and began to lay waste the land, and the Phocians immediately sent ambassadors to Sparta to ask for help. They pointed out that it was not they who had started the war; they had only gone against the Locrians in self-defence.

The Spartans were glad enough to have a pretext for a 5 campaign against the Thebans, since they had been angry with them for some time. First, the Thebans had claimed the tithe due to Apollo at Decelea; they had refused to follow the Spartans against Piraeus and were accused of having persuaded the Corinthians also to refuse. The Spartans also remembered that the Thebans had not allowed Agesilaus to sacrifice at Aulis and had thrown down from the altar the victims that had been sacrificed already; and they had failed to join Agesilaus on his campaign in Asia. The Spartans calculated, too, that this was just the right moment for leading an army against Thebes and putting an end to Theban insolence. After the victories of Agesilaus, everything was going well for them in Asia, and they had no other war on their hands in Greece.

* Unless the detailed narrative of *Hell. Oxy.* 18 is wholly awry, Xenophon has got the wrong Locrians, the Opuntians being the eastern Locrians.

6   It was in this way that the city of Sparta saw the situation, and the ephors gave the orders for general mobilization. They sent Lysander to Phocis with instructions to get together the forces of the Phocians, the Oetaeans, Heracleans, Malians and Aenianians, and to come with them to Haliartus. Pausanias, who was to be in supreme command, agreed to meet him there on the day that they had fixed. Lysander carried out all the tasks that had been assigned to him and, in addition, in-

7   duced the people of Orchomenus to revolt from Thebes. But Pausanias, when the sacrifices for crossing the frontier had turned out favourably, marched to Tegea, and stayed there, sending out officers to assemble the allied troops and waiting for the arrival of the troops from the Laconian cities outside Sparta.

It was now clear to the Thebans that a Spartan army was going to invade their country, and they sent ambassadors to

8   Athens.* The speech they made was as follows: 'Athenians, you may feel indignant with us for voting in favour of such savage reprisals against you at the end of the war. But you would be wrong. It was not the city of Thebes that voted

7   then; it was just one man who happened at that time to have a seat at the council of the allies. When, on the other hand, the Spartans asked us to join them in attacking Piraeus, the whole city voted and the whole city said "no". Indeed, it is mainly because of you that the Spartans are angry with us, and so we think it only fair that you should come to the help

9   of our city. And we think that those of you especially who used to belong to the party holding Athens ought to be willing to take the field against the Spartans. Remember how they put you in power as an oligarchy, and of course made you hated by the democracy; then they arrived with a great force; they professed to be your allies, and in fact they handed

*One would never guess from Xenophon what the decree of alliance (Tod, *G.H.I.*, II, no. 101) makes certain, *viz.* that the alliance was with the whole Boeotian Confederacy.

you over to the democrats. So far as they had anything to do with it, you might as well be dead; it was this people of Athens here assembled who saved you.

'Now we are all aware, men of Athens, that you would 10 like to get back the empire which you used to have. Surely this is most likely to happen if you go to the help of all victims of Spartan injustice. There is nothing to be afraid of in the fact that their power is so widely extended; indeed, this is rather an additional reason for confidence. Remember your own case. It was when you had most subjects that you made most enemies. And they only concealed their hatred of you during the time when they had no one to support them if they revolted; but as soon as the Spartans came forward as leaders they soon showed what they really thought about you. So now if people see Thebes and Athens falling into line 11 together against Sparta, you can be quite sure that those who hate Sparta will soon show themselves in full numbers.

'If you look into the matter, you will see at once that what we say is the truth. Can you think of anyone who is still in favour of them? Certainly not the Argives, who have been their enemies from the beginning of history. As for the 12 Eleans, they have now become enemies, too, after losing so much land and so many cities. And what about the Corinthians, the Arcadians and the Achaeans? In the war with you they, at the urgent entreaties of Sparta, took their share in all the hardships and danger and expense; but when the Spartans had achieved their object, did they ever get any share of the power or glory or money that was won? Far from it. The Spartans, now that things have gone well for them, think it perfectly proper to set up their own helots as governors, and meanwhile treat their free allies as though they were slaves. And as for the people whom they got to revolt 13 from you, they have made their deception quite clear. What they gave them was not freedom but a double measure of

servitude. These people are now under the absolute authority not only of governors but also of the Committees of Ten
which Lysander set up in each city.* And now consider the
king of Asia; it was his aid that contributed most to Sparta's
victory over you, but, by the way he is being treated now,
he might just as well have been fighting with you against
Sparta.

14   'Is it not likely, then, that, if you come forward in your
turn to take the lead of all those who have been so obviously
injured, you will become much the greatest power that has
ever existed? As you know, when you had your empire, your
authority was confined to countries that were accessible by
sea; but it could now be exercised everywhere – over us, and
the Peloponnesians, and those who were subject to you before and even over the king himself with his enormous resources. As for us, you know yourselves what good allies we
were to the Spartans. But you can expect us to be altogether
stouter allies to you than we were then to them. For now it
is not a question of helping islanders or Syracusans or strangers; it is in defence of Thebes herself that we are taking up
arms.

15   'This, too, is a point that should be understood: this greedy
and arrogant dominion of Sparta is much easier to destroy
than was the empire which you had. You had a navy while
your subjects did not; the Spartans, few in number themselves, are greedily dominating people who are many times
as numerous as they and also just as well armed.

      'These, then, are our proposals. Please believe us, Athen-
ians, when we say that in our opinion we are inviting you to
take a course which promises much more benefit for Athens
than for Thebes.'

16   So he ended his speech. Very many Athenians rose to
speak in agreement with him, and there was a unanimous
vote to send help to the Thebans. Thrasybulus told the am-

      *This was not true of 395 B.C. (cf. III.4.2).

bassadors that this vote was their answer. He then made the following point: 'Although Piraeus is not fortified,' he said, 'we are nevertheless going to run the risk of repaying you with a greater favour than we have received. You did not join in the Spartan attack on us; we are going to fight with you against the Spartans, if they attack you.'

The Thebans then went away and made preparations for 17 their defence, and the Athenians got ready to help them. And in fact the Spartans did not delay any longer. King Pausanias with the troops from Sparta and from the rest of the Peloponnese, except the Corinthians, who refused to follow him, was now marching into Boeotia. Lysander, with his army from Phocis, Orchomenus and the districts in that area, had reached Haliartus ahead of Pausanias, and, when he got there, was not 18 content to remain inactive and wait for the Peloponnesian army to arrive. Instead, with the troops he had, he marched up to the walls of Haliartus. First he attempted to persuade the people to revolt from Thebes and become independent, but some of the Thebans inside the city prevented them from doing so. He then made an assault on the wall. News of this 19 reached the Thebans and they came running to the rescue with their hoplites and cavalry. It is not clear whether they fell upon Lysander before he was aware that they were coming, or whether he saw them coming but still stood his ground because he felt confident of winning. What is certain is that the battle was fought quite close to the wall, and a trophy stands there by the gate of Haliartus. In this battle Lysander was killed and his army fled to the mountains hotly pursued by the Thebans. However, when the Thebans had 20 reached steep ground in the pursuit, and found that they had to move along difficult narrow paths, the enemy hoplites turned round and hurled their javelins and other missiles down on them. They struck down two or three who were leading the pursuit, rolled rocks down the hill on the rest and then began to attack with great spirit. So the Thebans were driven down the hill and more than two hundred of them were killed.

21   For the rest of that day the Thebans were in low spirits. It seemed that they had lost just as much as they had gained. Next day, however, they found that the Phocians and all the rest had gone away in the night to their own states, and at this they became very much happier at what they had done. But now Pausanias appeared with the army from Sparta, and the Thebans once again began to think that they were in an extremely dangerous position. Indeed, by all accounts, their army appeared thoroughly cowed and no one had much to 22 say for himself. Next day, however, the Athenians arrived. They formed up in line of battle with the Thebans, and Pausanias neither advanced against them nor showed any sign of wanting to fight. This made the Thebans feel much more confident.

    Pausanias now called a meeting of his regimental commanders and commanders of fifties to discuss whether to join battle or to get back the bodies of Lysander and those who 23 had fallen with him by making a truce. The following facts had to be weighed up by Pausanias and the Spartans who shared responsibility with him: Lysander was dead, and his army had been defeated and had run away; the Corinthians had refused outright to take part in the expedition, and those allies who were serving with them were showing very little enthusiasm; also to be considered was the problem of cavalry, of which the enemy had a great many while they had very few; most important of all was the fact that the bodies of the dead lay directly under the wall, so that even if they won a battle it would not be easy to recover them because of the enemy troops on the towers. For all these reasons they decided to get the bodies back under a truce.

24   The Thebans, however, said that they would only give the bodies back if the Spartans agreed to leave their country. The Spartans were glad enough to accept these terms and,

after taking up the bodies, retreated from Boeotia. After this arrangement had been made the Spartans went away in a very dejected frame of mind, while the Thebans behaved with the utmost insolence. If a Spartan so much as set foot on any portion of their land, they would chase him back into the road with blows.

So ended this campaign of the Spartans. Pausanias, how- 25 ever, was put on trial for his life when he reached home. He was charged with having failed to arrive in time to meet Lysander at Haliartus, although he had agreed to be there on the same day; with taking back the bodies of the dead under truce, instead of trying to recover them in battle, and with having allowed the Athenian democrats to get away, when he had them in his power at Piraeus. Since, in addition to all this, he failed to put in an appearance at his trial, he was condemned to death. However, he escaped to Tegea and died there from an illness.* So much for the events in Greece during this period.

*He was still alive in 380 B.C. when his son Agesipolis died. Cf. Tod, *G.H.I*, II, no. 120, for the memorial he erected. So the end of Book III was written after that date.

BOOK FOUR

CHAPTER 1

Agesilaus in Pharnabazus' satrapy (395–394 B.C.)

AT the beginning of autumn Agesilaus reached the part of 1
Phrygia that was governed by Pharnabazus.* He burned the
crops, ravaged the land, and won over the cities either by
force or by their voluntary surrender. Spithridates then sug- 2
gested that he should go to Paphlagonia where, he said, he
would arrange a conference between Agesilaus and the king
of the Paphlagonians and make him an ally. To win over
some nation from the king of Persia was just what Agesilaus
had long been wanting to do, and so he was very glad to fall
in with this suggestion.

When he reached Paphlagonia king Otys came to him and 3
made an alliance with him; it appeared that he had been summoned to go to the king of Persia, but had refused to do so.
Spithridates also persuaded Otys to detach for service with
Agesilaus a force of 1,000 cavalry and 2,000 peltasts. Agesi- 4
laus was grateful to Spithridates for all this and said to him:
'Tell me, Spithridates, would you not be willing to give
your daughter to Otys?'

'Much more willingly than he would take her,' said
Spithridates. 'She is the daughter of an exile, and he is a king
with much land and much power.'

That was all that was said on this occasion about the

*For the gap between Agesilaus' leaving the coast of Asia Minor
(III.4.29) and his arrival in Pharnabazus' satrapy and for the details
of his march as far east as Gordium (which is about fifty miles west
of Ankara), see *Hell. Oxy.* 21. Xenophon prefers to allow ample
space to the pretty story of the wedding; the Oxyrhynchus Historian
spends no more than five lines on the meeting with the Paphlagonian
king, whom he names Gyes (22.1 f.).

5 marriage. However, before Otys went away he came to
see Agesilaus to say good-bye to him. Agesilaus, after asking Spithridates to withdraw, began the conversation in
6 the presence of the thirty Spartan officers. 'Tell me, Otys,'
he said, 'what sort of a family does Spithridates come from?'

'As good as any in Persia,' replied Otys.

'Have you noticed,' said Agesilaus, 'what a very good-
looking son he has?'

'Indeed I have,' said Otys. 'As a matter of fact I dined with
him yesterday.'

'They say,' said Agesilaus, 'that his daughter is even better-
looking.'

7 'By Zeus,' said Otys, 'she certainly is a very beautiful
woman.'

'Well,' said Agesilaus, 'now that you have become my
friend, may I give you my advice? I should advise you to
marry the girl. She is very beautiful, and what can be nicer
for a husband than that? Her father comes from an excellent
family and had such authority that, when he was injured by
Pharnabazus, he was able to avenge himself. As you see,
Pharnabazus is now an exile from every part of his country.
8 And I think you can be sure that he is just as capable of
doing good to a friend as he is of avenging himself on his
9 enemy Pharnabazus. There is another point too; if this
arrangement is made you will not only be connected with
Spithridates but also with me and the other Spartans, and,
since it is we who control Greece, with the rest of Greece
as well. Finally, if you do this, you will have the most splendid marriage that has ever been seen. What other bride has
ever been escorted home by as many cavalry and peltasts
and hoplites as will be there to escort your bride to your
house?'

10 Otys then asked: 'Can you tell me, Agesilaus, whether
what you are saying has the approval of Spithridates
too?'

'By the gods,' said Agesilaus, 'it was not he who told me to speak as I have been speaking. The fact is that, though I am remarkably pleased when I get my own back on an enemy, I really believe that I'm still more delighted if I see my way to doing some good to a friend.'

'Well, then,' said Otys, 'why not find out if Spithridates 11 himself would be pleased with the idea?'

'Herippidas,' said Agesilaus, 'I should like you all to go to him and try and get him to see things in the same way as we do.'

Then, after they had been some time away, Agesilaus said: 12 'What do you think, Otys? Shall we call him in and talk to him ourselves?'

'As a matter of fact,' said Otys, 'I think he would be more easily won over by you than by all the rest put together.'

When they came back again Herippidas said: 'There is no 13 point, Agesilaus, in reporting the whole conversation word for word. The upshot is that Spithridates says that he'll be glad to do whatever you think best.'

'Then this is what I think best,' said Agesilaus. 'You, 14 Spithridates, should give your daughter to Otys, and may the wedding be a lucky one! And you, Otys, are to marry her. But we will not be able to bring the girl here by land until the spring.'*

'But, by Zeus,' said Otys, 'what is to prevent her being brought by sea at once, so long as you are willing?'

They then shook hands in solemn ratification of this agree- 15 ment and so sent Otys on his way. Realizing how impatient he was, Agesilaus manned a trireme at once and ordered Callias, a Spartan, to go and fetch the girl. He himself now marched to Dascylium.†

*For Agesilaus' plans for spring 394 B.C., cf. n. at IV.1.41.

†Xenophon omits the story of the Spartan commander at the Hellespont sailing with five ships into the Lake Dascylitis (the exact

It was in Dascylium that Pharnabazus had his palace. All around the place there were numbers of large villages, very well stocked with provisions, and also some very beautiful wild animals, kept either in enclosed parks, or in the open
16 country. A river full of all kinds of fish ran past the palace and there were also plenty of birds to be caught by those who knew how to go about it. Here he spent the winter. Provisions for the army were obtained either on the spot or by foraging expeditions.

17 Since they never encountered any set-backs, the soldiers had got into the habit of collecting their supplies carelessly and without taking due precautions. And there was one occasion when Pharnabazus, with two scythed chariots and about four hundred cavalry, came on them when they were
18 scattered all over the plain. When the Greeks saw him bearing down on them, they ran to join up with each other, about seven hundred all together; but Pharnabazus did not waste time. Putting the chariots in front, and following behind
19 them himself with the cavalry, he ordered a charge. The chariots, dashing into the Greek ranks, broke up their close formation, and the cavalry soon cut down about a hundred men. The rest fled and took refuge with Agesilaus, who happened to be close at hand with the hoplites.

20 Four or five days later Spithridates heard that Pharnabazus was camping about twenty miles away in a large village
21 called Caue. He immediately informed Herippidas, who was very anxious to have some spectacular achievement to his credit and who asked Agesilaus to let him have 2,000 hoplites, 2,000 peltasts, and a cavalry force consisting of the cavalry of Spithridates, the Paphlagonians and any Greeks whom he
22 could induce to come with him. Agesilaus agreed to do so, and Herippidas proceeded to sacrifice and went on till the

_____

location of which is unsure) and collecting the army's booty. Cf. *Hell.*
Oxy. 22.4, part of what was evidently a much fuller account of winter
395–4.

late afternoon, when the omens turned out favourably. He then ordered the troops to have their meal and then report in front of the camp. However, by the time it got dark, less than half of the various detachments had shown up. Never- 23 theless Herippidas, who did not want to be laughed at by the other Spartan officers if he gave the whole idea up, set off with what troops he had, and at dawn fell upon Pharnabazus' 24 camp. Many of the outposts, who were Mysians, were killed; the main body took to flight and the camp was captured. They found there numbers of drinking cups and other articles of the sort that one would expect Pharnabazus to have; also considerable quantities of baggage and of baggage animals. For Pharnabazus was afraid to establish himself in any one 25 place, in case he should be surrounded and besieged, and therefore he was always on the move, like the nomads, and took great care to keep secret the places where he camped.

When the Paphlagonians and Spithridates came in with 26 the property they had captured, Herippidas posted his divisional commanders and captains in their way and took everything away from them, his idea being to have great quantities of booty to turn in to the officials responsible for disposing of it. But Spithridates and the Paphlagonians would not put up 27 with being treated like this. They considered that they had been both insulted and injured, and so they packed up and went off by night to join Ariaeus in Sardis, thinking that they could trust him, since he also had revolted from the king and made war on him. As for Agesilaus, he was more upset by the 28 desertion of Spithridates, Megabates and the Pamphylians than by anything else that happened on the campaign.*

*Spithridates hoped that Ariaeus, who had joined in the revolt of Cyrus in 401 B.C., would secure him a pardon rather than punish him as a traitor. Agesilaus was much enamoured of Spithridates' son (*Hell. Oxy.* 21.4), and Xenophon felt it necessary in his encomium to deny that there were any improprieties (*Ages.* V.4 ff.). So perhaps that was why Agesilaus was so upset, but it is also possible that Agesilaus hoped

29   There was a citizen of Cyzicus called Apollophanes, who
had long been a friend of Pharnabazus and had recently become friends with Agesilaus. He now told Agesilaus that he
thought he could arrange a meeting between him and Phar-
30 nabazus to discuss peace. After receiving Agesilaus' reply, he
obtained the proper pledges for a truce and brought Pharnabazus with him to a place that had been agreed upon. Here
Agesilaus and his escort of the thirty Spartan officers were
lying on the grass waiting for them. Pharnabazus appeared
dressed in clothes that would have been worth a lot of gold,
and then his servants came forward to spread down for him
the kind of soft rugs on which the Persians sit. However,
when Pharnabazus saw that there was no sort of ostentation
or finery about Agesilaus, he was ashamed to make a display
of his own luxury and lay down on the grass too, just as he
31 was. First they greeted each other, and then Pharnabazus
held out his right hand. Agesilaus grasped it with his own,
and Pharnabazus, being the elder of the two men, began the
conversation as follows:
32   'I want to remind you, Agesilaus, and you other Spartans,
that when you were at war with the Athenians I was your
friend and your ally. I made your fleet strong by providing
money, and on land I fought on horseback at your side, and
drove your enemies into the sea. And you cannot accuse me,
as you can Tissaphernes, of any double-dealing towards you
33 at any time in either word or deed. That is my record towards you, and now, because of you, I find myself in such a
position that I cannot even get a meal in my own country
unless, like the wild animals, I come across something that
you may have left behind. My father left me beautiful houses
and parks full of trees and wild animals, and these were a

---

to use Spithridates both as a guide (*Hell. Oxy.* 21.4) and as an induce-
ment to other Persian grandees to revolt (cf. IV.1.36 f.) when the
campaign of 394 began (cf. n. at IV.1.41). Characteristically, Xenophon leaves us guessing.

delight to me. Now all the trees are cut down, all the houses
burned. Maybe I do not understand the meaning of honour
and of justice. If so, perhaps you will demonstrate to me that
this behaviour of yours is the right behaviour for men who
are repaying kindnesses that they have received.'

When he had spoken all the thirty Spartan officers were 34
filled with shame and no one uttered a word. Finally, Agesilaus spoke. 'I think, Pharnabazus,' he said, 'that you know
that in Greece also citizens of different states make binding
friendships together. But when their states are at war, these
same men will fight with their fatherlands even against their
friends, and it may happen that they will actually kill each
other. So it is with us today. We are at war with your king
and we are forced to treat as hostile everything that belongs
to him. But for yourself, there is nothing that we would
like better than to become friends of yours. And if, in joining 35
us instead of the King, it was a question of your changing one
master for another, I myself should certainly not advise it.
In fact, however, by joining us you have the chance of living
in the enjoyment of your own possessions, without doing
homage to any man and without any master at all. And, as
I see it, it is better to be free than to have all the money in the
world. This, however, is not what we are advising – that you 36
should be free and at the same time poor. What we suggest
is that you should, by using us as your allies, add, not to the
King's empire, but to your own, and that you should bring
into subjection to yourself those who are now, like you,
slaves of another. And so, if you become free and rich at the
same time, what else could you desire to make you completely happy?'

'Then,' said Pharnabazus, 'shall I tell you frankly what I 37
propose to do?'

'I think you should,' said Agesilaus.

'Well, then,' said Pharnabazus, 'if the King sends down
someone else to take over my command and tells me to serve

under him, I shall want to become a friend and ally of yours. However, so powerful, it seems, are pride and ambition, you can be quite sure that, if he gives the command to me, I shall make war on you to the very best of my ability.'

38   When he heard this, Agesilaus grasped his hand and said: 'You are a good man, Pharnabazus. And, knowing you as I do, all I pray is that you may come to be our friend. Of one thing you may be sure. I am now going to leave your land as fast as I can, and, even if there is war, we shall keep our hands off you and yours, so long as we have it in our power to march against anyone else.'

39   With these words he ended the conference. Pharnabazus mounted his horse and rode away, but his son by Parapita, a boy who was still at the most beautiful age, stayed behind and ran up to Agesilaus: 'I should like you, Agesilaus,' he said, 'to become my friend.'

'And I,' said Agesilaus, 'shall be glad to be your friend.'

'Remember, then,' said the boy, and he immediately gave his javelin, an extremely fine one, to Agesilaus. After accepting it, Agesilaus took from the neck of the horse of his secretary, Idaeus, a magnificent trapping and gave it as a return gift, and the boy leapt on his horse and rode after his
40   father. Later, however, when Pharnabazus was away, the son of Parapita was deprived of his lands by his brother and forced into exile. Then Agesilaus gave him all the help he could. Among other things was this. The boy had fallen in love with the son of Eualces, an Athenian, and Agesilaus, for his sake, tried his best to get this Athenian, who was much taller than the boys of his age, allowed to enter for the men's 200 yards at Olympia.

41   So, after this interview, Agesilaus immediately left the territory of Pharnabazus, as he had promised. It was already near the beginning of spring. When he reached the plain of Thebe, he camped near the temple of Artemis of Astyra and began to get together a large army in addition to the troops

he had already. He was planning to march as far as possible into the interior, with the idea of detaching from the king all the nations through which he should pass.*

* The sources suggest that Agesilaus planned in spring 394 B.C. no less than a new Anabasis into the heart of the Persian Empire (cf. *Hell. Oxy.* 22.4, Plut. *Agesilaus* 15, Xen. *Ages.* I.36, etc.), thus realizing the grandiose intention implied by his attempt to sacrifice at Aulis (III.4.3 f.). His performance in 395 B.C., when he had already passed through the satrapy of Lydia and the Royal Road to Susa was open before him, suggests that his achievement in 394 might have been much more modest (cf. *Hell. Oxy.* 12), perhaps no more than the cutting off of the westernmost satrapies (cf. Isocrates IV.144). However, Xenophon, like his hero, preferred Panhellenist big talk.

CHAPTER 2

Recall of Agesilaus. Spartan Victory at Nemea (394 B.C.)

1 WHILE Agesilaus was engaged in these activities the Spartans had received definite information about the sending of the money and of how a coalition of the most powerful states in Greece had been formed to make war on them.* In what seemed to them to be the present dangerous situation for Sparta, they considered that it was necessary to take the field 2 and began to make preparations accordingly. They also sent Epicydidas out at once to recall Agesilaus.

When Epicydidas arrived in Asia he explained the state of affairs to Agesilaus, and told him that Sparta asked him to come to the help of the fatherland as quickly as he could. 3 This was bitter news for Agesilaus to hear. He had splendid prospects in front of him and could see himself being robbed of them. Nevertheless, he called together the allies, told them what the orders were from home and said that it was a matter of necessity to go to the help of the fatherland. 'But,' he added, 'if everything goes well over there, you allies can be sure that I shall not forget you and that I shall come back 4 again to do what you want me to do.' There were many who burst into tears when they heard him speak, but they all voted in favour of going to Sparta with Agesilaus and then, if things went well there, of bringing him back again with them to Asia.†

*The organization of the Grand Alliance of the Corinthian War, briefly referred to at III.5.2, is formally described by Diodorus (XIV.82) and implied by Xenophon's account of the debate before the battle of Nemea (IV.2.10 ff. and cf. IV.2.18). Xenophon did not care to describe constitutions (cf. n. at VII.4.33).

†For the Panhellenist folly of Agesilaus, shared by Xenophon, see

The troops, then, got ready to follow him. He left Euxenus 5
in Asia as governor, and gave him a garrison of at least 4,000
men so that he would be able to protect the cities. He could
see that most of the soldiers preferred to stay in Asia rather
than go on a campaign against Greeks and so, since he wanted
to have with him the best troops available and as many as
possible of them, he offered prizes to whichever city produced the best force, and to whichever captain of mercenaries joined him with the best-equipped company of hoplites,
of archers and of peltasts. The cavalry commanders were also
told that a special prize would be given to the one who produced the best-mounted and best-equipped squadron. So as 6
to make them understand that they would have to make sure
of the quality of their troops, Agesilaus announced his intention of awarding the prizes on the Chersonese, after they
had crossed from Asia to Europe. The greater part of the 7
prizes consisted of magnificently made armour, both for
hoplites and for cavalrymen; there were also gold crowns,
and altogether the prizes cost at least four talents. However,
the result of this great expense was that the army acquired
for itself arms worth huge sums of money. After the crossing 8
of the Hellespont, Menascus, Herippidas and Orsippus were
appointed as judges on the side of the Spartans, and for the
allies one judge was appointed from each city. When the
decisions were made, Agesilaus marched on with the army
by the same route as that followed by the King of Persia *
when he invaded Greece.

Meanwhile, the ephors had ordered general mobilization. 9
Since Agesipolis † was still a child, the state appointed Aristo-
demus, a member of the royal family and the boy's guardian,

Cawkwell, *Classical Quarterly*, 26, 1976, pp. 66–71. The liberation
from Persia of the Greek cities of Asia was a pipe-dream, until it
became part of the subjection of Greece to Macedon.

* Xerxes.

† Son of Pausanias.

10 to command the army. So the Spartan army took the field, and their enemies also had brought their forces together. First they met to discuss how they could fight the battle to
11 the best advantage of themselves, and at this meeting Timo-. laus of Corinth spoke as follows: 'Friends and allies, there seems to me an important parallel to be drawn between the Spartans and the courses of rivers. Rivers at their sources are not big and are easy to cross; but as they flow on, other
12 streams join them and make the original current stronger. It is just the same with the Spartans. At the point from which they start, they are alone by themselves, but as they advance and gather forces from the cities on their way, they become more numerous and more difficult to fight with. I also consider what happens when people want to get rid of a wasps' nest. If they try to catch the wasps on their way out of the nest they very often get stung; but if they set the nest on fire when the wasps are still inside, they destroy the wasps with no damage to themselves. Bearing all this in mind, I think that it would be best to fight the battle in Sparta itself, if possible, and, if not, as near to Sparta as we can.' *

13 This seemed a good proposal and the allies voted in favour of it. They then occupied themselves in discussions on who should hold supreme command, and tried to reach an agreement as to the number of ranks in which the whole army should be drawn up in depth.† This was in order to see to it that the individual cities did not draw up their contingents in such great depth as to provide the enemy with an opportunity to outflank the whole line. But while these discussions were going on the Spartans had marched out of their own country

*It seems unlikely that, before Epaminondas in 370–69 invaded Laconia, for centuries inviolate (cf. Plut. *Pelopidas* 31, etc.), anyone would advocate such a strategy. Perhaps Timolaus' speech is anachronistic, a mark of 'late' composition.

†Cf. n. at IV.2.1.

and, having already picked up the Tegeans* and Mantineans, were on the road along the coast. Both armies, in fact, 14
were on the march, and at about the time when the Corinthians and their allies were near Nemea, the Spartans and
theirs were at Sicyon.

The Spartan and allied army invaded Corinthian territory
by way of Epieicia and at first suffered considerable casualties from the missiles and arrows of the enemy light troops
on the heights to their right. But once they had come down 15
the hills to the sea they could march ahead on level ground,
burning and laying waste the land as they went. Meanwhile,
the main Corinthian army had fallen back and camped with
the dried-up river-bed† in front of them. The Spartans advanced until they were not much more than a mile away,
then camped where they were and made no move for the
time being.

I will now describe the numbers and composition of the 16
two armies. On the side of the Spartans the figures were as
follows. Of hoplites there were about six thousand from
Sparta herself and the vicinity; nearly 3,000 were provided
by the Eleans, Triphylians, Acrorians and Lasionians; 1,500
came from Sicyon, and at least 3,000 from Epidaurus, Troezen, Hermione and Halieis. Then there was a cavalry force of
about six hundred. About three hundred Cretan archers, too,
followed the army, and in addition to these there were at
least 400 Marganian, Letrinian and Amphidolian slingers.
The Phliasians, however, said that they were in a sacred
period of truce and so did not join the expedition.

* Xenophon omits the Tegeans in the order of battle in §16, though
they took part (§19).
† Xenophon does not trouble himself or his readers with precise
topography. He knows the places he is talking about and expects
others to do the same. But the 'dried-up river-bed', the Nemean
charadra, was familiar enough to many in the 350s by reason of a
minor engagement there in the mid 360s (cf. Aeschines II.168).

17   The army opposing these contained the following numbers of hoplites. There were about six thousand from Athens
and, so it was said, about seven thousand from Argos; the
Boeotians (since Orchomenus sent no troops) only produced
5,000; 3,000 came from Corinth and from the whole of
Euboea at least 3,000. As to cavalry, there were about eight
hundred from Boeotia (the Orchomenians not having sent
any), about six hundred from Athens, about a hundred from
Chalcis in Euboea and about fifty from the Opuntian Locrians. The greater part of the light troops were with the
Corinthian section of the army, since the Ozolian Locrians,
the Malians and the Acarnanians were all serving with the
Corinthians.*

18   This, then, was the force available to each side. The Boeotians, so long as their position was on the left wing, showed
absolutely no enthusiasm for joining battle. But when the
Athenians took over their place opposite the Spartans and
they themselves took over the right wing and were faced by
the Achaeans, they immediately declared that the sacrifices
had turned out favourably and sent round orders to make
ready for battle.†

First, so far from paying any attention to the plan of draw-
ing up the line in sixteen ranks, they made their own phalanx
exceedingly deep. Then, in leading the advance, they inclined
to the right so as to outflank the enemy with their wing. The

*It is to be noticed that Xenophon is imprecise about all the forces
engaged in this battle; elsewhere for the battles of Haliartus, Coronea,
Leuctra and Mantinea he does not give any sort of indication. To be
precise about the size of the forces engaged is one of the prime duties
of a military historian, but Xenophon is writing memoirs, not history.

† Xenophon imputes cowardice and bravado to the Boeotians but
it is evident that, when they had their turn as commanders, they seized
the chance and fought a battle which Xenophon perhaps did not
understand; for the concentration of force and the oblique movement
to the right seem to foreshadow their tactics at Leuctra (cf. n. at
VI.4.15). For Xenophon's attitude to Thebes, cf. Introduction p. 35 ff.

Athenians, not wanting to leave a gap in the line, followed their lead, though they were well aware of the danger of being encircled. However, since there was a lot of natural cover, the Spartans were not immediately aware that the enemy were advancing. It was only when the paean was sounded that they realized what was happening, and then they quickly ordered their whole army to prepare for battle. When their whole line was drawn up, with the allied troops in the positions assigned to them by Spartans in charge of this operation, word was passed along to keep in contact with those leading the advance. It was the Spartans themselves who took the lead and they, like the Boeotians, inclined to their right with the result that they extended so far beyond the opposing left wing that only six tribes of the Athenians found themselves engaged with the Spartans, the other four being opposite the Tegeans.

When the armies were less than 200 yards apart, the Spartans sacrificed the customary goat to Artemis the Huntress and then led the charge on the enemy. Those out beyond the enemy line were told to wheel inward so as to take them in the rear. When they came to close quarters all the Spartan allies were defeated by the troops to which they were opposed, except for the men of Pellene. Both they and the Thespians against whom they were fighting stood their ground and fell where they stood. But the Spartans themselves drove back the portion of the Athenian army which was in front of them and, wheeling behind them with their extended wing, killed large numbers. They then marched on, with scarcely a casualty and in good order. They marched past the four tribes of the Athenians, since they had not yet returned from the pursuit, so that none of these were killed except for the ones who had fallen in the fighting against the Tegeans at the beginning of the battle. But the Spartans did encounter the Argives on their way back from the pursuit. Here the story is that just when the first polemarch was going

to attack them in front, someone shouted out, 'Let their first ranks go past!' This was done and then, as the Argives were running past, the Spartans attacked and struck down great numbers of them, since their blows were directed at their exposed right sides. They also attacked the Corinthians as they were returning and some of the Thebans too, many of
23 whom they killed. After this the defeated troops first of all fled to the fortifications of Corinth, but the Corinthians shut them out, so they went back again and camped in their old camp. The Spartans also retired to the place where they had first engaged the enemy and put up a trophy there. And this concludes the account of this battle.

Spartan
wins

CHAPTER 3

Agesilaus in Greece. Battle of Coronea (394 B.C.)

MEANWHILE Agesilaus was on his way from Asia, coming 1
to the help of Sparta as fast as he could. When he was at
Amphipolis,* Dercylidas arrived with the news that the
Spartans had won a victory, that they themselves had only
lost eight men while their enemies had lost very great numbers. He added, however, that there had been a certain number of casualties among the Spartan allies. Agesilaus then 2
asked: 'Would it not be a good thing, Dercylidas, for the
cities who are sending troops with us to hear of this victory
as soon as possible?'

'Yes,' said Dercylidas, 'I should say that the news would
certainly put them in better heart.'

'And who could be a better messenger than you,' said
Agesilaus, 'since you were actually present at the battle?'

Dercylidas was always a man who liked being abroad, so
he was very glad to hear this. 'Are these your orders?' he
said.

'They are,' said Agesilaus, 'and I also want you to tell them
that if this present campaign of ours also turns out well, we
shall be back again with them, just as we said.'

Dercylidas then set off at once for the Hellespont, and Ag- 3
esilaus, after marching through Macedonia, came to Thessaly.

---

*Amphipolis is named here only. The recovery of the city, one
of the principal assets of the Fifth-Century empire, was the main preoccupation of Athens for over twenty years from 368 onwards, but
Xenophon cared for none of these things. Only, when the matter
touched Spartan diplomacy, did the war for Amphipolis get passing
reference – for those who know what he is referring to (cf. n. at
VII.I.36).

Here his army suffered from constant harassing attacks on its rear by troops from states allied with the Boeotians – Larissa, Crannon, Scotussa, Pharsalus, in fact, all Thessaly,

4 except for those who happened then to be exiles. For some time Agesilaus led the army forward in a hollow square, with half his cavalry in front and the other half at the rear. However, the Thessalians continued to slow up the march by making charges on the rear-guard, so he sent back to the rear all the cavalry in the van except for his own personal guard.

5 The two forces formed up against each other, but the Thessalians thought it would be unwise to engage in a cavalry battle in such close proximity to the hoplites; so they turned round and retired slowly, with the Greeks following cautiously after

6 them. Agesilaus saw that both sides were making a mistake. He therefore sent his own guard of picked cavalry and told them to pass on the word to the others, and then all together to go after the enemy as fast as they could and not give him a chance to face round.

7 As for the Thessalians, when they saw Agesilaus' men charging down on them so unexpectedly, some of them fled, some turned to face the charge and some, while trying to do

8 this, were caught with their horses only half turned. Polycharmus the Pharsalian, who was in command of their cavalry, turned round and fell fighting, as did the men who were with him. After this the Thessalians fled headlong, some being killed and others taken prisoner. Certainly they never stopped running until they got to Mount Narthacium.

9 On that day Agesilaus put up a trophy between Pras and Narthacium, and remained on the field of battle. He was particularly pleased with this action, seeing that with a cavalry force chosen by himself he had defeated the people who, more than all others, pride themselves on their horsemanship. Next day he crossed the Achaean mountains of Phthia and marched for the rest of the way through friendly country up to the Boeotian frontier.

When he was just about to cross into Boeotia it was ob- 10
served that the sun was appearing shaped like a crescent.
News followed that the Spartans had been defeated in the
naval action and that the admiral, Peisander, had been killed.
An account of how the battle had been fought was also given.*
It was, it appeared, near Cnidos that the two fleets had come 11
into contact. Pharnabazus with the Phoenician fleet was in
supreme command, and Conon, with the Greek contingent,
was posted in front of him. Peisander brought his ships into 12
line of battle opposite Conon, though it was evident that he
was greatly outnumbered by Conon's Greek fleet. The allied
ships on Peisander's left wing immediately fled. Peisander
himself came to close quarters with the enemy, but his trireme
was rammed and forced on shore. All the others who were
driven ashore abandoned their ships and got away as best
they could to Cnidos, but Peisander died fighting aboard his
ship.

This news had a very depressing effect on Agesilaus at first. 13
In weighing up the situation, however, he saw that most of
his troops were the kind of people who were glad enough to
share in any good fortune that came along, but that there
was no necessity to make them share in any difficulties which
might appear. He therefore altered the news. He announced
that it had been reported that Peisander had died after winning
a great victory on the sea. At the same time as the announce- 14
ment he offered sacrifices as though for good news and sent
portions of the sacrificed animals to numbers of people in the
army. As a result, when there was a skirmish with the enemy,
Agesilaus' men had the better of it, inspired as they were with
this story of a Spartan naval victory.

There were now drawn up against Agesilaus troops from 15

*The eclipse of the sun of 14 August 394 B.C. was for Xenophon a
divine sign of the naval disaster at the battle of Cnidos which, characteristically, he reports as a piece of news that reached him, not as
part of the naval war to which he devotes Chapter 8 of this book.

the following states: Boeotians, Athenians, Argives, Corinthians, Aenianians, Euboeans and both peoples of the Locrians. With Agesilaus were one regiment of Spartans which had crossed over from Corinth, half the regiment from Orchomenus, the emancipated helots from Sparta who had been serving with him in Asia, the foreign contingent under the command of Herippidas, the troops from the Greek cities in Asia and also those from the Greek cities in Europe which had joined him on the march; then also from the immediate neighbourhood he had been joined by hoplites from Orchomenus and Phocis. Agesilaus had a very great superiority in peltasts, but the cavalry on each side was about equal in numbers.

16 So much for the forces on each side. I will now go on to describe the battle itself and show how unlike it was to any other battle fought in our times.* The two armies met in the plain of Coronea, Agesilaus' army advancing from the Cephisus, and the Thebans and their allies from Mount Helicon. Agesilaus himself was in command of his right wing, and the troops from Orchomenus were on the extreme left of his line. On the other side, the Thebans led the right wing, and the Argives were on the left.

17 First, the two armies advanced towards each other in total

* Some have supposed that, since the battle of Leuctra was in fact the most remarkable battle of Xenophon's lifetime, this comment must have been written before 371 B.C; which is poor argument indeed. Xenophon took no trouble to discover what happened at Leuctra (cf. n. at VI.4.15), and the battle of Coronea was indeed unique in that it was a double battle, a sort of knock-out championship for military excellence. First, the Thebans beat their leading Boeotian rivals, the Orchomenians, while the Spartans beat their ancient Peloponnesian rivals, the Argives; then the Spartans beat the Thebans. (Agesilaus consciously chose to confront the Thebans, although he appears to have been criticized for taking the risk – cf. Plut. *Agesilaus* 18 – as Xenophon well knew; cf. §19.) Xenophon was there to witness one of his hero's finest hours.

silence; but when they were about two hundred yards apart the Thebans shouted out their war-cry and ran in at the double. Then, when there was still about a hundred yards between the armies, from the phalanx of Agesilaus came running out the troops under Herippidas. They were joined by the Ionians, Aeolians and Hellespontines, who all came running out with them and, getting within spear thrust of the enemy, routed the troops in front of them. As for the Argives, they did not even wait for Agesilaus and his troops to attack, but fled to Mount Helicon. At this point many of the mercenary troops were already offering garlands to Agesilaus when someone came in with the news that the Thebans had broken right through the troops from Orchomenus and were now in among the baggage train. Agesilaus immediately made his phalanx wheel round to the left and led them against the Thebans. They, however, had seen that their allies had fled to Mount Helicon and, wishing to break through to them, formed up in close order and came on resolutely. 18

Agesilaus' next action may, without any question at all, be described as courageous. One must own, however, that he certainly did not adopt the safest plan. He might have let the troops that were trying to break through pass by and then followed them up and given the ones in the rear a very rough handling, but instead of doing this he crashed into the Thebans front to front. So with shield pressed against shield they struggled, killed and were killed. In the end some of the Thebans broke through to Mount Helicon, but many others were killed on their way there. 19

Agesilaus himself had been wounded and, after the victory had been won, had been carried back to the phalanx, when some of his cavalry rode up. They informed him that about eighty of the enemy, still armed, were in the temple and asked him what should be done. In spite of the many wounds he had received, he still remembered what was due to heaven. 20

He told them to let the men go wherever they wished, and would not allow them to do anything wrong.

It was already late in the day, and so they had their dinner
21 and rested for the night. In the morning Agesilaus ordered the polemarch Gylis to draw up the army in battle order and to put up a trophy; everyone was to wear a garland in honour of the god and all the flute players were to play. The Thebans then sent heralds asking to be allowed to bury their dead under a truce. So the truce was made and Agesilaus went to Delphi, where he made an offering to the god of the tenth part of the proceeds from the booty. This came to no less than 100 talents.

Meanwhile, the polemarch Gylis retired with the army to
22 Phocis and from there invaded Locris. The soldiers spent nearly the whole day in carrying off plunder and food from the villages, but in the evening, when they were retiring, with the Spartans bringing up the rear, the Locrians followed them up with volleys of stones and javelins. The Spartans turned about and chased them off, killing a few, and after that they no longer followed in the rear, but went up on to the high ground to the right and shot down from there.
23 Again the Spartans attempted to chase them off, even going up the slope after them. But darkness was coming on; some fell in the rough ground or because they could not see what was in front; others were struck down by the enemy's missiles. In this fighting the polemarch Gylis was killed, as were Pelles, one of his comrades, and all together about eighteen of the Spartan officer class, some stoned to death, some dying of javelin wounds. Indeed, all of them might have been killed if some of the men who were having dinner in camp had not marched out to their help.

CHAPTER 4

Revolution in Corinth. Fighting in the Peloponnese
(393–391 B.C.)

AFTER this the various contingents of the army dispersed to their cities and Agesilaus also sailed back home. The Athenians, Boeotians, Argives and their allies now based themselves on Corinth and carried on the war from there, and the Spartans and their allies based themselves on Sicyon. With the enemy constantly close at hand, the Corinthians could see their own land being laid waste in front of their eyes and many of their own people being killed; they observed, however, that, in the case of their allies, their countries were enjoying peaceful conditions and their fields were under cultivation. Thus most of the Corinthians, including all the best elements in the state, began to desire peace and to agitate for it. This did not escape the notice of the Argives, Athenians, Boeotians, together with those Corinthians who had taken money from the King and those who had become most clearly responsible for the war. Realizing that unless the peace party were suppressed, there was a strong likelihood that Corinth would revert to her alliance with Sparta, they made plans for a massacre. The first point in their plan showed a total disregard for religion. Other people, even if a man is legally condemned to death, do not execute him on the day of a sacred feast; but these men chose the last day of the festival of Artemis Euclea, because they thought that on that day they would catch and kill the greatest number of people in the market place. So different individuals were told whom they were to kill and, when the signal was given, they drew their swords and began to strike their victims down. Men were killed while standing in a group of friends, or sitting down, or in the theatre, or even sitting as judges in musical or dramatic competitions. As soon as the news of what was happening got about, all the people of the better classes fled, some to the statues of the gods in the market place and some to the altars. (What followed next shows both in those who gave the orders and in those who carried them out a contempt for religion and a total disregard for all the conventions of civilized life.) The butchery went on actually in the holy places, and many of those who were in no danger of being struck down themselves, but who were ordinary decent people, were utterly revolted at the sight of such impiety.

4 Many of the older men were killed in this way, for a greater proportion of them happened to be in the market place. The younger men, however, owing to Pasimelus,* who had suspected what was going to happen, had stayed quietly in the gymnasium of Craneium. Here they heard the noise of shouting, and then there arrived various people who had managed to escape from the massacre. The young men then rushed up to the citadel of Acrocorinth, and when they were attacked 5 there by the Argives and the rest they beat the attack off. But when they were discussing what to do next, the capital fell down from one of the columns, although there was no earthquake and no wind at the time. And then when they sacrificed, the omens from the slaughtered animals turned out in such a way that the prophets said that it would be better for them to go down from the citadel. First, then, they retired across the Corinthian frontier with the intention of going into voluntary exile. However, their friends and mothers and sisters came out to them and tried to persuade them to change their minds, and there were even some of the people now in power who guaranteed under oath that they would be per-6 fectly safe. Under these conditions some of them did go back

---

*Pasimelus was still alive in the 360s (VII.3.2), and was no doubt known to Xenophon. His conversation perhaps furnished much of what Xenophon has to say about events around Corinth in the Corinthian War. Cf. n. at IV.4.6.

to their homes. However, they soon saw that the men in power were behaving like tyrants; it was evident, too, that their state was being abolished as a separate entity; boundary stones had been removed, their fatherland was now called Argos instead of Corinth, and while they were forced to enjoy the rights of Argive citizenship, which they did not want, they had less influence in their own state than did the resident aliens. Some of them, therefore, came to think that life under these conditions was not worth living; but, they reflected, to try to make their fatherland Corinth again, as it always had been, to restore freedom, to purify the city from the stains of blood and to give it an orderly government – would not such an attempt, if successful, entitle them to be called the saviours of their fatherland, and, if unsuccessful, allow them to meet with the kind of death which is most praised of all, coming, as it does, to those who have striven for what is most glorious and honourable and good?*

Two men, Pasimelus and Alcimenes, now undertook to 7 wade through a swollen river and try to make contact with the Spartan polemarch, Praxitas, who was on garrison duty with his regiment at Sicyon. When they reached him, they

* This account is coloured by the prejudices of men like Pasimelus; the plan to unite Corinth and Argos was perhaps popular enough (cf. V.1.34). Xenophon appears also to be muddled about the chronology of the movement. Andocides III.26 f. shows that the union had not been effected by the date of the Peace Congress in Sparta of 392–1, as is indeed shown by the separate representation of Corinth and Argos at the Congress in Sardis and the remark that the Argives 'desired' the union (IV.8.13 and 15). It appears to have been realized shortly before Iphicrates was sent to the Hellespont in perhaps late 390, a consequence of the Spartan disaster at Lechaeum (cf. IV.8.34 and Diod. XIV.92.1). But in the mind of a Pasimelus passion obscured such niceties. It is not surprising that Xenophon's account of what happened when the Spartans were brought in to the Long Walls of Corinth differs in detail from the account in Diodorus (XIV.86) whose information may have come from a more dispassionate source.

told him that they would be able to give his troops entry
into the walls which go down to Lechaeum. Praxitas believed them. He knew from the past that these two men were
reliable. He then organized matters so that the regiment
which was on the point of leaving Sicyon should remain as
well, and made plans for the entrance into the fortifications.

8 Partly by luck and partly by management an occasion arose
when these two men were on guard at the gate where the
trophy stands, and Praxitas took the opportunity and came
up with his regiment, the troops from Sicyon and all the
Corinthian exiles who were with him. When he reached the
gate he felt apprehensive about entering, and wished to send
someone whom he could trust to investigate what was going
on inside. The two Corinthians brought in the man chosen
by Praxitas, and showed him everything with such obvious
sincerity that he went back and reported that there was no
question of deception and that all was just as they had said.

9 Praxitas then entered the gate. The walls here, however, are
a considerable distance apart from each other, and when his
men formed up in battle order, they thought that there were
too few of them. So they put up a stockade and dug as deep
a ditch as they could in front of them to serve as protection
until they were reinforced by their allies. They had also to
consider the garrison of Boeotians in the harbour to their rear.

After this night entry they were left unmolested for the
whole of the next day; but on the following day the Argives
came hurrying up to the support of their friends. They found
that the Spartans were drawn up facing the extreme right of
their own line; next to them were the troops from Sicyon
and then the Corinthian exiles, about a hundred and fifty in
number, with their flank on the eastern wall. They then made
their counter-dispositions. Iphicrates with his mercenaries
was by the eastern wall, then the Argives themselves and

10 then on the left wing the Corinthians from the city. Feeling
complete confidence in their numerical superiority, they
attacked at once, defeated the men from Sicyon and, after

breaking through the stockade, pursued them down to the sea and killed many of them there. But Pasimachus, the Spartan cavalry commander (though his force was a very small one), saw the men of Sicyon being beaten back. He told his men to tie their horses to trees and then, taking their shields from the fugitives, advanced against the Argives with a body of volunteers. The Argives, seeing the Sigmas on the shields, assumed that these were more Sicyonians and felt no apprehension at all. It was then, so the story goes, that Pasimachus, running into battle, said: 'By the twin gods, Argives, you will find you have made a mistake about these Sigmas.' So, fighting with his small party against greatly superior numbers, he was killed as were many of those with him.

Meanwhile, the Corinthian exiles had defeated the troops 11 opposite them, and had pushed on farther inland till they were near the wall of the city itself. As for the Spartans, they had seen the enemy victorious in the sector held by the men of Sicyon, and they now marched out from the stockade to go to the rescue, keeping the stockade on their left. But when the Argives heard that the Spartans were in their rear, they turned round again and rushed out of the stockade at the double. Those of them who were on their extreme right were killed by the Spartans, who could thrust and strike at their unprotected sides, but those who were close to the wall fell back towards the city in a dense throng and with no sort of order. However, when they met the Corinthian exiles and discovered that they were enemies, they turned back again. Some of them now climbed up the steps to the ramparts, leapt down from the wall and were killed; others were herded together by the enemy and struck down at the foot of the steps; others were trodden under the feet of their own people and were suffocated.

As for the Spartans, they were at no loss about whom to 12 kill next, for this was certainly an occasion when God gave them an opportunity beyond anything they could have prayed for. Here was a great mass of their enemies delivered over to them in a state of utter panic, offering their unprotected sides, with no one making the least effort to fight and everyone doing everything possible to ensure his own destruction: what can one call this except an instance of divine intervention? Certainly on this occasion so many fell in such a short time that the dead bodies seemed to be heaped together like heaps of corn or piles of wood or stones. The Boeotian garrison in the harbour were also killed, some on the walls and some up on the roofs of the shipyards where they had climbed for safety.

13 After this the Corinthians and Argives carried away their dead under truce, and reinforcements arrived for the Spartans from their allies. When these had all assembled, Praxitas decided first of all to demolish a section of the walls * big enough to allow passage for an army. He then led the whole army out in the direction of Megara and took by storm first Sidus and then Crommyon. Before going back again he left garrisons in both these fortresses. Next he fortified Epieicia so that it could be used to protect the outlying country of his allies. He then disbanded the army and went back himself by the road to Sparta.

14 From this time on neither side sent out large expeditionary forces. Instead, the cities in each alliance sent contingents for garrison duty either in Corinth or in Sicyon and these forces merely guarded the fortifications. Both sides, however, employed forces of mercenaries and used them vigorously in carrying on the war.†

*From Corinth to Lechaeum.

†Somewhere hereabouts are to be set the diplomatic exchanges which began with the Congress at Sardis which Xenophon describes in his account of the naval war in Chapter 8 (IV.8.12–15) and concluded with the abortive Peace Congress in Sparta which he neglects entirely, one of the most astonishing omissions of the *Hellenica* (cf. n. at IV.8.15). The operations of the next two paragraphs (§§15 and

This was the time when Iphicrates invaded the territory of 15
Phlius and set an ambush while he went plundering with a
few troops. The men from the city came out against him
without having taken sufficient precautions and were killed
in enormous numbers. Previously they had not allowed the
Spartans inside their walls because they were afraid they
might bring back those who claimed that they had been
exiled because of their pro-Spartan sympathies, but after
this victory of Iphicrates, they were so terrified of an attack
from Corinth that they sent for the Spartans and handed
over their city and their citadel to them to guard. As for the
Spartans, though they were certainly friendly to the exiles,
they never even raised the question of their restoration during all the time they held the city, and when they thought
that the Phliasians had recovered their confidence they went
away again, giving them back their city and their laws just
as they had been when they took the place over.

Iphicrates and his men also made a number of invasions 16
into Arcadia, carrying away plunder and launching attacks
on walled towns. For the Arcadian hoplites were so terrified
of the peltasts that they never once came out into the open
against them. On the other hand, the peltasts were so frightened of the Spartans that they would not go within a javelin's
throw of Spartan hoplites. For it had happened once that
some of them had been killed after the younger men among
the Spartans had pursued and caught them up even over this
distance. However, if the Spartans looked down on the pel- 17
tasts, they looked down much more on their own allies. The
Mantineans, for instance, had once gone out against peltasts
who had run forward from the wall going down to Lechaeum,
and had not only fallen back before the javelins of the peltasts

16) may be misplaced by Xenophon and belong properly where
they seem to be put by Diodorus (XIV.91.3), viz. after the disaster
in Lechaeum of 390 B.C. But chronological woolliness does not
suffice to explain his silence about the peace negotiations.

but had also lost a number of men as they fled. Because of this the Spartans were fond of making the disrespectful remark that their allies were as frightened of peltasts as children are of bogey-men.

18   The Spartans, with one regiment and the Corinthian exiles, used to set out from Lechaeum and make various expeditions all round the city of Corinth. The Athenians meanwhile, frightened of Spartan military might and thinking that, now that the long walls of the Corinthians had been destroyed, they themselves were in danger of Spartan attack, decided that the best thing to do would be to rebuild the walls that had been demolished by Praxitas. So they came out in full force, bringing masons and carpenters with them, and within a few days had finished rebuilding the wall towards Sicyon and the west. They made a really excellent job of it, and then went to work with rather less hurry on the eastern wall.

19   The Spartans now made an expedition against the Argives. It had occurred to them that these people were living comfortably off their own land and were actually enjoying the war. Agesilaus was in command of this expedition. After laying waste the whole territory of Argos, he came straight from there over the pass of Tenea to Corinth and captured the walls that had been rebuilt by the Athenians. His brother Teleutias was also in this action, supporting Agesilaus by sea with about twelve triremes. This was certainly something to make their mother happy. For on the same day one son captured the enemy's fortifications, and the other, on sea, his ships and dockyards. After this achievement Agesilaus disbanded the army of his allies and led the home army back to Sparta.*

*The comparatively brief notice of this campaign of 391, contrasted with the fullness of the campaign of 390 (IV.5.1 ff.) and those of the two following years (IV.6.1 ff. and 7.1 ff.), suggests that Xenophon took no part in it.

CHAPTER 5

Campaign at Corinth. The Spartan Disaster near Corinth
(390 B.C.)

AFTER this the Spartans were informed by the Corinthian 1
exiles that the people in the city were keeping all their cattle
safely in Piraeum, and that a large proportion of the population were being fed from this source. They therefore made
another expedition into Corinthian territory, Agesilaus being
again in command. He went first to the Isthmus, because this
was the month when the Isthmian games are held, and on
this occasion the Argives were there and were offering the
sacrifice to Poseidon, just as though Argos were Corinth.
However, as soon as they heard that Agesilaus was coming
they got very alarmed indeed and went back to the city by
the road leading to Cenchreae, leaving behind the animals
that had been sacrificed and all the preparations for the feast
that were being made. But Agesilaus, though he saw what 2
they were doing, did not pursue them. Instead, he encamped
in the sacred precinct and sacrificed to the god himself, and
stayed there until the Corinthian exiles had made the sacrifice
and held the games in honour of Poseidon. But when Agesilaus had left the Isthmus the Argives held the Isthmian games
all over again. So in that year in some of the events various
competitors were beaten twice and the same people were
twice proclaimed winners.

On the fourth day Agesilaus led his army against Piraeum. 3
He found that large forces were ready to defend the place
and, after his men had had their breakfast, he withdrew in
the direction of Corinth, wishing to give the impression that
the city was going to be betrayed to him. As a result the
Corinthians, fearing that there might be some people prepared to do this, sent to Iphicrates and asked him to come

215

with the greater part of the peltasts. Agesilaus found that
Iphicrates and his force had gone past his lines during the
night, and so he turned round and led his army towards
Piraeum as soon as it was dawn. He himself went by way of
the Hot Springs, but he sent one regiment up along the top
of the ridge. For that night, then, he was in camp at the
Hot Springs, and the regiment bivouacked in its commanding
4 position on the heights. It was on this occasion that Agesilaus
won a lot of credit for showing even in a small matter the
most timely consideration for his men. None of the men
carrying supplies for the regiment had brought fire, and the
weather was very cold, partly because of the high altitude
and partly because there had been rain and hail that evening.
They had also made the ascent in light summer clothing.
However, when they were sitting about shivering in the dark
and with little enthusiasm for their dinner, Agesilaus sent up
to them two or more men carrying fire in earthenware pots.
The men carrying fire went up by different routes to the
summit, and soon there were a number of large fires to be
seen, as there was plenty of wood available. All the soldiers
rubbed themselves down with oil, and many of them started
dinner all over again.

It was on this night, too, that the temple of Poseidon was
seen to be on fire; but no one knows who started the fire.*

5 When the people in Piraeum realized that the heights were
in enemy hands, they gave up all thought of resistance and
fled to the Heraeum, men and women, slaves and freemen,
together with the greater part of the cattle. Agesilaus with the
army then took the road along the coast, while the regiment
descended from the heights and captured the fortified port of
Oenoe. They carried off all the property inside, and indeed

---

*For Xenophon the fire in the temple would have been an ill
portent before the Disaster; but he is perhaps exempting Agesilaus
from any blame, when others had suggested that by sending up fire
to the troops Agesilaus was really responsible.

all the soldiers that day collected a lot of valuables from the country districts. As for the people who had taken refuge in the Heraeum, they came out and surrendered unconditionally to Agesilaus. He decided that those who had had a hand in the massacre should be handed over to the exiles and that the rest should be sold.

The prisoners, in great numbers, then came out from the 6 Heraeum. It was a great haul of booty. And now embassies began to come in from a number of states. Envoys, in particular, were there from Boeotia to ask what they could do to obtain peace. Agesilaus treated these Boeotians with studied contempt. Though Pharax, who was officially in charge of Theban interests in Sparta, was standing by them to introduce them, he pretended not to notice their existence. He merely sat down in the circular building near the lake and contemplated the quantities of booty which were being brought out. Some Spartans from the camp, armed with their spears, were marching along as guards for the prisoners and everyone there was staring at them. I suppose it is because good luck and victory seem always to make people especially worth looking at.

But while Agesilaus was still sitting there, looking pleased 7 and satisfied with his achievements, a horseman came galloping up. His horse was drenched with sweat, and he would say nothing to all those who questioned him about his news until he had come close to Agesilaus. He then leaped down from his horse, ran up to him and, with the most miserable expression on his face, told him of what had happened to the regiment in Lechaeum. As Agesilaus heard the news he sprang to his feet at once, seized his spear and ordered the herald to summon the regimental and company commanders and the commanders of the allied contingents. These all 8 came running up and he told them (since they had not yet had breakfast) to eat what they could and then follow after him as quickly as possible. He himself and his tent

217

companions went on ahead without taking their meal.
Agesilaus led the way, his companions came next, and then his
bodyguard of spearmen, fully armed, hurried along behind.

He had already gone past the Hot Springs and come into
the plain of Lechaeum when three horsemen rode up with
the news that the bodies of the dead had been recovered. On
hearing this, he ordered the troops to halt and stand at ease;
then, after giving them a short rest, he led them back again
to the Heraeum. Next day he held a sale of the prisoners and
captured property.

9   Next the Boeotian ambassadors were summoned and asked
to explain why they had come. They now made no mention
of peace, but merely said that, if there was no objection, they
would like to go through the lines into the city to join their
own soldiers. Agesilaus laughed and said: 'I happen to know
that what you really want to see is not your own soldiers
but the good fortune which has come to your friends. You
want to see with your own eyes how great that has been.
Well,' he went on, 'stay with me and I will take you there
myself. If you are with me, you will get a better idea of
exactly what has happened.'

10   Agesilaus meant what he said. Next day, after making the
sacrifices, he led the army to the city. He did not throw down
the trophy that had been set up but he cut down and burned
all the fruit trees left in the area, thus making it clear that no
one was willing to march out and oppose him. As for the
Theban ambassadors, he did not let them go directly to the
city but sent them back by sea to Creusis.

A disaster such as this one had been was something to
which the Spartans were quite unused, so there was great
distress in the Laconian army – except in the cases of those
whose sons, fathers or brothers had fallen where they stood.
Those whose relatives had so died went about like men who
had won some great prize, with radiant faces, positively
glorying in their own suffering.

It was in the following way that the regiment had met with 11
disaster. The people of Amyclae, whether they are on a campaign or are for any other reason abroad, always go home for
the festival of the Hyacinthia so as to sing the hymn to
Apollo. So, on this occasion, Agesilaus had left behind at
Lechaeum all men from Amyclae who were in the army.
The polemarch * in command of the garrison there, after
instructing the allied troops in the garrison to guard the wall,
went himself with the regiment of hoplites and the regiment
of cavalry to escort the Amyclaeans past the city of Corinth.
When they were at a distance of three or four miles from 12
Sicyon, the polemarch turned back towards Lechaeum, taking with him the hoplites, of whom there were about six
hundred. He told the commander of the cavalry to follow
with his regiment after they had escorted the Amyclaeans as
far as they asked him to go. They were quite aware that
there were great numbers both of peltasts and hoplites in
Corinth, but because of their previous successes they dis-
counted any danger of any attack from that quarter. How- 13
ever, the generals in Corinth – Callias, the son of Hipponicus,
who was in command of the Athenian hoplites, and Iphicrates, who commanded the peltasts – saw that the Spartans
were neither in great force nor protected by peltasts or
cavalry, and came to the conclusion that it would be safe to
attack them with their own peltasts. If they marched along the
road, they could be shot at with javelins on their unprotected
side and mowed down; and if they tried to pursue their
attackers, it would be perfectly easy for peltasts, light and fast
on their feet, to keep out of the way of hoplites. After reaching this conclusion, they led their men out. Callias drew up 14
his hoplites in battle formation not far from the city, and
Iphicrates with his peltasts attacked the regiment of Spartans.

And now as the javelins were hurled at them, some of the

* The incompetent polemarch is not given a name, although Xenophon is likely to have known it. See Introduction p. 37 f.

Spartans were killed and some wounded. The shield-bearers were told to take up the bodies and carry them back to Lechaeum, and these were the only men in the regiment who really* got away unscathed. The polemarch then ordered the infantry in the age groups 20 to 30 to charge and drive 15 off their attackers. However, they were hoplites pursuing peltasts at the distance of a javelin's throw, and they failed to catch anyone, since Iphicrates had ordered his men to fall back before the hoplites came to close quarters. But when the Spartans, in loose order because each man had been running at his own speed, turned back again from the pursuit, Iphicrates' men wheeled round, some hurling their javelins again from in front while others ran up along the flank, shooting at the side unprotected by the shields. In fact, in the very first pursuit they shot down nine or ten and after this they began to press their attacks with still greater confidence. 16 Then, as things were going very badly, the polemarch ordered another pursuit, this time with the men of the age groups 20 to 35. But in falling back from this pursuit even more men were killed than before. Now, when the best men had already been killed, the cavalry came up and they once again attempted a pursuit with the cavalry in support. However, when the peltasts turned to run, the cavalry charge was mismanaged. Instead of going after the enemy until they had killed some of them, they kept, both in their advance and their retreat, a continuous front with the hoplites. So it went on, the same actions with the same results, and, while the Spartans were continually losing in numbers and in resolution, their enemies became bolder and bolder, and more and 17 more joined in the attack. Not knowing what to do they formed up in a body on a small hill which was less than half a mile from the sea and rather over two miles from Lechaeum.

* There were about three hundred and fifty survivors (cf. §§12 and 17), but only those who under orders carried the bodies back survived, in Xenophon's view, honourably.

And the men in Lechaeum, seeing what was happening, embarked in small boats and sailed along the shore until they came opposite the hill. The Spartans were already at their wits' end, suffering as they were and being destroyed without being able to do anything about it; and now when, in addition to all this, they saw the hoplites bearing down on them, they broke and ran. Some plunged into the sea and a few attached themselves to the cavalry and got safely to Lechaeum. But in all the fighting and in the flight about two hundred and fifty of them were killed. This, then, was the 18 action that had taken place.

Afterwards Agesilaus went away, taking with him the defeated regiment and leaving another one behind in Lechaeum. On his march home he led his troops into the cities as late as he could in the day and started off in the morning at the earliest possible hour. In the case of Mantinea he went past it while it was still dark, having left Orchomenus before dawn. He considered that it would be hard indeed for his soldiers to be faced with the sight of the Mantineans showing pleasure in the disaster that had happened to them.

After this action things went very well with Iphicrates in 19 other enterprises also. Garrisons had been placed in Sidus and Crommyon by Praxitas after he had captured these fortresses, and Agesilaus had put troops into Oenoe at the time when Piraeum was seized. Now all these places were taken by Iphicrates. The Spartans and their allies, however, still occupied Lechaeum. As for the Corinthian exiles, as a result of the disaster which had happened to the regiment, they no longer went by land from Sicyon past Corinth. Instead, they sailed along the coast to Lechaeum and used this as a base for setting out on raiding expeditions which, though causing them much trouble, also did much damage to their enemies in the city.

Spt Achaeons v Acarnany

Spt Acarnanian Achaeans

CHAPTER 6

Agesilaus' Acarnanian Campaign (389 B.C.)

1 THE Achaeans were in possession of Calydon, which in the past had belonged to Aetolia, and they had made the people of Calydon Achaean citizens. Now, however, they were obliged to keep a garrison in the place because the Acarnanians, supported by some Athenians and Boeotians (since they were allied with the Acarnanians), were bringing up an army against it. Finding themselves in difficulties, the Achaeans sent ambassadors to Sparta who, when they had arrived, claimed that the Spartans were not treating them fairly.

2 'We Achaeans,' they said, 'join up with you Spartans whenever you give the word and follow you wherever you lead the way. But now, when we are being besieged by the Acarnanians and their Athenian and Boeotian allies, you are showing no consideration for us at all. And we simply cannot go on with things as they are now. Either we shall have to take no further part in the war in the Peloponnese and all cross over to make war against the Acarnanians and their allies, or else we shall have to make peace on the best terms we can get.'

3 The object of this speech was to suggest a threat that they would leave the Spartan alliance unless the Spartans did something for them in return, and, after the speech was made, both the ephors and the assembly agreed that it was necessary to join the Achaeans in an expedition against the Acarnanians. So they sent out Agesilaus with two regiments of Spartans and appropriate numbers of allied troops. The Achaeans, however, marched out in full force.

4 When Agesilaus had crossed over, all the Acarnanians in the country districts took refuge in the towns and all their

cattle were driven into the interior so as to be out of reach of the army. Agesilaus, on reaching the enemy frontier, sent to the general assembly of the Acarnanians at Stratus and told them that unless they abandoned their alliance with the Athenians and Boeotians and chose instead to become allies of the Spartans and Achaeans, he would lay waste their country section by section, not leaving any portion of it unharmed. And, since they refused to come to terms, this is what he did. 5 He marched on methodically devastating the land and thus not advancing more than a mile or two every day. Because the army was advancing so slowly the Acarnanians, thinking this a safe thing to do, brought their cattle down from the mountains and went on cultivating the greater part of their land. But on the fifteenth or sixteenth day after he had cross- 6 ed the frontier Agesilaus, who considered that by this time the enemy was full of confidence, after making a sacrifice early in the morning led the army before evening on a twenty-five mile march to the lake round which were nearly all the cattle belonging to the Acarnanians. Here he captured great numbers of cattle and horses, all sorts of other stock and very many slaves as well. After making this haul, he stayed where he was for the following day and then sold all the booty.

And now a large force of Acarnanian peltasts appeared. 7 Agesilaus was camping on the slopes of the mountain and the peltasts, hurling their missiles and sling-stones from the highest ridges, while suffering no casualties themselves, forced the army to go down to the plain, even though the men had already started to make ready for their evening meal. At nightfall the Acarnanians went away and the soldiers posted sentries and lay down to sleep.

Next day Agesilaus began to lead the army back. The road 8 leading out of the meadows and low-lying ground by the lake was a narrow one, as there were mountains round it in every direction. These heights were occupied by the Acarnanians who hurled down their javelins and missiles on the

right flank of the army, and then began to come down to the lower slopes, from which they attacked more boldly and made things so difficult that in the end the army found it
9 impossible to move forward. When the hoplites and cavalry moved out from the phalanx to chase their attackers off, they did no damage, since the Acarnanians were quickly on safe ground whenever they fell back. Seeing how difficult it was for his men to get out through the narrow pass while they were exposed to these attacks, Agesilaus decided to drive back the very large number of enemy troops who were attacking them on the left, since on the high ground in this direction there was easier going both for hoplites and horses.
10 While he was making the sacrifice the Acarnanians kept up a continuous pressure. Hurling stones and javelins they came in close and inflicted a number of wounds. Then Agesilaus gave the order; the men in the age groups 20 to 35 ran forward from the hoplites, the cavalry charged and Agesilaus
11 himself followed them up with the rest of the army. The Acarnanians who had come down from the mountains to hurl their weapons were quickly routed and cut down as they tried to escape uphill; but the hoplites of the Acarnanians and most of their peltasts were drawn up in battle order on the summit and there they stayed. They let loose with all their weapons and with volleys of spears wounded some of the cavalry and killed some of the horses. However, when they were very nearly within close fighting range of the Spartan hoplites, they broke and ran and on that day about three hundred of them were killed.
12 After this Agesilaus put up a trophy. He then went through the country cutting down the trees and burning the crops, and also, under pressure from the Achaeans, made regular assaults on some of the cities, but failed to capture any of them.

When autumn was already in the air he prepared to leave
13 the country. The Achaeans, however, thought that, since he

had failed to gain control of a single city, whether by force or diplomacy, he had accomplished nothing worth while, and they urged him, even if he would do nothing else, at least to stay there long enough to prevent the Acarnanians from sowing their seed. Agesilaus told them that this suggestion was directly contrary to their interests. 'I shall march here again next year,' he said, 'and the more these people sow, the more anxious they will be to make peace.'

He then marched away overland through Aetolia. It was a 14 route which, whatever the size of the army, would be impossible to take except with the consent of the Aetolians. They, however, allowed him to go through, since they hoped that he would help them to recover Naupactus. On reaching the part of the coast opposite Rhium he crossed over from there and so returned to Sparta. The sea passage from Calydon to the Peloponnese was blocked by the Athenians with their triremes based on Oeniadae.

CHAPTER 7

Spartan Operations against Argos (388 B.C.)

1 WHEN the winter was over and at the very beginning of
spring Agesilaus once again called up troops for service
against the Acarnanians as he had promised the Achaeans that
he would do. When they heard of this the Acarnanians came
to the conclusion that, since their cities were in the interior,
they would be just as effectually under siege if their enemies
destroyed their corn as if they undertook regular siege operations at close quarters; they therefore sent ambassadors to
Sparta, made peace with the Achaeans and became allies of
Sparta. So ended the Acarnanian affair.

2 After this the Spartans decided that it would be unsafe for
them to march against either Athens or Boeotia while leaving
a hostile state in their rear and on their own borders – and
particularly one so powerful as Argos. They therefore ordered mobilization against Argos. Agesipolis realized that it
would be his duty to lead the invasion army and, after the
sacrifices made at the frontier turned out favourably, he went
to Olympia and consulted the oracle there, asking the god
whether he would be acting righteously if he refused to accept the holy truce suggested by the Argives; he pointed out
that they had begun to talk about the holy months not at the
correct times but only when the Spartans were on the point
of invading their country. The god signified to him that it
was in accordance with his religious duties not to accept a
truce which had been offered in a dishonest manner. He then
went straight from Olympia to Delphi and consulted Apollo
in his turn, asking whether he, too, on this question of the
truce held the same opinion as his father Zeus. Apollo
answered that he most certainly did.

3 It was only then that Agesipolis marched out with the army

from Phlius, where it had been assembling while he was away visiting the holy places. He invaded Argos by way of Nemea and the Argives, realizing that they had not the power to stop him, sent out, as the custom was, two heralds with garlands round their heads who claimed the observance of a holy truce. Agesipolis, however, refused to accept this. His reply was that the gods did not consider that the plea was a just one. So he went forward and spread terror and dismay both in the country districts and in the city.

On the first evening that he was in the Argive country, 4 while he was seated at dinner and when the after-dinner libations had already been poured, there was an earthquake. All the Spartans, with those in the king's own company taking the lead, sang the hymn to Poseidon, and the rest of the army assumed that they would now go back again, since Agis had, on another occasion when there was an earthquake, withdrawn his army from Elis. But Agesipolis said that if the god had sent the earthquake when he was just going to invade, it would appear that he was forbidding the invasion; now, however, when the invasion had already begun, the god, in his view, was encouraging him to proceed. And so on the 5 next day he sacrificed to Poseidon, and then led his troops on farther into the country. Agesilaus, of course, had recently led an army into Argos, and now Agesipolis, after finding out from the soldiers how close to the wall Agesilaus had led his men or to what depth he had laid waste the country, tried in every way to go one better himself, like an athlete competing in the pentathlon. There was an occasion when he 6 crossed the trenches round the city wall and only withdrew when he came under fire from the towers; and once, when most of the Argives had gone to 'the Laconian',* he came so close to the gates that the Argives on guard shut out the

*We do not know what this topographical feature was, if indeed the text is not corrupt. It is inconceivable that the Argives had gone far from the city. Characteristically, Xenophon felt no need to explain this term, nor in §7 'the enclosure'.

Boeotian cavalry who wanted to come in, since they feared that the Spartans might force their way in with them. The result was that the cavalrymen had to cling to the wall, spread-eagled under the battlements like bats, and had it not been for the fact that the Cretan archers happened to have gone off plundering to Nauplia at the time, many men and horses would have been shot down.

7   After this, when Agesipolis had made his camp near the enclosure, a thunderbolt fell in the camp, killing some men directly and some from the shock. Later, when he wished to build a fort on the passes into Argive territory on Mount Celusa, he made a sacrifice, and it was found that the livers of the victims were without lobes. At this he led the army back and disbanded it. His invasion had done much harm to the Argives, since it had been entirely unexpected.

CHAPTER 8

The War at Sea (394–389 B.C.)

THE war by land, then, was fought as described above. I shall   1
now describe what was happening at sea and in the cities on
the sea during the period when all the above events were
taking place. I shall pass over those actions that are not worth
mentioning, dealing only with what deserves to be remembered.

First of all, then, Pharnabazus and Conon, after the naval
victory over the Spartans, sailed from island to island and to
the cities on the coast, driving out the Spartan governors and
putting heart into the cities by telling them that they proposed to leave them to govern themselves and had no intention of building fortified posts inside their walls. This was   2
good and pleasant news for the people of the cities to hear,
and they gladly sent gifts to Pharnabazus as tokens of friendship. Conon, it appears, was advising Pharnabazus, and
Pharnabazus was acting in accordance with this advice. If,
Conon said, Pharnabazus acted as described above, all the
cities would be friendly; but if, on the other hand, he made   *alliance*
it clear that his intention was to subdue them, each single one
of them would be capable of causing a lot of trouble, and
there would also be the risk that the Greeks in general, if
they got to hear of it, would unite together.

Pharnabazus disembarked at Ephesus, and from there be-   3
gan to march by land to his own province. He gave Conon
forty triremes and instructed him to meet him at Sestus. For
Dercylidas, who had for long been an enemy of Pharnabazus,
had been at Abydus at the time of the sea battle and instead
of abandoning his post, like the other Spartan governor, had
held on to the city and kept it loyal to the Spartans. He had

called an assembly of the people of Abydus and spoken to
4 them as follows: 'My friends, you have been on good terms
with our city in former days, but now you have the opportunity to show yourselves real benefactors to us Spartans.
There is nothing remarkable about being loyal when things
are going well; what is remembered and remembered for
ever is when people stand by their friends in their times of
misfortune. It is certainly not the case that just because we
were defeated in the naval action we have now ceased to
count. You will remember, I think, that even in former days,
when Athens ruled the seas, our city was perfectly capable of
doing good to its friends and harm to its enemies. And now,
the more that the other cities, swayed by a shift in fortune,
turn away from us, the greater in sober fact will your steadfastness appear to be. Some of you may be afraid that we
shall be exposed to a siege here both by land and sea. You
must reflect that there is not yet a Greek fleet on the sea and
Greece will not tolerate any attempt that the Persians may
make to control the sea. Thus in helping herself, she will at
the same time become your ally.'

5   After hearing this speech the people of Abydus, so far from
raising any objections, were most willing to follow Dercylidas. They gave a good reception to those Spartan governors
who took refuge with them, and they sent for others who
were at a distance. Then, when numbers of valuable men had
been collected in Abydus, Dercylidas crossed over to Sestus
as well, which is opposite Abydus and not more than a mile
away. Here he gathered together all those who owed their
holdings of land in the Chersonese to the Spartans, and he
also received the governors who had been driven out of their
cities on the European side and told them that they in particular had no reason to be downhearted. He pointed out
that even in Asia, which had always belonged to the King,
there was Temnus, by no means a powerful city, and Aegae
and other places as well where people could live without
being the King's subjects. 'And now,' he went on, 'where

could you find a stronger place than Sestus or one more difficult to take by siege? Without both an army and a naval force it could not be besieged at all.' With arguments such as this he prevented the people in this area also from losing their nerve.

This was the state of affairs which Pharnabazus found both 6 in Abydus and in Sestus, and he issued a proclamation to the effect that unless the people of these towns drove out the Spartans, he would make war on them. They refused to obey, and he then ordered Conon to shut them off from the sea, while he himself laid waste the land around Abydus. He made no progress, however, towards securing their submission and went back home, after instructing Conon to try to win over the cities on the Hellespont in order to raise as large a fleet as possible before the spring. He was angry with the Spartans because of the way he had been treated by them, and his particular desire was to sail to their country and take what revenge he could.

So they spent the winter. At the beginning of spring Phar- 7 nabazus manned a large number of ships and hired a force of mercenaries as well. Then, with Conon, he sailed through the islands to Melos and, using Melos as a base, went on to Spartan territory. The first place at which he put in was Pherae, where he laid waste the land, and then went on to make landings at other points along the coast, doing all the damage he could. Then, since he was apprehensive about the lack of harbours, the possibility of relief forces arriving and the shortage of food supplies, he quickly changed course and sailed away to Phoenicus in the island of Cythera, where he came to anchor. The people of Cythera abandoned their 8 walls since they feared they would be taken by storm, and Pharnabazus allowed them a safe conduct to the Spartan mainland. He then repaired the fortifications and left behind a garrison of his own in Cythera, with Nicophemus, an Athenian, as governor.

Next he sailed to the isthmus of Corinth, where he

encouraged the allies to continue energetically with the prosecution of the war, and to show the King that they were men whom he could trust.* After leaving them all the money he had available he sailed off home. Conon, however, asked to be allowed to keep the fleet. He said that he could support it by contributions from the islands, and that he proposed to sail to Athens and to help his countrymen rebuild the Long Walls and the fortifications of Piraeus. 'I can think of no action,' he said, 'which would hurt the Spartans more. By doing this you will not only have given the Athenians something for which they will be grateful but will have really made the Spartans suffer. You will make null and void that achievement of theirs which cost them more toil and trouble than anything else.'

This proposal was welcomed by Pharnabazus. He not only sent Conon to Athens but gave him additional money for the rebuilding of the walls. And Conon, when he arrived, erected a great part of the fortifications, using his own crews for the work, hiring carpenters and masons and meeting all other necessary expenses. There were other parts of the walls, however, which had been rebuilt by the Athenians themselves with the help of volunteers from Boeotia and other states.

Meanwhile, the Corinthians used the money left by Pharnabazus for manning ships. They appointed Agathinus as admiral and controlled the sea in the gulf around Achaea and Lechaeum. The Spartans on their side also manned a fleet under the command of Podanemus. He, however, was killed in an engagement which took place, and Pollis, the vice-admiral, was wounded and went home. The fleet was then taken over by Herippidas. Meanwhile Proaenus, the Corinthian, had replaced Agathinus in command of the Corinthian fleet. He abandoned Rhium, and the Spartans took the place

* That the opponents of Sparta could be invited to show themselves loyal to the Great King was, in Xenophon's eyes, disgraceful.

over. Afterwards Teleutias arrived to take over the command from Herippidas, and he once again controlled the waters of the gulf.

The Spartans now heard that Conon was not only rebuild- 12 ing the walls of Athens with the King's money but was also, from this same source, maintaining his fleet and winning over for Athens the islands and the cities on the coast of the mainland. It seemed to them that if they informed Tiribazus, the King's general, of this, they would either bring him over into alliance with them or, at least, stop him from maintaining Conon's fleet. So, when they had reached this conclusion, they sent Antalcidas to Tiribazus, instructing him to inform Tiribazus of what was happening and to try to bring about peace between Sparta and the King.

When the Athenians heard of this, they sent out an em- 13 bassy, too, consisting of Conon himself, together with Hermogenes, Dion, Callisthenes and Callimedon. They also invited their allies to send ambassadors with them, and ambassadors came from the Boeotians, from Corinth and from Argos.

When their embassies arrived, Antalcidas addressed Tiri- 14 bazus and told him that he had come because he wanted peace as the King himself desired. 'The Spartans,' he said, 'are putting forward no claim against the King for the Greek cities in Asia, and are content that all the islands and the other cities should be governed according to their own laws. And now, when we are willing to agree to all this, what reason can the King have for being at war with us, and spending all the money he is spending? Under these conditions no one could undertake a campaign against the King. The Athenians could not unless we took the lead; and we could not, if the cities were independent.'

Tiribazus was delighted to hear these proposals from An- 15 talcidas; but to the other side there was no reality in them. The Athenians were afraid to agree that the citizens and

233

islands should be self-governing, in case they should lose control of Lemnus, Imbros and Scyros; the Thebans feared that they might have to grant independence to the Boeotian cities; and the Argives thought that, if peace was concluded on these lines, they would not be able to continue with their cherished plan of holding Corinth as a part of Argos. So the proposed peace came to nothing and the ambassadors returned to their various cities.*

16   Tiribazus thought that it would be unsafe for him to side openly with the Spartans unless he had the authority of the King. However, he gave money secretly to Antalcidas, with the idea that, if the Spartans manned a fleet, the Athenians and their allies might be more ready to make peace. And he imprisoned Conon on the ground that he was doing harm to the King, and that the case put forward by the Spartans was a true one. After doing this he went to see the King himself in the interior, to tell him what the Spartans had said and that he had arrested Conon, and to ask what he should do about all these things.

17   The King, when Tiribazus had joined him in the interior, sent down Struthas to take charge of affairs on the coast. Struthas, however, remembering all the harm that the King's country had suffered from Agesilaus, was strongly in favour of the Athenians and their allies. So the Spartans, seeing that Struthas was behaving like an enemy to them and like a friend to the Athenians, sent Thibron to make war on him. And Thibron after crossing over into Asia and basing himself on Ephesus and the cities in the plain of the Maeander (Priene, Leucophrys and Achilleum), laid waste and plundered the King's territory.

*Xenophon astonishingly omits the negotiations in Sparta, of which we learn from Andocides III. For the relation between the Congress which Xenophon describes and the one he does not, cf. Cawkwell, *Classical Quarterly*, 26, 1976, p. 271 n. 13 – and p. 276 n. 25 for the crucial Fragment 149 of Philochorus.

As time went on Struthas noticed that every time Thibron **18**
sent out a party of troops the operation was carried out in an
undisciplined and over-confident manner. He therefore sent
a cavalry force into the plain with orders to charge the enemy,
surround them and get away with whatever they could.
Thibron happened to have just finished breakfast and was
engaged in throwing the discus with the flute player Thersander, who was not only a good flute player but, as an admirer of all things Spartan, a keen competitor in physical
prowess. Struthas could see that the advance party of enemy **19**
troops were few in number and were coming on in no sort
of order, and he now appeared himself at the head of a large
and compact body of cavalry. The first to be killed were
Thibron and Thersander, and their fall was followed by the
flight of the rest of the army. Large numbers were killed in
the pursuit, though there were some who managed to escape
to the friendly cities, and more still had been left behind in
camp because they had not been told in time that the expedition was setting out. For this was one of many cases when
Thibron set out on a raid without even issuing orders to his
men. And so this affair ended.

Now those of the Rhodians who had been banished by the **20**
democratic party came to Sparta, where they pointed out
that the Spartans ought not to allow Athens to subdue
Rhodes and thus gain such a powerful position for themselves.
Realizing that if power went to the democracy the whole of
Rhodes would go over to Athens, while if the richer classes
were in power the island would be on their side, the Spartans
manned eight ships for the exiles and appointed Ecdicus to
command them. With these ships they also sent out Diphri- **21**
das with orders to cross over to Asia in order to safeguard the
cities which had welcomed Thibron; he was to take over
whatever was left of Thibron's army, to raise another army
from all possible sources, and to carry on the war against
Struthas.

Diphridas proceeded to carry out these instructions and things went well with him. In particular he succeeded in capturing Tigranes, who had married Struthas' daughter, together with his wife as they were travelling to Sardis. He got a large ransom for them, and was thus able to start at once

22 hiring mercenaries. Diphridas had just as attractive a personality as Thibron, and as a general he was both more efficient and more enterprising. He was not the slave of bodily pleasure and he always stuck to the job in hand.

Ecdicus meanwhile sailed to Cnidos, where he discovered that the democrats were in power throughout Rhodes, in control both by land and sea, and in possession of twice as many triremes as he had himself. He therefore stayed in

23 Cnidos and made no move; but when the Spartans heard that he had too small a force to be able to help their friends they sent instructions to Teleutias, who was in command of the twelve ships in the gulf around Achaea and Lechaeum, telling him to sail round to Ecdicus, to send him home and to take over himself the responsibility for those who wanted to be their friends and to do what harm he could to their enemies.

When he reached Samos Teleutias got seven more ships from there. He then went on to Cnidos and Ecdicus returned

24 home. By the time he reached Rhodes Teleutias had a fleet of twenty-seven ships, since on his way there he had met with Philocrates, the son of Ephialtes, who, with ten ships, was sailing from Athens to Cyprus in order to bring help to Evagoras, and he had captured all ten of them. In this incident both sides were acting directly contrary to their own interests: the Athenians, who enjoyed the friendship of the King, were sending help to Evagoras, who was fighting against the King; and Teleutias, although the Spartans were at war with the King, was destroying a force that was sailing against the King. After seizing the ships, Teleutias sailed back to Cnidos, where he disposed of his booty, and then set out

again for Rhodes and there supported those who were on the side of Sparta.

It now appeared to the Athenians that the Spartans were 25 once again growing powerful on the sea, and they sent out Thrasybulus, from the district of Steiria, with forty ships to take counter-measures. Sailing out on this mission he decided not to operate in Rhodes for the following reasons. He thought it would be difficult to do much harm to the pro-Spartan party there, since they held a fortress and had Teleutias with his fleet to support them; and, on the other hand, it seemed unlikely that the pro-Athenian party there could be subdued by their enemies, holding, as they did, all the cities, being in greater number, and having already been victorious in battle. He therefore sailed for the Hellespont. There was 26 no enemy force to oppose him in that area and it seemed to him that he would be able to do some good service there for Athens. He learned that Amedocus, the king of the Odrysians, and Seuthes, who held power in the coastal area, were on bad terms with each other, and his first step was to bring about a reconciliation between them and to make both of them friends and allies of Athens. Now that they were friendly he thought that the Greek cities along the coast would also be more inclined to be pro-Athenian.

Things here, then, were going satisfactorily, and the same 27 was true of the cities in Asia now that the King had become friendly to the Athenians. Thrasybulus sailed next to Byzantium, where he distributed contracts for collecting the dues on ships sailing out of the Pontus. He also changed the government in Byzantium from an oligarchy to a democracy. The result of this was that the common people of Byzantium were glad to see as many Athenians as possible present in their city.

His next step was to win over the people of Calchedon also 28 and make them friends of Athens. He then sailed out again through the Hellespont and came to Lesbos, where he found that all the cities except Mytilene were on the side of the Spartans. Before undertaking operations against any of them he assembled together in Mytilene the 400 hoplites from his own ships and also the exiles from the Lesbian cities who had taken refuge in Mytilene; to these he added the best fighting material to be found among the Mytilenaeans themselves. He pointed out that in the event of his reducing the cities all had something to look forward to; the Mytilenaeans would become the dominant state in Lesbos; the exiles, by combining together against each separate city, would end up by recovering, each and all, their own cities; and as for the marines aboard his own ships, by making Lesbos friendly to Athens they would find that they had secured a great deal of money for themselves. After encouraging them with these prospects he put them in order of battle and led them against Methymna.

29 The Spartan governor here was Therimachus, and as soon as he heard that Thrasybulus was marching against him, he went to meet him on the frontier with a force composed of the marines from his ships, the Methymnaeans themselves and all the exiles from Mytilene who happened to be there. A battle was fought in which Therimachus was killed in the actual fighting and many others were killed in the pursuit.

30 After this Thrasybulus won over a certain number of the cities and raised money for his troops by plundering the lands of those who refused to join him. He was in a hurry to get to Rhodes, and in order to make sure that his army there, too, would be as strong as possible he collected contributions from various cities. Aspendus was one of these, and when he arrived there he anchored his fleet in the river Eurymedon. He had already received the money from the people of Aspendus when a number of them, infuriated by some acts of brigandage committed on their property by his soldiers, rushed into the camp by night and cut him down in his tent.

31 This, then, was the end of Thrasybulus, who had won the

reputation of being a very good man indeed.* In his place
the Athenians appointed Agyrrhius and sent him out to take
over the naval command. Meanwhile the Spartans had been
informed that the right to collect the ten-per-cent duty on
vessels sailing out of the Pontus had been sold at Byzantium
by the Athenians, that the Athenians also held Calchedon,
and that the other cities of the Hellespont were going in the
same direction because of the friendship of Pharnabazus for
the Athenians. They decided that it was a situation where
something had to be done. No fault was found with Dercy- 32
lidas, but Anaxibius, owing to the fact that the ephors had
become friends of his, succeeded in getting himself sent out
to Abydus as governor. He promised that, if he were given
money and ships, he would also make war against the Athenians and put an end to their successes in the Hellespont. The 33
ephors gave him, therefore, before sending him out, three
triremes and enough money to hire 1,000 mercenaries. On
his arrival he raised a mercenary force, and in his land operations won over some of the Aeolian cities from Pharnabazus,
and marched against others which had been in active hostility
to Abydus, taking his army through their territory and laying
it waste. Then, in addition to the ships he had already, he
manned three others from Abydus and brought into harbour
all merchant ships belonging to Athens or her allies which he
could find.

The Athenians heard of what was going on and, fearing 34
that all the good work done by Thrasybulus in the Hellespont might go for nothing, sent out Iphicrates to deal with

*Xenophon's commendation of Thrasybulus was due perhaps to
shared Panhellenism (cf. Cawkwell, *Classical Quarterly*, 26, 1976, pp.
275–7). By contrast, Agyrrhius who replaced him is named here only
in the *Hellenica*. He was perhaps too much of a financier to interest
Xenophon, but he was also 'a man of the people' (Demosthenes
XXIV.134). The real opposites to Thrasybulus, *viz*. Epicrates and
Cephalus, passed unmentioned.

the situation with a force of eight ships and about one thousand two hundred peltasts. Most of them were from the force he had commanded at Corinth. For after the Argives had incorporated Corinth in their own city they said they had no further need of Iphicrates' men (he had, in fact, put to death some of the pro-Argos party). He had then returned to Athens and happened to be still there.

35 He now came to the Chersonese, and for the first part of this campaign both he and Anaxibius carried on the war by sending out parties to raid each other's territory. After some time, however, Iphicrates received news that Anaxibius had gone off to Antandrus, taking with him his mercenaries, the Spartan troops in his command, and 200 hoplites from Abydus. It was reported that he had succeeded in bringing over Antandrus to his side. Iphicrates guessed that after leaving a garrison there he would come back again, bringing the troops from Abydus home, and so he crossed over by night to the least inhabited part of Abydene territory, went up into the mountains and there set an ambush. He ordered the triremes which had brought him across to sail on at dawn up the straits along the coast of the Chersonese so as to make it appear that he had sailed up the Hellespont, as he often did

36 do, in order to collect money. This action was justified by events. Anaxibius did return. They say that on that day the sacrifices he made did not come out well, but he treated them with contempt, considering that he was marching through friendly country to a friendly city. He was told, too, by those who met him that Iphicrates had sailed off in the direction of Proconnesus. Not many precautions, then, were

37 taken on the march. Nevertheless, so long as Anaxibius' army was on level ground, Iphicrates kept his men hidden. He waited until the troops from Abydus in the van were already in the plain of Cremaste, where their goldmines are, and the rest of the army following them were on the downward slope, with Anaxibius and his Spartans just beginning the

descent. It was at this moment that Iphicrates led his men out
of the ambush and charged towards Anaxibius at the double.
Anaxibius realized that his position was hopeless. He could 38
see his troops stretched out in a long line of march and on a
narrow route, and it seemed to him plainly impossible for
those who had gone ahead to come back up the hill to his
relief. He saw, too, that the sight of the ambush had put
everyone into a state of terror, and he said to the men with
him: 'My friends, for me the only honourable thing to do is
to die here. As for you, try to get away as fast as you can
before the enemy are on us.' After these words he took his 39
shield from the man who was carrying it and fell fighting
where he stood. But the young man with whom he was in
love stayed by him, and so did about twelve of the Spartan
governors who had come to join him from their cities. All of
these fought and died with him. The rest of his men took to
flight and were cut down fleeing. Iphicrates' men pressed the
pursuit right up to the city, killing about two hundred of the
rest of the army and about fifty of the hoplites from Abydus.
After this action Iphicrates went back again to the Chersonese.

BOOK FIVE

CHAPTER 1

Naval operations round Aegina. Teleutias' raid on the Piraeus.
Antalcidas and the King's Peace (389–386 B.C.)

WHILE the Athenians and Spartans were conducting these 1
operations in the area of the Hellespont, Eteonicus was again
at Aegina. Up to now there had been normal commercial relations between Aegina and Athens, but now, with war
being openly carried on by sea, Eteonicus, with the approval
of the ephors, encouraged all who wanted to do so to carry
out raids on Attica. The Athenians, under pressure from these 2
raids, sent out to Aegina a force of hoplites under the general
Pamphilus. They built blockading walls round the city on the
land side and blockaded it from the sea with the triremes. It
happened, however, that Teleutias had arrived in the islands
on a mission to collect money. Hearing of the blockade he
came to the help of the Aeginetans and drove off the Athenian fleet. Pamphilus, however, succeeded in holding on to
the fortifications on the land.

After this Hierax arrived from Sparta as admiral and took 3
over the fleet.* Teleutias sailed home, but what a glorious
occasion this was for him! When he was going down to the
sea on his way back, there was not a single one of the

* Much confusion has resulted from the presumption that Xenophon
has given the names of all the Spartan admirals in the Corinthian War.
Teleutias had been admiral presumably for a year from autumn 392,
although Xenophon does not say as much at IV.8.11, and had continued in command though not in office until relieved by Hierax
here in autumn 389. For the missing admiral of 390–89, cf. Aeschines
II.78 and Cawkwell, *Classical Quarterly*, 26, 1976, p. 272 n. 14. The
matter is not trifling. If Xenophon had been carefully composing a
history, an exact framework of Spartan admirals would have been
essential, and this omission is tell-tale of his method and intention.

soldiers who did not grasp his hand; one put a wreath on his head, another crowned him with ribands; and those who came late, when his ship was already under way, nevertheless threw garlands into the sea and prayed that he would have
4 every kind of good fortune. In describing this scene I know that I am not telling of anything which cost money or involved danger or showed any particular skill. But, by Zeus, I think it is very well worth a man's while to consider this question – how had Teleutias conducted himself so as to make the men under his command feel like this about him? For this is the achievement of one who is a man indeed, and this by itself is worth more than the expense of quantities of money or the facing of all sorts of dangers.*

5 Hierax now sailed back to Rhodes with the fleet, except for twelve triremes which he left in Aegina, with his vice-admiral Gorgopas as governor of the place. And now it was not so much the Aeginetans in the city as the Athenians in their fortifications who were under siege. In fact, after passing a decree the Athenians in Athens manned a large number of ships and, in the fifth month, brought back from Aegina their men from the fortifications. After this they were once again troubled by raiders and by the activities of Gorgopas. They manned thirteen triremes against him and chose Eunomus as admiral to command them.

6 After Hierax had arrived at Rhodes the Spartans sent out Antalcidas as admiral. This was a step which, in their view, would have the additional advantage of giving very great pleasure to Tiribazus. When he arrived at Aegina Antalcidas took with him the fleet of Gorgopas and sailed to Ephesus. He then sent Gorgopas and his twelve ships back to Aegina, and put Nicolochus, his vice-admiral, in command of the rest. Nicolochus set out for Abydus, wishing to help the

*Xenophon here professes disrespect for the conventional matters of history. His aim is to display virtue, though typically he does not elucidate until §13.

people there, but turned aside to Tenedos where he laid the country waste and raised money. He then sailed to Abydus. Meanwhile the Athenian generals who were in Samothrace, 7 Thasos and other places in the area joined forces and set out to bring help to the people of Tenedos. Finding that Nicolochus had gone to Abydus they went there and, using the Chersonese as their base, blockaded him and his twenty-five ships with their own fleet of thirty-two ships.

Meanwhile, Gorgopas on his way back from Ephesus fell in with the Athenian squadron under Eunomus. For the moment he fled into Aegina, which he reached just before sunset. He then disembarked his men at once and gave them their evening meal. Eunomus waited for a short time and then 8 sailed on. As night was coming on, he showed the customary light and led the way himself so that the ships following him would not go astray. Gorgopas at once got his men aboard and came after him, following the light at a distance so as not to be seen or discovered in any way. Instead of shouting, the boatswains gave the time to the rowers by clapping stones together, and the rowers brought their oars in and out with the least possible noise. When Eunomus' ships were 9 close inshore near Cape Zoster in Attica, Gorgopas gave the trumpet signal for attack. On some of Eunomus' ships the men were just disembarking; others were still letting down their anchors, and others were still sailing into the anchorage. The action was fought by moonlight and Gorgopas captured four triremes which he took in tow and brought to Aegina. The rest of the Athenian ships fled into Piraeus.

It was after this that Chabrias was sailing out to Cyprus to 10 bring help to Evagoras. He had 800 peltasts with him and ten triremes, and in addition he got more ships and a force of hoplites from Athens. Now with the peltasts under his own command he made a night landing in Aegina and set an ambush in a valley beyond the Heracleium. At dawn, as had been arranged, the hoplites from Athens, under the command

of Demaenetus, arrived and marched inland to a point about
two miles beyond the Heracleium where the so-called Tripyr-
11 gia is. As soon as Gorgopas heard of this he marched out
against the invaders with the Aeginetans, the marines from
his ships and eight Spartans of the officer class who happened
to be with him. He also proclaimed that all free men from
the crews of his ships should join up with him, so that many
of these came too, each with whatever weapon he could lay
12 his hands on. When their vanguard had gone past the ambush, Chabrias' men came out of hiding and at once hurled
down javelins and stones on the enemy. The hoplites who
had landed from the ships came into action simultaneously.
The men in the van, who were not marching in any close
order, were quickly killed and among the dead were Gorgopas himself and the Spartans. As soon as these had fallen,
the rest also turned and broke. About one hundred and fifty
of the Aeginetans were killed, and at least 200 foreigners, a
figure which includes aliens resident in Aegina, and sailors
13 from the ships who had run up to join the force. After this
the Athenians sailed the sea just as in peacetime. For the
Spartan sailors refused to row for Eteonicus in spite of his
attempts at compulsion, since he was not giving them their
pay.

After this the Spartans again sent out Teleutias to take over
the command of this fleet,* and the sailors were delighted to
see him arrive. He called an assembly of them and there
14 made the following speech: 'Comrades in arms, I have not
brought any money with me here. But with the help of

*The text is dubitable and it is sensible to avoid the translation
'admiral'. But if Xenophon meant by the word *nauarchos* 'admiral',
he was using it inexactly, for the office could be held once only
(II.1.7); the only possible exception is Pollis (V.4.61), which is the
name of an admiral in the 390s (*Hell. Oxy.* 19.1), but there may have
been two admirals of the same name, separated by nearly a generation.
Cf. nn. at V.1.3 and VI.2.4 for Xenophon's lack of interest in a careful
framework of admirals.

God and if you all do your part, I shall try to see that you get all the supplies that it is possible to get. You know well that when I am in command of you it is for you, your lives and safety, that I pray just as much as for myself. As for food and drink, you may be surprised if I tell you that I would rather see you well supplied than myself. Nevertheless, I swear that I would choose to go without food for two days myself rather than have you go without food for one day. And just as in the old days my door, as you all know, was always open for anyone who wanted to come in and ask me for anything, so it will be open now. So when you have all 15 the provisions which you could ask for, then you will see me living pretty well too; but if you see me putting up with extremes of cold and heat and with lack of sleep, then you can expect that you, too, will be enduring the same things. And I do not ask you to do these things just because they are unpleasant but only so that by means of them you may get hold of something good. Think, comrades, of our city. 16 Think of Sparta. She has the name of a happy prosperous place; but you can be sure that honour and prosperity did not come to her through idleness. No, it was because she was willing to suffer hardship and willing to face danger whenever necessary. You too, as I know very well, used to show yourselves good men. Now I want you to show yourselves better still. In this way we shall be happy to suffer hardships together, and happy to share all together in the good things that are coming. And what can make one happier than this – 17 not to have to curry favour from anyone, Greek or foreign, in order to get our pay, but to be strong enough to get our own supplies for ourselves and to get them from the most honourable source? You can be sure of this – in time of war when one gets all one needs from the enemy, one will not only be feeding oneself but also winning fame among all men.'*

*This speech serves to show why Teleutias was commended at

18   When he had made this speech, they all shouted out, telling him to give them any orders necessary and they would
obey them. He, as it happened, had just finished sacrificing.
'Well, my friends,' he said, 'go off now and have your evening meal, just as you were going to do. I would then like you
to get ready food for yourselves for one day. Then come
quickly to the ships so that we may sail where God wants
us to go, and may get there at the right time.'

19   When they arrived, he got them aboard the ships, and
sailed by night into the harbour of Athens, giving the men
periods of rest and relaxation between the spells of rowing.
People may think that it was sheer madness on his part to
sail with twelve triremes against an enemy with huge naval
resources, but if anyone does think like this, he should con-
20   sider the factors with which Teleutias was reckoning. He
considered that the Athenians, now that Gorgopas was dead,
were taking fewer precautions than usual about their harbour; and even if there were triremes lying at anchor there,
he thought that it would be safer to sail against twenty of
them in the harbour at Athens than against ten of them anywhere else. He knew that when they were on active service
the sailors would be quartered aboard their ships, but when
they were at Athens the captains would be sleeping in their
own houses and the sailors would be quartered one in one
21   place, one in another. He was bearing all this in mind when
he sailed on this venture.

Now, when they were rather less than a mile from the har-

V.1.4. It was not just his concern for his men's welfare, but perhaps
too his laudable Panhellenist sentiments, so reminiscent of Callicratidas' in I.6.7. By implication Teleutias sneers at Antalcidas begging
money from Persia and promises to provide by plundering the enemy
(the true Spartan way, as the Panhellenist Cimon had long ago remarked – Plut. *Cimon* 14.4), a promise he proceeded to redeem by
raiding the Piraeus (§18–24). Teleutias echoed the sentiments of his
step-brother, Agesilaus, and his encomiast, Xenophon. Cf. Cawkwell,
Classical Quarterly, 26, 1976, pp. 66–71.

bour, he stayed quietly where he was and rested his men. At the first sign of dawn he led the way forward. His instructions were that they were not to sink or damage any merchant vessel with their own ships, but they were to try to disable any trireme which they saw lying at anchor; they were also to take in tow merchant ships which were loaded, and to board, wherever possible, the larger ones and carry off the people on board. In fact, some of his men actually jumped ashore at the Exhibition wharf, seized hold of merchants and shipowners and carried them off. Teleutias, then, had done 22 what he meant to do. As for the Athenians, some, hearing the noise, ran from indoors into the streets to find out what the shouting was about; others, who were out of doors, ran to their homes to get their arms, and others to the city to report the news. And then the whole body of Athenians, cavalry and hoplites, came to the rescue, thinking that Piraeus had been captured. Meanwhile Teleutias was sending the 23 captured merchant ships to Aegina. He had instructed three or four of his triremes to escort them there, and with the rest he sailed along the coast of Attica. As he was sailing out of the harbour he was also able to capture numbers of fishing craft and ferry-boats full of people coming in from the islands. When he reached Sunium he also captured some trading vessels, some carrying corn and others various kinds of merchandise. After doing all this he sailed back to Aegina. 24 Here he sold the booty and gave his men a month's pay in advance. And so he went on making voyages in these waters and capturing whatever he could. In this way he kept his ships fully manned and his sailors ready and glad to obey his orders.

Now Antalcidas came back to the coast with Tiribazus. He 25 had succeeded in coming to an arrangement by which the King would join in the war on the side of Sparta, unless the Athenians and their allies would accept the peace which he, the King, was dictating. When Antalcidas heard that

Nicolochus and his fleet were being blockaded at Abydus
by Iphicrates and Diotimus, he marched to Abydus. Here he
took over the fleet and sailed out of the harbour by night
after spreading the report that he had been sent for by the
people of Calchedon. In fact, he came to anchor at Percote
26 and stayed there without making any move. Meanwhile, the
Athenians under Demaenetus, Dionysius, Leontichus and
Phanias heard that he had set sail and went after him in the
direction of Proconnesus. Antalcidas waited until they had
sailed past him and then turned about and came back to
Abydus. He had heard that Polyxenus was coming with the
ships, twenty of them, from Syracuse and Italy, and he
wanted to have this force with him as well. Soon afterwards,
however, Thrasybulus, from the deme of Collytus, came
sailing in from Thrace with eight ships, wishing to join up
27 with the rest of the Athenian fleet. As soon as Antalcidas received the information from his scouts that eight triremes
were sailing in, he ordered the crews of his twelve fastest
ships to go aboard, and told the captains, if they were short
of men, to make up the number from the crews of the ships
left behind. He kept these ships as far as possible out of sight
and waited for Thrasybulus. Then, when the Athenian ships
were sailing past, he set out in pursuit and the Athenians, as
soon as they saw him, tried to get away. He quickly overhauled the slowest sailors of the Athenian ships with his own
fastest ships, but he told his leading formation not to attack
the enemy ships that were falling behind, and continued to go
after the ones in front. When he had captured them, the other
Athenian ships in the rear, seeing that their leading ships were
being captured, lost all heart for action and were themselves
captured even by Antalcidas' slower ships. So in the end all
eight were taken.

28   His fleet was now increased by the twenty ships which
came from Syracuse; others came from the part of Ionia
under the authority of Tiribazus; and more still had been

manned from the country controlled by Ariobarzanes. For Antalcidas was an old friend of Ariobarzanes and Pharnabazus had already gone away to the interior. He had been called to the King's court, for it was at this time that he married the King's daughter. So Antalcidas now had a fleet of more than eighty ships and controlled the sea. He was able, too, to prevent the ships from the Pontus from sailing to Athens; instead, he forced them to sail to harbours in territory allied to Sparta.

As for the Athenians, they were now very anxious indeed to make peace. They could see the size of the enemy's fleet and they feared that, now that the King had become an ally of the Spartans, they might be overwhelmed as they had been before. They were also suffering privation because of the raiders based on Aegina. The Spartans, too, were tired of the war. They had to keep a garrison of one regiment at Lechaeum and another one at Orchomenus; they had to keep an eye on all their allies in order to prevent the ones they trusted from being destroyed by the enemy, and the ones they distrusted from revolting; and there was continual action, going now one way and now another, round Corinth. Even the Argives were now willing to make peace. They knew that the Spartans were mobilizing an army against them, and they were also aware that the pretext of the sacred months was no longer going to be of any use to them. The result was that when Tiribazus called a meeting of all who wished to subscribe to the peace terms which he was bringing to them from the King, all parties came to the meeting with alacrity. When they were assembled, Tiribazus showed them the King's seal on the document and then read out its contents, which were as follows: 'I, King Artaxerxes, regard the following arrangements as just: 1. The cities in Asia and, among the islands, Clazomenae and Cyprus should belong to me. 2. The other Greek cities, big and small, should be left to govern themselves, except for Lemnus, Imbros and Scyros, which should belong to Athens, as in the past. And if either of the two parties refuses to accept peace on these terms, I, together with those who will accept this peace, will make war on that party both by land and by sea, with ships and with money.'

32 After hearing this pronouncement the ambassadors from the various states referred the matter back to their governments. All the others swore that they would abide by these conditions,* but the Thebans claimed that they should take the oath in the name of all the Boeotians. Agesilaus, however, refused to accept their oaths as valid unless they swore that, as was written in the document from the King, all cities, big and small, should be self-governing. The Thebans replied that they had not received instructions to this effect. 'Then go back again,' said Agesilaus, 'and ask. And you can tell your government this too – that unless they do as I have said, they will not be included in the peace.'

33 The Theban ambassadors then went away. Agesilaus, however, hating the Thebans as he did, wasted no time. He won over the ephors to his way of thinking and then made the sacrifices preparatory to a campaign. The offerings at the frontier turned out well and, on reaching Tegea, he sent horsemen round the country to hurry on the mobilization of the Perioeci, and also sent Spartan officers to the various allied cities. But before he had moved on from Tegea the Thebans arrived and said that they would allow the cities to be self-

* Xenophon presumes that his readers will know that there was a Congress in Sparta, as the narrative of §33 implies, nor does he bother to transcribe or even describe the precise terms of the King's Peace which were probably detailed (cf. Isocrates 4.120). By chance we learn from an inscription (Tod, G.H.I., no. 118) that the King of Persia was involved in the exchange of oaths. Onlywhen the accursed Thebans took over Sparta's role are such discreditable facts made explicit (cf. VII.1.39 and nn. at VI.2.1 and VI.3.18). For the sanctions clause of the Peace, cf. n. at V.2.11. So Xenophon avoids the obvious and the unmentionable.

governing. So the Spartans went back home, and the Thebans were forced to agree to the treaty, leaving the cities of Boeotia independent.

The Corinthians, however, still kept the Argive garrison 34 in their city. Agesilaus now announced his intentions here also. He would make war, he said, on the Corinthians, if they failed to send away the Argives, and on the Argives, if they did not leave Corinth. Both parties were frightened by this prospect, and so the Argives left Corinth, and Corinth once again became a separate independent state. Those who had taken part in the massacre themselves and those who shared the responsibility for it left the city of their own accord. The rest of the citizens were happy to receive back again those who had been exiles before.

When all this had been done and the cities had sworn to 35 abide by the terms dictated by the King, armies and fleets were alike demobilized. Thus after the war which followed the destruction of the walls at Athens there occurred this first peace * between Sparta on the one hand, and Athens and her allies on the other. In the actual fighting the Spartans had 36 just about held their own, but now, as a result of what is known as 'the Peace of Antalcidas', they appeared in a much more distinguished light. It was they who had been the chief supporters of the King's peace; by insisting on the independence of the cities, they had gained in Corinth an additional ally; they had attained what had long been an object of their policy by making the Boeotian cities independent of Thebes;

* The King's Peace was renewed in 375 B.C. (VI.2.1 and n.), and Xenophon seems to have been aware of this when he wrote these words. Some have postulated a break in composition at the end of Chapter 1 of Book V as if the Peace was a natural stopping place, but it was only so for as long as Spartan power was unchallenged, and from the Liberation of Thebes and the foundation of the Second Athenian Confederacy in 378 B.C. the King's Peace must have seemed to close a chapter but not to end a book. Writing after 375, Xenophon must have felt no temptation to stop with the events of 386.

and they had also, by threatening Argos with invasion unless she left Corinth alone, put a stop to the Argive plan of taking that city over.*

*Xenophon omits to remark on the effect of the Peace on Athens which was to put a stop to the vainglorious attempt of Thrasybulus and his successors to re-establish the Athenian Empire.

CHAPTER 2

Spartan intervention in Mantinea and Phlius (385–384 B.C.). Despatch
of a force to attack Olynthus and occupation of the Theban Cadmea
(382 B.C.). Campaign against Olynthus (382 B.C.).

THINGS, then, had gone just as the Spartans wanted and they 1
now turned their attention to those of their allies who had
been against them in the war or had been more inclined to
the side of their enemies. These, the Spartans decided, should
be punished or reorganized in such a way that disloyalty
would become impossible. First, they sent to the people of
Mantinea and ordered them to demolish their fortifications, *Mant*
saying that, unless this was done, they could not feel confident that Mantinea would not side with their enemies. They 2
pointed out that they had taken note of the fact that Mantinea had sent corn to the Argives when Sparta had been at
war with Argos; also that there had been times when the
Mantineans, under pretext of a sacred truce, had not served at
all in the Spartan armies, and other times when they had indeed taken their place in the army, but had served badly and
unwillingly.* They were also, said the Spartans, perfectly
conscious of the fact that the Mantineans were envious of
any successes which Sparta might have, but were delighted if
things went wrong for her. Then, too, it was being said that
this was the year when the Mantineans would be no longer
covered by the thirty years truce made after the battle of
Mantinea.† So when the Mantineans refused to tear down 3

* There is nothing in Xenophon's account of the Corinthian War
to explain these charges against Mantinea.

† The account of Thucydides (V.81.1) shows that the thirty years
truce between Sparta and Mantinea had expired before the King's
Peace. Xenophon has erred.

their fortifications, Sparta ordered mobilization against
them.

Agesilaus asked the authorities to excuse him from taking
command of the invading force, saying that Mantinea had
done much to help his father in the wars against the Messenians. It was Agesipolis, therefore, who took over this command, even though his own father was on very friendly terms
✓ indeed with the leaders of the democratic party in Mantinea.*

4   On entering Mantinean territory he first laid waste the
land.† Even then, however, they would not destroy their
fortifications, and so he dug a trench all round the city. Half
of his army did the digging, while the other half stayed under
arms in front of them as a protection. When the trench had
been finished, he went on without fear of interruption to
build a wall round the city. He found out, however, that,
since last year's harvest had been a good one, there was plenty
of corn inside the city, and it seemed to him that he was going to be up against difficulties if it became necessary to call
upon both Sparta and her allies to suffer the hardships of very
extended service abroad. So he dammed up the river, a very
5 large one, which flows through the city. Once the outflow
of the river had been stopped, the level of the water rose
above the foundations of the houses and above those of the
city wall. As the moisture began to affect the lower layers of
bricks, the upper ones also were weakened; first cracks began
to appear in the wall and then signs of collapse. The Mantineans tried for some time to prop it up with timbers and
did everything they could think of to prevent the tower from

* Xenophon hints that Agesilaus did not give his real reason for
avoiding the command. What that was, we are left to speculate.

† According to Diodorus (XV.5.5) the Mantineans had appealed to
Athens for help and been declined, and according to Pausanias
(IX.13.1) and Plutarch (*Pelopidas* 4) Epaminondas and Pelopidas
served in a Theban contingent sent to help the Spartans. Xenophon
cared for none of these things.

collapsing. But they could not keep pace with the effects of the water; they feared that if any section of the circuit of fortification were to collapse they would become prisoners of war, and so they said that they would agree to demolish their walls. But the Spartans now refused to make peace unless they also agreed to split up the population and live in separate villages. It seemed to the Mantineans that they had no choice, and so they agreed to this too. And now the pro- 6 Argive party and the leaders of the democratic party thought that they would be sure to be put to death. But the father of Agesipolis persuaded his son to guarantee that these men (there were sixty of them) should be allowed to leave the town in safety. And so from the city gates along both sides of the road Spartan troops stood with their spears watching these people coming out. They hated them, but still they were better able to keep their hands off them than were the members of the aristocratic party in Mantinea. I have recorded this incident as a fine example of good discipline.

After this the fortifications were demolished, and the Man- 7 tineans were split up into four separate villages just as they used to be in ancient times. They did not like it at first, since they had to pull down the houses which they had and build new ones. Owners of landed property, however, were pleased with what had happened. They now lived nearer to their estates, which were in the neighbourhood of the villages, and they had also got rid of all the trouble they had had with the demagogues since their government was now run on aristocratic lines. In future the Spartans sent to them not just one mobilization officer but one for each village, and they came in from their villages to join the army much more willingly now than they did when they were under a democracy. So ended this campaign at Mantinea. It was a campaign which taught people at least one thing, and that is not to let a river run through the walls of one's city.*

*In this paragraph Xenophon expounds the secret of Spartan

8   The exiles from Phlius had observed that the Spartans were looking into the way in which their various allies had behaved towards them during the war, and now, thinking that this was the right moment for them, came to Sparta and put forward their case. They pointed out that so long as they had been at home in Phlius the city had welcomed the Spartans inside its walls and its forces had joined in all expeditions made under Spartan leadership; but that after they had been driven into exile the people of Phlius had refused to follow Spartan leaders anywhere and, while they would receive everyone else, would not receive Spartans inside their walls.

9 After they had listened to the exiles, the ephors came to the conclusion that this was something which should be dealt with. So they sent to Phlius and said that the exiles were friends of Sparta and had been unjustly driven out. They added that in their view what should be done was that the exiles should be recalled, but should be recalled not as a result of compulsion but with the consent of their own people. The people of Phlius, when they received this message, were afraid that, supposing the Spartans did march against them, there would be people in Phlius quite prepared to let the enemy inside the city. For there were not only a number of relatives of the exiles inside the city and others who, for one reason or another, were friends of theirs but also, as one will find in most cities, there was a party which wanted a change

10 of government and was in favour of recalling the exiles. Such considerations as these were enough to make the people of Phlius apprehensive; they therefore voted that the exiles

---

power in the Peloponnese, *viz.* prevention of urbanization, and support of and from the landed aristocracy, and his final remark, which is a sour comment on the Mantineans' failure to apprehend the real point of it all, suggests that this chapter was written after the rebuilding of Mantinea after the battle of Leuctra (VI.5.3 ff.). Cf. nn. at VII.4.35 and 5.1 for Xenophon's attitude towards the Spartan order in the Peloponnese.

should be recalled and that all property that had been un-
questionably theirs should be given back to them, and that
those who had bought any of this property should be com-
pensated from public funds; all cases where there was any
dispute between present and past owners should be settled in
the courts. In this way and at this time the question of the
exiles from Phlius was dealt with.

Ambassadors now came to Sparta from Acanthus and 11
Apollonia.* These are the biggest cities in the neighbourhood
of Olynthus. The ephors were informed of the purpose of
this embassy and introduced the ambassadors to an assembly
of the Spartans and their allies. Cligenes from Acanthus then 12
made the following speech: 'Spartans and representatives of
the allies, there is a very dangerous situation arising in Greece
and we do not think that you have noticed it. Now most of
you, we assume, are aware that Olynthus is the biggest city
in the Thracian area. The Olynthians induced other cities to
combine with them on the basis of one system of laws and a
common citizenship; they then went on to take over some
of the larger cities. Their next objective was the liberation of
the cities of Macedonia from the Macedonian king, Amyntas, and as soon as the nearest cities had come over to them 13
they were quick to take the next step and proceed against
the more distant and the larger ones. When we left they were
already in control of a large number of Macedonian cities,
and among them is Pella, the biggest of them all. We discovered also that Amyntas was abandoning his cities and
indeed had been already virtually driven out of the whole of

*Xenophon's inadequate account of the King's Peace (cf. n. at
V.1.32) has left us with the task of guessing the precise terms of the
sanctions clause of the Peace (which is to be presumed from the re-
newal of 372–1, etc. – cf. nn. at VI.2.1 and VI.3.18). The narrative of
the Acanthian appeal and the various expeditions against Olynthus
are almost all that we have to go on. Cf. Cawkwell, *Classical Quarterly*,
23, 1973, p. 52 f. Characteristically, Xenophon does not make
explicit the legal reason for the Acanthian appeal to Sparta.

Macedonia.* And now the Olynthians have sent to us and
to the people of Apollonia. They say that unless we come
and take part in the campaign, they will march against us.

14 'Now, Spartans, what we want to do is to keep the constitution we have always had and to live independently in our
own cities. But unless we get help, we shall be forced to join
the Olynthian league. Let us point out that now already they
have at least 800† hoplites and a much greater number of
peltasts; and, if we join them, they will have more than 1,000
15 cavalry. When we left there were ambassadors from Athens
and Thebes already there, and according to our information
the Olynthians have voted to send ambassadors of their own
to these states in order to negotiate an alliance. Now suppose
that all the resources of Olynthus were added to the existing
power of Athens and Thebes; you will recognize, I think,
that the situation then would be no longer an easy one for
you to handle. Then, too, Potidaea on the isthmus of Pallene
is controlled by Olynthus; you can be sure that all the other
cities on that stretch of land will come under the same control. That these cities are already terrified can be proved by
the fact that in spite of their hatred for Olynthus they did not

* In Diodorus' account of this affair (XV.19) the appeal to Sparta
is made by Amyntas of Macedon and the Acanthians do not come
into it. There were thus two views. Amyntas was not, as far as we
know, a party to the King's Peace (cf. Aelius Aristides *Panathenaicus*
172), and Sparta had, legally speaking, no business supporting him
against Olynthus which was a party. The other view was that the
autonomy of Acanthus and Apollonia, both parties to the Peace, was
threatened and Sparta was obliged to help. Athens began by taking
the Diodoran view; Thebes persisted in it to the point of negotiations for an alliance with Olynthus (V.2.15, 34) and making a proclamation which implied that Sparta was in the wrong (V.2.27).
Xenophon displays no doubts about the legality of the Spartan action.
To judge by the political allegiance of the initial commanders, it was
Agesilaus who was responsible.

†This figure seems much too small, and corruption in the manu-
script is suspected.

dare to send ambassadors with us to explain their feelings to
you. And here is another point for you to consider: after all 16
the trouble you have taken to see that Boeotia does not become united, does it make sense for you to turn a blind eye
on this much greater concentration of power* which is taking place and growing strong not only on land but also on
the <u>sea</u>? For what is there to prevent its growth? There is
plenty of timber for shipbuilding on the spot; there are revenues coming in from numbers of ports and trading posts;
and there is no shortage of manpower since there is no shortage of food. <u>And then they have as neighbours the Thracian</u> 17
<u>tribes who are not under a king.</u> These Thracians are already
making diplomatic advances to them; if they came under
their control, here would be another great accession of power
to them. And with the Thracians on their side, the next allur-
ing prospect would be the goldmines of Mount Pangaeum.
And you can be sure that not one of the things we have been
saying here has not been said a thousand times over among
the people of Olynthus. Their pride and self-confidence are 18
quite indescribable. Indeed, it seems that heaven has so ordered things among men that these qualities must increase
with the increase of power.

'Spartans and allies, we have given you our account of
conditions in this area. Now it is for you to make up your
minds whether they are such as to require intervention. And
you should take note of this point too. This power which we
have described as great is still capable of being challenged.
The cities which have been forced against their will to share
a common citizenship with Olynthus will soon revolt if they
see that there is any opposition. But this league may not be so 19

---

* The Chalcidic League, formed in 432 and dissolved in theory in
421, must have been dissolved in fact by the King's Peace, Olynthians
having fought against Sparta in the Corinthian War (Isaeus V.46).
But Xenophon neglects to fill in any of the historical background to
the debate.

easy to dissolve once the various peoples have become closely bound to each other by intermarriage and by property relationships (which have been already voted) and once they recognize that it pays to be on the side of the winner – as in the case of the Arcadians who, when they go on a campaign with you, keep their own property safe and also have the opportunity of taking the property of others.'

20   After this speech the Spartans invited their allies to speak, and asked them to give what each considered to be the best advice for the Peloponnese as a whole and for the allies themselves. A number of speeches were then made – and particularly by those who wanted to say what the Spartans wanted to hear – in favour of raising an army, and it was decided that each state should send its contingent for a total force of

21   10,000 men. It was also agreed after discussion that any state which so wished should be allowed to send money instead of men at the rate of three Aeginetan obols for each man, and that for states which normally sent cavalry the rate for each cavalryman should be a sum equivalent to the pay of four

22   hoplites; and if any state failed to send its proper contingent, the Spartans should be empowered to fine that state two drachmas a day for each man.

23   When these decisions had been made, the delegates from Acanthus rose up to speak again and pointed out that, while the proposals just passed were excellent in themselves, they could not be carried into effect quickly. They therefore recommended that while the main army was assembling, a commander should be sent out as quickly as possible, with a force from Sparta of such a size as would be compatible with setting out at short notice, and with contingents from other states. If this was done, they said, the cities which had not yet gone over to Olynthus would remain firm, and the ones which had been forced into alliance would become less de-

24   pendable allies. This proposal also was approved. The Spartans sent out Eudamidas as commander with a force of about

~~two thousand men. This force was made up of~~ emancipated
~~helots, Perioeci and Sciritans.~~

Before setting out Eudamidas asked the ephors to allow his
brother Phoebidas to see to the calling up of the troops which
had been allotted to him and which he had left behind, and
then to lead them out to him.* He himself went on to Thrace.
He sent garrisons to those cities which asked for them, and he
won over Potidaea. This city came over to him voluntarily,
although it was already an ally of the Olynthians. He made it
his base, and carried out from there such operations as can be
carried out by a force inferior to that of the enemy.

By now Phoebidas had got together the rest of Eudamidas' 25
troops and was setting out with them. When they reached
Thebes, they camped outside the city, near the gymnasium.
In Thebes two parties were struggling for power, and it so
happened that among the chief magistrates of Thebes were
two men, Ismenias and Leontiades, each of whom hated the
other and each of whom led one of the two political clubs.
Ismenias, because of the hatred he felt for Sparta, never even
went near Phoebidas. Leontiades, on the other hand, did all
he could to make himself agreeable and, when he had estab- 26
lished friendly relationships, spoke to him as follows: 'Phoebidas, today you have an opportunity to do a very great
service to your country. If you follow me with your hoplites,
I shall lead you into the Acropolis. Once this is done, you
may consider that Thebes will be entirely under the control
of Sparta and of us who are your friends. Now, as you can 27
see, it has been publicly proclaimed that no Theban citizen
is to join you in the expedition against Olynthus; but if you

*Xenophon's picture of an advance force split in two is curious.
If Eudamidas took two thousand with him, and Teleutias was to
take ten thousand (§§20, 37), the role of Phoebidas is surprising. In
Diodorus (XV.19.3 and 20.3) things are differently arranged, and
there can be no confidence that Xenophon has not got it all somewhat
awry.

join us in carrying out our plan, we will immediately supply you with large forces both of hoplites and of cavalry. In this way, you will bring a large army with you when you join your brother, and, while he is still waiting to subdue Olynthus, you will already have subdued Thebes, a very much greater city than Olynthus.'

28 These words had an intoxicating effect on Phoebidas who was a man with such a passion for doing something distinguished that he would prefer it to life itself. He was not, however, thought to be a reasonable man or of really good judgement.* When he had agreed to the plan, Leontiades told him to start marching away, just as he had been prepared to do. 'At the right time,' said Leontiades, 'I will come to you and then show you the way myself.'

29 On this day, because the women were celebrating the Thesmophoria in the Cadmea, the Council was meeting in the portico in the market place; since it was summer and midday, the streets were empty, and it was at this point that Leontiades rode out to Phoebidas, got him to turn back and led him straight to the Acropolis. After seeing Phoebidas and his troops established there, he gave him the key of the gates and told him not to let anyone inside the Acropolis unless he himself gave the order. He then went straight to the meeting 30 of the Council and, when he had arrived, made the following speech: 'My friends, the Spartans are now in control of the Acropolis, but there is no reason to be dismayed about that. They declare that they have come here with no hostile intentions against anyone except those who are wanting to start a war. Now the law directs that a chief magistrate may arrest any man guilty of doing things which deserve the death penalty. I therefore arrest this man Ismenias on the charge that he is a war-monger. And I order the captains and

*This sentence is Xenophon's oblique rebuttal of the charge that Phoebidas had been put up by Agesilaus to the seizure of the Cadmea (cf. Diod. XV.20.2, Plut. *Agesilaus* 24).

those who have been detailed to help them to step forward now, to seize this man and to take him where you have been instructed to take him.'

Those, naturally, who were in the plot were present and 31 did what they were told. They all joined in arresting Ismenias, while those who knew nothing of what was afoot and were in the opposite party to that of Leontiades either fled from the city at once in terror for their lives, or for the time being retired to their homes. But when they heard that Ismenias was imprisoned in the Cadmea, then the whole party of Androclidas and Ismenias, about three hundred of them altogether, retired to Athens.

The Thebans now chose another chief magistrate to take 32 the place of Ismenias, and directly after this Leontiades set out for Sparta. Here he found that the ephors and most of the citizens were displeased with Phoebidas because he had carried out this operation without any authorization from the state. Agesilaus, however, expressed himself as follows: 'If the action of Phoebidas is harmful to Sparta, then he deserves to be punished. If, on the other hand, it will do Sparta good, we should remember our established rule that in such cases a man may use his own initiative. The point to be examined, therefore, is simply this: has this action been good or bad for Sparta?' *

Leontiades then came before the assembly and made the 33 following speech: 'Spartans, the hostility of the Thebans to you was something which you yourselves, before this recent action had taken place, used to talk about constantly. You saw that they were invariably friends to your enemies and enemies to your friends. You remember how they refused to march with you against the Athenian democratic government

* Xenophon neglects to notice that Phoebidas was fined, nor in §35 does he deny or give currency to the story that it was Agesilaus who persuaded the Spartans to maintain the occupation of the Cadmea (Diod. XV.20.2, Plut. *Agesilaus* 23) – an account in two senses partial.

in Piraeus, who were bitter enemies of yours, and how, on the other hand, they marched themselves against the Phocians, because they saw that you were friendly to them.

34 And now in the full knowledge that you were making war on the Olynthians, Thebes was arranging an alliance with Olynthus. In the past you always had to keep an eye on Thebes and were always waiting to hear the news that she was forcing the rest of Boeotia into subjection. But now, after this action which we have carried out, you need have no more fear in that quarter. All you will have to do is to send a short message and you will get from Thebes all the help you want, that is if you show the same consideration for us as we have shown for you.'

35 After hearing this the Spartans decided that, since the Acropolis had been seized, they would maintain a garrison there and that they would put Ismenias on trial. As judges they sent out three men from Sparta and one from each of the allied states, large and small. No charges were made until the court was actually in session. They then accused Ismenias of having worked in the interest of foreigners, of having made friends with the Persian satrap against the interests of Greece, of having taken money from the king, and of being chiefly responsible, with Androclidas, for all the disorders which had

36 taken place in Greece. Ismenias defended himself against all these charges, but failed to convince the court that he had not been very deeply implicated in treasonable activities. He was therefore condemned and put to death. Leontiades and his party now held power in Thebes and gave the Spartans even more help than they were asked to give.

37 After all this the Spartans were much more enthusiastic about the joint expeditionary force against Olynthus. They sent out Teleutias as governor, provided their own full contingent of the total army of 10,000, and sent around dispatches to the allied states instructing them in accordance with the decision of the allies to march with Teleutias. All were glad to be serving under Teleutias, a man known for

his gracious behaviour to his subordinates, and in particular the Thebans, since Teleutias was a brother of Agesilaus, were glad to join him with both hoplites and cavalry.

He did not hurry on the march, taking care to see that no 38 harm was done by his troops on the way to any friends of Sparta and also that he should get together as large a force as possible. He also sent messengers on ahead to Amyntas asking him, if he really wanted to regain his power, to hire mercenaries and to distribute money to the kings in the area so as to induce them to become his allies. He sent to Derdas too, the ruler of Elimia, pointing out that the Olynthians had already overthrown the greater power of Macedonia and were not likely to leave the lesser power alone unless someone put a stop to their insolent aggressiveness. These mea- 39 sures resulted in his having a very large army indeed by the time he reached the country of his allies. He entered Potidaea, and from there set out in order of battle into the enemy's country. On the way to Olynthus he refrained from burning the crops and cutting down the trees, his idea being that either of these actions would slow down his march both on the way there and on the way back. The right thing to do, he considered, was to wait until he was withdrawing and then to cut down the trees as obstacles in the way of any force that might be coming after him.

He halted the army about a mile and a half from the city 40 and himself took command of the left wing. In this way he would advance in the direction of the gates from which the enemy came out; the rest of the line, made up of the forces of the allies, stretched away to the right. Also on the right he posted the cavalry from Laconia and Thebes and all the Macedonian cavalry who were there; he kept by him Derdas and his cavalry, about four hundred in number; this was a force of which he thought highly, and also he wanted to do a favour to Derdas so that he should be glad that he had come.

After the enemy had come out and formed up in line in 41

front of the city wall, their cavalry in massed formation charged down on the Laconians and Boeotians. They struck Polycharmus, the Spartan cavalry commander, down from his horse and covered him with wounds as he lay on the ground; they killed others, and in the end forced the cavalry on the right wing to turn and run. As the cavalry fled, the infantry on their left began to give way. Indeed, the whole army might well have been defeated if Derdas and his force had not charged directly at the gates of Olynthus. At the same time Teleutias advanced with his own troops in order

42 of battle. Seeing this, the Olynthian cavalry feared that they might be cut off from the gates; they turned round and retreated as fast as they could, and many of them were killed by Derdas as they rode past him. The Olynthian infantry also retreated to the city, but, since the wall was near, not many of them were killed.

43 After Teleutias had won this victory, he set up a trophy and only then, as he was withdrawing, began to cut down the trees. He went on with the campaign throughout the summer and then dismissed the Macedonian army and Derdas' cavalry. The Olynthians, however, kept on making raids on cities which were allied with Sparta and succeeded in carrying off booty and killing men.

CHAPTER 3

Death of Teleutias at Olynthus. Sieges of Phlius and Olynthus

AT the very beginning of the following spring the Olynthian 1
cavalry, about six hundred in number, made a raid into the
territory of Apollonia. Appearing about midday, they scattered over the country and engaged in pillage. It so happened
that on this same day Derdas had arrived with his own cavalry and was having his morning meal in Apollonia. When he
saw the raiders he made no immediate move, but saw that
his horses were saddled and bridled and that their riders were
fully armed. The Olynthians now came riding up insolently
right into the suburbs and even up to the city gates and it
was at just this moment that Derdas with his men in close
battle order charged out on them. As soon as they saw him, 2
the Olynthians turned and ran, and he, once they were in
flight, did not stop pursuing them and cutting them down
for twelve miles until he had driven them right up to the
wall of Olynthus. It was said that Derdas killed about eighty
cavalrymen in this action. From then on the enemy were
more inclined to keep inside their fortifications and only cultivated a very small proportion of their land.

Later on, however, there was an occasion when Teleutias 3
had marched up to the city of Olynthus so as to destroy any
trees or any piece of cultivated ground belonging to the enemy that might have been overlooked. While he was on his
way the Olynthian cavalry rode out quite calmly, crossed the
river that flows past Olynthus, and kept on their way towards the army facing them. When Teleutias saw them he
was enraged at their audacity and at once ordered Tlemonidas, the commander of the peltasts, to charge them at the
double. The Olynthians, when they saw the peltasts charging 4

down on them, calmly retired and went back across the river.
The peltasts, however, came after them in a mood of over-
confidence, following them across the river as though they
were pursuing troops in full flight. As for the Olynthian
cavalry, they turned about and made their charge at the
exact moment when it seemed to them that the peltasts who
had crossed the river would still be easy to deal with, and there
they killed Tlemonidas himself and more than a hundred
5 of his men. When Teleutias saw what was going on he was
infuriated. Snatching up his arms he led the hoplites straight
into battle and told the peltasts and the cavalry to pursue the
enemy and to go on pursuing him. Now it has often happened before that, when a pursuit is pressed too close to a city
wall, the pursuers have a hard time getting back again. So
on this occasion when the soldiers became exposed to the
fire of missiles from the towers, they were forced to retire
in a disorderly manner, all the time guarding themselves
6 from the missiles. It was at this moment that the Olynthians
charged out with their cavalry and with their peltasts in
close support; in the end their hoplites also charged out and
fell on the already broken Spartan line. There Teleutias fell
fighting. As soon as this had happened the troops around him
gave way at once; soon there was no one to stand his ground
and the whole army was in flight, some for Spartolus, some
for Acanthus, some for Apollonia and the majority for
Potidaea. So they fled in all directions and the enemy pursued them as they fled, killing very great numbers of men
and putting an end to this army as an effective force.
7   In my opinion, however, disasters such as these teach men
this lesson with regard to anger: one ought not to punish even
a slave in anger; for masters who have lost their tempers often
do more harm to themselves than they inflict; but in dealing
with enemies it is utterly and entirely wrong to launch an
attack under the influence of anger and without deliberation.
Anger does not look ahead, whereas deliberation is just as

concerned with avoiding harm oneself as with inflicting it on the enemy.*

When the Spartans heard what had happened they decided, 8 after they had discussed the matter, that a large force ought to be sent out so as to put an end to the pride of the victors and to make sure that all the work done already should not be wasted. Once the decision was made they sent out King Agesipolis as commander and gave him, as they had given Agesilaus when he was in Asia, a staff of thirty Spartans of the officer class. Many of the better class Perioeci, too, went 9 with him as volunteers; also aliens belonging to the so-called 'Spartan-trained'; also bastard sons of Spartan officers, a very fine-looking body of men and one well acquainted with the ideals of the city.† There were also volunteer contingents from the allied states, and cavalry from Thessaly who wanted to become known to Agesipolis. Amyntas, too, and Derdas joined in with even greater enthusiasm than before. So Agesipolis set out against Olynthus.

The people of Phlius had been specially commended by 10 Agesipolis for sending him a large sum of money for the expedition and for sending it so promptly. It now occurred to them that, with Agesipolis abroad, Agesilaus would not march against them; it could never happen, they thought, that both Spartan kings would be out of Sparta at the same time. They therefore brazenly refused to restore any of their rights to the men who had come back from exile. The exiles claimed that all disputed matters should be dealt with by an impartial court, but the Phliasians forced them to put their cases before courts inside the city and paid no attention to them when they pointed out that there could be no fair trial

---

*A good instance of Xenophon's moralizing method. Cf. VII.2.1 and n.

†The scantiness of information elsewhere than in Xenophon concerning the complexity of the Spartan social system attests his intimacy with the state. Cf. n. at III.3.6.

11 where the criminals constituted the jury. As a result of this, however, not only did the restored exiles come to Sparta to complain of the behaviour of their people but others also came with them from Phlius and said that even among the Phliasians themselves there were many who thought that the exiles were being badly treated. This angered the government at Phlius, and they imposed a fine on all who had gone 12 to Sparta without being authorized by the state. Those who had been fined were now frightened to go back. They remained in Sparta and expressed their views, which were as follows: 'These people who are acting so high-handedly are the people who exiled us and who shut their city against you; they bought up our property and are illegally refusing to give it back; they have now managed to get a fine imposed on us for coming to Sparta, and their aim is that no one in the future will dare to come here to tell you what is going on in our country.'

13   It seemed to the ephors that the Phliasians were indeed behaving outrageously and they ordered mobilization. Agesilaus was far from displeased at this decision, for the friends of his father Archidamus were in the party of Podanemus, now among the restored exiles, and his own friends were 14 in the party of Procles, the son of Hipponicus. As soon as the sacrifices at the frontier had turned out satisfactorily he set out with no delay on the march. A number of embassies came to meet him and offered him money not to invade. He replied: 'The object of this expedition is not to do harm but 15 to do good to those who have been harmed.' In the end they said that they would do anything he asked, only they begged him not to invade. He told them again that he could not trust their promises since they had broken their word once before; what was required was some action upon which he could rely. 'What sort of action have you in mind?' they asked, and he replied: 'The same as before. And when you did that you suffered no harm from us.' By this he meant the

handing over of their Acropolis, and as they refused to do 16
this, he invaded their country, quickly built a wall round
their city and kept it under siege.

There were a number of Spartans who complained that for
the sake of a few individuals they were making themselves
hated by a city of more than 5,000 men. Indeed, the Phliasians, just in order to stress this fact, were in the habit of
holding their assemblies in a place where they would be
visible to the army outside. Agesilaus, however, found a
means of dealing with this. He told the exiles that whenever 17
they were visited by any of their friends or relations from
the city they should form special messes of their own with
any of these people who were willing to join in the army
training; they should give them money for their needs,
should see to it that they were all provided with arms and
not hesitate to borrow money for all this. The exiles followed
these instructions and in the end could produce a body of
more than 1,000 men, all in excellent physical condition, well
trained and magnificently armed. So finally, the Spartans
said that these were just the sort of comrades-in-arms whom
they wanted to have.*

While Agesilaus was occupied with this situation, Agesi- 18
polis had marched straight on from Macedonia and halted
near Olynthus. Then, since no one came out against him, he
laid waste any parts of the country which had so far been
untouched, and went on to the territory of cities allied with
Olynthus, destroying their crops. In the case of Torone he
made an attack on the city and took it by storm. In the middle 19
of these operations, at the height of summer, he fell ill with
a burning fever. Before then he had seen the shrine of

*Xenophon here comes near to making explicit the difference
between Agesilaus and his opponents, led by the other royal family,
about how Sparta should keep control of places remote from herself
(Cf. Cawkwell, *Classical Quarterly*, 26, 1976, pp. 71–82). Xenophon
makes Agesilaus win the day here.

Dionysus at Aphytis and now he felt a longing for its shady
arbours and cool limpid waters. So he was carried there still
living, but on the seventh day from the beginning of his illness
he died outside the sanctuary. His body was placed in honey
and taken back to Sparta, where it was given a royal burial.

20   One might have expected that Agesilaus, when he heard
this news, would have been pleased, as one is at the death of a
rival, but in fact he wept and mourned for the loss of a com-
rade; for, of course, the Spartan kings mess together when
they are at Sparta. And in all their conversations about their
young days, hunting, horsemanship or love affairs, Agesipolis
was excellent company for Agesilaus. He also treated him,
as the elder man, with becoming respect in all relations which
arose out of their shared quarters. To take the place of Agesipolis the Spartans sent out Polybiades as supreme commander
at Olynthus.

21   Agesilaus meanwhile had already been in front of Phlius
longer than the time for which it was assumed that the enemy's food supply would last. This is an example of what a
difference it makes to be able to control one's appetite; for
the Phliasians had voted that only half the normal corn ration
should be issued, and had carried out this decision, with the
result that they held out under siege for twice the time that
22   might have been expected. There was a man called Delphion,
too, who is a good example of how very much more effective daring can be than cowardice. He was regarded as a
brilliant personality and he gathered round him 300 of the
Phliasians. With these he was not only able to prevent the
party who wanted to make peace from taking any action
but could also arrest and keep under guard anyone whom he
distrusted. He could also compel the mass of the people to
do their guard duty, could keep a good watch on them, and
see to it that they remained faithful. Often, too, he would
make a sally from the town with his 300 men, and drive back
one detachment or another of the besieging troops at various

points of the circuit of the surrounding wall. However, a 23
time came when these picked men, search as they would,
could find no more food in the city; they then sent to
Agesilaus and asked him to give them safe conduct to go on
an embassy to Sparta; they had decided, they said, to surrender their city unconditionally to the Spartan government.
Agesilaus gave safe conduct to the embassy, but he was angry 24
with them for treating him as though he lacked authority
himself, and he sent to his friends in Sparta, through whom
he had it arranged that all decisions with regard to Phlius
should be left to him. Meanwhile he kept the city under
closer siege than ever so that no one inside could escape. In
spite of this, Delphion and a man who had been branded as
a criminal and who had often stolen arms from the besiegers
managed to get away by night.

Messengers now came from Sparta to say that the state 25
authorized Agesilaus to make whatever decisions he thought
best with regard to Phlius. Agesilaus then decided as follows:
fifty men from the restored exiles and fifty from those at
home should in the first place form a commission to settle
the question of who should be allowed to live and who
should be put to death in the city, and next they should draw
up a constitution for the future government. He left behind
him a garrison and six months' pay for the troops to serve in
it, and they were to remain there until all these things had
been settled. After making these arrangements he allowed
the allied contingents to disperse and led his own troops back
to Sparta. So ended the operations at Phlius. They had taken
a year and eight months.

Now, too, Polybiades forced the Olynthians to send an 26
embassy to Sparta to sue for peace. They had been reduced to
the extremities of famine, unable either to get any food from
their own land or to import any by sea. Their ambassadors,
who came with full powers to Sparta, concluded an agreement to have the same foreign policy as Sparta, to join any

expedition led by Sparta and to become an ally. After swearing to abide by this agreement they returned to Olynthus.

27   Things had certainly gone well for Sparta. The Thebans and the rest of the Boeotians were entirely under control, the Corinthians had become perfectly reliable, the Argives, finding that the pretext of the sacred months was no longer any help to them, had had their pride humbled, and while the Athenians were left isolated, all allies of Sparta who had shown any hostile feelings had been brought to heel. Thus it appeared that now at last Spartan supremacy had been well and truly established.

CHAPTER 4

The Liberation of Thebes (Winter 379 B.C.). Sphodrias' attempt to take the Piraeus by surprise (378 B.C.). Trial of Sphodrias. Agesilaus' invasions of Boeotia (378 and 377 B.C.). Athenian naval victories: Naxos (376 B.C.) and Alyzia (375 B.C.)

MANY examples could be given both from Greek and foreign history to show that the gods are not indifferent to irreligion or to evil doing.* Here I shall mention only the case which occurs at this point in my narrative. The Spartans had sworn to leave the cities independent, and then they had seized the Acropolis of Thebes. Now they were punished by the action of these men, and these men alone, whom they had wronged, although before that time they had never been conquered by any nation on earth; and as for the Thebans who had brought them into the Acropolis with the aim of enslaving their city to Sparta so that they might act as dictators there themselves, it took only seven men from the exiled party to put an end to their government. I shall now tell the story of how this happened.†

*There seems to be a curious dichotomy in Xenophon's mind: Sparta was punished for her wrongful acts, but Agesilaus, who was largely responsible for them, is shielded from censure and remained for Xenophon 'a completely good man' (*Ages*. I.1).

† Plutarch (*Pelopidas* 7–13) describes fully the part played by Pelopidas in the Liberation, and according to the summary of his career in Diod. XV.81 (deriving doubtless from the great Greek historian of the second half of the Fourth Century, Ephorus) all accounts agreed in allotting him the leading role. Xenophon does not even name him and his account is therefore 'Hamlet without the prince'. Xenophon came to hate Pelopidas and named him only in connection with the Theban attempt to woo the King of Persia in 367 (VII.1.33 ff.). The hatred probably stemmed from Pelopidas' part in the invasion of the Peloponnese in 370–369 B.C., and the

res *istar2e*
occur
in
Ath.

2   There was a man called Phillidas who worked as secretary to Archias and the other polemarchs and was, it appears, extremely efficient both in this job and in others. While on a visit to Athens on some business or other he met Melon, one of the Thebans in exile at Athens and an acquaintance from earlier days. Melon heard from Phillidas all the news about the polemarch Archias and about the dictatorial behaviour of Philippus, and he realized that Phillidas hated the state of affairs in Thebes even more than he did himself. So, after each had given the other pledges of his good faith, they plan-

3   ned their course of action. Next Melon chose six out of the best men among the exiles and set out with them by night. They carried no other arms except daggers, and came first into the country district outside Thebes. Then, after spending the day in a deserted spot, they came to the gates as though they had been working in the fields, arriving just at the time when the last of the labourers were coming in. Once inside the city they spent the night and the following day at the

4   house of a man called Charon. Meanwhile, Phillidas was making all the necessary arrangements for the polemarchs with regard to the feast in honour of Aphrodite which they always celebrate at the end of their period of office. For some time he had been promising them that he would bring them some of the most beautiful and respected ladies in Thebes and now, he said, was the time when he would really do this. As for the polemarchs, they were looking forward to spend-ing a very pleasant night indeed. That was the type of person

5   they were. Now when they had finished dinner and, with the willing help of Phillidas, had rapidly got drunk, they kept on asking him to bring in their mistresses. He went out of the room and came back with Melon and his men, having dressed three of them up as ladies and the rest as their maids.

---

studious avoidance of his name here argues that this chapter was not written before the 360s.

He brought them to the anteroom of the treasury in the 6
polemarchs' building, and then went in by himself to
Archias and the others and told them that the women said
that they would not come in if any of the servants were in
the room. The polemarchs immediately ordered them all to
leave, and Phillidas, after giving them some wine, sent them
off to the house belonging to one of them. He then brought
in the 'mistresses' and conducted each to a seat beside each
of the polemarchs. The agreement was that, as soon as they
had sat down, they should unveil themselves and stab the
men at once. So, according to one version of the story, the 7
polemarchs were killed. According to another version Melon
and his men came in dressed as revellers and killed them in
this way.

Next Phillidas took three of the men and went to the house
of Leontiades. He knocked at the door and said that he wanted to deliver a message from the polemarchs. It so happened
that Leontiades was there by himself, still reclining on his
couch after dinner; his wife was sitting by him, doing some
work with wool. Since he considered Phillidas perfectly
trustworthy, he told him to come in. So they entered the
house, killed Leontiades and terrified his wife into keeping
quiet. When they left they told her that the door must
remain shut, and threatened to kill everyone in the house if
they found it open.

After this action Phillidas took two of the men and went to 8
the prison, where he told the prison governor that he was
bringing a man from the polemarchs to be kept in custody.
As soon as he opened the door, they immediately killed him
and then released the prisoners, whom they quickly armed
with weapons which they took down from the portico. They
led them to the shrine of Amphion and told them to stand
there under arms. They then immediately issued a proclama- 9
tion telling all Thebans, cavalry and hoplites alike, to come
out into the streets, since the tyrants were dead. So long as it

Spartan leaders
in Thebes fooled
again

was dark, the citizens, not knowing what to believe, stayed where they were; but as soon as it was light and it became clear what the facts were, then both the hoplites and the cavalry came running out quickly with their arms to join in the revolt. The returned exiles also sent horsemen over the border to a contingent of Athenian troops who were there with two of the generals. They knew why the horsemen had been sent ⟨and marched in to bring their help⟩.*

10 Meanwhile the Spartan governor in the Acropolis, as soon as he had heard the proclamation in the night, had sent to Plataea and Thespiae for help. But when the Theban cavalry saw the Plataeans coming they went out to meet them and killed more than twenty of them. After this action they returned to the city and, since by this time the Athenian force† from the frontier had also arrived, made an attack on the 11 Acropolis. The defenders of the Acropolis realized that they were few in number, and could see with what enthusiasm this whole force was moving up against them; there were also promises being made of large prizes to the first man to break in to the Acropolis. As a result of all this the defenders were frightened, and said that they would withdraw if they were allowed to do so in safety and retaining possession of their arms. The Thebans were glad to agree to this offer; a

*There is a lacuna in the text which the bracketed words attempt to fill.

†In Diodorus (XV.25 f.) not only is this help to the Theban exiles mentioned but also the Thebans are said to have formally appealed to Athens for help and the Athenians to have sent a force of five thousand hoplites and five hundred cavalry. The orator Dinarchus (I.39) spoke of a decree that sent the Athenians out to help the Theban exiles besieging the Spartan garrison in the Cadmea. As long as the Nineteenth-Century view of Xenophon prevailed, these notices were considered fancy and embroidery, but the Athenian force of peltasts under Chabrias in V.4.14 needs explanation, and it is coming to be generally recognized that Xenophon's silences can never be used to prove that an event reported elsewhere did not take place. Cf. Cawkwell, *Classical Quarterly*, 23, 1973, pp. 56 ff.

truce was made, oaths were exchanged, and they were allowed to go on these terms. However, when they were in the 12
open the Thebans seized and killed all whom they recognized
as belonging to the party of their enemies. A few of them
were rescued and brought to safety by the Athenians, who
had come in across the frontier with their supporting force,
but the Thebans even seized and butchered the children of
their victims, if they had any children.

When the Spartans heard what had happened they put to 13
death the governor* who had abandoned the Acropolis instead of waiting for the relief force, and they ordered mobilization against Thebes. Agesilaus said that it was more than
forty years since he reached military age, and pointed out
that just as other men of his age were no longer compelled to
go on foreign service, so, it would seem, the same rule should
apply to kings also. This was what he said, and so he did not
serve on this campaign; but this was not the reason why he
stayed behind. The real reason was that he knew well enough
that if he took command the citizens would say 'Here is
Agesilaus turning the state upside down because he wants to
come to the help of tyrants.' He therefore left them to make
whatever decisions they liked about the whole affair, and the 14
ephors, after listening to the men who had been driven out
of Thebes after the massacre, sent out Cleombrotus (this
being his first command) in the middle of the winter.

Chabrias with a force of Athenian peltasts† was guarding
the road that goes through Eleutherae, but Cleombrotus

*The governor (the harmost) had done badly and so joined the
company of the eminent Spartans whom Xenophon did not care to
name. Cf. IV.5.11, and VII.1.17.

†Cf. n. at V.4.10. Chabrias cannot have been one of the two generals who were punished for helping the Theban exiles on their
journey (§§9 and 19), for he was in command later in 378 (Diod.
XV.32 f.). His task here was evidently to stop the Spartans reaching
Boeotia and argues that Athens was more involved than Xenophon
cares explicitly to say.

283

made his ascent of the mountain by the road leading to Plataea. At the top of the pass his peltasts, going ahead of the rest of the army, fell in with the men who had been freed from the prison and were now guarding the pass, about a hundred and fifty in strength. Apart from a few who may have escaped, the peltasts killed every one of them. Cleombrotus then marched down to Plataea, which was still 15 friendly, went on to Thespiae and from there to Cynoscephalae in Theban territory, where he encamped. He stayed there for about sixteen days and then went back again to Thespiae. Here he left Sphodrias as governor with a third of each contingent of allied troops, and also gave him all the money which he had brought with him from Sparta, telling him to use this for hiring an additional force of mercenaries.

16 While Sphodrias was busy with all this, Cleombrotus himself led his own forces back home by the road through Creusis. His soldiers would have been quite unable to answer the question whether they were at war with Thebes or not, since, after leading the army in an invasion of Theban territory, he had then gone away again, having done the least 17 possible damage. However, while he was on the march back, a most extraordinary wind-storm arose and some people regarded this as an omen of what was going to happen later. There were many instances of the storm's violence; in particular, when he had left Creusis with the army and was crossing the mountains that slope down to the sea, numbers of pack-asses with their loads were swept down the precipices, and numbers of shields were wrested away from the 18 soldiers and fell into the sea. In the end many of the men were unable to march forward with all their arms and left their shields behind scattered about on the heights, lying on the ground with the concave surfaces filled with stones. That day they had whatever sort of an evening meal they could get at Aegosthena in Megarian territory. Cleombrotus then

disbanded the army and they all went back to their various homes.

The Athenians, meanwhile, were alarmed at the sight of 19 this deployment of Spartan power. So far from the war being still confined to Corinth, the Spartans were now going past Attica and invading the territory of Thebes. They therefore put on trial the two generals who had collaborated with Melon in the rising against Leontiades and his party. One of these they put to death, and they exiled the other, who had got away before the verdict was given.*

On their side the Thebans also were alarmed at the prospect of having to fight against the Spartans entirely by themselves. So they thought out the following plan. By a bribe, so it was said, they induced Sphodrias, the Spartan governor at Thespiae, to invade Attica, so that he might force Athens into war with Sparta. Sphodrias agreed to this, and made out that he was going to seize Piraeus, which had still no gates to protect it. After giving his troops an early dinner, he led them out from Thespiae, saying that before dawn they would be in Piraeus and at the end of their march. However, 21 when the sun rose he was still at Thria. He now made no attempt to disguise his presence but seized cattle and looted houses on his way back.

Meanwhile some of the people who had fallen in with him

---

*At this point Xenophon omitted any notice of the foundation of the Second Athenian Confederacy, one of the most celebrated of his silences. Only at VI.3.19 does it emerge that Athens was at the head of an alliance of states on behalf of which she might have sworn oaths (cf. n. *ad loc.*). Elsewhere he pointedly avoids explicit reference (cf. n. at V.4.64). He plainly did not choose to record an anti-Spartan alliance. Only when Athens came to Sparta's help in 370–69, does he enlarge on Athenian relations with Sparta (VI.5.33–52, and VII.1.1–14). That the Confederacy was founded before the raid of Sphodrias is the theme of Cawkwell, 'The Foundation of the Second Athenian Confederacy', *Classical Quarterly*, 23, 1973, pp. 47–60. Cf. n. at V.4.34.

during the night had fled to the city, and told the Athenians
that a huge army was marching against them. The Athenians,
cavalry and hoplites, had armed themselves at once and were
22 ready to defend the city. There also happened to be at the
time some ambassadors from Sparta staying at the house of
Callias, who looked after Spartan interests in Athens. Their
names were Etymocles, Aristolochus and Ocyllus. When the
Athenians heard the news of what was happening, they seized
these men and kept them under guard on the assumption that
they, too, were implicated in the plot. They, on the contrary, were absolutely dumbfounded by the whole affair.
They pointed out in their defence that if they really had
known that there was a move to capture Piraeus, they could
not conceivably have been such fools as to put themselves
into Athenian hands and actually to stay in the house of the
citizen who was looking after Spartan interests, just where
23 they could be most quickly found. They said, too, that it
would soon be clear to the Athenians also that the government of Sparta had no more to do with this attempt than
they had, and they asserted that they were convinced that it
would soon be found that Sphodrias had been put to death
by Sparta. It was concluded therefore that the ambassadors
24 were not implicated in the affair and they were released. And
in fact the ephors did recall Sphodrias to stand trial for his
life. Sphodrias, however, was too frightened to appear and
disobeyed the summons. Nevertheless, in spite of the fact
that he failed to appear, he was acquitted. And many people
considered that this was the most unjust verdict given in a
Spartan court. The reason why it was given is as follows.
25 Sphodrias' son, Cleonymus, had just grown out of boyhood and was the best looking and the most popular of all
the young men of his age. And it happened that Archidamus,
the son of Agesilaus, was in love with him. Now the friends
of Cleombrotus, who moved in the same circles as Sphodrias,
were inclined to acquit him, but they were afraid of Agesilaus

and his friends and also of the people who were uncommitted to either party, since it did seem that Sphodrias had done something really serious. It was in this situation that Spho- 26 drias addressed Cleonymus as follows: 'My son, you may be able to save your father's life if you go to Archidamus and beg him to win the goodwill of Agesilaus for me at my trial.' When he heard this Cleonymus summoned up the courage to go to Archidamus, and to ask him for his sake to become the saviour of his father. Archidamus, on his side, 27 seeing the tears falling from Cleonymus' eyes, wept with him as he stood beside him and, when he heard what the request was, replied: 'O Cleonymus, I must tell you that I my-self do not dare to look my father in the face. If I want to get something done in the city, I go with my request to anyone rather than him. But all the same, since it is you who are asking me, you can be sure that I shall try to do everything I can to get this done.' He then left the mess, went to his home 28 and retired to rest. He got up at dawn and watched to be sure that he did not miss his father when he left the house. But when he did see him on his way out, he first of all gave way to any citizen who happened to be there and wanting to speak to Agesilaus; next he stood aside for any foreigner, and then even for any of the servants who had any request to make. Finally, when Agesilaus came back from the Eurotas and went indoors again, Archidamus went away without even having come near him. And on the following day it was exactly the same thing again. Agesilaus had a shrewd idea of why it was 29 that he was following him about, but asked him no questions and let him be. As for Archidamus, he was, naturally enough, longing to see Cleonymus, but did not see how he could go and visit him until he had talked with his father about Cleo-nymus' request. And Sphodrias' friends, who saw that Archi-damus was no longer coming to see Cleonymus, whereas he used to be constantly there, were in a great state of anxiety, since they feared that he had been reprimanded by Agesilaus.

30 However, in the end Archidamus did manage to pluck up the courage to approach Agesilaus and to say, 'Father, Cleonymus tells me to beg you to save his father. I, too, beg you to do this, if it is possible.'

Agesilaus replied: 'So far as you are concerned, I don't blame you. But I don't see how I could avoid being blamed myself by the state if I failed to declare guilty a man who has made money for himself by harming Sparta.'

31 For the time being Archidamus had nothing to say to this and went away, submitting to the justice of what his father had said. Later, however, whether on his own initiative or at the suggestion of someone else, he went to Agesilaus and said: 'Father, if Sphodrias had done nothing wrong, I know that you would have acquitted him. Now, as it is, even if he has done something wrong, can you not forgive him for our sakes?'

Agesilaus replied: 'Well and good, if such an action as that could turn out honourably for us,' and when he heard this Archidamus gave up hope and went away.

32 Now a man who was a friend of Sphodrias, during a conversation with Etymocles, said: 'I suppose that all of you who are friends of Agesilaus will want to condemn Sphodrias to death.'

Etymocles replied: 'By Zeus, if so we shall be acting differently from Agesilaus. Certainly he always says the same thing to everyone with whom he discusses the matter. He says that the idea of Sphodrias' being innocent is an impossibility, but, on the other hand, it is a hard thing to put to death one who in childhood, boyhood and youth has consistently acted well and honourably; Sparta needs soldiers like this.'

33 When he heard this, the friend of Sphodrias went and told Cleonymus, who was delighted and went at once to Archidamus and said: 'Now we know that you really care for us. And you, Archidamus, can be sure that we, too, shall try to take care that you will never feel ashamed of our friendship.'

And he was as good as his word. While he lived, all his actions were those of a good and noble Spartan, and at Leuctra, after falling three times, he died first of his citizens and deep in the enemy ranks fighting for his king with Dinon the polemarch.* Certainly his death caused Archidamus terrible pain; but he had kept his promise; he had brought him honour and not shame. It was in this way, then, that Sphodrias was acquitted.

And now the pro-Boeotian party in Athens pointed out to 34 the people that Sparta, so far from punishing Sphodrias, had actually commended him for intriguing against Athens. As a result the Athenians built gates for Piraeus, fitted out ships, and did all they could to help the Boeotians.†

The Spartans on their side ordered mobilization against 35 Thebes and asked Agesilaus to take command of the expeditionary force, since they thought he would be a more intelligent leader than Cleombrotus. Agesilaus said that he would never go against any decision made by the state and proceeded to get ready for the campaign.‡ He knew that it 36 would be difficult to invade Theban territory unless he had first occupied the passes of Cithaeron and he came to an agreement with the Cletorians who were at war with the people of Orchomenus and had a mercenary army serving with them. According to the agreement this mercenary army

*Cf. VI.4.14. This passage shows that Xenophon's account of 378 B.C. was written after the battle of Leuctra (371 B.C.).

†The Spartans commended Sphodrias, because he had sought to nip the Second Athenian Confederacy in the bud (cf. n. at V.4.19). The narrative of Diodorus (XV.28 and 29) suggests that the building of the gates and equipment of a fleet were the practical effects of a declaration that the King's Peace had been rendered by Sparta null and void, and that full help for the Boeotians was the effect of admitting Thebes to the Confederacy. (Cf. Cawkwell, *Classical Quarterly*, 23, 1973, pp. 51 ff.). Xenophon prefers the concrete to the formal (cf. n. at III.5.2.)

‡Xenophon is pleased to record this sample of the wit of Agesilaus, whose enmity towards Thebes (V.1.33) was unwavering. Contrast Agesilaus' avoidance of the command against Mantinea (V.2.3).

37 was to be at his disposal, if he needed it. Then, after the sacrifices for crossing the frontier had turned out satisfactorily and before he himself had got as far as Tegea, he sent a message to the commander of the mercenaries at Cletor, gave him a month's pay for his men and instructed him to occupy Cithaeron before he arrived. He told the people of Orchomenus that, so long as his army was in the field, they must abstain from all warlike action; indeed, he said that if any state at all attacked a neighbour during the period of his own campaign, he would, in accordance with the resolution of the allies, first of all march against that state.

38 After crossing Cithaeron he came to Thespiae and, using this city as a base, marched into the territory of Thebes. Here he found the plain and all the most valuable part of the land protected by a trench and a stockade. He constantly moved his camp, and after breakfast each day used to lead his men out to lay waste the country on his side of these obstacles, and the enemy, ready to give battle, moved along keeping pace
39 with him inside the stockade. On one occasion, when he had already started to go back to his camp, the Theban cavalry, who had not been visible until this moment, suddenly charged out through the exits which had been built in the stockade. In Agesilaus' army the peltasts were either on their way back to dinner or were getting ready to go, and as for the cavalrymen, some were still dismounted and others just in the act of mounting. So, charging down on them in this state, the Thebans cut down great numbers of the peltasts, and among the cavalry two Spartans of the officer class, Cleas and Epicydidas, one of the Perioeci, Eudicus, and several of the exiles from Thebes. All these were killed when still dismounted.
40 Agesilaus now turned about and brought the hoplites to the rescue; his cavalry, too, charged the Theban cavalry, and the hoplites of the first ten age groups ran in to the attack with them. (The Thebans, however, behaved like men who have got drunk in the middle of the day.) They stood up to the

charge so as to throw their spears, but they threw their spears when the attackers were still out of range. They then turned about, but even with all that start twelve of them were killed.

Agesilaus had observed that it was always after breakfast 41 that the enemy, just like his own troops, appeared on the scene. So, after making the sacrifices at dawn, he led his army forward as fast as possible and made his way inside the stockade at an unguarded point. He then burned and destroyed the country inside right up to the walls of the city. After this had been done he retired again to Thespiae and built fortifications for the Thespians. He left Phoebidas there as governor, and himself recrossed the mountains to Megara where he disbanded the allied contingents and led the Spartan troops back home.*

After this Phoebidas kept on sending out plundering ex- 42 peditions to seize Theban property and organized raids to devastate the land. Wishing to get their own back, the Thebans marched into Thespian territory with their whole army. Once they were inside the borders Phoebidas kept so close to them with his peltasts that he stopped them from moving out in any direction from the main body of their troops. The result was that the Thebans became extremely discouraged and retreated much faster than they had advanced; the drivers of the mules threw away whatever farm produce they had taken and made off rapidly for home; indeed, the army was in a real state of terror.

Such being the conditions, Phoebidas pressed his attack 43 boldly. He had the peltasts with him and had ordered the hoplites to follow in battle order. He now entertained the hope of routing the Thebans; he was leading on his own

---

*The part of Chabrias in this campaign and especially the famous tactic, whatever it was (cf. J. Buckler, *Hesperia*, 41, 1972, pp. 466 ff.), which was commemorated at Athens by a statue, escapes Xenophon's pen (cf. Diod. XV.32.5, and 33.4, etc.). Chabrias had saved the accursed Thebans on that occasion and silence was best.

men with the greatest confidence, calling on the rest of his
army to join in the attack and ordering the Thespian hoplite
44 force to come up in support. However, in their retreat the
Theban cavalry had come to an impassable ravine. Here they
first gathered into a compact body and then, not seeing how
they were to get across, turned back to face the enemy. There
were not many peltasts in front of them and the first ones
of these fled in terror of the cavalry who, as soon as they
saw this, took the lesson to heart and charged on against the
45 others. There Phoebidas and two or three men with him fell
fighting, and at this the whole mercenary force turned and
ran. In their flight they came to the Thespian hoplites, men
who had previously done a lot of boasting about how they
would never give way to the Thebans. In spite of this, however, they, too, turned and ran, though there was not even
a regular pursuit as it was now so late in the day. Not many
were killed, but the Thespians went on running until they
were inside their city walls.

46   After this the ambitions of the Thebans were rekindled.*
They sent out forces against Thespiae and the other neighbouring cities. From these cities the democratic parties had
withdrawn and taken refuge in Thebes, since in all of them
oligarchical governments had been set up, as previously in
Thebes. Consequently, the pro-Spartan party in these cities
were now in need of aid. However, after the death of
Phoebidas the Spartans merely sent over by sea a polemarch
and one regiment for the garrisoning of Thespiae.

*The vagueness of the Greek is hard to render in translation, but
behind the words there probably lies a fact which Xenophon was by
no means concerned formally to record, viz. the refoundation of the
Boeotian Confederacy, albeit on the new basis of a democracy centred
on Thebes. Cf. Cawkwell, Classical Quarterly, 22, 1972, pp. 259 and
275 f. Plutarch (Pelopidas 15) mentions a Spartan defeat at Tanagra
and the death of Panthoidas, the harmost, not the sort of thing
Xenophon thought worth mentioning, but perhaps to be connected
with these Theban operations of winter 378–7 B.C.

When spring came round the ephors again ordered mobili- 47
zation against Thebes and, as before, asked Agesilaus to take
command. Agesilaus, holding as he did the same views as
previously about invading Boeotia, sent a message to the
polemarch at Thespiae before even holding the sacrifices for
crossing the frontier, and told him to occupy the heights
above the road over Cithaeron and to hold the position until
he arrived himself. Then, after crossing Cithaeron, he made 48
it look as though he was going on first to Thespiae by sending messengers there, asking that a market should be organized there for his men, and that embassies should wait for
him there. As a result the Thebans sent strong forces to guard
the route leading from Thespiae into their country. Agesilaus, 49
however, on the following day, after holding the sacrifices at
dawn, advanced by the route to Erythrae. In one day he did
what would be a normal two days' march for an army and
suddenly appeared behind the line of the stockade at Scolus
before the Thebans had got back from keeping guard at the
point where he had entered their country last year. After
doing this he devastated all the country to the east of Thebes
as far as the frontier of Tanagra. (At this time Tanagra was
still held by Hypatodorus and his party who were pro-
Spartan.) He then began to retire, keeping the fortifications
of Tanagra on his left.

The Theban army, however, had slipped out of the city 50
and were drawn up in battle order facing him on the hill
known as the Old Woman's Breast. Behind them was the
ditch and the stockade, and they thought this a good position
in which to fight a battle, since in front of them the ground
was somewhat shut in and not easy to cross. Agesilaus, however, when he saw what the position was, did not move
against them at all; instead, he turned aside and marched in
the direction of Thebes. As for the Thebans, they began to 51
fear for the safety of their city which was undefended.
Abandoning the position where they had been drawn up,

they went off at a run towards Thebes by the road to Potniae,
which was the safer route. And I must say that this idea of
Agesilaus seemed a beautiful one: he had led his army right
away from the enemy and by doing so was making them
retreat at the double. And all the same, while they were running past, some of the polemarchs with their regiments were
52 able to charge out on them. The Thebans, however, hurled
their spears down from the heights and one of the polemarchs,
Alypetus, was struck and killed, though even from this height
the Thebans were driven down. Then the Sciritans and some
of the cavalry climbed up and charged in among the last of
53 the Thebans as they hurried on past them to the city. When
they were near the wall, however, the Thebans turned, and
when the Sciritans saw this they fell back at a faster than
walking pace. Not a single one of them was killed, but all
the same the Thebans put up a trophy, on the grounds that
after climbing the hill the Sciritans had retired again.*

54 Agesilaus meanwhile, when it was time to do so, retired,
and made a camp in the place where he had seen the enemy
drawn up in battle order. Next day he set off on the road to
Thespiae. The peltasts who were in Theban service as mercenaries followed him up boldly on his march and kept
shouting out to Chabrias, blaming him for not joining them.
But the Olynthian cavalry, who were now, in accordance
with the peace terms, serving with the Spartans, wheeled
round and, bearing down on the peltasts, chased them up a
slope and killed great numbers of them; for men on foot are
easily overtaken by cavalry when going uphill where riding
conditions are good.

55 When Agesilaus arrived at Thespiae he found the citizens

*Diod. XV.34 gives a somewhat different account of this battle.
The sarcastic remark of Xenophon about the Thebans preening themselves on unreal triumphs recalls his aspersions on Theban valour at
Haliartus (III.5.21 f.). At VII.5.12 he exposes the vehemence of his
feelings about the 'fire-breathers'. Cf. n. at IV.2.18.

in a state of violent party strife. Those who professed to be
pro-Spartan wanted to put their enemies, among whom was
Menon, to death; but Agesilaus would not allow them to do
this. Instead, he brought the two sides together and made
them swear oaths to keep the agreement. He then went back
again, crossing Cithaeron by the road to Megara, where he
dismissed the allied contingents, and led the Spartan troops
back home.

It was now two years since the Thebans had brought in 56
crops from their land, and they were suffering greatly from
the shortage of corn. So they put men aboard two triremes
and sent them with ten talents to Pagasae to buy corn. However, while they were engaged in making the purchase,
Alcetas, the Spartan in command of the garrison at Oreus,
manned three triremes, taking every precaution that this fact
should not be reported. He then captured both the corn and
the triremes, on the return voyage from Pagasae and made
prisoners of the men on board, who were at least 300 in
number. He kept these men under guard in the Acropolis
where he had his own quarters. They say that in Oreus there 57
was a boy who was often with Alcetas. He was a fine attractive boy and Alcetas used to come down from the Acropolis
and spend his time with him. This carelessness of his was
observed by the prisoners who seized the Acropolis, whereupon the city revolted and, as a result of this, the Thebans
could now bring in corn easily.*

At the beginning of the following spring, Agesilaus was 58
confined to his bed. At Megara, when he was leading the
army back from Thebes, he had ruptured a vein while he
was going up from the shrine of Aphrodite to the government offices. The blood from his body had then poured into

*The deeds and misdeeds of the Spartan Alcetas in Euboea engage
the pen of Xenophon; those of the Athenian Chabrias are unmentioned, although they included ravaging of the territory of Oreus
(Diod. XV.30).

his good leg, causing excessive swelling in the lower leg and unendurable pain. A Syracusan surgeon had opened the vein at the ankle, but once the blood had begun to flow, it poured out day and night, and in spite of everything they did, they could not stop it, until he lost consciousness, and then it did stop. So, after he was carried back to Sparta, he was ill for the rest of the summer and all through the winter.

59   However, at the very beginning of spring the Spartans again ordered mobilization and called upon Cleombrotus to take over the command. He reached Cithaeron with his army, and his peltasts went on ahead to seize the heights above the road before the enemy could occupy them. But some Theban and Athenian troops were already in possession of these heights. They allowed the peltasts to ascend up to a certain point, then, when they were close to them, rushed out on them, drove them down and killed about forty of them. This event made Cleombrotus conclude that it was impossible to cross Cithaeron into Theban territory; so he led back the army and dismissed it.

60   There was now a meeting of the allies at Sparta, at which speeches were made to the effect that this war was being prosecuted with lack of energy and that the result would be that they would all be worn down by it. It was claimed that Sparta and her allies could man far more ships than were available to Athens and could starve her into submission; the same ships could be used to transport an army across to Thebes by whichever route they preferred, either through Phocis or through Creusis. On the basis of all this they manned sixty triremes, and Pollis took command of them as admiral. And in fact there was nothing mistaken about these decisions (Athens really was now in a state of siege.) Her corn ships got as far as Gerastus, but could no longer sail on along the coast from there since the Spartan fleet was in the waters round Aegina, Ceos and Andros.

The Athenians saw that there was only one thing to do.

They manned their ships themselves and, under the command of Chabrias, fought a naval engagement with Pollis.
In this battle they were victorious, and as a result corn could
now be brought in to Athens.*

NAXOS.

Next the Spartans made preparations for transporting an 62
army across the gulf to invade Boeotia, but the Thebans asked
the Athenians to send a force round the Peloponnese. They
calculated that, if this were done, it would be impossible for
the Spartans to guard their own land and the allied cities in
their own area and at the same time to send across the gulf a
force large enough to be effective against Thebes. The Athen- 63
ians, angry as they were with the Spartans because of what
Sphodrias had done,† were perfectly willing to send out the
expedition round the Peloponnese. They manned sixty ships
and appointed Timotheus as commander.

So there was no enemy invasion of Theban territory either
in the year when Cleombrotus was in command of the army,
or in the year when Timotheus sailed round the Peloponnese. As a result, the Thebans marched confidently against the
neighbouring cities of Boeotia and once again gained control
of them.

After sailing round the Peloponnese Timotheus went 64
straight on to Corcyra and took the island over. However,

*The battle of Naxos is fully recounted by Diodorus (XV. 34 f.),
who gives precise numbers for each side and the location and circumstances of the battle, whereas Xenophon contents himself with a
round number for the Spartan side and the merest mention that a
battle took place. A large omission is to be suspected in the conse-
quences of the battle. In mid 375 (cf. n. at VI.2.1) a Royal Rescript
from Artaxerxes reached Greece, and it seems likely enough that
after the serious naval defeat Sparta sent an embassy to Persia to say
it was time for the King to intervene (in the spirit of Isoc. IV.120).
Such trafficking with the Mede was shameful in the eyes of Agesilaus
and of Xenophon, who therefore omits it.

†No word of the formal obligations of the Second Athenian Confederacy emerges. Cf. Introduction p. 35, and nn. at V.4.19 and 64
and VI.3.19.

he did not enslave the inhabitants nor banish individuals nor change the constitution. The result of this conduct was to make all the states in that area better disposed towards Athens.* But by now the Spartans had manned a fleet against him and had sent out Nicolochus, a man of great energy and daring, as admiral. As soon as he sighted the ships under Timotheus he engaged him without any delay, even though six of his own ships (the ones from Ambracia) were not with him. So with fifty-five ships he fought against the sixty ships of Timotheus, and on that occasion he was defeated and

66 Timotheus put up a trophy at Alyzia. But when Timotheus' ships had been hauled ashore for refitting, Nicolochus, who had now been joined by the six Ambraciot triremes, sailed out to Alyzia where Timotheus was, and, since Timotheus did not put out to meet him, he also put up a trophy on the nearest islands. But when Timotheus had refitted the ships he had already and had manned others from Corcyra he had altogether more than seventy – a fleet obviously greatly superior to the enemy's. But he kept on sending to Athens for money. He needed a lot, since he had a lot of ships.

* 'Better disposed' is a vague reference to the fact, of which we are apprised by an inscription (Tod, *G.H.I.*, II, no. 126), *viz.* that Corcyra, Acarnania and Cephallenia joined the Second Athenian Confederacy in 375. (Cf. previous note.) The seemingly gratuitous comment about the conduct of Timotheus is in all probability a sharp comment on the scandalous behaviour of Chares when he was in the same western area in the late 360s (Diod. XV.95.3) – which strongly argues that the end of Book V was written in the 350s.

BOOK SIX

CHAPTER 1

Growing Power of Jason of Pherae (375 B.C.)

WHILE the Athenians and Spartans were engaged in these 1
operations the Thebans had subdued the Boeotian cities and
next were moving into Phocis. So now the Phocians sent an
embassy to Sparta and said that unless they received aid it
would be impossible for them to avoid following the lead of
Thebes. The Spartans then sent an army across the gulf to
Phocis. King Cleombrotus was in command, and with him
were four regiments of Spartan troops and a corresponding
proportion of their troops from all the allies.*

It was just about this time, too, that Polydamas of Pharsa- 2
lus arrived from Thessaly to make an appeal to the Spartan
assembly. Polydamas was very well known all over Thessaly,
and in his own city was regarded as a man of such honour and
distinction that when the people of Pharsalus became involved
in very bitter party strife, they handed over the Acropolis to
him and entrusted him with the task of collecting the revenue
and of spending whatever portion of it was prescribed by law
on religious purposes and general administration. He, on his 3
side, used the money for guarding the Acropolis, which he
kept safe for them, and for the administration of the state.

---

*Xenophon omits to mention that two of these regiments (*morai*)
sustained a serious defeat at the hands of the Theban Sacred Band
commanded by Pelopidas (Plut. *Pelopidas* 16–19, Diod. XV.37), a
highly ominous preliminary to the battle of Leuctra. He must have
heard about it, but it was no part of his purpose to give the Thebans
the credit they deserved. It was perhaps mere carelessness that he
omitted also to notice the recall of this Spartan force after the Peace
later in the year, but the omission should not gull the unwary into
thinking that the army that fought at Leuctra (VI.4.2) had been in
Phocis for four years.

He gave a yearly account and, whenever there was a deficit, made it good out of his own fortune, paying himself back whenever there was a surplus of revenue. Then, too, he showed the real Thessalian love for hospitality and for doing things in a big way. When he arrived at Sparta he made the following speech:*

4 'Spartans, I, like all my ancestors of whom we have record, act as your representative in my own country and am honoured by you with the title of "benefactor". It seems right, then, for me to come to you if I am in any difficulty, and to let you know if things begin to be dangerous for you in Thessaly. I am certain that you, too, know the name of Jason. He is very powerful and very famous. Now, after making a treaty with my city, Jason spoke to me as follows:

5 "Polydamas, whether your city liked it or not, I could still bring it over to my side, as you can see for yourself, if you look at these facts. I have as my allies most of the cities of Thessaly and these include the most powerful ones. Moreover, I subdued them when you, acting with them, were in the field against me. You know too, I imagine, that I have a foreign mercenary army of up to 6,000 men. In my opinion there is no city which would find it at all easy to face this army in battle. No doubt there are other cities which could send out a force equally strong in numbers; but armies made up of citizens must include some men who are already past and some who have not yet reached their prime. And there are very few people in each city who keep constantly in good physical training. But no one serves in my mercenary army unless he can stand physical hardship as well as I can myself."

6 And he himself – for I must tell you the truth – not only has

*Xenophon presents the affairs of Thessaly through the mouth of Polydamas of Pharsalus, perhaps because that was how he knew of them. (See Introduction p. 26.) Hence the laudatory introduction to the speech and the near absence of Larissa, which is only mentioned at VI.4.33 f., from the account of Jason and his successors.

a magnificent physique but enjoys putting it to the test. In fact, he tries out his own men every day, marching at their head in full armour whether on the parade ground or on a campaign. Any mercenary troops of his whom he finds slack, he gets rid of, but when he sees men who are fond of hardship and fond of the dangers of war, he rewards and honours them, doubling, trebling and quadrupling their pay, giving them special gifts, and also medical attention when they are ill and every mark of distinction when they are buried. The result is that all the mercenaries in his service know that good conduct in war will guarantee them a life full of honour in which they will lack for nothing.

Jason + mercenary

'He told me too (though I knew this already) that now the 7 Maracians, the Dolopians and Alcetas, ruler of Epirus, are subjects of his. "And so," he said, "what have I to fear? Why should I not expect to subdue you easily? Indeed, people who do not know me might reasonably wonder what I am waiting for and why I am not marching against Pharsalus at this moment. The reason, of course, is that I think it is in every way better to have your voluntary, rather than forced, co-operation. If you were under compulsion, you would be planning to do all the harm to me you could, and I on my side should be wanting to keep you as weak as possible. But if I persuade you to join me of your own accord, obviously we shall both do whatever we can to strengthen each other. Now I know, Polydamas, that your country looks to you 8 for guidance. If you arrange for her to be friendly to me, I promise that I will make you, after myself, the greatest man in Greece. And now listen to what my offer of second place here means and do not believe anything I say until you have weighed it up and found it true. This, I think, is clear enough to us – that if I were joined by Pharsalus and all the cities dependent upon you, I should have no difficulty in becoming Lord of all Thessaly; also that, when there is a Lord of Thessaly, he can call on a cavalry force of 6,000 and a hoplite

9 army of more than 10,000. And when I see the physique of these men and their fine spirit, I think that, if these men were properly led, there is no race on earth to whom the Thessalians would think it right to defer. And here is another point: Thessaly itself is a very flat country and all the people round this central plain are subject to Thessaly whenever a Lord of Thessaly is acknowledged; now these people are nearly all javelin men, so that one may reasonably assume that our
10 force will have the advantage in peltasts also. Then the Boeotians and all other states now at war with Sparta are allies of mine and I can assure you that they would accept my leadership, too, if only I free them from the Spartans. As for the Athenians, I am quite sure that they also would do anything to become allies of ours, but I myself am not in favour of entering into friendly relations with them,* because, in my view, I should find it even easier to take over
11 power on sea than on land, and I think that the following considerations will show you that my calculations are reasonable. It is from Macedonia that the Athenians get their timber, and, with Macedonia under our control, we shall clearly be able to build many more ships than they can. And as for manning these ships, it seems reasonable to suppose that here, too, we, with our large population of first-rate serfs, will be in a better position than the Athenians. The same is true with regard to supplying the crews. Is it not likely that we, who have so much corn that we export it abroad, shall be better able to do this than the Athenians, who have not even enough for them-
12 selves unless they buy it elsewhere? Financially, too, it seems clear that we shall be in the stronger position; we do not look to wretched little islands for our revenues but can draw upon the races of a continent; for, once there is a Lord of Thessaly,

*Since Xenophon gives no account of the Second Athenian Confederacy, and so does not record the adhesion of Jason in autumn of this very year (cf. Tod, *G.H.I.*, II, no. 123, l.111), these words read oddly to those who know the sequel.

all the peoples around us pay tribute. And I am sure you know that the reason why the King of Persia is the richest man on earth is that he gets his revenue from a continent and not from islands. Yet I think that it would be easier to subdue him than to subdue Greece. For I know that in Persia everybody except for one man is educated to be a slave rather than to stand up for himself, and I know to what extremities the King was brought by comparatively small forces – the one that marched with Cyrus and the one with Agesilaus.'

'This is what he said to me. I told him that what he said 13 certainly deserved consideration, but for us, who were friends of Sparta, to desert her and go over to her enemies when we had no complaints to make against her was not a thing that I could contemplate. He then congratulated me on the sentiments that I had expressed and said that, since this was the sort of man I was, it made him all the keener to have me with him, and he encouraged me to come to you and tell you the truth, namely, that he proposes to march against Pharsalus unless we come over to him voluntarily. He told me to ask for help from you, and then said: "Supposing that the gods grant you the power to persuade them to send you a force big enough to make war with me, well and good; we will see how the war turns out and abide by the result. But if you come to the conclusion that they are not giving you adequate help, no one, I think, could then blame you if you were to do the best thing possible for your city, which honours you."

'This, then, is the subject about which I have come to you, 14 and I am describing the whole thing to you as I see it myself and as I have heard it from him. And, Spartans, this is what I think: if you send us a force that will appear not only to me, but also to the other Thessalians, big enough to make war on Jason, then the cities will revolt from him. They are all frightened, not knowing where this man's power is going to turn next. But if you are under the impression that it will be enough to send a force of emancipated helots under a ✓

305

commander who is not a Spartan king, then my advice is that
15 you do nothing at all. For you can be sure that the war will
have to be fought against a really strong force and against a
man whose generalship is of the highest quality – one who,
whether his methods are those of plain force, of working in
the dark or of seizing an unexpected advantage, very seldom
fails to achieve his objects. He can use the night-time as well
as the day-time and when he wants to move fast, he will put
breakfast and dinner into one meal so as not to interrupt his
work. He will not think it right to rest until he has reached
the point for which he set out and done all that had to be
done. And he has trained his men to behave in the same way,
although he also knows how to gratify the feelings of his
soldiers when they have won some success as the result of
extra hard work. So all who follow him have learned this too
16 – that one can have a good time also, if one works for it. Then,
too, he is more self-controlled than any man I know with
regard to all bodily pleasures. These never take up his time
and prevent him from doing what has to be done. Now,
then, I ask you to consider this question and to tell me, as is
your duty, both what you will be able to do and what you
intend to do.'

17   This was the speech of Polydamas. The Spartans put off
replying to it for the time being. They spent the next day and
the one after in reckoning up the number of regiments which
they had serving abroad, and those, too, in the neighbourhood of Sparta for use against the Athenian triremes and for
wars on their own frontiers. They then gave their reply and
said that at present they were not able to send out a force
adequate to aid Pharsalus, and they told Polydamas to return
home and make the best arrangements he could both for
18 himself and for his city. So he went away, after expressing
his admiration for the straightforward way in which Sparta
had dealt with him.

On his return he begged Jason not to force him to give up

the Acropolis of Pharsalus, since he wanted to go on holding it in the interests of those who had entrusted him with it. But he gave his own children to Jason as hostages and promised him that he would persuade the city to join his alliance voluntarily and also to help Jason become Lord of Thessaly. Thus, after guarantees had been given on both sides, the people of Pharsalus were at peace, and Jason was soon appointed Lord of Thessaly by general consent. After reaching this posi- 19 tion he assessed the numbers of cavalry and hoplites which each city was able to provide. He found that he could count on more than 8,000 cavalry (including the cavalry of the allies); his hoplites were reckoned at at least 20,000 and, as for peltasts, he had enough to take on the rest of the world; it would be a hard enough job just to count the cities which provided them. Jason also sent orders to all in the area to pay the same tribute as had been fixed in the time of Scopas.

So things went in Thessaly. I shall now return to the point in my narrative when I digressed in order to tell what Jason was doing.

CHAPTER 2

Peace of 375 B.C. Action in Corcyra. Brilliant Campaign of Iphicrates
(373–372 B.C.)

1 As already mentioned, the Spartan and allied army was
gathering together in Phocis and the Thebans had withdrawn
to their own territory and were guarding the passes. As for
the Athenians, they could see that owing to their help the
power of Thebes was growing, yet no money came in to
them from Thebes for the upkeep of their fleet, and they
themselves were being exhausted by extraordinary taxation,
raids on their coast from Aegina and garrison duties throughout their country. With all this in mind they felt a desire to
put an end to the war, and they sent ambassadors to Sparta
and there concluded a peace treaty.*

2 Two of the Athenian ambassadors sailed directly from
Sparta and, in accordance with a decree of the city, told
Timotheus to sail back home, as there was now a state of
peace. However, on his way back Timotheus took the
opportunity to put ashore in their country the exiles from
3 Zacynthus. The Zacynthians in the city then sent to Sparta
and reported how they had been treated by Timotheus, and
the Spartans immediately † came to the conclusion that the

*The Peace of 375 B.C. was in form comparable to the King's
Peace of 387–6 and was made in response to a Rescript from the King
of Persia, but because of the great victory of Timotheus at Alyzia
(V.4.65), Athens was accorded in the Sanctions Clause a share of the
hegemony (cf. Philochorus F 151, Nepos *Timotheus* 2.2, etc.). Timotheus was accorded a hero's welcome at Athens, and Isocrates must
have been alluding to this Peace when later he called for a restoration
of the King's Peace (VIII.16; cf. XV.109 f.). Xenophon's laconic
statement conceals much.

†Xenophon has nodded here. Peace was made in 375 and war

Athenians had committed a hostile act and once more began
to fit out a fleet. The fleet was to be of sixty ships with
varying contingents from Sparta herself, Corinth, Leucas,
Ambracia, Elis, Zacynthus, Achaea, Epidaurus, Troezen, Hermione and Halieis. They put Mnasippus in command with 4
the rank of admiral* and instructed him to keep a watch on
Spartan interests in general in those waters, and in particular
to sail against Corcyra. They also sent to Dionysius† and
pointed out that it would be in his interests, too, for Corcyra
not to be under the control of Athens.

Mnasippus, then, sailed for Corcyra as soon as his fleet had 5
assembled. In addition to the Spartan troops serving with
him, he had at least 1,500 mercenaries. On landing he found 6
himself master of the country and went about laying waste
the land, which was very beautifully planted and in a fine
state of cultivation. There were magnificent houses, too,
which he destroyed, and well-stocked wine-cellars on the
country estates. The result was, so it was said, that his soldiers got such a taste for luxurious living that they would
drink no wine unless it had a fine bouquet. They also made
off with great numbers of slaves and cattle from the fields.
He then camped with his army on a hill less than a mile from 7
the city and between the city and the country, so that from
this position he could cut off any Corcyraeans who tried to
get out to their land. And he had a camp made for his sailors
on the other side of the city, in a position from which he
thought they would be able to see in good time any ships

resumed in 373 (cf. Cawkwell, *Historia*, 12, 1963, pp. 83 ff.). Timotheus may have taken some time over the restoration of the Zacyn-
thian exiles, regarding the task as a duty of Athens in her new role
as part-hegemon of the Peace, but that could hardly fill the gap.

*Xenophon nods again? Diod. XV.45.4 and 46.2 names two other
Spartan naval commanders sent out before Mnasippus. For Xeno-
phon's indifference to a proper framework of nauarchies, see nn. at
V.1.3 and V.1.13.

†Tyrant of Syracuse.

that were approaching and would prevent them from sailing in. In addition to this he had ships on patrol at the mouth of 8 the harbour whenever the weather permitted. In this way he kept the city in a state of siege.

The Corcyraeans were now in a desperate position. Because of the enemy's superiority on land, they were getting no food in from their farms, and because of his naval superiority they were importing nothing by sea. They therefore sent to Athens and begged the Athenians to come to their help. They pointed out that if Athens were to be deprived of Corcyra she would be throwing away a great advantage and at the same time putting additional strength into her enemies' hands. No other state, they said, except Athens herself could produce more ships and more money than Corcyra. Then, too, Corcyra was well situated for all operations in the Gulf of Corinth or against cities in that area, well situated, too, as a base for raids on Spartan territory, and for Epirus just opposite, and also for the coast route from Sicily to the Peloponnese, its position was unrivalled.

10 The Athenians, after listening to this, came to the conclusion that this was a matter to be taken in hand very vigorously. They sent out Ctesicles * as general with a force of about six hundred peltasts, and they asked Alcetas to help in getting 11 them across to Corcyra. They were, in fact, brought across by night to a place somewhere in the country from which they made their way into the city. The Athenians also voted that sixty ships should be manned and chose Timotheus to 12 take command of them. Timotheus, however, found it impossible to find crews in Athens and sailed off to the islands to recruit men from there. In his view it was a very serious undertaking and one which required organization to sail round the Peloponnese against a well-equipped and ex-13 perienced fleet. But the Athenians could not forgive him for

* For a different order of events, see Diod. XV.46 and 47, which is preferable (cf. Cawkwell, *Historia*, 12, 1963, p. 85 f.).

what they considered was letting slip the best time of the year for the voyage and they deprived him of his command, appointing Iphicrates to take his place. As soon as he was 14 made general Iphicrates went vigorously to work on manning the ships and saw to it that the captains did this work too. He also obtained from the Athenians the state ships *Paralus* and *Salaminia* and any other ships that were cruising round Attica. 'If things go well in Corcyra,' he said, 'I shall send plenty of ships back to you.' In the end his whole fleet came to about the number of seventy.

Meanwhile the people of Corcyra were suffering terribly 15 from hunger. There were so many desertions that Mnasippus had it proclaimed that all deserters would be sold as slaves. But deserters still kept coming in, and in the end he actually had them driven back with whips. However, those in the city would not allow them back again inside the wall, considering them no better than slaves, and many of them died outside. Seeing all this, Mnasippus thought that the city was 16 already as good as his, and he began to treat his mercenaries differently from before. He had already discharged some of them, and by this time he owed the remainder as much as two months' pay. This was not, as was said, because he was short of money. In fact, since this was an expedition overseas, most of the allied states had sent him money instead of men. The people in the city could now see from their towers that 17 the enemy posts were not so well guarded as before and that the soldiers were dispersed about the country. So they made a sortie, captured some of them and cut down others. When 18 Mnasippus saw what was happening, he put on his armour and came to the rescue with all the hoplites he had, and he ordered the captains and senior officers to lead out the mercenaries. Some of the captains replied that it was not easy to 19 keep men in a proper state of discipline unless they were given their supplies, and at this Mnasippus struck one of them with a stick and one with the spike of his spear. The result was that all the troops following him out of camp were in low spirits themselves and antagonistic to him personally. There can be no worse state of mind for men going into battle.

20   After he had formed his men in line Mnasippus himself defeated the enemy troops in front of the gates and pressed on after them in pursuit. But when they were near the wall, they faced about and hurled stones and javelins from the shelter of the raised memorials in the cemetery. Other enemy troops came charging out from the other gates and fell in a compact body on the extreme end of the Spartan line, where the men

21 were drawn up only eight deep. The Spartans, now considering their line at its end was too weak, tried to draw it back and wheel it round behind the rest of the line. But as soon as they began the movement to the rear, the enemy, assuming that they were running away, launched another attack and the Spartans no longer continued the movement so as to face the front; and then the troops next to them began

22 to take to flight also. As for Mnasippus, he was being strongly attacked by the enemy in front and so could not go to the help of that part of his army which was in distress, and meanwhile he was being left with fewer and fewer men. In the end the whole enemy force made a massed attack on Mnasippus and his men, who by this time were very few, and the citizens, who saw what was happening, came out of the town

23 and joined in the attack. They killed Mnasippus and then all together pressed on with the pursuit. In fact, they might well have captured the camp itself, stockade and all. As it happened, however, when the pursuers came in sight of the crowd of camp-followers, menials and slaves, they turned back again, imagining that these people were capable of putting up a resistance.

24   Next, then, the Corcyraeans put up a trophy and gave back the bodies of the dead under truce. And now the forces in the city were much more sure of themselves than before, while the troops outside were in a state of very low morale indeed.

It was rumoured that Iphicrates would arrive at any moment and it was a fact that the Corcyraeans were now manning their own ships. Hypermenes, who was second in 25 command to Mnasippus, manned every ship he had there in the fleet and sailed round to the stockade. He filled all his transports with slaves and booty and then ordered them to sail away. He himself with the marines and those of the soldiers who had survived the battle stayed behind and guarded the stockade; but in the end they too, in a state of great dis- 26 order, went aboard the triremes and sailed away, leaving behind them quantities of corn and wine and also many slaves and soldiers who were sick. They were thoroughly terrified of the prospect of being caught on the island by the Athenians. And so they got safely away to Leucas.

Now Iphicrates from the beginning of his voyage round 27 the Peloponnese had been always and in every way prepared to engage the enemy in battle. At the very start he had left his large sails behind in Athens, just as though he was sailing into battle. And even when he had a good wind for sailing, he made very little use of his small sails. So, by having the men row all the way, he kept them in better physical shape and got more speed out of the ships. Often, too, when his 28 force was just ready to take the morning or the evening meal, he would order the leading ships of the column to come about away from the shore in whatever place it was and form into line, then he would turn the line around again so that the triremes were facing the land, and at a signal make them race to the shore. And it was something to be really proud of to be the first to get water or whatever else was wanted and to be the first to get one's meal. On the other hand, those who came in last were made to suffer for it: they were defeated by the others in all these points, and at the same time they had to put to sea together with the others when the signal was given. So, while those who had got there first did everything at their leisure, the ones who were last had to do

29 everything in a hurry. Then too, if he happened to be taking a meal in enemy territory, his policy for posting sentries was as follows: he not only, as was right and proper, posted them on land, but he also hoisted the masts of his ships and had men to keep a look-out from their tops. These men, of course, from their higher point of view could see much farther than those posted on the level ground. And when he was taking his evening meal or sleeping, he would allow no fires inside the camp during the night, but he would have lights burning in front of his army, so that no one could approach without being observed. But, if it was good weather, he often put to sea again as soon as the meal was over. If there was a good breeze, they took their rest while sailing, and if they had to row, he would give the sailors rest by
30 turns. And during the voyages by day he would use signals and lead the fleet sometimes in column and sometimes in line of battle. Thus while sailing out they had at the same time received training and had become versed in all the tactics for naval engagements before they reached the sea which, so they thought, was controlled by the enemy. Nearly always they took both their morning and evening meals in enemy territory, yet, since nothing except what was necessary was done, Iphicrates always put to sea again and was well on his way before the enemy's forces arrived to dislodge him.
31 At the time of Mnasippus' death Iphicrates happened to be near the Sphagiae islands off Laconia. After reaching Elis and sailing past the mouth of the Alpheus, he anchored beneath the headland known as the Fish. Next day he put to sea from there on his way to Cephallenia. He was sailing with his fleet drawn up in such a way that he would be fully prepared to go into battle, should the occasion arise. This was because the account he had had of the death of Mnasippus had not come from any eye-witness, and he suspected that it might have been made up to deceive him. He was consequently on his guard; but when he arrived at Cephallenia he really

did get reliable information and he allowed his forces to rest.

I know, of course, that when people are expecting to fight 32 a naval action all these tactical exercises and all this training are quite usual. But what I admire in the conduct of Iphicrates is this: when he had to arrive quickly in an area where he expected to engage the enemy, he found a way by which his men would be none the worse trained tactically because of having to make the voyage, and the voyage would be none the slower because of the training given to the men.

Iphicrates received the submission of the cities in Cephal- 33 lenia and then went on to Corcyra. Here he heard that ten triremes from Dionysius were on the way as reinforcements to the Spartans. First he went personally to reconnoitre the ground and find a place from which any ships approaching could be seen and from which signals back would be visible inside the city. Here he put men on watch and arranged with 34 them the signals they should give to indicate when the enemy were approaching and when they were at anchor. He then detailed twenty of the captains to follow him as soon as the herald gave the word, and he told them that if anyone failed to follow him, he could be quite sure that the punishment would not fall short of what it should be. And now, when 35 the signals came to show that the enemy were approaching and when the herald gave the call to action, the general enthusiasm was really something worth seeing. There was not a man among those who were to sail who did not run to get aboard. Sailing up to the place where the enemy triremes were, Iphicrates found that the crews of all except one ship had gone ashore. Melanippus the Rhodian, however, after advising the others not to stay there, had manned his own ship and was sailing out to sea. Even though he met the ships of Iphicrates he still managed to get away. But all the ships from Syracuse together with their crews were captured. Iphicrates cut off their beaks and towed the triremes into the 36

harbour of Corcyra; as for the prisoners he came to an arrangement by which each man should pay a fixed sum as ransom, except for Crinippus who was in command. He kept Crinippus under guard with a view to getting a very large ransom for him or else selling him as a slave; but Crinippus took things so badly that he died by his own hand. Iphicrates let the rest go after accepting Corcyraeans as guar-
37 antors for the ransom money. He now maintained most of his sailors by letting them do work on the land for the Corcy-raeans, and with the peltasts and hoplites on the ships he crossed over into Acarnania. Here he gave help, where help was needed, to the cities that were friendly and made war against the Thyrians, a nation of first-rate fighters who live
38 in a place of great natural strength. He also took the fleet from Corcyra, now about ninety ships, and sailed to Cephallenia where he raised money. Some contributions were voluntary, others enforced. Then he made preparations for launching attacks on Spartan territory, for winning over all the enemy cities in the area who were willing to join him, and for mak-ing war upon those who would not.
39   In my view, of all the campaigns of Iphicrates this was one of the most remarkable, and I also admire him for asking the Athenians to appoint as his colleagues Callistratus and Cha-brias. Callistratus, the popular speaker, was far from friendly to him and Chabrias was regarded as a very good general. It seems to me, then, that he was acting wisely if he thought that they were intelligent men and therefore wanted to have their advice; and if, on the other hand, he regarded them as opponents and yet was bold enough to give them the chance of seeing that neither his energy nor his planning could be criticized, then that seems to me to show what confidence the man had in himself.

CHAPTER 3

Renewal of the Peace (371 B.C.). Isolation of Thebes

WHILE Iphicrates was so engaged, the Athenians took note
of the fact that the Plataeans, who were their friends, had
been expelled from Boeotia and had come to them as refugees; and the Thespians, too, were begging Athens not to
allow them to be left without a city. They therefore no
longer thought kindly of the Thebans, though they were
deterred from making war on Thebes partly by a sense of
shame and partly because they calculated that a war would
not be in their own interest. However, they were certainly
unwilling to go on co-operating with Thebes in her actions
when they saw her marching against the Phocians, who were
old friends of Athens, and destroying other friendly cities,
cities, too, which had proved reliable in the Persian wars.
As a result of all this the Athenian people voted that peace
should be made. First they sent a deputation to Thebes to
invite the Thebans to come with them, if they wished to do
so, to Sparta in order to negotiate a peace, and then they
sent ambassadors to Sparta themselves.* Among the ambassadors appointed were Callias, the son of Hipponicus;
Autocles, ⟨the son of⟩ Strombichides; Demostratus, the
son of Aristophon; Aristocles, Cephisodotus, Melanopus and
Lycaethus. The popular speaker Callistratus was also one of
the party.† He had promised Iphicrates that, if he was

* Considering that Thebes was a member of the Second Athenian
Confederacy and that in it decisions on peace could not be taken by
Athens without the prior consent of the Allied Synedrion (Tod,
G.H.I., no. 127), one finds Xenophon's account of the preliminaries
very curious.

† It is unclear whether Xenophon meant that Callistratus was one

allowed to go home, he would either send money for the fleet or else make arrangements for peace. This was why he was at Athens at the time and serving in the peace-making mission.

When the ambassadors were introduced to the assembly of the Spartans and their allies, the first of them to speak was Callias, the torch-bearer at the Mysteries. He was the kind of man who enjoyed being praised by himself just as much as by others. On this occasion he began to speak more or less as follows:

4   'Spartans, I must remind you that I am not the only one of my family to hold the position of your diplomatic representative in Athens. No, my father's father received it from his father and handed it down to his descendants. And I want to make this point clear to you too, namely, that Athens has always had a particular regard for my family. It is among us that she looks for her generals when there is a war, and when she wants a cessation of hostilities, we are the ones whom she sends out as peace-makers. I myself have before now already come here twice in order to arrange for an end to fighting and on both of these missions I succeeded in negotiating peace both for you and for us. Now I am here for the third time, and I think that now much more than ever before it is

---

of the elected ambassadors, or just happened to be present, in that sense 'of the party'; as a general, he was probably not an elected ambassador, though no distinction is made in §10 when he begins to speak. Why does Xenophon give only seven names of elected ambassadors (when ten would be normal) and patronymics for only three of that seven (or, if the Manuscripts are exactly followed, eight and two)? Carelessness is perhaps the right explanation; he simply could not remember and did not care to find out. (C. J. Tuplin, *Liverpool Classical Monthly*, 1977, pp. 51 ff. argued that the text may have been corrupted and that Xenophon may have given the full list, but since Xenophon gave the names as being 'among the ambassadors appointed' he himself seems to have been conscious that he was not giving the full list.)

right that I should achieve my aim of bringing about a reconciliation. For I see that now it is not a case of your think- 5
ing one thing and us another. On the contrary both you and
we are grieved and angry about the destruction of Plataea
and Thespiae. Is it not reasonable that, since we think in the
same way, we should be friends rather than enemies? You
will, no doubt, agree that wise men do not go to war for
trifling differences. But if we are, in fact, in complete agreement, is it not absolutely absurd for us not to make peace?
The right thing to have done would have been for us not to 6
have made war on each other in the first place, since, accord-
to the tradition, the first foreigners to whom our ancestor
Triptolemus revealed the mysteries of Demeter and Core
were Heracles, who founded your state, and the Dioscuri,
who were your citizens; and the Peloponnese was the first
place on which he bestowed the seed of the fruit of Demeter.
Surely, then, it must be wrong for you ever to come and
destroy the crops of those very men from whom you received the seed, and it must be equally wrong for us not to
want you, to whom we gave the seed, to enjoy the greatest
possible abundance of its produce. And if it is really true
that it is divinely ordained that there should be wars among
men, then what we should do is to be as slow as we can to
start a war and as quick as we can to end it, once it has begun.'

After Callias Autocles, who was regarded as a particularly 7
accomplished speaker, made the following speech: 'Spartans,
I am well aware that what I am going to say will not be quite
what you will enjoy hearing. All the same I am of opinion
that when people want the friendship that they are making to
last for as long as possible, they ought to point out to each
other the reasons why they were at war. Now you are always
saying: "The cities must be independent," but it is you yourselves who are the greatest obstacle to this independence. The
first clause you put into any treaty with your allied cities is
this, that they must follow you wherever you lead. What has

8 that got to do with independence? You make enemies of other powers without any previous consultation with your allies, and then you lead your allies against them. And so it often happens that these so–called "independent" states are forced to march against people who want to be on the best possible terms with them. But where you show yourselves most utterly opposed to the idea of independence is in the fact that you set up your own government – of ten in one city, of thirty in another – and with regard to these men in power what you aim at is not that they should govern in accordance with the laws, but that they should be strong enough to hold down the cities by force. This makes it look as though what gives you pleasure is dictatorship and not 9 constitutional government. And then at the time when the King directed that the cities should be independent, you appeared to be thoroughly convinced that the Thebans would not be acting in accordance with the King's prescription unless they allowed each one of their cities to rule itself and to live by whatever laws it chose. But after you had seized the Cadmea, you deprived even the Thebans themselves of their independence. But if one is going to make friends with other people, one should not first of all claim everything due to one from others and then take up the attitude of grabbing for oneself everything else one can.'

10 This speech of Autocles was followed by a general silence. However, he had succeeded in giving pleasure to those who were angry with the Spartans. The next speaker was Callistratus, who said: 'Spartans, it must be admitted, I think, that mistakes have been made both by us and by you. But I do not think that one ought never to have anything more to do with people who make mistakes. I observe that no one in the world goes through life without making them. And I think that when people have made mistakes they are sometimes easier to deal with, especially if, like us, their mistakes 11 have been followed by punishment. In your own case, too, I

notice that a number of things have gone wrong because of ill-considered actions which you have taken, among which, no doubt, was the seizure of the Cadmea in Thebes. Now, certainly, as a result of the wrong you did to the Thebans, all those cities which you so much wanted to be independent are once again under Theban authority. Therefore I hope that now, after we have been taught that it does not pay to seize more than we are entitled to, we shall once again come to a reasonable and friendly understanding. Now there 12 are some people about who want to stop peace being made, and they are slandering us by saying that we have not come here because we want your friendship, but simply because we are afraid that Antalcidas may arrive with money from the King. You can easily see how stupid this argument is. Surely it is well known that the King's message was to the effect that all the cities in Greece should be independent. Then why should we, who agree with the King and have followed his direction, be frightened of him? Or does anyone imagine that the King wants to spend money on making others great? What he really wants, of course, is to have his own policies carried out for him without spending any money at all himself.

'Well, then, why have we come? It is not because we are 13 in any difficulties, as you can easily, if you like, find out by looking at the situation on sea or on land at the present moment. Then why are we here? Obviously because some of our allies are acting in a way which we do not like. And maybe also because we should like to show you the gratitude which we very rightly felt towards you when you saved us from destruction. And now I should touch also on the question of self-interest. As you know, all the cities of Greece are divided among those who are on our side and those who are on yours, and in each individual city there is a pro-Spartan party and a pro-Athenian party. Now if you and we became friends, would there be any quarter from which either of us could reasonably expect trouble? Certainly, if you were with us, no one would be powerful enough to do us any harm on land; and, with us on your side, no one

15 could hurt you by sea. And after all, do we not all know this – that wars are constantly breaking out and constantly coming to an end, and that even if we do not want peace now, we shall want it again some time? Why, then, should we wait for the time when we shall have had a lot of trouble and be at the end of our resources? Why not make peace as quickly as we can, before we have suffered something past curing?

16 Personally, I do not admire the athlete who after constantly winning in the games and after having won a great reputation is so fond of competition that he never stops until all his training ends in defeat. Nor do I admire the gambler who doubles his stakes after one lucky throw. I observe that most

17 people of that sort end up by having nothing at all. Should not we also recognize this fact, and never become involved in a fight where one either wins all or loses all? Should we not rather become friends while we are still strong and still successful? In this way you will help us and we shall help you to a position in Greece even greater than we have had in the past.'

18 These speeches by the Athenians won approval and the Spartans also voted for peace.* The terms were that governors should be withdrawn from the cities, all forces, both

---

*Literally, 'the Spartans also voted to accept the peace'. Did they accept it from the Athenians and allies or from the Persian king? Diod. XV.50.4 asserts the latter, and Dionysius of Halicarnassus *Lysias* 12, who almost certainly drew on the reliable Philochorus, says that the Peace involved the King of Persia. But, when Xenophon wrote so fully, can he have omitted to notice such an important fact? Many have refused to think him capable of such an omission, without remarking that there is a far more astonishing omission for all the alleged 'fullness', *viz.* the famous altercation between Epaminondas and Agesilaus (Nepos *Epaminondas* 6.4, Plut. *Agesilaus* 28). Xenophon eschewed the unpalatable.

naval and military, should be disbanded, and that the cities should be left independent. It was provided that in any case of violation of these terms, any state which so desired should be free to go to the help of the injured party, but that, if a state did not desire to do this, there should be no legal obligation for it to do so. On these terms the Spartans took the 19 oath for themselves and their allies, and the Athenians and their allies took the oath separately, city by city.* The Thebans also signed with the other cities which were taking the oath, but on the following day their ambassadors appeared again and demanded that the signature should be altered so as to read 'the Boeotians' instead of 'the Thebans' as signatories. However, Agesilaus replied that he was not going to change anything in what they had signed and sworn to in the first place; if, however, they did not want to be included in the treaty, he was prepared, on their instructions, to strike out their names. So, with all the other 20 states at peace, and with no one having any complaints except against the Thebans, the Athenians held the view that now there was a good chance that the Thebans would be, as they say, cut down to size. As for the Thebans themselves, they went back home in a state of profound discouragement.

*Only from this single sentence of the whole of the *Hellenica* could one suspect that Athens had allies on whose behalf she might have sworn, i.e. members of a league. For Xenophon's attitude to the Second Athenian Confederacy, see Introduction p. 42.

CHAPTER 4

Battle of Leuctra (371 B.C.).
Death of Jason (370 B.C.). His successors

1 AFTER this the Athenians withdrew their garrisons from the
cities and sent out to Iphicrates and his fleet, instructing him to
give back everything which he had seized after the time when
2 the oaths were sworn in Sparta. The Spartans also withdrew
their garrisons and governors from the cities. There remained, however, the question of Cleombrotus and his army
in Phocis. Cleombrotus asked the home authorities what he
was to do and Prothous said that in his opinion they should
first disband the army, as they had sworn to do, and send
round to all the cities asking them to make whatever contributions they could to a fund to be placed in the temple of
Apollo; they should then, if any state failed to allow the
cities to be independent, again call together those states who
were willing to support the cause of independence and lead
them against those who were opposing it; by doing this, he
said, it seemed to him that they would be most likely to win
the favour of the gods and also provoke the least possible
3 discontent from the cities. However, when the Spartan assembly heard this from him they considered that he was talking
utter nonsense. It looks as though they were already being
impelled by some divine power.* They sent to Cleombrotus
telling him not to disband his army, but to lead it directly
against the Thebans unless they agreed to leave the cities
independent. Cleombrotus found that the Thebans, so far
from agreeing to this, were keeping their own army intact

* According to Plut. *Agesilaus* 28, it was Agesilaus who insisted
on not recalling Cleombrotus – not a detail which Xenophon would
choose to mention.

so that they would have a force with which to meet him. He therefore led his army into Boeotia.

Cleombrotus did not invade by the route which the Thebans had expected him to take and where they had a force on guard in a narrow pass. Instead, he went by way of Thisbae by an unexpected route over the mountains. Arriving at Creusis he captured the fortifications, and took twelve triremes belonging to the Thebans. After this action he marched 4 inland and camped at Leuctra in the territory of Thespiae. The Thebans were encamped on a hill opposite and not far away. They had no allies with them apart from the Boeotians. It was now that his friends went to Cleombrotus and said: 'Cleombrotus, if you let the Thebans get away without 5 fighting a battle, the chances are that Sparta will make you suffer for it to the limit of her ability. They will remember against you the time when you got as far as Cynoscephalae and then did no damage to Theban territory, and also the other time later when the army you led was beaten back from the frontier, although Agesilaus always managed to invade by way of Cithaeron. So if you have any consideration for yourself or any wish to see your country again, you must lead the way into battle against these men.' And while his friends said this, his enemies were saying: 'Now it will become clear whether this man is really on the side of the Thebans, as people say that he is.'

All this talk had the effect of making Cleombrotus eager to 6 join battle. And on the other side, the leaders of the Thebans calculated that if they did not fight, the cities round them would revolt and they themselves would be besieged; moreover, if the people of Thebes were deprived of necessities, there was a risk that the city itself would turn against them. Many of these Theban leaders had been in exile before, and they now reckoned that it would be better to die in battle than to go into exile again. They also found a certain en- 7 couragement in the oracle which says that the Spartans must suffer a defeat at the place where stands the monument to the virgins who are supposed to have killed themselves because they had been raped by some Spartans. So the Thebans put garlands on this monument before the battle. Reports also came to them from Thebes to the effect that the doors of all the temples were opening of their own accord and that the priestesses were saying that the gods were giving clear signs of victory. It was also said that the arms in the temple of Heracles had disappeared, showing that Heracles himself had set out for the battle. Now there are some people who say that all these reports were fabricated by the Theban

8 leaders, but as far as the battle was concerned, everything certainly went badly for the Spartans, and everything, including luck, was on the side of the Thebans.

It was after the morning meal that Cleombrotus held his last council of war. They had been drinking a bit at midday, and it was said that the wine had a certain stimulating effect

9 on them. When both sides were getting under arms and it was already clear that there was to be a battle, first of all there began to withdraw from the Boeotian army all the people who had been providing the market and also some of the baggage carriers and others who did not want to fight. Now the Spartan mercenaries under Hieron, the peltasts from Phocis, and the Heraclean and Phliasian cavalry wheeled round behind these people, attacked and routed them, and drove them back to the Boeotian camp. The effect was to make the Boeotian army much larger and more closely

10 massed than it was before. Next, since between the two armies the ground was level, the Spartans stationed their cavalry in front of the phalanx and the Thebans stationed their cavalry opposite them. The Theban cavalry, as a result of the war with Orchomenus and with Thespiae, was in good training, but the Spartan cavalry at that time was in very

11 poor shape. This was because the horses were kept by the very rich, and it was only after an order for mobilization

that the appointed cavalryman appeared to get his horse
and whatever arms were given him; he then had to take the
field at once. Also the men who served in the cavalry were
the ones who were in the worst physical condition and the
least anxious to win distinction. So much for the cavalry on   12
each side. As for the infantry, it was said that in the Spartan
order of battle each half-company advanced three files
abreast, so that the phalanx was not more than twelve men
deep. The Thebans, on the other hand, were drawn up in
a massed formation of at least fifty shields in depth. They
calculated that, if they proved superior in that part of the
field where the king was, all the rest would be easy.

Now Cleombrotus began to advance; but first of all, and   13
even before his troops had realized that he was going into
battle, the cavalry had already engaged and the Spartan contingents had very quickly been worsted. Then in their flight
they had fallen foul of their own hoplites, and at the same
moment the companies of the Thebans were also coming in
to the attack. Nevertheless, Cleombrotus and the men with
him were at first having the better of things in the fighting.
This is clearly proved by the fact that they would not have
been able to take him up and carry him off while still alive
unless those fighting in front of him had at that time been
winning. But after Dinon, the polemarch, had been killed,   14
and Sphodrias too, who was one of the king's tent-com-
panions, together with his son, Cleonymus, then the king's
horse-guards and the troops known as 'the polemarch's own'
and all the rest gave way before the Theban masses. And the
Spartan left wing, seeing that their right was being pushed
back, gave way too. Nevertheless, although many had been
killed and they had suffered a defeat, once they had crossed
the ditch in front of their camp, they halted and grounded
arms at the place from which they had started out (though
it should be added that their camp was not on entirely level
ground; there was a slope uphill). And at this point there

were some of the Spartans who could not bear to contemplate what had happened and who said that they ought to prevent the enemy from putting up a trophy and that, instead of recovering the bodies of their dead under a truce,
15 they ought to win them back by fighting. The generals, however, could see that of the whole Spartan army nearly a thousand had been killed; they saw, too, that out of the 700 Spartans of the officer class who had been there, about four hundred had fallen; and they realized that none of their allies had any heart left for fighting, while some of them were not even displeased by the way things had gone. So they called a meeting of those best qualified to decide, and discussed what to do. All agreed that it would be best to recover the dead under a truce, and so they sent a herald to ask for this. The Thebans then put up their trophy and gave back the bodies under truce.*

16 It was on the last day of the festival of the Gymnopaedia that the messenger sent to report this disaster arrived in Sparta. The men's chorus was in the theatre at the time. When the ephors heard what had happened, they were deeply grieved as, indeed, they were bound to be, yet instead of putting an end to the performance, they let the chorus go through with it to the end. Also, while they gave the names of all the dead to the relatives concerned, they told the women to bear their suffering in silence and to avoid any cries of lamentation. And on the following day you could see† those whose relatives had been killed going about in public looking bright and happy, while as for those whose relatives

---

*Xenophon's account of Leuctra is quite inadequate as a piece of military history. Epaminondas and Pelopidas are not named and their plans and actions not explored. Some help is provided by Diod. XV.51–6 and Plut. *Pelopidas* 20–23, but much is uncertain. For two different reconstructions, see J. K. Anderson, *Military theory and practice in the age of Xenophon* (1970), pp. 192–220, and Cawkwell, *Classical Quarterly*, 22, 1972, pp. 260–63.

† 'Foreigners' were allowed to attend the Gymnopaedia (cf. Xen. *Mem.* I.2.61), and Xenophon may have been there in 371 B.C.

had been reported living, there were not many of them to be seen, and those who were to be seen were walking about looking gloomy and sorry for themselves.

The next step taken by the ephors was to call up the two 17 remaining regiments, bringing in men who were forty years above the minimum age for service; and they also sent out all men up to the same age who belonged to the regiments now serving abroad. For in the original expedition to Phocis only the age groups up to 35 from the minimum had been serving. In addition, they ordered out those who at the time of the first expedition had been left behind because of official duties. Since Agesilaus had still not recovered from his illness, the 18 state ordered his son, Archidamus, to take command. The Tegeans marched with him willingly, since at that time Stasippus and his party, who were pro-Spartan and influential in Tegea, were still alive. The Mantineans too, coming in from their villages, supported him strongly, being then governed by an aristocracy. Corinth, Sicyon, Phlius and Achaea also came in perfectly willingly, and other states also sent troops. Meanwhile, both the Spartans themselves and the Corinthians were manning triremes, and they asked the Sicyonians to join them in this, the intention being to carry the army across the gulf in these ships. Archidamus then 19 made the sacrifices for crossing the frontier.

Immediately after the battle the Thebans had sent a messenger, crowned with garlands, to Athens. There they not only reported the extent of the victory that had been won but urged the Athenians to come and help them, saying that it was now possible to make the Spartans pay for all that they had done to them. The Athenian Council happened to be in 20 session on the Acropolis. After they had heard what had happened, it became clear to everyone that they were very far from pleased; they did not offer the herald any hospitality, and they said nothing in reply to his request for aid. And so he left Athens.

The Thebans now sent in all haste to their ally Jason, and

among themselves tried to work out how the future was
21 likely to go. Jason at once manned triremes, as though he was
going to send naval assistance, but he actually came into
Boeotia himself by land, bringing his mercenary army and
his personal cavalry force. He marched through Phocis, in
spite of the fact that there was a bitter, undeclared war going
on between him and the Phocians. In many of their cities he
appeared before their eyes before they even knew he was on
his way. Certainly before they could get any army together
by calling up their scattered contingents, he was already far
beyond their reach – a good example of how speed often
counts for more than force when it comes to getting things
done.

22   When he arrived in Boeotia, the Thebans suggested that
now was the time to engage the Spartans. They proposed
that he with his mercenaries should attack from the heights,
while they moved in from the front. Jason, however, argued
against them. He pointed out that they had had a great success
and questioned the value of now risking a decisive battle in
which, while they might gain more still, they might also lose
23 what they had won already. 'Do you not see,' he said, 'that
in your own case it was when you were really up against it
that you won the victory? One can suppose, then, that the
Spartans too, if forced into the same situation, will fight it
out to the end regardless of their lives. It seems, too, that
heaven takes pleasure in raising up the small and bringing
24 down the great.' These were the arguments he used to divert
the Thebans from their plan of risking a decisive battle. He
then pointed out to the Spartans what a difference there was
between a defeated and a victorious army. 'If,' he said, 'you
want to forget the disaster that has happened to you, I should
advise you to get your breath back again and rest; then,
when you have regained strength, you can go into battle
against men who are undefeated. As it is, you can be sure
that some, even among your own allies, are already nego-

tiating with the enemy about a pact of friendship. I advise
you, then, to do everything you can to secure a truce. This
is what I want myself, and I am acting out of a desire to see
you safe – partly because my father was your friend and
partly because I act as your diplomatic representative in
Thessaly.'

This was what he said, but it may be that he was acting in 25
this way with the aim of keeping the two powers in opposition so that each one of them should need his help.

In any case the Spartans, after hearing him, asked him to
negotiate a truce for them. Then, when it was reported that
a truce had been made, the polemarchs issued the order that
after the coming meal all troops should have their baggage
packed so as to be ready to set out during the night and be
climbing Cithaeron by daybreak. Actually, as soon as dinner
was over and before the men had rested, they ordered a start
to be made and at the very beginning of the evening led the
way by the route going through Creusis, relying not so much
on the truce as on keeping their intentions secret. They had a 26
very difficult march, going away, as they were, by night and
in fear and by a hard road. Arriving at Aegosthena in the
territory of Megara they met the army under Archidamus.
There they waited until all the allies had joined them, and
then Archidamus led back the whole army together as far as
Corinth. From there he disbanded the allied contingents and
led the Spartan forces back home.

Jason, on his way back through Phocis, captured the outer 27
city of the Hyampolitans, devastated their land, and killed a
number of their men. He went through the rest of Phocis
without undertaking any operations, but when he reached
Heraclea he destroyed the fortifications there. This, clearly,
was not because he was under any apprehension that, with
this pass open, anyone might march against his own dominions; what he really had in mind was the possibility of some
power seizing Heraclea and its narrow pass and so being able

to impede him from marching wherever he wanted to in Greece.

28   So he returned to Thessaly, a great man indeed. He had been legally appointed Lord of Thessaly; he controlled great forces of mercenaries, both infantry and cavalry, and these forces had been trained to the highest pitch of efficiency. He was greater still in the strength of his alliances, many states being allied with him already and others being anxious to do so too. When one considers that there was no power on earth that could afford to disregard him, one may say that he was the greatest man of his times.

29   Now when the time of the Pythian festival was approaching Jason sent round to his cities orders for them to produce cattle, sheep, goats and swine for the sacrifice. It is said that the contributions required of each city were very moderate, and yet that no less than 1,000 cattle and more than 10,000 of the other animals were brought in. He also proclaimed an offer of a crown of gold as prize to the city which raised the

30 finest bull to lead the procession in honour of the god. And he ordered the Thessalians to be ready to take the field at the time of the Pythian festival. His intention, so they say, was to take personal charge both of the religious assembly and of the games. However, to this day no one knows what his intentions were with regard to the sacred treasure. It is said that when the people of Delphi asked the god what they should do if he tried to take any of this treasure, Apollo answered that he would look after that matter himself.*

31   However that may be, this great man with all his great designs had just finished holding a review and inspection of

*When Xenophon was writing the second part of the *Hellenica*, i.e. in the 350s, the sacred treasure of Delphi was being used by the Phocians. He was unsure about the intentions of Jason, although his early death (§31) was suggestive. About the actions of the Phocians he could have no doubt, and their ruin in 346 at the end of the Sacred War was for him, as for the Greeks generally, only to be expected.

the cavalry from Pherae, had taken his seat, and was giving his answers to those who came to him with any request, when he was struck down and killed by some young men who came up to him pretending that they had some quarrel among themselves. Those of his bodyguard who were there 32 rushed to his help and one of the young men, still in the act of striking at Jason, was run through with a lance and killed. Another was caught while mounting his horse, and died of the many wounds he received. But the rest leapt on the horses which they had waiting for them and got safely away. In most of the Greek cities to which they came they were honoured – a fact which clearly shows that the Greeks were really seriously frightened that Jason might seize an absolute and irresponsible power.

After his death his brothers Polydorus and Polyphron were 33 appointed Lords of Thessaly. While the two of them were travelling to Larissa, Polydorus was killed at night while he was asleep, and it looked as though this sudden death, with no apparent reason for it, must have been the work of his brother. Polyphron now ruled for a year, and he made this 34 Lordship of his into something more like a dictatorship. In Pharsalus he put to death Polydamas and eight others of the best citizens, and he exiled numbers of people from Larissa. While still behaving in this way he was himself killed by 35 Alexander, who claimed to be avenging Polydorus and putting an end to the dictatorship. But as soon as he got into power he showed his intractable temper to the Thessalians as their Lord, and to the Thebans and Athenians as their enemy. On land and sea he acted like a lawless freebooter. Such was his character and he, too, was killed. The murder was done by his wife's brothers, but it was his wife who planned it. She told her brothers that Alexander was planning to de- 36 stroy them, and she hid them in her house for the whole of one day. Alexander came home drunk and, after she had received him and put him to bed, she carried his sword out of the bedroom, leaving the light burning inside. Seeing that her brothers hesitated to go in and attack Alexander, she told them that unless they did so at once, she would wake him up. And when they did go in, she shut the door and held it tight by the knocker until her husband had been killed. The reason 37 for her hatred of her husband is variously explained. Some say it was because Alexander once imprisoned a beautiful young boy, with whom he was in love, and when she begged for him to be released, he took him out and killed him. Others say that, since his wife was bearing him no children, Alexander was sending to Thebes and proposing marriage to Jason's widow. These are the reasons given for the plot made against Alexander by his wife. As for those who carried it out, the eldest of the brothers, Tisiphonus, has, up to the time when this was written, been holding power in Thessaly.*

*Tisiphonus acceded, according to Diod. XVI.14.1, in 357–6 and was replaced in 353 (Diod. XVI. 35). So we can be confident that chapter 4 of Book VI was composed in the 350s.

CHAPTER 5

Agesilaus in Arcadia (370 B.C.). Theban invasion of Laconia
(Winter 370–369 B.C.). Athens sends help to Sparta

So much for the events in Thessaly in Jason's time and from 1
the time of his death until the rule of Tisiphonus. I shall now
return to the point from which I started this digression.

Archidamus, then, had led back the army sent out to relieve the force at Leuctra. The Athenians were now concerned with the thought that while the Peloponnesians still
considered themselves bound to follow the leadership of
Sparta, the Spartans themselves were not in the same situation as that to which they had brought Athens. They therefore sent round to the cities and invited all those who wished
to share in the peace on the terms sent down by the King to
send delegations to Athens. A meeting was held and a reso- 2
lution was passed that they and all who wished to share in
the peace should take the following oath: 'I will abide by the
peace terms sent down by the King and by the decrees of the
Athenians and their allies. And if anyone makes war on any
of the cities which have taken this oath, I will come to the
help of that city with all my strength.' *

*Diodorus omits notice of this Peace, perhaps because it did not
come at the end of a war but merely reaffirmed in essence the terms
of the Peace before Leuctra, though under somewhat different management, *viz.* at the instigation of Athens. Much is therefore obscure,
a good indication of how much in the dark we would be if we had
only Xenophon to enlighten us on the first four decades of the Fourth
Century. The one important development appears to be 'the decrees
of the Athenians and their allies'. The only decree then passed, at
which we can guess, was the recognition of Athens' right to recover
Amphipolis (cf. Aeschines II.32). See n. at VI.5.37 for the question of
whether the Spartans took part.

Everyone was pleased with this oath except for the Eleans,
who objected to having to admit the independence of the
Marganians, the Scilluntians* and the Triphylians, since they
3 claimed that these cities belonged to them. The Athenians,
however, and all the rest voted that, as in the terms written
down by the King, all cities, big and small alike, should be
independent. They then sent out officials to administer the
oath, and instructed them to go for this purpose to the highest authorities in each city. All took the oath except for the
Eleans.

As a result of this the Mantineans too, on the assumption
that they were now completely independent, met together
and voted that Mantinea should be made into one city and
4 that it should be fortified with walls. To the Spartans, on the
other hand, it seemed quite intolerable that such a thing
should be done without their authority. They therefore sent
Agesilaus as their representative to Mantinea, since he was
thought to have long-standing family ties of friendship with
the Mantineans. When he arrived, the authorities would not
call a meeting of the whole people for him to address; instead, they told him to say what he wanted to them personally. He then promised them that, if they would halt work on
the fortifications for the time being, he would arrange things
so that they would be able to save money on the project and
5 also carry it out with full Spartan approval. They replied
that a resolution had been passed by the whole citizen body
that the fortifications should be built at once; it was therefore impossible to stop work. After this Agesilaus went away
in an angry mood; but it did not seem possible to send an
army against them, since the peace had been made on the
basis of independence for the cities. Meanwhile, some of the

*This is the only place in the *Hellenica* where Xenophon alludes
to Scillus, the place where he lived from the late 390s until the Eleans
marched against it and Xenophon and his sons had to flee (Diogenes
Laertius II.53). For Xenophontic reserve, see Introduction p. 32 f.

cities in Arcadia sent men to help the Mantineans in the work, and the Eleans contributed three talents towards the expense of the fortifications.

While the Mantineans were occupied in this way, among 6 the Tegeans the party led by Callibius and Proxenus were agitating in favour of forming a united state of Arcadia with the provision that whatever was passed in the general assembly should be binding on the various cities in the union.* The party of Stasippus, on the other hand, were for leaving things in Tegea as they were and for following the constitution of their ancestors. In the council of magistrates the party of 7 Callibius and Proxenus were defeated, but, thinking that if they could rally the whole people together they would have the advantage in numbers, they came out openly in arms. Seeing this, Stasippus and his party also took up arms. They were indeed inferior in numbers, but they joined battle, killed Proxenus and a few of the men with him, and drove the others back in flight. However, they did not press the pursuit, since Stasippus was the sort of man who disliked killing many of his own fellow-citizens. The followers of 8 Callibius had retreated to a position under the city wall and the gates on the side towards Mantinea. As their enemies were making no further moves against them, they stayed here quietly and reorganized themselves. Long before this they had sent to Mantinea asking for help to be sent, but they now proceeded to enter into peace talks with the party of Stasippus. Then, as soon as it could be seen that the Mantineans were approaching, some of them leapt up on to the wall, calling for help as quickly as possible and shouting out to the

*Xenophon in characteristically allusive fashion (cf. Introduction p. 34 f.) gives no formal account of the foundation of the Arcadian Federation, let alone of the building of the Federal capital, Megalopolis (cf. VII.5.5). The chief elements of the Federal constitution emerge, unexplained, at VII.4.33 f. Xenophon writes for those who know.

Mantineans to hurry; others from inside opened the gates to
9 them. Seeing what was happening, Stasippus and his party
rushed out of the gates leading to Pallantium and before their
pursuers could catch up with them fled for refuge into the
temple of Artemis, where they shut themselves in and stayed
as they were. But their enemies crowded after them, climbed
up the temple, tore off the roof and hurled down tiles on
them. The men inside, seeing that there was nothing else to
do, told them to stop and promised that they would come
out. As soon as their enemies had them in their hands, they
bound them, threw them into a wagon and carried them
back to Tegea. There they and the Mantineans sentenced
them and put them to death.

10 While this was going on, about eight hundred of the
Tegeans in the party of Stasippus had fled to Sparta as exiles.
Later, the Spartans decided that in accordance with their
oaths* they ought to take action both on behalf of the
Tegean dead and of the exiles. So they marched against
Mantinea on the grounds that the Mantineans had violated
their oaths by making an armed attack on the Tegeans. The
ephors ordered mobilization, and the state instructed Agesilaus
to take command.

11 Most of the Arcadians were assembling at Asea, but the
Mantineans were staying at home to keep a watch on the
Orchomenians, who had refused to join the Arcadian League
because of their hostility towards Mantinea, and had actually
received into their city the army of mercenaries under Polytropus which had been brought together at Corinth. The
Heraeans and the Lepreans also were serving in the Spartan
army against Mantinea.

*Xenophon does not bother to explain that the 'oaths' in question
are those sworn after Leuctra (VI.5.3). Some have therefore tried to
explain the Spartan action in terms of the constitution of the Peloponnesian League – improbably, since wars between member states
were in certain circumstances permissible (cf. Thuc. V.65.4 and
IV.134).

As soon as the sacrifices for crossing the frontier turned out 12
favourably, Agesilaus started his march into Arcadia. He
seized the frontier city of Eutaea where he found the old men,
the women and the children still living in their houses, while
the men of military age had gone off to join the Arcadian
army. In spite of this he did no harm to the city; he let the
people go on living there, and his troops paid for whatever
they took to meet their needs. If there was any looting at the
time when they entered the city, Agesilaus saw to it that the
property was found and restored. He remained here waiting
for the mercenaries under Polytropus and occupied the time
in repairing those parts of the city wall which were in need
of repair.

Meanwhile the Mantineans had marched against Orcho- 13
menus. Their attack on the city wall ended badly for them
and a number of them were killed. In their retreat they had
got as far as Elymia and, though the Orchomenian hoplites
had stopped pursuing them, Polytropus and his men were
still at their heels, attacking with great audacity. At this point
the Mantineans, realizing that unless they could beat back
these attacks they were going to lose numbers of men from
the javelins, turned about and charged all together against
their pursuers. There Polytropus fell fighting; the rest fled, 14
and great numbers of them would have been killed if it had
not been for the arrival of the Phliasian cavalry, who rode
round to the rear of the Mantineans and made them give up
the pursuit. After this action the Mantineans went back
home.

When Agesilaus heard what had happened he came to the 15
conclusion that the mercenaries from Orchomenus would
not now be joining him, and went forward with his own
force. On the first day he had the evening meal in the territory of Tegea, and on the day after crossed into Mantinean
territory and camped at the foot of the mountains west of
the city. There he laid waste the land and carried off property
from the farms. Meanwhile the Arcadian force that had

16 gathered at Asea came to Tegea by night. On the next day
Agesilaus was encamped between two and three miles from
Mantinea when the Arcadians from Tegea, a very large army
of hoplites, appeared. They were marching along the foot of
the mountains between Mantinea and Tegea, and were aiming at joining up with the Mantineans. There were Argives
with them too, but these were not in full force. Some of
Agesilaus' advisers now tried to persuade him to attack this
force while it was still alone, but Agesilaus feared that while
he was marching against them the Mantineans might come
out from their city and attack him in the flank and rear. He
therefore thought that the best thing to do was to let them
join forces and then, if they wanted to fight a battle, to engage them in the open and in regular formation.

17 The Arcadians, then, had now all joined up together. But
now also the peltasts from Orchomenus and the Phliasian
cavalry, who had made their way past Mantinea during the
night, appeared just as Agesilaus was sacrificing in front of
the camp at dawn. Their appearance caused the Spartans to
fall hurriedly into line and Agesilaus himself to retire inside
the camp. However, when they were recognized as friends
Agesilaus obtained favourable omens, and then, after breakfast, led the army forward. Then in the evening he camped,
without realizing quite what his position was, in the valley
behind the town of Mantinea. This is a very narrow valley
18 with mountains all round. Next day he was sacrificing at
dawn in front of the army when he saw that troops were
coming out of Mantinea and forming up on the mountains
above the rear of his column. He decided that he must lead
his army out of the valley as quickly as he could, but he
feared that if he led the way himself the enemy would fall
upon his rear. He therefore made no forward move, but
turned to face the enemy in line; he then ordered the men at
the rear to march up towards him behind the line. In this
way he managed to lead them out of the valley and, while

he was doing so, his phalanx was growing stronger all the
time. When it was double its original depth, he marched out 19
into the plain with the hoplites still in this formation, then
extended the army again into a line nine or ten shields deep.
The Mantineans, however, were no longer coming out from
their fortifications. The Eleans, who were with them, had
persuaded them not to fight a battle until the Thebans arrived, and said that they were certain that the Thebans would
be coming,* because they had themselves lent the Thebans,
at their request, ten talents for their expenses in bringing up
their forces. When they heard this the Arcadian army stayed 20
quietly in Mantinea. As for Agesilaus, he was anxious enough
to lead his army away, since it was already mid-winter;
nevertheless, he stayed for three days where he was, quite
near the city of Mantinea, so as not to give the impression
that he was hurrying away because he was frightened. On
the fourth day, after an early breakfast, he led the army away
with the intention of camping at the place where he had
camped after originally leaving Eutaea. But as not a single 21
Arcadian appeared he led them straight on by the quickest
route to Eutaea, even though it was very late. He wanted to
get his hoplites away before they even saw the enemy's camp-
fires, so that no one could possibly say that this withdrawal
was being done out of fear. He had, he considered, done
something to restore Spartan morale: he had invaded Arcadia, he had laid waste the country, and no one had shown
any willingness to engage him in battle. When he reached

*Xenophon omits all account of arguably the most important
diplomatic affair of his age, *viz.* the Arcadians' appeal to Athens in
late 370 B.C., which Athens rejected, and their recourse to Thebes
which led to the Theban expedition to the Peloponnese in winter
370–69 B.C. (Diod. XV.62.3, Demosthenes XVI.12) – an odd omission, since the Athenian rejection must have pleased him. Perhaps
the pleasure was overborne by the pain of the Thebans seizing their
chance. Possibly he heard very little about it all, just as he evidently
heard a great deal about the negotiations of VI.5.33 ff. and VII.1.1 ff.

Laconia, he dismissed the Spartans of the officer class to their houses and the Perioeci to their various cities.

22 When Agesilaus had gone, the Arcadians, still in full force, heard that his army had been disbanded. They therefore marched against the Heraeans, who had not only refused to join the Arcadian League * but had joined the Spartans in invading Arcadia. Crossing into their country they burned the houses and cut down the trees. They did not leave Heraea until it was reported that the Theban army which was marching to help them had arrived in Mantinea. Then they went to join up with the Thebans.

23 When the two armies were united, the Theban view was that things had turned out very well for them: they had brought help to the Arcadians, but there was now no enemy to be seen in the land. But the Arcadians, Argives and Eleans urged them to lead the way into Laconia as quickly as possible, pointing out how many men they had in their own army and lavishing praise on the Theban army. And, in fact, proud as they were of their victory at Leuctra, all the Boeotians were now becoming trained soldiers; they were followed, too, by the Phocians, now their subjects, the Euboeans from every city in the island, both the Locrian peoples, the Acarnanians, the Heracleans and the Malians; they also had cavalry and peltasts from Thessaly. Seeing all this, and maintaining that there was a real shortage of manpower in Sparta, the Arcadians begged the Thebans not on any account to turn back without invading Spartan territory.

24 The Thebans listened to all this, but also took into account the fact that Laconia was said to be a very difficult place to invade, and that all the easiest routes into the country were, so they believed, well guarded. And, in fact, Ischolaus was at Oeum, in Sciritis, with a force of emancipated helots and about four hundred of the youngest of the exiles from Tegea; and there was another force on guard at Leuctrum, above

*Cf. n. at VI.5.6.

Maleatis. They also took into account the fact that the Spartan army could be concentrated quickly and that the Spartans would be likely to fight nowhere better than in their own country. In view of all this they were not very enthusiastic about the project of invading Laconia.*

However, some people came in from Caryae to say that 25 that area was undefended; they promised to act as guides themselves and told the Thebans to put them to death if they were found to be playing them false. Then, too, some of the Perioeci were there to beg for Theban intervention; they undertook to revolt if only the Thebans appeared in the country and said that even now the Perioeci were refusing to obey the calling-up orders issued by the Spartans of the officer class. After hearing all this and hearing the same story from every source, the Thebans were won over. They invaded with their army by way of Caryae, while the Arcadians took the route by Oeum in Sciritis.

Here, if Ischolaus had gone forward to make his stand at 26 the difficult part of the pass, no one, so they say, could have got up this way anyhow. However, since he wanted to make use of the Oeans as allies, he stayed in the village. So the whole force of the Arcadians reached the pass. Here Ischolaus and his men met them face to face and were victorious in the fighting. However, the enemy were attacking them also from the rear and the flank; climbing up to the roofs of the houses they hurled down stones and javelins. There, then, Ischolaus was killed and the whole of his force was destroyed, apart from a few who may have got away without being recognized. After this action, the Arcadians marched to join the 27

*These hesitations of the Thebans, their reluctance to march into Laconia until they heard that the Arcadians had already done so (§27), hardly accord with what we hear elsewhere of Epaminondas' determination not to leave the Peloponnese until he had done what he came to do (Pausanias IX.14.5 ff., etc.). Cf. Cawkwell, *Classical Quarterly*, 22, 1972, pp. 266 ff. For Xenophon's omission of the name and deeds of Epaminondas prior to VII.1.41, see Introduction p. 35 f.

Thebans at Caryae, and the Thebans, when they heard of what the Arcadians had done, marched down from the mountains with much more confidence than they had shown so far. Making straight for Sellasia, they burned and pillaged the place, but on reaching the plain, they camped there in the ground sacred to Apollo. On the next day they marched on again.

They never even tried to cross the bridge and march against Sparta; they could see the hoplites ready to meet them and drawn up inside the ground sacred to Athena Alea. So keeping the Eurotas on their right, they went past the city, burning and plundering the houses which they found full of 28 valuables. As for the Spartans, the very sight of the smoke seemed unendurable to the women, who had never seen an enemy in their lives; but the men of the officer class, posted in detachments here and there, guarded this city of theirs, which was without fortifications; they looked few and they were few. The government also decided to issue a proclamation to the helots promising that all who volunteered and were accepted for military service and took part in the war 29 should be guaranteed their freedom for the future. It was said that at first more than 6,000* came forward to enlist, with the result that, when they were drawn up in battle order, they, too, caused alarm, since there seemed to be far too many of them. However, when the mercenaries from Orchomenus remained loyal and help also came in from Phlius, Corinth, Epidaurus, Pellene and a few other states, the Spartans began to feel less apprehensive about the men whom they had enlisted.

30 Meanwhile the invading army had marched on as far as

*According to Diod. XV.65.6, the figure was 1,000. Since the readiness of helots to fight for Sparta instead of joining in her destruction is one of the most important facts on which to base our notions of Spartan society, it is a pity that there is no way of knowing whether Xenophon is correct. The figure in the text of Diodorus may be due to corruption.

Amyclae. Here they crossed the Eurotas. Wherever the Thebans camped they guarded their position by cutting down trees and stacking as many of them as possible in front of their lines. The Arcadians, however, took none of these precautions; their habit was to go out of camp and turn to looting the houses.

It was on the third or fourth day of the invasion that the cavalry advanced to the racecourse in the sanctuary of Poseidon the Earth-holder; there were the Thebans in full force, the Eleans and all the Phocians, Thessalians and Locrians who were serving. Drawn up in line to face them were the Spartan 31 cavalry, apparently in very inconsiderable numbers. But, in fact, the Spartans had set an ambush of about three hundred of the younger hoplites in the house of the Tyndaridae, and these three hundred came running out at the same moment as their cavalry charged. The invaders failed to stand up to this attack and gave way. However, when the pursuit was over and the Theban army stood its ground, they settled down in camp again. There now seemed rather more reason for con- 32 fidence that they would make no further move against the city of Sparta; and, in fact, their army did leave its present position and marched off on the road towards Helos and Gytheum. They burned all towns on their way which were unfortified, and they made an attack lasting for three days on Gytheum, where the Spartans have their dockyards. Some of the Perioeci, too, not only took part in this attack but served throughout along with the troops following the Thebans.

When the Athenians heard of all this they were in some 33 perplexity about what their policy towards Sparta should be and, following upon a resolution of the Council, an Assembly was held. It so happened that there were in Athens at the time some ambassadors from Sparta and from the other allies who still remained loyal to her. It was natural, then, that these Spartans – Aracus, Ocyllus, Pharax, Etymocles and Olontheus – should speak, and nearly all of them spoke in much the same terms. They reminded the Athenians that throughout history in every great crisis Athens and Sparta had stood together for the right; Sparta had helped to drive the tyrants from Athens, and Athens had willingly sent help to Sparta when she was in difficulties with the Messenians.

34 And they referred to those happy days when the two were acting in concert, reminding their audience of how together they had driven back the Persians and of how, when Athens was chosen by the Greeks to be the leader of the naval forces and the guardian of the common funds, Sparta had supported the decision; and of how Athens on her side had given her support to the unanimous choice of

35 all the Greeks that Sparta should act as leader by land. In fact, one of the ambassadors actually said something like this: 'If you and we, my friends, would agree together, there is a very good prospect that, as the saying goes, we could make mincemeat of the Thebans.'

The Athenians, however, were not in a very receptive mood. There was a general kind of murmur to the effect that 'this is what they say now, but when they were doing well,

36 they turned against us. They thought that the most impressive of the Spartan arguments was that after their victory in the Peloponnesian War, they had opposed the Thebans, who had been in favour of the total destruction of Athens. A very great deal was said to show that the Athenians were bound by their oaths to come to the help of Sparta. The argument was that the Arcadians and those with them had marched against Sparta not because Sparta had done them any injury, but only because she had gone to the help of the Tegeans, and she had done this because the Tegeans were being attacked by the Mantineans in violation of the oaths sworn.* These

*For the oaths, cf. n. at VI.5.6. The important debate about whether Sparta took part in the Congress at Athens after Leuctra (VI.5.2 f.) turns on the interpretation of §§36 and 37 (with §6). In such matters it never occurred to Xenophon to explain fully.

words, too, caused a certain amount of uproar in the Assembly; some said that the Mantineans were quite right to avenge the people in Proxenus' party who had been killed by the party of Stasippus; while others maintained that, by the fact of marching against Tegea, they were in the wrong.

While the Assembly was attempting to sort out these 37 problems, a Corinthian called Cliteles rose to speak. He spoke as follows: 'With regard to which party was originally in the wrong, I should say, Athenians, there is perhaps room for disagreement; but as for us, can anyone accuse us of having, since the peace was made, marched against any other city, or taken anybody else's property, or laid waste anybody else's land? Yet in spite of this the Thebans have come into our country, have cut down our trees, burned our houses and stolen our property and our cattle. Surely, then, you must be violating your oaths if you fail to come to our assistance, when we are so clearly the victim of aggression. And these oaths, you will remember, were the ones which you were so anxious should be sworn to by all of us to all of you.'

This speech of Cliteles seemed to the Athenians to be making a perfectly fair and correct point, and they shouted out in approval.

Next, Procles, a Phliasian, rose to speak. He said: 'It is 38 clear, Athenians, I think, to everyone that, with Sparta out of the way, the first people whom the Thebans would march against would be you. They think that you are the only people who would stand in the way of their domination over the whole of Greece. If this is so, I should say that in taking 39 the field to help the Spartans you would be helping yourselves at the same time. The Thebans are no friends of yours and they live on your frontier; to have them as the first power in Greece would be, I imagine, much more awkward for you than to have your enemies living at some distance from you. Also it would be more to your interest to help yourselves while there are still people to fight at your side than to wait until your potential allies are destroyed, and then be forced to fight the final battle against the Thebans entirely by yourselves.

40   'Some of you may fear that if the Spartans come off safely this time, they are still quite likely to cause you trouble in the future; but you must remember that what is to be feared is great power in the hands of people whom one has injured, not in the hands of those whom one has helped. Remember this too – that for individuals and states alike the right course is to acquire some solid advantage when they are at their strongest, so that if they ever lose power they may have, as the result of their previous efforts, something to fall back

41 upon. And now heaven has offered you the opportunity of helping Sparta in her hour of need and, by so doing, of acquiring for all time to come the Spartans inescapably as your friends. Certainly it seems to me that there would be more than a few witnesses of the good treatment that Sparta would be receiving from you; yes, and the gods will know of this too, the gods who see all things now and for ever; both your allies and your enemies know also what is happening, and so does the whole world, Greeks and foreigners alike. There is no one to whom this question does not matter.

42 So that if the Spartans did appear to be acting badly towards you, how could anyone ever again show any enthusiasm about them? But, of course, one must expect that they will behave well rather than badly; indeed they, more than any other people in the world, seem to have consistently aimed

43 at winning praise and avoiding dishonourable actions. And there is another point, too, to remember. If at any time in the future Greece should be again threatened by a foreign power, is there anyone you would trust more than the Spartans? Are there any others you would be more glad to have as your comrades-in-arms than these men whose countrymen, standing at Thermopylae, chose to a man to die fighting rather than to live and let the barbarian into Greece?

These Spartans, fighting at your side, have shown themselves good men in the past, and there is every reason to suppose that they will do so in the future. Is it not right, then, that you and we, too, should be willing to give them our help unreservedly?

'It is also worth your while to show this willingness to help 44 for the sake of those allies whom they still have with them. You can be sure that those who have remained loyal to Sparta in her misfortunes would be ashamed if they failed to show their gratitude to you. We who are willing to take our share of the danger that threatens Sparta may seem to you small states; but you should reflect that, if your city comes in with us, we who are helping Sparta will no longer be a collection of small states. As for me, Athenians, I always used to 45 admire this state of yours from what I heard of it – namely, that refuge and help was available here for all who were oppressed and all who were in terror. But now it is no longer hearsay; I can see with my own eyes the Spartans, the most famous people in Greece, and all the friends who have proved most loyal to them all coming here to you and asking you to help them. I also see the Thebans, who after the last war failed 46 in their attempts to get the Spartans to enslave you, now asking you to turn a blind eye to the destruction of those who then saved you.

'Now that is a fine story that is told about your ancestors – that they refused to allow the Argives who died in the famous expedition against Thebes to remain unburied. But you would be doing something finer still in not allowing these living Spartans either to be humbled or to be destroyed. That 47 was a fine action, too, of yours when you checked the arrogance of Eurystheus and saved the lives of the sons of Heracles; but it would be a finer one still if you saved not only the founders of the state but the whole state as well. And what would be the finest thing of all would be this. After the war the Spartans saved you by a vote and with no risk to them-

349

selves; but you would be going to their aid with arms in
48 your hands and at the hazard of your lives. Now even we
who have come here together to urge you by our speeches
to help good and brave men are proud of what we are doing.
As for you, you have often been friends and often enemies
of the Spartans. Would it not appear as extraordinarily gen-
erous of you if you remembered not the harm but the good
which they have done you, and if you rewarded them for
this not only on your own account but on account of all
Greece, because it was on behalf of all Greece that they have
shown themselves good and brave?'

49 After the speeches there was further discussion, and the
Athenians refused to listen to any speakers who argued
against the views expressed. They voted to go to the help of
Sparta in full force, and chose Iphicrates as commander.
When his sacrifices had turned out well, he ordered his men
to be under arms in the Academy for their evening meal.
They say, however, that many were there before Iphicrates
himself put in an appearance. After this Iphicrates led the
way forward and his troops followed him, thinking that he
was leading them towards some glorious action. On reaching
Corinth, he waited about for several days and immediately,
and for the first time, his men began to blame him for this
loss of time. In the end he did lead them forward and they
willingly followed him wherever he took them, and willingly assaulted any fortified position against which he led them.

50 As for the enemy forces in Spartan territory, many of the
Arcadians, Argives and Eleans had already gone away. They
lived only just across the frontiers and they were driving away
the cattle and carrying off the plunder that they had taken.
The Thebans and the rest also wanted to withdraw, partly
because they saw their army growing smaller every day,
partly because provisions were becoming more difficult to
find; much of the supply had been used up, and much, too,
had been carried away or laid waste or burned. Besides this it

was now winter, so that by now everyone wanted to get away.

As they began to retire from Spartan territory, so Iphi- 51 crates led the Athenian army back from Arcadia to Corinth. Now Iphicrates no doubt showed himself a good general on other occasions and there I have no fault to find with him. But as for his actions on this campaign, I find that they were all either quite useless or positively harmful. His purpose was to guard the road by Oneum so that the Thebans would not be able to get back home; but meanwhile he left unguarded the best pass of all, which leads past Cenchreae. Then, when 52 he wanted to find out whether the Thebans had got past Oneum, he sent out the entire cavalry force of the Athenians and the Corinthians to act as scouts. And yet a few men are just as good as a lot for seeing what is happening. Moreover, if it should be necessary to retreat, it would be much easier for a small force than for a large one to find an easy route and to retire in their own time. But could anything be more absurd than to send out a large force which is still inferior to the enemy? And, in fact, since his cavalry, being in great numbers, were in a widely extended line, they found themselves very often on very difficult ground when they had to retreat. The result was that at least twenty of them were killed. On this occasion, then, the Thebans made their way home just as they pleased.*

* And so Xenophon gets the Thebans home without a single word about the most important achievement of the campaign, *viz.* the refoundation of Messene (Diod. XV.66, Pausanias IX.14.5, etc.). How 'holy Messene at last takes back her children' (Pausanias IX.15.6) was too painful a matter for Xenophon to recount or even to allude to, although the fact of the city's independent existence had to emerge later (VII.1.27, 36, etc.).

BOOK SEVEN

CHAPTER 1

Alliance of Athens and Sparta formalized. Second Theban invasion of the Peloponnese (Summer 369 B.C.). Independent attitude of Arcadians towards Thebes. The 'tearless battle' (Summer 368 B.C.). Negotiations with Persia (367 B.C.). Epaminondas' invasion of Achaea. Rise of Euphron of Sicyon

NEXT year ambassadors from Sparta and her allies came with full powers to Athens to discuss the precise terms of the treaty of alliance between Athens and Sparta. After many foreigners and many Athenians had said that the alliance should be on absolutely equal terms, Procles the Phliasian made the following speech:

'You have decided, Athenians, that it is a good thing for you to make the Spartans your friends. Now, it seems to me, there is another point to consider: how can this friendship be made to last as long as possible? In my view it will be most likely to last if we make the treaty along just those lines which will give most advantage to each of the parties concerned. On most points there is a very general agreement already; what we have to consider now is the question of the supreme command. Now your Council has proposed that Athens should have the supreme command on sea and Sparta by land. And in my opinion this division of responsibility seems to be not merely a human expedient but something ordained by providence and by the way things are. In the first place, you live in a position which might have been created just for this. Most states which are dependent on the sea are situated round about your state, and they are all weaker than your state. Also you have harbours – an essential for the exercise of naval power. Moreover, you have a large fleet of triremes, and it has always been your policy to

4 keep on adding to your navy. And as for the skills required in seafaring, all these are very much your own. Then, too, you are far ahead of everyone else in experience of naval matters. Most of you get your livelihood from the sea, and, consequently, while you are engaged in your private business you are at the same time gaining experience for naval operations. And here is another point: more triremes at one time can put to sea from your harbour than from any other in the world – and this is a point that counts for a lot in the matter of leadership, since all men like best to join up with the power

5 that is the first to show its strength. And from heaven, too, you have been granted success in this. You have fought very many and very great battles on the sea and of these you have lost only a very few; nearly always you have won. It is natural then that the allies would be happiest in facing the

6 perils of the sea if they had you to lead them. This naval training and discipline of yours is something which is natural to you and which you have to have, as is evident from the fact that in the war which Sparta once fought with you and which lasted many years they were able to control your land, but could make no progress at all towards really destroying you. But when in the end heaven gave them the control of the sea, you were at once completely in their power. This makes it clear enough that for you everything depends on the sea.

7 This is something in the nature of things, and therefore you cannot be fairly expected to surrender the supreme naval command to the Spartans. In the first place, they admit themselves that they lack your experience in naval affairs; and then it is true that in naval actions they are not facing the same risks as you are. They are risking merely the men aboard the triremes, but you risk wives, children, your whole state.

8 'So much for the situation from your point of view. Now let us look at it from the angle of the Spartans. Firstly, they live away from the coast; therefore, so long as they control

the land they can live their lives perfectly well even if they are cut off from the sea. This is a fact which they recognize themselves, and so from the very beginning of boyhood they are trained and disciplined for land warfare. And in the most important point of all, obedience to one's commander, they excel on land just as you do by sea. Then, too, just as you can 9 do by sea, so they on land can mobilize a very large force in a very short time; and, consequently, it is natural that here it would be to them that allied armies would rally with the greatest confidence. And just as heaven has granted you success on sea, so it has granted success to them on land. In the numerous land battles which they have fought, they have suffered very few defeats and have nearly always won. And 10 that military training and discipline are just as essential to them as naval training and discipline are for you is evident from the facts of history. In your long war with them you often defeated them on the sea, but came no nearer to winning the war as a result. But as soon as they met with one defeat on land, their wives, their children, their whole state were immediately endangered. From their point of view, 11 then, it would obviously be a monstrous thing to turn over to others the supreme command on land, when they themselves are the best-trained people there are for land operations. I say, then, that the proposal made by your Council is the one which I also have spoken for and the one which I believe to be the best in the interest of both parties. And I pray that you in this discussion may have the good fortune to take the course which is best for us all.'

This speech was loudly applauded by the Athenians and 12 also by the Spartans who were present. However, Cephisodotus now came forward. 'Athenians,' he said, 'you do not see how you are being deceived. Just listen to me, and I will soon show you. As things are, you are to have the supreme command by sea. Now if the Spartans are your allies, they will obviously send out Spartans as captains and possibly also

as marines; but equally obviously, the crews will be either
13 helots or mercenaries. These will be the people under your
orders, then. But when the Spartans ask you to put an army
into the field, obviously you will send your hoplites and
your cavalry. They, then, will be in command of Athenian
citizens, while you will be in command merely of their slaves
and of the people who count for least among them. Answer
me,' he said, 'Timocrates of Sparta. Did you not say just now
that you had come to make the alliance on absolutely equal
terms?'

'I did say that,' replied Timocrates.

14 'Then,' said Cephisodotus, 'what could be fairer than for
each party to hold each command, naval and military, by
turns? For you to have your share in it, if there is any advantage in holding the naval command, and for us to have our
share in whatever advantages there are in the command by
land?'

After listening to this speech, the Athenians changed their
minds and voted that each party should hold the command in
turn for periods of five days at a time.

15 Both powers now, together with their allies, put armies
into the field and went to Corinth. It was decided that they
should all join in guarding Oneum. And so, while the Thebans and their allies were still on the march, they posted their
forces so as to guard the various points in Oneum, with the
Spartans and Pelleneans guarding the most accessible area.
The Thebans and the allies camped in the plain at a distance
of four miles from the troops on guard. They worked out
the time at which they thought they should start in order to
reach their objective at dawn, and then marched against the
16 guard-post held by the Spartans. They had judged the time
perfectly correctly and fell upon the Spartans and Pelleneans
just when the night-watches were ending and when the men
were getting out of bed and beginning to go to their various
posts. So the Thebans fell on them and struck them down.

It was a case of men all keyed up for action and in good order
against men taken unawares and in no order at all. Those of 17
the Spartans who got away with their lives escaped to the
nearest high ground, and here it would have been perfectly
possible for them to have held their position. Their general *
could have got as many hoplites and peltasts as he wanted
from the forces of the allies, and supplies could have been
brought in safely from Cenchreae. However, he failed to do
this. Just when the Thebans were very worried about how
they could manage to make the descent on the side towards
Sicyon and were thinking of going back again, he made a
truce with them which in most people's opinion was more
to their advantage than to his own. So he went away and
took with him the troops under his command.

The Thebans now descended into the plain without risk, 18
joined up with their allies, the Arcadians, Argives and Eleans,
and at once moved against Sicyon and Pellene. They also
marched against Epidaurus and laid waste the whole country
of the Epidaurians. On their way back they marched in a way
that showed the utmost contempt for all their enemies, and
when they came near the city of Corinth they charged at the
double towards the gates one goes through on the way to
Phlius with the idea of bursting into the city if the gates happened to be open. But some light troops came out from the 19
city and met the picked troops of the Thebans † within about
a hundred yards of the walls. They climbed up on to the
burial monuments and other high places and hurled down
stones and javelins. They killed a great number of the

* Cf. n. at IV.5.11.

† This is the sole reference in Xenophon to the Sacred Band. He
omits its glorious moments, at Tegyra (cf. n. at VI.1.1) and at Leuctra
(cf. Plut. *Pelopidas* 23), but records a reverse. (Admittedly, it could
have happened under Xenophon's own eyes, if he was watching
from Acrocorinth.) Comparison with Diod. XV.68 and 69 reveals
the inaccuracy and selectiveness of Xenophon's account.

Thebans in the front ranks and finally put them to flight and pursued them for about half a mile. After this the Corinthians dragged the dead bodies to the shelter of the wall. They gave them back under an armistice and then put up a trophy. All this had the effect of putting fresh heart into the allies of the Spartans.

20   Just after these actions the force sent by Dionysius to help Sparta sailed in. There were more than twenty triremes and they brought Celts, Iberians and about fifty cavalry. Next day the Thebans and their allies, formed up in separate detachments, filled the whole plain from the sea to the hills by the city and destroyed all property in the plain that was of value. The cavalry of the Athenians and of the Corinthians, seeing the strength and the numbers of the opposition, kept

21   their distance from the enemy army. But the cavalry sent by Dionysius, in spite of their small numbers, rode along the enemy's line either as individuals or in small detachments and charged down on them, hurling their javelins. When the enemy moved out against them, they would fall back, and then face about and hurl their javelins again. And in the course of all this they would dismount and have a rest; and if they were attacked while they were dismounted, they would easily leap on their horses and ride away. But if the enemy pressed his pursuit far from the main army, they would turn on them while they were going back again, and with volleys of javelins give them a very rough time. Thus they made the whole enemy army either advance or retreat just as they pleased.

22   After this, however, the Thebans only remained for a few days and then went home, as did the forces of their allies. The troops sent by Dionysius then invaded the territory of Sicyon. In a battle on the plain they defeated the Sicyonians and killed about seventy of them, and they took the fortress of Deras by storm. After these actions this first force sent out by Dionysius sailed back to Syracuse.

Up to this time the Thebans and all the rest who had seceded from the Spartan alliance had acted and fought in full agreement under the leadership of the Thebans. But 23 now there came upon the scene a man from Mantinea called Lycomedes. His family was among the noblest; he was richer than anyone and he was also ambitious. He succeeded in filling the Arcadians with a sense of their own importance. According to him it was the Arcadians and the Arcadians alone who could call the Peloponnese their fatherland, since they were the only indigenous people who lived there; the Arcadians were also the most populous race in Greece and were physically the strongest. They were also, he declared, the bravest and, as a proof of this, he stated that when anyone wanted to hire mercenaries, none were preferred to the Arcadians. It was also true, he pointed out, that Sparta had never invaded Athenian territory nor had Thebes invaded the territory of Sparta without Arcadian help. 'So,' he said, 24 'if you are wise, you will give up following invariably the leadership of other people. In the past you followed the Spartans and made them great. Now if you thoughtlessly follow the leadership of Thebes without claiming that you should share the command with them, you will very likely find that they are just another sort of Spartans.'

The effect of this propaganda was to make the Arcadians vastly proud of themselves; they adored Lycomedes and thought he was the only man in the world, and they appointed as their leaders just the men whom he told them to appoint. But the Arcadians could also feel proud because of their actual achievements. When the Argives had invaded 25 the territory of Epidaurus and had had their retreat blocked by the mercenaries under Chabrias and by the Athenians and Corinthians, it was the Arcadians who went to the rescue and, faced not only by enemy armies but also by very difficult country, freed the Argives from a position of real blockade. They also marched against Asine in Laconia, defeated the Spartan garrison, killed Geranor, a Spartan of the officer class who had been made polemarch, and laid waste the suburbs of Asine. And whenever they wanted to take the field, they were never put off by darkness or bad weather or long distances or difficult mountains. Thus, certainly at this time, they considered themselves much the strongest of the Greeks.

26 As a result of this the Thebans not unnaturally began to feel rather jealous of the Arcadians and not so friendly as they had been. The Eleans, too, had asked the Arcadians to give them back the cities of which they had been deprived by the Spartans, but found that the Arcadians were quite indifferent to what they said. On the other hand, they treated with great respect the Triphylians and others who had revolted from Elis, on the grounds that these people claimed to be Arcadians. As a result the Eleans also felt hostile to the Arcadians.

27 In this state of affairs, with each of the allied powers full of the sense of their own importance, Philiscus of Abydus came from Ariobarzanes, bringing a large sum of money with him. His first step was to call together at Delphi a peace conference of the Thebans, their allies and the Spartans. However, when they arrived there, they took no steps towards consulting the god about the way in which peace might be brought about; instead, their deliberations were entirely among themselves. When the Thebans would not agree that Messene * should be subject to Sparta, Philiscus started to raise a large mercenary army in order to fight on the side of the Spartans.

28 While these negotiations were going on, the second force sent out by Dionysius to help Sparta arrived. The Athenians maintained that this force should go to Thessaly as a threat to Thebes,† but the Spartans wanted it to go to Laconia, and it

* This is the first mention of the refounded Messene. Cf. n. at VI.5.52.

† This is the sole reference in the *Hellenica* to the Theban involvement in Thessaly. Cf. Introduction pp. 25–8 and VII.5.4.

was the Spartan plan that won the approval of the allies.
So these troops from Dionysius sailed round to Sparta,* and
Archidamus took them over and with them and his citizen
troops set out on a campaign. He captured Caryae by storm
and put to death all the prisoners he took. From there he
moved straight on with his army against Parrhasia in Arcadia
and devastated the country. The Arcadians and Argives now
came to the rescue and Archidamus retired and camped on
the hills above Melea. While he was there Cissidas, the
commander of the troops sent by Dionysius, said that the
time for which he had been told to stay was now up and,
as soon as he had stated this, went away by the road leading
to Sparta. However, while he was marching away the Mes- 29
senians occupied a narrow pass on the road and tried to cut
him off. He then sent a message back to Archidamus asking
for help and Archidamus actually did come and help him.
However, just when they reached the branch road leading to
Eutresia the Arcadian and Argive armies appeared. They
were marching towards Laconia and they, too, aimed at
cutting Archidamus off from his way home. There is some
level ground at the point where the road to Eutresia joins
the road to Melea, and it was here that Archidamus turned
aside and drew up his troops in order of battle. It is said, too, 30
that he went along the lines and encouraged the men in the
following words: 'Fellow-citizens, we must now show what
we can do and so be able to look people in the face. Let us
leave to those who come after us the Sparta which we received from our fathers. Let there now be an end to our
feeling ashamed of ourselves before our wives and our children and the older men and the foreigners – we who were
once the admiration of the whole of Greece!'

---

* 'Sailed round' shows that this synod of the Spartan alliance met
at Corinth, the headquarters of the war, where too Xenophon kept
watch on policy and events. But he eschews formal explanation of
what is to him obvious (cf. Introduction p. 34).

31 They say that after these words lightning and thunder, showing the favour of the gods to him, came from a clear sky. It so happened, too, that on the right wing there was a sanctuary and statue of Heracles. And they say that as a result of all this the soldiers were filled with such might and such confidence that they all pressed on forward, and it was quite a job for their officers to restrain them. And when Archidamus led the charge only a few of the enemy waited till they came within range of the spears. These were killed. The rest turned in flight and were cut down in great num-
32 bers by the cavalry and by the Celts. When the battle was over and he had put up a trophy, Archidamus at once sent Demoteles the herald to Sparta to report how great a victory had been won and how, though vast numbers of the enemy had fallen, not a single Spartan had been killed. They say, too, that when the people in Sparta heard the news they all burst into tears, beginning with Agesilaus, and the members of the Council and the ephors. And indeed it seems that tears can equally express both joy and sorrow. However, the Thebans and the Eleans were almost as pleased as the Spartans themselves with what had happened to the Arcadians – so much had they already come to dislike them for their arrogance.*
33 Theban policy had been continuously directed towards securing supremacy in Greece, and the Thebans now thought that an embassy to the King of Persia might gain them some advantage. So they now sent round to their allies on the pretext that Euthycles, the Spartan, was also at the King's court. Their delegation consisted of Pelopidas for the Thebans, Antiochus, the boxing and wrestling champion, for the Arcadians, and Archidamus for the Eleans. (He was accompanied by Argaeus. The Athenians too, when they

*Xenophon omits the foundation of Megalopolis, the need for which this campaign of Archidamus had made plain. (Cf. Diod. XV.72.4; Pausanias VIII.27.8 misdates it.)

heard of what was happening, sent Timagoras and Leon to see the King.*

When they all arrived, Pelopidas had a very great advan- 34 tage over the rest in dealing with the Persian King. He was in a position to say that his countrymen were the only ones in Greece who had fought on the King's side at Plataea, that they had never since then undertaken a campaign against the King, and that the reason why the Spartans had made war against them was just because they had refused to join Agesilaus in his attack on Persia and had not allowed him to sacrifice to Artemis at Aulis, the place where Agamemnon had sacrificed before setting out to Asia to capture Troy. It 35 also greatly contributed to Pelopidas' renown that the Thebans had been victorious in the battle of Leuctra and that they were known to have laid waste the territory of Sparta. And Pelopidas pointed out that the Argives and the Arcadians had been defeated by the Spartans when they had not got the Thebans with them. The Athenian, Timagoras, backed up Pelopidas in all these statements and so stood next to him in the King's regard.

Pelopidas was then asked by the King what he wanted to 36 have put into writing for him. He replied that Messene should be independent of Sparta, that Athens should draw up her ships on land,† and that if Sparta and Athens refused, the rest should make war on them, and that if any city failed to join in the campaign, they should first march against that

*Here Pelopidas makes his entry in the pages of the *Hellenica*, a mere twelve years after his illustrious career had begun. From Xenophon's prejudicial account the truth emerges that the Spartans had appealed to Persia for aid and that Pelopidas only went to stop it. (See Introduction pp. 37 and 40 and nn. at V.4.1, VI.2.1, VI.3.18.) But shameless Theban 'medizing' had to be exposed (cf. V.2.35). So in §34 Pelopidas is represented as catching Persia's favour with references to Thebes' treacherous conduct.

†A reference to Athens' war to recover Amphipolis, for which cf. n. at IV.3.1.

37 city. These terms were written down and read to the ambassadors, upon which Leon remarked in the King's hearing: 'By Zeus, Athenians, it looks as though it was high time for you to be looking for some other friend instead of the King.' When the King was told by his secretary what the Athenian had said, he added a clause to the document saying: 'And if the Athenians know of any fairer way to deal with the situation, let them come to the King and tell him what it is.'

38 So the ambassadors returned home, and the Athenians put Timagoras to death after Leon had accused him of refusing to share quarters with him and of having worked hand in glove with Pelopidas in all the negotiations. As for the other ambassadors, Archidamus of Elis approved of what the King had done because he had treated the Eleans with more distinction than the Arcadians; Antiochus, however, because the Arcadian League had been belittled, would not accept the King's gifts, and told the Arcadian Assembly of Ten Thousand that, while the King had masses of bakers, cooks, waiters and door-keepers, all his research had failed to discover any men capable of standing up to Greeks in battle. He also said that in his view the great wealth of the King was mere trickery; even the golden plane tree, about which there was such a song, was not big enough to give shade to a grasshopper.*

39 The Thebans now called together representatives from all the cities to hear what the King had written. The Persian who came with the document showed the King's seal and read the contents of the letter. The Thebans then said that those who wanted to be friends of the King and of themselves should swear to abide by these terms. However, the representatives from the cities replied that they had been sent to listen to a report, not to swear to adopt it, and they told the Thebans that, if they wanted oaths sworn, they would have to send to

*Debunking Persia was a favourite Panhellenist pastime. Doubtless these witticisms gave pleasure to Xenophon and his friends.

the various cities concerned. Lycomedes, the Arcadian, in fact went further and said that it was not the right thing to hold this congress in Thebes anyway; it should be held in whatever place there was fighting to be done. The Thebans were angry with him for this and told him that he was disrupting the alliance, whereupon he refused even to take his seat at the congress and went right away, taking with him all the representatives from Arcadia.

So, since the delegates at the meeting refused to take the 40 oath in Thebes, the Thebans sent ambassadors to the cities to tell them to swear to abide by the terms stated in the King's letter. They reckoned that no single city by itself would risk incurring both their hostility and that of the King at the same time. However, when the ambassadors came to Corinth, the first city to be asked, the Corinthians stood firmly against the proposal and replied that they had no wish to enter into any sworn compacts with the King; and the other cities followed their lead and answered in the same terms. So this attempt of Pelopidas and the Thebans to become the leading power in Greece came to nothing.

Epaminondas,* on the other hand, now wished to win 41 over the Achaeans to the side of Thebes so that the Arcadians and the other allies would be more inclined to follow Theban guidance. He therefore decided that they should march against Achaea and persuaded Peisias, general of the Argives, to occupy Oneum in advance. Peisias found out that Oneum was being carelessly guarded by Naucles, the commander of the mercenaries employed by Sparta, and by Timomachus, the Athenian, and so he seized the hill above Cenchreae by night. He had 2,000 hoplites with him, and supplies for seven days. Within these seven days the Thebans arrived and cross- 42 ed over the pass at Oneum. They and all the allies, led by

*Epaminondas is thus named for the first time. For Xenophon's treatment of Epaminondas, see Introduction p. 35 f. and Cawkwell, *Classical Quarterly*, 22, 1972, pp. 254 ff.

Epaminondas, then marched against Achaea. Epaminondas was here urgently approached by the aristocratic parties in Achaea, and by his own influence brought it about that the men of good family should not be exiled, nor should there be any changes of the constitution. Then, after receiving guarantees from the Achaeans that they would join the alliance in all sincerity and would follow wherever the Thebans led, he went back home again. However, he was accused by the Arcadians and the anti-aristocratic parties in Achaea of having settled things in that country in a way profitable to Sparta and of then going away. So the Thebans decided to send governors to the Achaean cities, and these governors, when they arrived, drove out the aristocrats with the aid of the people and set up democracies in Achaea. However, the exiles quickly joined forces and marched against each one of the cities in turn. Being very numerous they got themselves restored and took control of the cities again. And now, after their restoration, they no longer steered a middle course but fought most willingly for Sparta. Thus the Arcadians found themselves hard pressed by the Spartans on one side and the Achaeans on the other.

44   Up to now Sicyon had been governed in accordance with the traditional laws. But now Euphron, the man who, of all the citizens, had the most influence with the Spartans, wished also to be first in his relations with the enemies of Sparta. He told the Argives and the Arcadians that if the men of the wealthy classes remained in control of Sicyon, quite obviously the city would, at the first opportunity, go over to Sparta again. 'But if,' he said, 'a democratic government is set up, you can be sure that the city will remain loyal to you.' And he went on to say: 'If you will be there to help, I will be the one who will call a meeting of the people. In this way I shall give you an assurance of my own good faith and at the same time shall make the city a firm and reliable ally to you. You must understand that the reason why I am doing this is be-

cause I, like you, have for a long time found the arrogance of
the Spartans intolerable, and I should be delighted to escape
from being a slave to them.' After hearing this, the Arcadians 45
and Argives gladly stood by to support him. He then at once
called a meeting of the people and, in the presence of the
Argives and Arcadians, declared that in future the constitution was to be on a basis of equal rights for all. At this meeting he told them to elect as generals whomsoever they
pleased and they chose Euphron himself, Hippodamus,
Cleander, Acrisius and Lysander. When this had been done
Euphron appointed his own son, Adeas, to the command of
the mercenary troops, after depriving Lysimenes, their previous commander, of his post. He proceeded at once to win 46
the personal loyalty of some of these troops by treating them
with special consideration, and he brought in others in addition, sparing neither the public funds nor the treasures sacred
to the gods. He also made use of the property of those whom
he had banished as pro-Spartans. As for those in the government with him, he made away with some of them by
treachery and banished others. In this way he got everything into his own hands and was quite evidently a dictator.
And he secured the compliance of his allies in all this partly
by bribery and partly by willingly making use of his mercenaries to fight at their side in all their campaigns.

CHAPTER 2

Exploits of the Phliasians (370–366 B.C.)

1 WITH things going in this way the people of Phlius found themselves in great difficulties and were suffering from a shortage of food. The Argives had built fortifications on Mount Tricaranum, above the Heraeum, as a base for attack on Phlius, and the Sicyonians were fortifying Thyamia on the frontier. In spite of this the people of Phlius remained steadfast allies of Sparta. And I shall write of this in some detail. For if one of the great powers does some fine and noble action, all the historians write about it; but it seems to me that if a state which is only a small one has done numbers of great and glorious things, then there is all the more reason for letting people know about them.*

2 The Phliasians, then, had become friends of Sparta when Sparta was at her greatest. Later, when the Spartans were defeated at the battle of Leuctra, when many of the Perioeci had revolted, together with all the helots and indeed nearly all the allies, and when, one might almost say, the whole of Greece was marching against Sparta, the people of Phlius still remained faithful and went to Sparta's help, even though they had as enemies the most powerful states in the Peloponnese, Arcadia and Argos. It then fell to their lot to cross over into Prasiae last of all those who were then serving in the allied army, namely the Corinthians, Epidaurians, Troezenians, Hermionians, Halieians, Sicyonians, and Pellenians,

3 for they had not yet seceded from Sparta. The Spartan

---

*For Xenophon and 'all the historians', see Introduction p. 22. For Xenophon's essentially moralizing purpose, see Introduction p. 43 f. The incidents in this chapter are again and again confined to a single day, and there is no attempt to set them properly in context. His purpose is made plain at VII.2.16 and 3.1.

commander went on ahead with those who had crossed
first, leaving the Phliasians behind. Even so, they did not
turn back. They hired a guide from Prasiae and, though the
enemy were all round Amyclae, somehow or other they got
through and reached Sparta. For this the Spartans conferred
many distinctions on them, including the gift of an ox which
they sent as a mark of friendship.

Later, when the enemy had retired from Sparta, the Ar- 4
gives were angry with the Phliasians because of the energetic
goodwill which they had shown to the Spartans, and they
invaded the territory of Phlius in full force and laid waste
their land. But even then the Phliasians would not give in.
In fact, when the Argives, having destroyed all that they
could, were going away again, the Phliasian cavalry sallied
out and went after them. The Argives had all their cavalry
and the companies of infantry who acted with them posted
to guard their rear, but the Phliasians, who were only sixty
strong, charged down and routed the entire rear-guard.
True enough that they did not kill many of them, but they
put up a trophy, with the Argives looking on, just as though
they had killed the whole lot.

There was also the time when the Spartans and their allies 5
were guarding Oneum and the Thebans were approaching
with the intention of crossing over the pass. At the same time
the Arcadians and Eleans were marching through Nemea in
order to join up with the Thebans, and some Phliasian exiles
approached them and said that if they would only show that
they were on their side, they would capture Phlius. Agreement was reached, and in the night the exiles and about six
hundred others with them stole up close to the wall with
scaling ladders. The sentries from Tricaranum then sent signals of the approach of enemy forces and at this moment,
when the attention of the city was diverted to this threat, the
party who wanted to betray the place signalled to the men
hiding below the wall to climb up. This they did and found 6

the guard-posts unmanned. They then went after the day
guards, ten in number (from each squad of five one man
being normally left as a day guard). They killed one in his
sleep and another after he had taken refuge in the Heraeum.
The rest of them had run away and jumped down from the
wall on the city side, and so the scaling party were in un-
7 disputed possession of the Acropolis. But when the noise of
shouting reached the city, the citizens came up to the rescue.
At first their enemies came out from the Acropolis and
fought in the space in front of the gates on the side of the city.
Then, as more and more came up and they were becoming
surrounded, they fell back again towards the Acropolis. The
citizens poured in after them; the space in the middle of the
Acropolis was cleared at once, but the enemy climbed up on
to the wall and the towers, hurling missiles and stabbing
downwards at those below, who defended themselves from
the ground and fought back from the steps leading up to the
8 wall. Next the citizens gained control of some of the towers
at various points on the wall and then made a combined
charge, fighting like madmen, on the party that had scaled
the walls. By their reckless daring as well as their fighting
qualities they now pushed the enemy back and penned him
into a smaller and smaller space. But just at this moment the
Arcadians and Argives appeared all round the city, and some
of them tried to dig through the wall of the Acropolis on
the upper side. As for the citizens inside, some were fighting
hand to hand with the people on the wall, others with those
who were still climbing up from outside and were on the
ladders, and others were engaged with those who had got
up on the towers. These last found fire in the tents and began
to set fire to the towers from below, bringing up sheaves of
corn which happened to have been cut in the Acropolis itself.
And now in terror of the flames the people on the towers
jumped off, and the people on the walls fell down from them
9 under the blows rained upon them and, once they had begun

to give way, it was not long before the whole Acropolis was clear of the enemy. Immediately, the Phliasian cavalry went out into action, and at the sight of them the enemy retired, leaving behind their ladders, their dead and some people still alive who had been lamed. At least eighty of the enemy had been killed in the fighting inside the city and in jumping down from the walls. Then, indeed, you might have seen the men clasping each others' hands in joy at their salvation and the women bringing them drink with tears streaming down their faces. This, in fact, really was an occasion when everyone present was weeping and laughing at the same time.

In the following year, too, the Argives and the whole Arcadian army invaded the territory of Phlius. The reason for these constant attacks which they made on the Phliasians was partly anger, and partly that, being on both sides of the country of Phlius, they were always hoping that the Phliasians would be forced to come to terms through lack of food. In this invasion also the Phliasian cavalry and crack troops, helped by some Athenian cavalry who were there, fell upon their enemies at the river crossing. They were victorious in the fighting, and for the rest of the day made the enemy retire under the shelter of the high ground just as if the crops in the plain belonged to friends and they were being very careful not to trample them down.

Then there was the occasion when the Theban governor at Sicyon marched against Phlius with the garrison under his own command, together with the Sicyonians and the troops from Pellene – which by this time was taking its orders from Thebes. Euphron also joined in the expedition with his private army of about two thousand mercenaries. The main body of the troops was coming down from the hills along Tricaranum in the direction of the Heraeum, with the intention of laying waste the plain; but their general had left the troops from Sicyon and from Pellene behind on the high ground facing the gates through which one goes to Corinth, in order to prevent the Phliasians from making a detour by that way and so getting above his men at the Heraeum.

12 But as soon as the men in the city saw that their enemies were marching towards the plain, the cavalry and the crack troops came out against them, and fought them in battle and prevented them from reaching the plain at all. Most of the day there was spent in long-range fighting with the troops of Euphron pressing their attacks only up to the point where the ground became suitable for cavalry, and the men from

13 Phlius only up to the Heraeum. When they thought the right time had come the enemy retired, making a detour over Tricaranum because the ravine in front of the wall prevented their marching towards the Pelleneans by the shortest route. The Phliasians followed them up the hill for a little way, then turned back and went at full speed against the Pelleneans and those with them by way of the road going

14 past the wall. The troops with the Theban general saw how the Phliasians were pressing on, and tried to race them so as to bring help to the Pelleneans before the others arrived. However, the cavalry got there first and charged down on the Pelleneans. For a time they stood up to the attack and the Phliasians retired; but then they launched another attack, together with the infantry who were coming up in support and began fighting hand to hand. And now the enemy gave way. Some of the men from Sicyon were killed and very

15 many of the men from Pellene – brave men too. After this the Phliasians put up a trophy and, as was natural, sang their paean loudly and clearly. Meanwhile the troops under the Theban general and Euphron made no attempt to interfere. In fact, they behaved as though they had been racing up to see a show. After this action the one party returned to Sicyon and the other to Phlius.

16 And here is another noble action done by the Phliasians: when they made a prisoner of Proxenus, from Pellene, they

let him go without a ransom, even though they themselves were short of everything. There is no question that men who did deeds like this must be called noble men and great warriors.

And it is perfectly clear that what made them able to keep 17 faith with their friends was their power to endure hardship. When they were cut off from the produce of their own land, they lived partly from what they could get from their enemies' land and partly by buying supplies from Corinth. Just to get to the market meant facing many dangers, and it was hard for them to find the price for what they bought, and hard to bring back safely the men who were bringing in their supplies; it was also very difficult to find people who would take a risk on providing baggage animals to do the carriage. There came a time when they were at the end of 18 their resources, and they arranged with Chares that he should escort their baggage train. And when he arrived in Phlius they begged him also to help convoy their non-combatants to Pellene. This was done; they left the non-combatants at Pellene and then, after bringing what they could and loading as many pack-animals as possible, they set off by night, quite aware that they would be ambushed by the enemy, but thinking that fighting was easier than being without food. The Phliasians with Chares led the way and when they met 19 the enemy they got to work at once. They fell upon the enemy, cheering each other on and shouting to Chares to come up and help them. So after winning a victory and driving the enemy off the road they got home safely with all their supplies.

Since they had gone through the night without sleep, they slept until late in the following day. But when Chares got up, 20 the cavalry and the best of the hoplites came to him and said: 'Chares, today you have the chance of doing something really splendid. The men of Sicyon are now fortifying a position on our frontier. They have a lot of men engaged on the building, but not very many hoplites. Now we, the cavalry and the strongest of the hoplites, will go ahead, and if you with the mercenaries come up after us, perhaps you will find the job already done for you and perhaps, as happened at Pellene, your appearance will turn the scale. But if you think there is any difficulty in this plan, make a sacrifice and consult the gods. In our view the gods will be even more strongly in favour of your doing what we suggest than we are ourselves. You can be sure of this, Chares: if you succeed, you will have secured a fortified base for operations against the enemy, you will have saved a friendly city, you will win the greatest distinction among your countrymen and become the most famous general among both your allies and enemies.'

21 Chares took their advice and proceeded to make a sacrifice. Meanwhile, the Phliasian cavalry were putting on their breastplates and bridling their horses, and their hoplites were making all the preparations proper for infantry men. Then they took up their arms and went to the place where Chares was sacrificing, but he and the seer met them on the way and told them that the sacrifices had turned out well. 'Wait for us,' they said, 'for we, too, shall be starting now.' Orders were given at once, and the mercenaries also rushed to arms 22 with a kind of enthusiasm that was almost miraculous. So Chares set out on the march and the Phliasian cavalry and infantry went ahead. They led the way at a great pace from the start, and then they began to run, and in the end the cavalry were riding at full gallop and the infantry were running as fast as men in line can run, and then came Chares following eagerly behind. It was a little before sunset and they found the enemy at the fortifications either bathing, or 23 cooking, or preparing bread, or making their beds. As soon as they saw the fury of the attack, they fled in terror, leaving all their supplies behind for these brave men, who used these provisions for their dinner (with more, too, which came

from home), poured out libations in thanks for their good
fortune, sang a paean and, after posting sentries, went to
sleep. During the night the news about Thyamia reached
Corinth, and the Corinthians, acting in the most friendly
way, called out all their teams of drivers and pack-animals,
loaded them with corn, and brought it into Phlius. And as
long as the fortifications were being built convoys were sent
in every day.

CHAPTER 3

Events in Sicyon. Murder of Euphron.

1 THIS completes my account of the Phliasians, of their fidelity to their friends, of their valour in war, and of how, though short of everything themselves, they remained steadfast in the alliance.

At about this time Aeneas the Stymphalian, who was now general of the Arcadians, decided that the state of affairs in Sicyon was unendurable. So with his army he went up to the Acropolis, summoned a meeting of the aristocratic party inside the city and sent for those who had been exiled without 2 a decree of the people. Euphron was terrified at this and fled to the port of Sicyon. He then called in Pasimelus from Corinth and, using him as an intermediary, handed over the port to the Spartans, thus again reverting to the Spartan alliance, and claiming that he had been faithful to Sparta all the time. According to him, when a vote was taken in Sicyon about whether to revolt from Sparta or not, he and 3 a few others had voted against; afterwards, and with a view to revenging himself on those who had betrayed him, he had set up a democracy. 'And now,' he said, 'all who were traitors to you have been sent into exile by me. And, having gained control of this harbour, I am now handing it over to you.' Many people heard him say these words; it is not so clear how many believed him.

4 But now, since I have begun the story of Euphron, I want to bring it to its close. While the parties of the aristocracy and of the democracy were at variance in Sicyon, Euphron obtained a force of mercenaries from Athens and once more seized power. Now, backed by the democratic faction, he was master of the city, but a Theban governor still held the Acropolis. Euphron realized that, so long as the Thebans

were in the Acropolis, he could not control the state, and he got together money and went off with the idea of using it to bribe the Thebans to banish the aristocrats and to put him in charge again. But the former exiles heard of his plans and 5 of where he was going and they, too, set out for Thebes. They saw him associating in a most friendly way with the Theban officials and they became frightened that he might succeed in his aims. So some of them were daring enough to assassinate him on the Acropolis while the Theban officials and council were holding a session there. The officials brought the perpetration of this action before the council and made the following speech: 'Fellow-citizens, we demand the 6 death penalty for these men who have killed Euphron. We observe that while good men never do anything unjust or sinful, and wicked men, when they do such things, try to do them without being noticed, these people in their reckless daring and their violence have gone beyond all bounds of human nature. In the presence of the magistrates and of you, who alone have the right to say who shall or shall not be put to death, they took matters into their own hands and killed this man. If these men, therefore, do not suffer the supreme penalty, who will venture to visit our city in the future? And what will happen to this city of ours if it becomes possible for anyone who likes to kill a man before he has even explained why he came here? We are therefore prosecuting these men as people who lack all sense of justice and right conduct and respect for the laws. They have shown the uttermost contempt for our city. It is for you, when you have heard the evidence, to inflict on them the punishment which you think that they deserve.'

After this speech of the officials, all except one of the mur- 7 derers of Euphron denied that they had done the act. This one, however, admitted it, and began to defend himself in some such words as these: 'I should like to point out, The- bans, that it is scarcely possible for a man to feel contempt for you when he knows that you have the power to do just what you like with him. What grounds for confidence, then, did I have when I killed this man here? Let me assure you that in the first place it was because I believed that what I was doing was right, and secondly, because I believed that you would reach a right decision in the matter. For I know how you yourselves dealt with the party of Archias and Hypates, whom you found to have acted just as Euphron did. You did not wait for a vote but punished them as soon as you were able to do so. And this was because you believed that people who are clearly villains and quite evidently traitors trying to make themselves dictators are already condemned

8 to death by the voice of mankind. Was not Euphron too, I ask you, guilty in all these respects? He took over our temples when they were full of offerings in silver and gold and he left them empty. And who could be more evident a traitor than Euphron? He was on the friendliest terms with Sparta, and then chose to support you instead. He gave guarantees to you and received guarantees from you, and then betrayed you again and handed over the harbour to your enemies. Was he not too, without any question, a dictator? A man who enslaved not only free men but also his own fellow-citizens, and who put to death and banished and deprived of their property not wrongdoers, but anybody he wanted to treat like this? Which meant the upper classes.

9 He then got back into the city with the help of the Athenians, your bitterest enemies, and he was in armed conflict with your governor; and when he found he could not drive him from the Acropolis, he got money together and came here. Now suppose he had come out openly against you with an army, you would actually have been grateful to me for killing him. As it is, he came with money instead to be used for bribing you and persuading you to put him back again in power in our city; then how can it be right for me to be put to death for giving him the punishment due to him? And when one is made to do something by force of arms, one is injured certainly, but at any rate not shown up

to be bad; but when one is bribed to act against the right, one is not only injured but also disgraced. Certainly, if he 10 had been an enemy of mine, but a friend of yours, I should be the first to admit that it would have been wrong of me to kill him in your city. But he was a traitor to you, and so just as much an enemy of yours as of mine. "All the same," someone may say, "he came here of his own accord." But if anyone had killed him while he was keeping out of the way of your city, he would have been praised for it. Are you really going to say that it was wrong to kill him now when he came here to do you still more harm than he had done already? Where can you point to legal agreements between Greeks and traitors or people who have changed sides twice or dictators? Then remember this too. You voted, as you 11 will recall, that from all cities of the alliance exiles should be subject to extradition. But what about an exile who returns without any general resolution of the allies? Can anyone say why such a person should not be put to death? Therefore, gentlemen, I declare that if you put me to death, you will be taking action on behalf of a man who was the worst of all your enemies; but if you decide that I acted rightly, you will be doing the right thing both for yourselves and for all your allies.'

After hearing this speech, the Thebans decided that Euph- 12 ron had got what he deserved. But Euphron's own citizens thought of him as a good man. They brought his body back and buried it in the market place, and they honour him as the founder of their city. And, indeed, it seems to be the case that the majority calls a man 'good' merely because he has benefited them.*

*Xenophon had watched events at Sicyon with interest and with contempt for Euphron, a man who had betrayed Sparta, and whose reconversion aroused scepticism (§3). Xenophon was bound to condemn a man who had carried out the revolutionary programme alluded to in §8, to condemn also the majority who regarded him highly.

CHAPTER 4

The diplomatic revolution and the Peace of Thebes (366–365 B.C.).
War between Elis and Arcadia. Preliminaries to Epaminondas' last
expedition to the Peloponnese

1 So much for the story of Euphron. I shall now return to the
point from which I began this digression.

While the Phliasians were still fortifying Thyamia and
Chares was still with them, Oropus was seized by the party
that had been exiled. The Athenians marched out in full force
against the city and recalled Chares from Thyamia; but then
the harbour of Sicyon also was recaptured by the Sicyonians
and the Arcadians. None of the allies of Athens sent help and
so the Athenians retired, leaving Oropus in the hands of the
Thebans pending a legal settlement.

2 Lycomedes heard that the Athenians were discontented
with their allies because, while they themselves were going
to much trouble on their behalf, not a single one of the allies
had given them any help in return. So he persuaded the
Assembly of Ten Thousand* to negotiate with Athens with
a view to making an alliance. At first some of the Athenians
were reluctant to accept the idea of becoming friends with
the enemies of Sparta, with whom they were themselves on
friendly terms, but after considering the matter they saw
that it was just as much in the interests of Sparta as of Athens
that the Arcadians should not be in need of the support of
Thebes, and so they accepted the Arcadian offer of an alli-
3 ance. After having arranged this, Lycomedes left Athens
and met his death in a way in which the hand of heaven can
most clearly be seen. Out of the many ships available, he
selected the one he wanted and agreed with the sailors that

*Cf. n. at VII.4.33.

they should put him ashore at the point which he chose himself. Then he chose to be landed just at the spot where the Arcadian exiles happened to be. So he met his death; but the alliance was now really in existence.

Demotion now made a speech in the Athenian Assembly 4 in which he said that while he approved of the negotiation of a treaty of friendship with the Arcadians, he thought that the generals should be instructed to see to it that Corinth also should be kept in a position where she could not be a threat to Athens. The Corinthians heard of this proposal, and at once sent sufficiently strong forces of their own men to all places garrisoned by Athenians and told the Athenians that they could go away, as they had no further need of garrisons. The Athenians did as they were asked to do, and when they all came in to Corinth from their various posts, the Corinthians proclaimed that if any Athenians had any complaints to make of ill-treatment, they should register their names and could be sure that justice would be done to them. Just at this moment Chares arrived at Cenchreae with 5 a fleet. He heard what had been done and said that he had information of a conspiracy against the state and had therefore come to help the Corinthians. The Corinthians expressed their gratitude, but were far from willing to allow his ships into the harbour and asked him to sail away. They also sent away the hoplites, after giving each man what was due to him. In this way, then, the Athenians left Corinth. How- 6 ever, they were bound by their alliance to send their cavalry to help the Arcadians if Arcadia were invaded. But they took no hostile action inside the territory of Sparta.

The Corinthians now began to take a serious view of their own security. Even before this they had been weak on land, and now the Athenians were added to the number of states unfriendly to them. So they decided to build up a mercenary army of both infantry and cavalry. With these troops under their leadership they succeeded both in safeguarding their

city and in doing much damage to their enemies in the immediate neighbourhood.* But they sent to Thebes asking
whether they could profitably send a delegation to obtain
7 peace. The Thebans said that peace could be obtained and
told them to come, and the Corinthians then asked whether
they could also go to their allies, so as to bring others into
the peace, if they wanted it, and let those who wanted war
go on fighting. The Thebans agreed with this too, and the
Corinthians went to Sparta, where they made the following
8 speech. 'Spartans, we have come to you as your friends, and
what we ask is this: if you can see any future for us if we go
on fighting to the end, then please explain it to us; but if you
consider that we are in a hopeless position, then join us in
concluding peace, if that is to your advantage too. There is
no one with whom we would rather share the blessings of
security than with you. But if you think that it is to your
advantage to carry on with the war, then we beg you to
allow us to make peace. If we are saved, perhaps there will
come a time when we can be useful to you again. But if we
are destroyed now, obviously we shall never be of any use
in the future.'

9   When they heard this the Spartans advised the Corinthians
to make peace. They also gave permission to any of their
other allies who were unwilling to carry on the war in their
company to stop fighting. But for themselves, they said they
would fight or take the lot that heaven sent them; they
would never submit to the loss of Messene – the land handed
10 down to them by their fathers. After receiving this reply the

*Xenophon omits to say that these mercenaries were used by
Timophanes to enforce measures which were perhaps akin to the
revolutionary programme of Euphron of Sicyon (VII.3.8) but which
made many Corinthians regard him as a tyrant, and that he was
murdered with the consent of his brother Timoleon (cf. Nepos
Timoleon I, Plut. *Timoleon* 4, Diod. XVI.65). Xenophon's view of
this famous fratricide is thus denied us. For Xenophontic reserve, see
Introduction p. 33 f.

Corinthians went to Thebes to make peace. The Thebans, however, wanted them not only to conclude peace, but also to join in an alliance. To this they replied that an alliance did not mean peace; it meant changing one enemy for another. And the Thebans greatly admired the Corinthians for refusing, even in their own great difficulties, to become involved in war with those who had been their benefactors. So they granted peace to the Corinthians, the Phliasians and those who had come with them to Thebes. The conditions were that each party should keep its own territory, and on these terms the oaths were taken.*

Now, since this was the basis for the treaty, the Phliasians 11 at once withdrew from Thyamia. The Argives had sworn to a peace on just these terms, but when they found that they could not arrange that the Phliasian exiles should stay at Tricaranum (the theory being that they could count this as their own territory), they occupied the place and kept it garrisoned. Just recently they had been laying it waste as though it was enemy land; but now they claimed that it was their own. And when the Phliasians proposed that the matter should be put up for arbitration, the Argives refused.

At about this time, and after the death of Dionysius I, his 12 son sent twelve triremes, under the command of Timocrates,

---

*About the Peace of Thebes opinion is sharply divided. Some accept the statement of Diod. XV.76.3 that it was a Common Peace, involving Athens (cf. Cawkwell, *Classical Quarterly*, 11, 1961, pp. 80 ff.). Others insist that, since Xenophon described it in such detail and gave no hint of it involving more than Corinth and some other Peloponnesian states, it must be regarded as much less than a Common Peace and nothing to do with Persia (cf. T. T. B. Ryder, *Koine Eirene*, 1965, pp. 83 and 137–9). But all arguments from Xenophon's silence are invalid (cf. n. at VI.3.18). Xenophon reported the whole affair from the viewpoint of the Corinthians and, since elsewhere he refused to record Persian influence (cf., e.g., n. at VI.2.1, and see Introduction p. 39 f.), it is no surprise if his account here is partial and misleading.

as reinforcements to the Spartans. On his arrival he helped them to capture Sellasia, and after this action sailed back to Sicily.

Soon after this the Eleans seized the town of Lasion which used to belong to them in the past but at this time had joined 13 the Arcadian League. The Arcadians took the matter seriously, mobilized their army and came to the rescue. In the Elean army that opposed them were included both the Three Hundred and the Four Hundred. Throughout the day the Eleans were encamped on more or less level ground opposite the enemy, and during the night the Arcadians climbed to the top of the mountains overlooking the Elean position. Then at dawn they began to march down on them. The Eleans could see that their enemies were approaching from higher ground and were also many times their number; but they were ashamed to retreat while they were still so far off. So they advanced to meet them and did not take to flight until they had met them in close fighting. They then lost many men and quantities of arms owing to the difficulty of the ground over which they were retreating.

14 After this successful action, the Arcadians marched against the cities of the Acrorians, capturing them all except for Thraustus. They then came to Olympia and built and garrisoned a stockade around the hill of Cronium. They were thus in control of the Olympian mountains, and they also seized Margana, which was betrayed to them by some of its citizens.

When things had reached this point the Eleans were completely disheartened, and the Arcadians now marched against the city of Elis itself. They actually got as far as the market place, but there the cavalry and the rest of the Eleans made a stand, drove the Arcadians out and, after killing some of them, put up a trophy.

15 From before this time there had been political dissension in Elis. The party of Charopus, Thrasonidas and Argaeus were trying to set up a democratic constitution, while the party of

Eualcas, Hippias and Stratolas were for an oligarchy. Now
the Arcadians, with their large army, seemed likely to be on
the side of those in favour of a democracy; so the party of
Charopus gained confidence and, after arranging with the
Arcadians for help, seized the Acropolis. However, the cav- 16
alry and the Three Hundred acted immediately. They went
up to the Acropolis at once and dislodged the men there, so
that about four hundred of the citizens, including Argaeus
and Charopus were forced into exile.

Soon afterwards the exiled party, with the help of some
of the Arcadians, seized Pylus. Since they now had in their
hands a strong position and also the large force of the Arcadian League on their side, a number of the democratic party
left Elis and joined up with them. Later on the Arcadians
invaded the territory of Elis again. They had been led to
believe by the exiles that the city would come over to them,
but on this occasion the Achaeans, now on friendly terms 17
with the Eleans, succeeded in preserving the city and the
Arcadians retired again without achieving anything except
the devastation of the Elean land. However, just as they were
leaving the country they heard that the Pelleneans were in
Elis, and, after a very long night march, they seized their
town of Olurus; for by this time Pellene had rejoined the
Spartan alliance. When the Pelleneans heard of the capture 18
of Olurus, they also made a long detour and got back again
as well as they could to their own city of Pellene. Afterwards
they carried on war not only with the Arcadians in Olurus
but also with the whole body of the democratic party in
their own country, even though they were very few in
number themselves. But in spite of this, they did not relax
their efforts until they had taken Olurus by siege.

The Arcadians now made another expedition into Elis. 19
When they were in camp between Cyllene and the city,
the Eleans made an attack on them, but the Arcadians stood
firm and defeated them. The Elean cavalry commander

Andromachus, on whose initiative, it was thought, this battle was fought, committed suicide; the rest returned to Elis. Also among those who died in the battle was Socleides, a Spartan of the officer class, who had just arrived; for by this time the Spartans were in alliance with Elis.

20 The Eleans were now in a difficult position in their own country and they sent ambassadors to the Spartans asking them also to take the field against the Arcadians. It seemed to them most likely that in this way the Arcadians, attacked on both sides, would grow tired of their enterprise. So now Archidamus marched out with the citizen army of Sparta and captured Cromnus. He left three of the twelve batta-

21 lions to garrison the place and then returned home. But the Arcadians, whose troops were all concentrated as a result of their expedition against Elis, came up to the relief, built a double stockade round Cromnus, and, in this safe position, kept the people there under siege. The city of Sparta was seriously perturbed by this blockade of her own citizens and again sent out an army. On this occasion, too, Archidamus was in command, and on his arrival he laid waste as much as he could of Arcadia and Sciritis and did everything to draw away, if possible, the besieging force from Cromnus. The Arcadians, however, disregarded all this and showed no more signs than before of moving.

22 Archidamus now observed a hill, over which the Arcadians had carried their outer stockade, and it seemed to him that he could capture it and that, with this hill in his possession, it would be impossible for the besieging troops below it to hold their position. He led his men round by a detour towards the place, and as soon as the peltasts who were running on ahead saw the Arcadian regular troops * outside the stockade, they charged down on them and the cavalry tried to join in the attack. But the Arcadians stood firm. They formed up in close order and stood there quietly. The Spartans then

*Cf. n. at VII.4.33.

charged again, but still the Arcadians did not give way; in fact, they began to advance. By this time there was a lot of shouting and Archidamus himself came up in support, turning off by the wagon road which goes to Cromnus. He led his men up in double file, just as they were on the march, and so, as the troops came to close quarters, the troops of 23 Archidamus, marching, as they were, along a road, were in column and the Arcadians were in close order, shield to shield. It soon became clear that the Spartans would not stand against the greater mass of the Arcadians; and almost at once Archidamus was wounded with a blow straight through the thigh; and there were severe casualties among those fighting in front of him. Among those killed were Polyaenidas and Chilon, who was married to Archidamus' sister; and altogether at least thirty fell in this engagement. The Spartans now retired along the road, but when they 24 came out on to open ground, they immediately formed up in line of battle against the enemy. The Arcadians still stood in close order, just as they were. They were inferior in numbers, but they were in much better heart than the Spartans, since they had attacked and driven back their enemies and inflicted losses on them. The Spartans, on the other hand, were greatly disheartened; they saw that Archidamus was wounded, and they had heard who had been killed – all brave men and indeed some of the most famous names in Sparta.

When the two armies were close together, one of the older 25 men shouted out: 'Friends, why should we fight? Why not make a truce and go away in peace?' Both sides welcomed the suggestion and a truce was made, after which the Spartans took up their dead and went away, and the Arcadians retired to the place where they had first begun to advance and put up a trophy there.

Now, while the Arcadians were busy at Cromnus, the 26 Eleans from the city marched first of all against Pylus and met with the Pylians who had been expelled from Thalamae. When the Elean cavalry came in sight they attacked without the slightest delay. Some they killed, others fled to a hill. However, as soon as the infantry came up these, too, were driven down, some being killed on the spot and others, about two hundred of them, taken prisoner. All prisoners who were foreigners were sold as slaves, and all who were exiles from Elis were slaughtered. Next the Eleans captured Pylus itself, with its inhabitants (since no one came to the help of the place), and also recaptured Margana.

27   Soon after the Spartans again marched against Cromnus. They came by night and overran the part of the stockade opposite the Argives. Then they called out to the Spartans who were under siege, and those who were nearest and who seized their chance quickly got out. Others, however, were intercepted by a large force of Arcadians who came up in support and then were shut up inside the stockade, captured and distributed to the various states. One lot went to the Argives, one to the Thebans, one to the Arcadians and one to the Messenians. The total number of prisoners, including Spartans of the officer class and Perioeci, came to more than a hundred.

28   Now that the Arcadians were no longer concerned with Cromnus, they again turned their attention to the Eleans. They put a stronger garrison into Olympia and, since an Olympic year was coming on, prepared to celebrate the Olympic Games together with the Pisatans, who claim to have been the first people to have had charge of the holy place. But when the month of the Olympic Games came round and the days had arrived when the great assembly gathers, who should appear but the Eleans? They had made their preparations openly; they had called on the Achaeans to help them; and now they came marching along the road

29 to Olympia. As for the Arcadians, they and the Pisatans were busy organizing the festal gathering, having had no idea that

the Eleans would march against them. They had already held
the horse-race and the first four events of the pentathlon.
The competitors who had got as far as the wrestling event
had left the racecourse and were now wrestling in the space
between it and the altar. By this time the Eleans in fighting
order had already reached the sacred precinct. As for the
Arcadians, they did not go forward to meet them; instead,
they formed into line along the river Cladaus, which flows
past the Altis and then into the river Alpheus. They had
allies, too, to back them up – about two thousand hoplites
from Argos, and about four hundred Athenian cavalry.
And now the Eleans formed up their line on the other side 30
of the river, made their sacrifices, and at once moved forward
into action. Before this time they had been looked down on
as soldiers by the Arcadians and Argives, and also by the
Achaeans and the Athenians. However, on this day they led
their allies into battle as though they were the bravest men
alive; the Arcadians were the ones they met first and they
routed them at once; they then stood firm against the
Argives, who came up in support, and were victorious over
these too. They then drove the enemy back to the space be- 31
tween the Council House and the temple of Hestia and the
theatre near by, fighting as bravely as ever and pushing the
enemy back towards the altar. However, stones and weapons
were raining down on them from roofs of the porticos, the
Council House and the temple of Zeus, while they themselves were fighting on ground level; some of them were
killed, and among these was Stratolas himself, the commander of the Three Hundred. After this they retired to their
own camp. But the Arcadians and their allies were so terrified 32
of what the next day might bring that they never even rested
during the night, spending the time in demolishing the splendid pavilions that had been built and using the material for
constructing a stockade. As for the Eleans, they advanced
again next day, but when they saw the strength of the

stockade and the numbers of men who had climbed up to
the roofs of the temples, they withdrew to their own city.
The courage that they had shown in battle was no doubt
something which a god by his inspiration could produce even
in a day, but it would take human beings a very long time
to produce such a quality in men who were not naturally
brave already.

33   The leaders of the Arcadians had now laid their hands on
the sacred treasure and were using it to maintain their regular army.* It was the Mantineans who first passed a vote that
this sacred treasure should not be touched. They then raised
in their own city the amount which was their own share for
the pay of the regular army and sent it off to the leaders of
the League. However, the leaders maintained that the
Mantineans were doing harm to the interests of the League,
and summoned their chief men to appear before the Assembly of Ten Thousand; then, when the Mantineans refused
to obey, they passed sentence on them and sent the regular
army to arrest those who had thus been condemned. But the
Mantineans shut their gates and would not allow the regu-
34 lars inside. As a result of this others, too, soon began to say
in the Assembly of Ten Thousand that the sacred treasure
ought not to be touched and that it was wrong to leave to
their children for ever afterwards such an act which would
merit the anger of the god. And so a resolution was passed
in the Arcadian Assembly forbidding the further use of the
sacred treasure. And now it was not long before all those
who could not afford to stay in the regular army without
pay began to melt away; on the other hand, those who could
urged each other on and began to join up, their idea being

*In these two sections the main elements of the Arcadian Federal
Constitution are presumed by Xenophon to need no explanation,
viz. the regular army (the so-called *eparitoi*) and the Assembly of Ten
Thousand. (Cf. VII.4.2 and 22.) For Xenophon's allusive manner,
see Introduction p. 34 and n. at VI.5.6.

that instead of being under the control of the regular army, they should control this army themselves. Then the Arcadian leaders who had been handling the sacred treasure realized that, if they were called upon to give an account of their transactions, they would be put to death. They therefore sent to Thebes and told the Thebans that unless they marched down into Arcadia the Arcadians would very probably go over again to the side of Sparta. So the Thebans 35 made preparations for a campaign; but those people who had the best interests of the Peloponnese at heart* persuaded the Arcadian Assembly to send ambassadors and tell the Thebans not to send an armed force into Arcadia unless they specially asked for it. At the same time as they were sending this message to the Thebans, they reckoned out among themselves that they did not really want a war. As for presiding over the temple of Zeus, they had no need to do this; it would be a more just and righteous thing to do if they gave back the presidency to the Eleans, and in this way, they concluded, they would please the god best. As this was just what the Eleans themselves wanted, both sides decided to make peace and an armistice was agreed upon.

The oaths were taken and sworn to by all, including the 36 Tegeans and the Theban governor himself, who happened to be in Tegea with 300 hoplites from Boeotia. Then the majority of the Arcadians, who were still staying in Tegea, held a feast with much merrymaking and pouring of libations and singing of paeans in celebration of the conclusion of peace. But the Theban governor and those of the Arcadian leaders who were anxious about having to give an account of their financial proceedings, backed by the Boeotians and their own party among the regular soldiers, shut the gates in the walls of Tegea and then sent to the merrymakers in the city and began to arrest all members of the aristocratic party. Since

*For Xenophon's ideal of 'the Peloponnese', see Introduction p. 39 and cf. VII.5.1. and n. at V.2.7.

Arcadians from all the cities were at the feast, and since all
of them were in favour of peace, it was natural that very
many arrests were made. The prison of Tegea was soon full
37 of prisoners and so was the town hall. Many, then, were in
prison, and many had jumped down outside the wall; many
also had been let out through the gates, since, apart from the
men who were apprehensive of being put to death, no one
had any ill feeling against anyone else. And it was particularly disturbing to the Theban governor and those who were
acting with him that they only managed to secure a very
few of the Mantineans whom they most wanted to arrest;
their city was close at hand and nearly all of them had gone
home.

38   When it was day and the people in Mantinea heard what
had happened, they sent at once to the other cities in Arcadia
and called on them to take up arms and guard the passes.
They themselves took the same precautions, and at the same
time they sent to Tegea and demanded the return of all
Mantineans who were held there; they also said that they
demanded that none of the other Arcadians there should be
held in prison or put to death without a trial. And they
guaranteed that, if anyone had any complaints to make
against these men, then the city of Mantinea would without
question produce before the general assembly of the Arcadians all against whom charges were made.

39   After hearing this, the Theban governor did not know
what to make of the affair and he released all the men under
arrest. Next day he called a meeting of any Arcadians who
wished to attend and defended himself by saying that he
had been deceived. He had heard, he said, that a Spartan
army was on the frontier and that some of the Arcadians
were going to betray Tegea to the enemy. His hearers knew
that he was telling lies about them, but they acquitted him
of guilt, though at the same time they sent ambassadors to
Thebes where they put in an accusation against him and said

that he ought to be put to death. Epaminondas was general 40 in Thebes at the time, and it is reported that he said that it had been a far more correct action to arrest the men than to let them go. 'It was on your account,' he told the ambassadors, 'that we mobilized for war. You then made peace without consulting us. We should be quite justified, I consider, in calling this an act of treason. You can be sure, however, that we are going to march into Arcadia and there we shall fight a campaign in the company of those who are on our side.'

CHAPTER 5

The Campaign of Mantinea (362 B.C.)

1 ALL this was reported to the general assembly of the Arcadians and also to the individual states. The inference made by the Mantineans, the Eleans, the Achaeans and all those Arcadians who had the interests of the Peloponnese at heart* was that the Thebans were quite clearly aiming to make the Peloponnese as weak as possible so that they might subjugate

2 it with the least possible difficulty. 'Why on earth,' they said, 'do they want us to be at war unless it is that they want each side here to do harm to the other side, with the result that both sides will need the help of Thebes? And why now, when we are telling them that we do not need them at the moment, are they getting ready to march out? Quite obviously they are preparing to take the field in order to do some harm to us.'

3 They also sent to Athens asking the Athenians for help, and ambassadors from the regular Arcadian army went to Sparta, too, and called upon the Spartans to join the common effort of resistance to any who might come to enslave the Peloponnese. As for the question of the leadership, they arranged on the spot that each state should hold it when inside its own territory.

4 Meanwhile, Epaminondas had started on his march. He had with him all the Boeotians, the Euboeans and great numbers of Thessalians, coming both from Alexander and from his opponents.† The Phocians, however, refused to join the expedition. They said that they were bound by their treaty

*Cf. n. at VII.4.35.　　　　†Cf. n. at VII.1.28.

to come to the help of Thebes if it was attacked, but there was nothing in the treaty that committed them to take part in a foreign invasion. Epaminondas, however, could reckon 5 on support in the Peloponnese itself from the Argives, the Messenians and those of the Arcadians who were on his side. These were the Tegeans, the Megalopolitans, the Aseans, the Pallantians and other cities which had to follow this line because they were small and surrounded by the above-named peoples.

Epaminondas, therefore, marched out with all speed; but 6 when he reached Nemea, he waited there in the hope of intercepting the Athenians on their way past. He reckoned that this would be a great thing for him and would have the effect of encouraging his own allies and of disheartening his opponents – that, in fact, any loss which the Athenians suffered would be all to the good of Thebes. Meanwhile, while 7 he was waiting at Nemea, all those forces opposed to Thebes were gathering at Mantinea.

Epaminondas now heard that the Athenians had given up their plan of marching by land; instead, they were going to go by sea, with the intention of marching through Spartan territory to the help of the Arcadians. He therefore left Nemea and came to Tegea. Now in my view this campaign 8 of his was not a lucky one, but I must say that both for planning and audacity this man cannot possibly be criticized. In the first place I approve of his decision to make his camp inside the fortifications of Tegea. Here he was in a safer position than he would have been outside, and also the enemy was less able to observe what he was doing. It was easier, too, for him to get whatever he needed from inside the city. And with the enemy encamped outside, he was able to see whether their dispositions were good ones or whether they were making any mistakes. He believed that he had the advantage in power over the enemy, but he could never be induced to initiate an attack when he saw that they had the

397

9 advantage in position. However, when he saw that time was passing and that no other city was coming over to his side, he realized that some action was necessary; otherwise, he could only expect ignominy instead of the fame that had been his before.

At this point he found that the enemy had taken up a strong position near Mantinea and were sending for Agesilaus and the Spartan army in full force; he heard, too, that Agesilaus was on the march and had already reached Pellene. So he ordered his men to have their dinner, and then led his
10 army straight to Sparta, and he would have taken the city, like a nest with no one to defend it, had it not been that by some providential chance a Cretan came and warned Agesilaus of the approach of the army. So Agesilaus, after receiving this information, got back to the city before Epaminondas reached it, and the Spartans of the officer class took up their posts and, though very few in number, were ready to defend it. All their cavalry were away in Arcadia, and so were all the mercenaries and three out of the twelve battalions.

11 When Epaminondas reached the part of the city where the Spartans of the officer class had their quarters, he made no attempt to break in at the point where his troops would have to fight on level ground and be exposed to missiles from the roof-tops, where, in fact, in spite of their numbers they would be at no advantage over their less numerous opponents. Instead, he occupied a position which, he thought, would give him the advantage, and proceeded to descend, rather than
12 climb up, into the city. As to what happened next, it is possible to maintain that the hand of heaven was involved, and also possible to say that, when men are desperate, no one can stand up to them. At any rate Archidamus, with less than a hundred men, went forward to the attack, got across some ground that appeared likely to impede him, and marched uphill against the enemy; and now these Thebans, these fire-

breathers, these conquerors of the Spartans, with their enormous superiority in numbers and with their advantage of the higher ground, failed to stand up to Archidamus and his men.* They gave way and those in the front ranks of Epaminondas' army were killed. But now the troops from inside the city, delighted with their victory, pressed their pursuit too far, and they, too, began to fall. It looks as though a line had been drawn by heaven, giving them victory only up to a certain point. So Archidamus put up a trophy at the place where his men had been victorious and gave back under an armistice the bodies of the enemy who had fallen there. Epaminondas calculated that the Arcadians would be marching to the help of Sparta and he had no wish to fight a battle with them and the combined Spartan army together, especially as they had done well, and his own men badly, in this engagement. So he marched back as fast as he could to Tegea. Here he rested his hoplites, but sent the cavalry on to Mantinea. In calling upon them for this further effort, he told them that in all probability all the cattle of the Mantineans were outside the city and all the people too, especially as it was harvest time.

So the cavalry set out. Meantime, the Athenian cavalry had started from Eleusis and had their evening meal at the Isthmus. Then they went through Cleonae and were now either very close to Mantinea or already taking up their quarters in the houses inside the wall. When the enemy force could be seen riding towards the city, the Mantineans begged the Athenian cavalry, if it was at all possible, to come to their help; all their cattle, they said, were outside the walls and so were the labourers and also many children and older men from among the free citizens. Neither the Athenians nor their horses had had anything to eat that morning, but when they heard what the Mantineans said, they rode out to the

___

*For Xenophon's bitter denigration of the Thebans as soldiers, see Introduction p. 36 f. and nn. at IV.2.18 and VI.5.24.

16 rescue. Now here again the gallantry of these men was truly admirable. They could see that the enemy greatly outnumbered them, and their cavalry had already suffered misfortune at Corinth; but they took no account of this, nor of the fact that they were going to fight against both the Thebans and the Thessalians, who were supposed to be the best cavalry in the world. Instead, they were ashamed to be on the spot and not doing anything to help their allies, and as soon as they saw the enemy, they came charging down on them, each man's heart on fire to win back the glory of their

17 fathers. By engaging in this battle they were responsible for the saving for the Mantineans of everything outside the walls. Good men among them were killed* and, very evidently, those whom they killed themselves were good men too; on each side no one had a weapon so short as not to reach the enemy with it. And the Athenians did not abandon their own dead; on the contrary, there were some of the enemy dead whom they gave back under a truce.

18 Epaminondas' campaign had now reached its time limit, and he realized that in a few days he would have to leave the Peloponnese. It was clear that if he were to leave behind him without protection the peoples to whom he had come as an ally, they would be encircled by their enemies and he would have utterly ruined his own reputation; with a large force of hoplites, he had been defeated by a few; at Mantinea he had been defeated in a cavalry battle; and, just because of his invasion of the Peloponnese, he had been responsible for the coalition of Sparta, Arcadia, Achaea, Elis and Athens. He therefore decided that it was impossible to leave the enemy country without fighting a battle. His calculation was as follows: if he won, he would make up for all his mistakes; and if he were to die in battle, it would be, he thought, a

*Xenophon forbears to name the most celebrated casualty of that action, his own son Gryllus (Diogenes Laertius II.54), who received a public burial at Mantinea (Pausanias VIII.11.6) and much else.

glorious end, for he would have died in trying to leave to his own country the dominion over the Peloponnese.*

It does not seem to me at all surprising that Epaminondas 19 should have thought along these lines. Ambitious men do think like this. What is more remarkable is the fact that he had trained his army to the point where his men never shrank from any hard work either by day or night, were ready to face every danger, and, however short they might be of food, were always willing to obey orders. For at this time, when 20 he gave them his final order to make ready for battle, the cavalry, at his command, were enthusiastically whitening their helmets, the Arcadian hoplites, just as though they were Thebans, painting the Theban device of clubs on their shields, and everyone in the army was sharpening spears and daggers and polishing shields.

Again noteworthy are the dispositions he made after he 21 had led the army out, ready for battle as they were. First, as was natural, he fórmed them into line. By doing this he made it look as though he was certainly preparing to join battle. But when the army was drawn up as he wished, instead of advancing by the shortest route towards the enemy, he led his men towards the mountains facing Tegea from the west. In this way he made the enemy think that he was not going to engage them that day. When he reached the 22 mountains, with his line fully extended, he grounded arms at the foot of the high ground and so gave the impression of getting ready to camp. All this had the effect of producing among the enemy a general relaxation; their mental eagerness for battle diminished and they were less careful about taking up their positions.

His next move was to bring up company after company to

*Thus Xenophon makes Epaminondas bring on the battle as a desperate last throw. But he is unlikely to have had any information about Epaminondas' feelings, and the paragraph is a mark of no more than hostile opinion.

the wing where he was himself and to wheel them into line, thus adding weight to the wedge-like formation of this wing.* And now came the moment when he gave the order to take up arms and led the advance, with his men following. Among the enemy, when they saw him advancing so unexpectedly, there was a total lack of steadiness. Some were running to take up their positions, others forming into line, others bridling their horses, others putting on their breast-plates. The general impression was one of people expecting
23 to suffer rather than to cause damage. Meanwhile, Epaminondas led his army forward prow on, as it were, like the ram of a trireme, believing that if he could strike and break through at any point, he would destroy the whole enemy army. His plan was to fight the battle with the strongest part of his army, and he had left the weakest part far in the rear, since he knew that if it were defeated, this would discourage the troops that were with him and give heart to the enemy. The enemy had drawn up their cavalry like a phalanx of hoplites in a line six deep and without infantry to act together
24 with the cavalry. But Epaminondas had formed up his cavalry, too, in a strong wedge-formation, and he had infantry with them in support, believing that, when he had broken through the enemy cavalry, he would have defeated the whole force opposed to him, since it is very difficult to find men who will stand their ground when they see any of their own side in flight. He also posted a force of cavalry and infantry on some hills opposite the Athenians on the left wing in order to prevent them coming to the help of the men on their right. Here the plan was to make the Athenians afraid of helping the men on the right, in case these troops of his should attack them from the rear.

*Unrelentingly, Xenophon does not take the trouble to describe the order of battle of either side. For that sort of thing one would have to have recourse to the works of historians. Diod. XV.84 ff. reproduces the account of Ephorus.

This, then, was the way in which he made his attack, and all his anticipations were fulfilled. By overwhelming the force against which he struck, he caused the whole enemy army to turn and fly. But he himself fell in this attack, and 25 after this those who were left, even though they had won, failed to take full advantage of the victory. The enemy phalanx was on the run, but the hoplites did not kill a single man of them, nor did they advance beyond the point where they had made their first impact. The enemy cavalry had also fled, but again the Theban cavalry did not pursue them and kill either cavalrymen or hoplites. Instead, they fell back timidly, like beaten men, through the routed lines of their enemies. The mixed force of infantry, cavalry and peltasts, who had shared in the victory of the cavalry, did indeed behave as though they had won and turned on the army's left wing, but here most of them were killed by the Athenians.

The result of this battle was just the opposite of what everyone expected it would be. Nearly the whole of Greece had 26 been engaged on one side or the other, and everyone imagined that, if a battle was fought, the winner would become the dominant power and the losers would be their subjects. But God so ordered things that both parties put up trophies, as for victory, and neither side tried to prevent the other from doing so; both sides gave back the dead under a truce, as though they had won, and both sides received their dead under a truce, as though they had lost. Both sides claimed 27 the victory, but it cannot be said that with regard to the accession of new territory, or cities, or power either side was any better off after the battle than before it. In fact, there was even more uncertainty and confusion in Greece after the battle than there had been previously.

Let this, then, be the end of my narrative. Someone else, perhaps, will deal with what happened later.

APPENDIX

Note on III. 4. 24

XENOPHON's account of these operations of Agesilaus in summer 395 B.C. is crucial for the understanding of the *Hellenica*. Clearly the account of Diodorus (XIV.80) derives from the *Hellenica Oxyrhynchia* 11 and 12. The differences are astounding. In Xenophon Agesilaus marched directly from Ephesus to Sardis, in Diodorus indirectly, by way of Mount Sipylus which separates the valleys of the Cayster and the Hermus. In Xenophon a battle was fought, apparently on the fourth day after three days without sight of the enemy, on the River Pactolus (which flows down past Sardis to the Hermus); it involved only the Persian cavalry and Tissaphernes was not present. In Diodorus the march up the Hermus was in a hollow square harassed by Tissaphernes in command of his full army (cf. *Hell. Oxy.* 11.3); no battle on the Pactolus is mentioned, though there is space on the *Hell. Oxy.* papyrus for a minor engagement at 'the river' (11.3, line 11); the surrounds of Sardis are ravaged (as in Xenophon's *Agesilaus* I.33 clearly, in the *Hellenica* §24 by implication); Agesilaus then turned, followed by Tissaphernes, and won a major battle with the aid of an ambush (cf. *Hell. Oxy.* 11.4, with Xenocles, whom Xenophon §20 had made joint commander of the cavalry, in charge); Tissaphernes and his army fled back to Sardis, and Agesilaus (after a wait of three days, *Hell. Oxy.* 12.1) proceeded to march up the valley of the Hermus (followed at a respectful distance by Tissaphernes, *Hell. Oxy.* 12.2) and over into the valley of the Maeander, intending to advance into Phrygia by way of Celaenae (*Hell. Oxy.* 12.3); but the omens were unfavourable, and he led his army back to the sea down the Maeander. Diodorus says (XIV.80.2) that this battle was half-way between Sardis and Thybarna, which latter name does not occur elsewhere, but a place Thymbrara is familiar to us and can be located up the valley of the Hermus near the later city of Philadelphia, on the plain of Castolus (cf. I.4.3, *Education of Cyrus* VI.2.11, and Dittenberger, *Orientis Graecae Inscriptiones Selectae*, II.488), and it is reasonable to suppose that 'Thybarna' in Diodorus is due to textual corruption of this name.

Some have struggled to argue that the account of the *Hellenica Oxyrhynchia* must be wrong because Xenophon was there and he could hardly have omitted such a glorious victory of his hero. But even if it were right to say that Diodorus' battle of the ambush is just a variant account of Xenophon's battle of the Pactolus, how are we to explain Xenophon's omission of any notice of the march into Phrygia? Unless the whole of the *Hellenica Oxyrhynchia* is here wildest fantasy, Xenophon has misled us very greatly at the least in that respect. Only those who believe that Xenophon was 'a really well-informed and truthful reporter' will shrink from the awful truth that here at least he has seriously failed us, a case of *inextricabilis error*.

MAPS

Pontus Euxinus

THRACE

0   50   100 miles

Aenus
Chersonesus
Cardia
Sestos
IMBROS
Lampsacus
Abydos
Hellespontus
Ilium
TROAD
Mt. Ida
Methymna
Antandrus
Adramyttium
Mitylene
LESBOS
Malea Pr.
Arginusae Is.
Phocaea
Cyme
Magnesia
Clazomenae
CHIOS
Erythrae
Teos
Colophon
Notium
Ephesus
SAMOS
Priene
Tralles
Miltetus
Iasus
Mt. Latmus
Halicarnassus
COS
Cos
Caunus
Cnidus
RHODES

Parinthus
Selymbria
Byzantium
Chalcedon
Propontis
PROCONNESUS
Cius
Astacus
Parium
Cyzicus
Dascylium
BITHYNIA
R. Rhyndacus
Scepsis
MYSIA
R. Caicus
R. Hermus
Sardis
R. Cayster
R. Maeander

Heraclea
Pontica

PHRYGIA

Gordium

R. Cogamus

Celaenae

CARIA

PAMPHYLIA
R. Eurymedon
Aspendus

LYCIA

H. A. Shelley

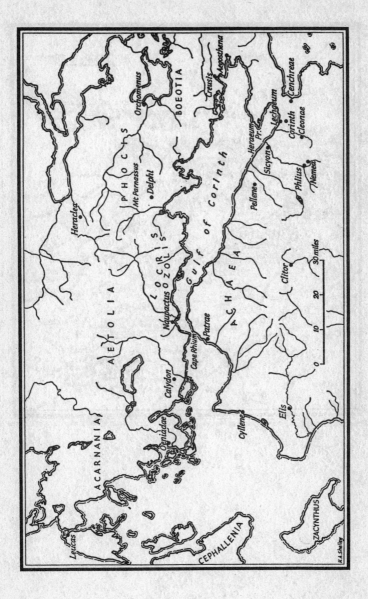

THESSALY

• Crannon

• Scotussa

Pherae •

Pharsalus • Pagasae •

ACHAEA PHTHIOTIS

0   10   20 miles

Othrys Mts

R. Sperchius

AENIANIA • Narthacium
M A L I S   • Histiaea

Heraclea   Thermopylae

E U B O E A

L O C R I S

P H O C I S   Opus

Mt Parnassus Daulis   Orchomenus

L O C R I S   Delphi

Chaeronea   L. Copais

Lebadea

Coronea   • Haliartus   Thebes •   • Tanagra   Oropus

B O E O T I A   Chalcis

Thespiae   Eretria

Leuctra   • Scolus

Creusis   Plataea   Erythrae   **Decelea**

Mt Cithaeron   • Eleutherae

Aegosthena   **A T T I C A**

G u l f   o f   C o r i n t h

A C H A E A   Heraeum   Eleusis

Pr. •   Megara   Piraeus   • Athens

Sicyon •   Lechaeum   Salamis

• Clitor   Corinth   Cenchreae   Crommyon

Phlius •

H. A. Shelley

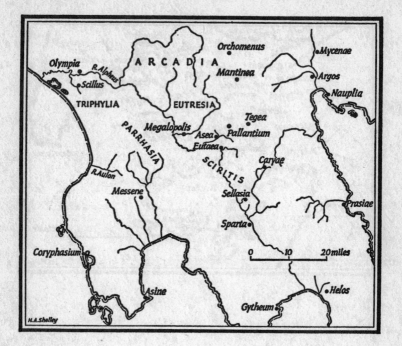

H.A.Shelley

0   10   20 miles

C H A L C I D I C E

Apollonia

Acanthus

Spartolus

A C T E

Olynthus

Potidaea

Thermaic Gulf

P A L L E N E

S I T H O N I A

Mende

Torone

Posidium Pr.

Scione

H. A. Shelley

INDEX

Abarnis (promontory), 102
Abydus, Abydenes, 53f., 63, 100,
141, 229ff., 239, 247, 252
Academia, 105, 350
Acanthus, Acanthians, 261, 264, 272
Acarnania, Acarnanians, 198, 216,
222ff., 342
Achaea, Achaeans, 64, 155f., 198,
222f., 232, 236, 309, 329, 367, 387,
390, 396, 400
Achaea (Phthiotic), 202
Achilleum, 153, 234
Acragas, 77, 108
Acrisius (Sicyonian), 369
Acrocorinth, 208
Acrorians, of Elis, 197, 386
Adeas (Sicyonian), 369
Adimantus (Athenian), 72, 86, 103
Aegae (in Mysia), 230
Aegina, Aeginetans, 104f., 245ff.,
296
Aegospotami ('Goats' River'), 101
Aegosthena (in Megara), 284, 331
Aeneas (Stymphalian), 378
Aenesias (Spartan), 110
Aenianians, 176, 204
Aeolis, Aeolians, 142, 144, 148, 152,
168, 205, 239
Aeschines (Athenian), 109, 111
Aetolia, Aetolians, 222, 225
Agamemnon, 165, 365
Agathinus (Corinthian), 232
Agesandridas (Spartan), 53, 67
Agesilaus (Spartan king), 159f.,
164ff., 185f., 194f., 204ff., 214,
222ff., 227f., 254f., 258, 267,
273ff., 283, 286ff., 289, 294f., 305,
323, 325, 336, 339ff., 398
Agesipolis (Spartan king), 195, 226,
258, 273, 275f.
Agesistratus (Spartan), 110
Agis (Spartan king), 59, 105f., 109
155f., 159
Agyrrhius (Athenian), 239
Alcetas (Spartan), 295
Alcetas (Molossian king), 303, 310

Alcibiades (Athenian), 54ff., 65f., 68,
70ff., 75f., 101f., 119
Alcibiades (cousin of Alc.), 63
Alcimenes (Corinthian), 209
Alea (epithet of Athena, sanctuary
of, in Sparta), 344
Alexander (of Pherae), 333f., 396
Alexias (Athenian), 99
Alexippidas (Spartan), 110
Alpheus, R., 157, 314, 391
Altis (sacred enclosure at Olympia),
391
Alypetus (Spartan), 294
Alyzia, 298
Amedocus (Odrysian king), 237
Amphidolians, 156f., 197
Amphipolis, 201
Amyclae, Amyclaeans, 344, 371
Amyntas (Macedonian king), 261,
269, 273
Anaetius (Athenian), 109
Anaxibius (Spartan), 239ff.
Anaxicrates (Byzantian), 68
Anaxilaus (Byzantian), 68
Androclidas (Theban), 174, 267f.
Andromachus (Elean), 387
Andros, Andrians, 72f., 77, 103, 296
Angenidas (Spartan), 110
Antalcidas (Spartan), 233f., 246,
251f., 321
Antandrus, 57, 67, 99, 240
Antigenes (Athenian), 65
Antiochus (Arcadian), 364, 366
Antiochus (Alcibiades' steersman), 75
Antiphon (Athenian), 118
Antisthenes (Spartan), 149
Anytus (Athenian), 119f.
Apaturia (Athenian festival), 87
Aphytis, 276
Apollo, 160, 175, 226, 324, 332, 344
Apollonia, Apollonians, 261f., 271
Apollophanes (Cyzicene), 190
Aracus (Spartan), 98, 111, 149f., 345
Arcadia, Arcadians, 156, 177, 213,
264, 338ff., 350f., 359, 361ff.,
370ff., 382ff., 398

417

READ MORE IN PENGUIN

In every corner of the world, on every subject under the sun, Penguin represents quality and variety – the very best in publishing today.

For complete information about books available from Penguin – including Puffins, Penguin Classics and Arkana – and how to order them, write to us at the appropriate address below. Please note that for copyright reasons the selection of books varies from country to country.

In the United Kingdom: Please write to *Dept. EP, Penguin Books Ltd, Bath Road, Harmondsworth, West Drayton, Middlesex UB7 ODA*

In the United States: Please write to *Consumer Sales, Penguin USA, P.O. Box 999, Dept. 17109, Bergenfield, New Jersey 07621-0120.* VISA and MasterCard holders call 1-800-253-6476 to order Penguin titles

In Canada: Please write to *Penguin Books Canada Ltd, 10 Alcorn Avenue, Suite 300, Toronto, Ontario M4V 3B2*

In Australia: Please write to *Penguin Books Australia Ltd, P.O. Box 257, Ringwood, Victoria 3134*

In New Zealand: Please write to *Penguin Books (NZ) Ltd, Private Bag 102902, North Shore Mail Centre, Auckland 10*

In India: Please write to *Penguin Books India Pvt Ltd, 706 Eros Apartments, 56 Nehru Place, New Delhi 110 019*

In the Netherlands: Please write to *Penguin Books Netherlands bv, Postbus 3507, NL-1001 AH Amsterdam*

In Germany: Please write to *Penguin Books Deutschland GmbH, Metzlerstrasse 26, 60594 Frankfurt am Main*

In Spain: Please write to *Penguin Books S. A., Bravo Murillo 19, 1° B, 28015 Madrid*

In Italy: Please write to *Penguin Italia s.r.l., Via Felice Casati 20, I–20124 Milano*

In France: Please write to *Penguin France S. A., 17 rue Lejeune, F–31000 Toulouse*

In Japan: Please write to *Penguin Books Japan, Ishikiribashi Building, 2–5–4, Suido, Bunkyo-ku, Tokyo 112*

In Greece: Please write to *Penguin Hellas Ltd, Dimocritou 3, GR–106 71 Athens*

In South Africa: Please write to *Longman Penguin Southern Africa (Pty) Ltd, Private Bag X08, Bertsham 2013*

PENGUIN AUDIOBOOKS

A Quality of Writing that Speaks for Itself

Penguin Books has always led the field in quality publishing. Now you can listen at leisure to your favourite books, read to you by familiar voices from radio, stage and screen. Penguin Audiobooks are ideal as gifts, for when you are travelling or simply to enjoy at home. They are produced to an excellent standard, and abridgements are always faithful to the original texts. From thrillers to classic literature, biography to humour, with a wealth of titles in between, Penguin Audiobooks offer you quality, entertainment and the chance to rediscover the pleasure of listening.

You can order Penguin Audiobooks through Penguin Direct by telephoning (0181) 899 4036. The lines are open 24 hours every day. Ask for Penguin Direct, quoting your credit card details.

Published or forthcoming:

Emma by Jane Austen, read by Fiona Shaw

Persuasion by Jane Austen, read by Joanna David

Pride and Prejudice by Jane Austen, read by Geraldine McEwan

The Tenant of Wildfell Hall by Anne Brontë, read by Juliet Stevenson

Jane Eyre by Charlotte Brontë, read by Juliet Stevenson

Villette by Charlotte Brontë, read by Juliet Stevenson

Wuthering Heights by Emily Brontë, read by Juliet Stevenson

The Woman in White by Wilkie Collins, read by Nigel Anthony and Susan Jameson

Heart of Darkness by Joseph Conrad, read by David Threlfall

Tales from the One Thousand and One Nights, read by Souad Faress and Raad Rawi

Moll Flanders by Daniel Defoe, read by Frances Barber

Great Expectations by Charles Dickens, read by Hugh Laurie

Hard Times by Charles Dickens, read by Michael Pennington

Martin Chuzzlewit by Charles Dickens, read by John Wells

The Old Curiosity Shop by Charles Dickens, read by Alec McCowen

PENGUIN AUDIOBOOKS

Crime and Punishment by Fyodor Dostoyevsky, read by Alex Jennings

Middlemarch by George Eliot, read by Harriet Walter

Silas Marner by George Eliot, read by Tim Pigott-Smith

The Great Gatsby by F. Scott Fitzgerald, read by Marcus D'Amico

Madame Bovary by Gustave Flaubert, read by Claire Bloom

Jude the Obscure by Thomas Hardy, read by Samuel West

The Return of the Native by Thomas Hardy, read by Steven Pacey

Tess of the D'Urbervilles by Thomas Hardy, read by Eleanor Bron

The Iliad by Homer, read by Derek Jacobi

Dubliners by James Joyce, read by Gerard McSorley

The Dead and Other Stories by James Joyce, read by Gerard McSorley

On the Road by Jack Kerouac, read by David Carradine

Sons and Lovers by D. H. Lawrence, read by Paul Copley

The Fall of the House of Usher by Edgar Allan Poe, read by Andrew Sachs

Wide Sargasso Sea by Jean Rhys, read by Jane Lapotaire and Michael Kitchen

The Little Prince by Antoine de Saint-Exupéry, read by Michael Maloney

Frankenstein by Mary Shelley, read by Richard Pasco

Of Mice and Men by John Steinbeck, read by Gary Sinise

Travels with Charley by John Steinbeck, read by Gary Sinise

The Pearl by John Steinbeck, read by Hector Elizondo

Dr Jekyll and Mr Hyde by Robert Louis Stevenson, read by Jonathan Hyde

Kidnapped by Robert Louis Stevenson, read by Robbie Coltrane

The Age of Innocence by Edith Wharton, read by Kerry Shale

The Buccaneers by Edith Wharton, read by Dana Ivey

Mrs Dalloway by Virginia Woolf, read by Eileen Atkins

READ MORE IN PENGUIN

A CHOICE OF CLASSICS

Aeschylus	**The Oresteian Trilogy**
	Prometheus Bound/The Suppliants/Seven Against Thebes/The Persians
Aesop	**Fables**
Ammianus Marcellinus	**The Later Roman Empire (AD 354–378)**
Apollonius of Rhodes	**The Voyage of Argo**
Apuleius	**The Golden Ass**
Aristophanes	**The Knights/Peace/The Birds/The Assemblywomen/Wealth**
	Lysistrata/The Acharnians/The Clouds
	The Wasps/The Poet and the Women/ The Frogs
Aristotle	**The Art of Rhetoric**
	The Athenian Constitution
	Ethics
	The Politics
	De Anima
Arrian	**The Campaigns of Alexander**
St Augustine	**City of God**
	Confessions
Marcus Aurelius	**Meditations**
Boethius	**The Consolation of Philosophy**
Caesar	**The Civil War**
	The Conquest of Gaul
Catullus	**Poems**
Cicero	**Murder Trials**
	The Nature of the Gods
	On the Good Life
	Selected Letters
	Selected Political Speeches
	Selected Works
Euripides	**Alcestis/Iphigenia in Tauris/Hippolytus**
	The Bacchae/Ion/The Women of Troy/ Helen
	Medea/Hecabe/Electra/Heracles

READ MORE IN PENGUIN

A CHOICE OF CLASSICS

Plautus	**The Pot of Gold and Other Plays**
	The Rope and Other Plays
Pliny	**The Letters of the Younger Pliny**
Pliny the Elder	**Natural History**
Plotinus	**The Enneads**
Plutarch	**The Age of Alexander** (Nine Greek Lives)
	The Fall of the Roman Republic (Six Lives)
	The Makers of Rome (Nine Lives)
	The Rise and Fall of Athens (Nine Greek Lives)
	Plutarch on Sparta
Polybius	**The Rise of the Roman Empire**
Procopius	**The Secret History**
Propertius	**The Poems**
Quintus Curtius Rufus	**The History of Alexander**
Sallust	**The Jugurthine War/The Conspiracy of Cataline**
Seneca	**Four Tragedies/Octavia**
	Letters from a Stoic
Sophocles	**Electra/Women of Trachis/Philoctetes/Ajax**
	The Theban Plays
Suetonius	**The Twelve Caesars**
Tacitus	**The Agricola/The Germania**
	The Annals of Imperial Rome
	The Histories
Terence	**The Comedies (The Girl from Andros/The Self-Tormentor/The Eunuch/Phormio/The Mother-in-Law/The Brothers)**
Thucydides	**History of the Peloponnesian War**
Virgil	**The Aeneid**
	The Eclogues
	The Georgics
Xenophon	**Conversations of Socrates**
	A History of My Times
	The Persian Expedition